AF600310

IF I LOSE MINE HONOUR I LOSE MYSELF: HONOUR AMONG THE EARLY MODERN ENGLISH ELITE

If I Lose Mine Honour I Lose Myself

Honour among the Early Modern English Elite

COURTNEY ERIN THOMAS

UNIVERSITY OF TORONTO PRESS
Toronto Buffalo London

Toronto Buffalo London
www.utppublishing.com

ISBN 978-1-4875-0122-8

Library and Archives Canada Cataloguing in Publication

Thomas, Courtney Erin, 1980–, author
If I lose mine honour I lose myself : honour among the Early Modern English elite / Courtney Erin Thomas.

Includes bibliographical references and index.
ISBN 978-1-4875-0122-8 (hardcover)

1. Social psychology – Great Britain – History – 16th century. 2. Social psychology – Great Britain – History – 17th century. 3. Honor – Social aspects – Great Britain – History – 16th century. 4. Honor – Social aspects – Great Britain – History – 17th century. 5. Reputation – Social aspects – Great Britain – History – 16th century. 6. Reputation – Social aspects – Great Britain – History – 17th century. 7. Upper class – Great Britain – History – 16th century. 8. Upper class – Great Britain – History – 17th century. I. Title.

HM1027.G74T46 2017 302.094209′031 C2017-901028-X

This book has been published with the help of a grant from the Federation for the Humanities and Social Sciences, through the Awards to Scholarly Publications Program, using funds provided by the Social Sciences and Humanities Research Council of Canada.

University of Toronto Press acknowledges the financial assistance to its publishing program of the Canada Council for the Arts and the Ontario Arts Council, an agency of the Government of Ontario.

Canada Council for the Arts Conseil des Arts du Canada

Funded by the Government of Canada Financé par le gouvernement du Canada

Contents

Illustrations

Acknowledgments

I was fortunate to receive funding at various stages in the development of this project from the Social Sciences and Humanities Research Council of Canada, the Whitney and Betty MacMillan Center for International and Area Studies at Yale University, the Beinecke Rare Book & Manuscript Library, the Leylan Fellowships in the Social Sciences, and other sources.

Research for this work was conducted at an array of North American and British archives and I would like to thank the archivists and librarians at the Folger Shakespeare Library (especially Georgianna Ziegler), the Beinecke Rare Book & Manuscript Library, the Yale University Microfilm Library, the Huntington Library (particularly Mary Robertson), the British Library, the Cambridge University Library, the Bodleian Library, the Surrey History Centre, and at the UK National Archives, for the time and assistance they offered me. I would also like to express my gratitude to the scholars in attendance at the various conferences, seminars, and colloquia in North America and England at which several portions of this project were presented between 2010 and 2015. In addition, Alan Bryson provided me with invaluable assistance on the transcription of several of the Cavendish letters – for which I am forever grateful. Portions of the fourth chapter of this work previously appeared in a 2013 article entitled "'The Honour & Credite of the Whole House': Family Unity and Honour in Early Modern England," and I am grateful to the *Journal of Social and Cultural History* (and Taylor & Francis Ltd, on behalf of the Social History Society) for their permission to print reworked portions of that earlier piece here.

I began this endeavour as a doctoral student at Yale University, and I am deeply grateful to many there for their advice and camaraderie. I am likewise indebted to many others for their support, whether offered in the form of insights into this project (often as probing questions and post-conference panel engagement which has been invaluable in shaping the work) or personal encouragement. In this regard I would like to warmly thank Sarah Eve Kelly, Brendan Kane, Krista Kesselring, Lisa Ford, Steve Hindle, Tim Stretton, Robert Tittler, Lisa Cody, Henry French, Andy Wood, Lindsay O'Neill, Sarah Cieglo, James Caudle, Alexandra Shepard, Paul Griffiths, Linda Pollock, Elizabeth Herman, Jennifer Wellington, Christopher Nixon, Daina and Stefan Esposito, Michael Meadows, Eric Lum, Siobhan Quinlan, Tara Forman, Charles Roeske, James Grant, Sarah Keyes, Jennifer Rolls, Shannon Green, Vanessa Grabia, Cindy Watt, Ellen Schoeck, Heather Hogg, Megan Caldwell, Hillary Taylor, Erin Glunt, Jennifer Ng, and Marita von Weissenberg.

My family, both immediate and extended, deserves a great deal of thanks; the brief remarks here are not sufficient to scratch the surface. My loving parents have made an indelible mark on this project – my mother and father, Judy and Ron Thomas, have provided seemingly boundless help, cheerleading, kindness, reassurance, assistance, and patience over the years, and lovingly edited all my works in progress since as far back as I can remember. The kindness and support offered to me by my partner, Shaun Badry, have likewise been immense. This project is the better for his interest in it, and in all my endeavours.

I also wish to express my great appreciation and indebtedness to Keith Wrightson, who has offered invaluable assistance, support, and guidance. His expertise, enthusiasm, and generosity of spirit seemed remarkable to me when I entered my doctoral program, and they remain so. Over the years he has been unfailing in his kindness and support, as well as in his willingness to engage critically with my ideas and assumptions; in short, a perfect mentor.

Finally, deepest gratitude is also due to the other members of my supervisory committee at Yale: Carlos Eire, Charles Walton, and Brendan Kane. Early on they all displayed a great deal of enthusiasm for the project and without their knowledge and assistance this study would not have been completed. In particular, I owe great thanks to Brendan for his many insightful suggestions and comments over the years, and for his support.

There are, of course, many more individuals who deserve to be thanked here and I hope they will forgive my brevity. The book itself is for Sarah Eve Kelly, who has ever been a source of support, laughter, friendship, and sage advice, and for my parents, who have made this and so many other things possible.

Abbreviations

BL	British Library, London, UK.
BOD	Bodleian Library, Oxford, UK.
BRBM	Beinecke Rare Book and Manuscript Library, New Haven, CT.
CUL	Cambridge University Library, Cambridge, UK.
FSL	Folger Shakespeare Library, Washington, D.C.
HL	Huntington Library, San Marino, CA.
HH	Hatfield House, Hatfield, UK (accessed online at http://cecilpapers.chadwyck.com/).
LH	Longleat House, Warminster, UK (accessed on microfilm at Yale University Library).
NA	National Archives, Kew, UK.
SHC	Surrey History Center, Woking, UK.

Brief Notes

This work retains the original spelling and punctuation when quoting sources directly. However, in instances in which quotations from such sources are difficult to understand, explanatory notes have been added in square brackets. All dates are presented in both new and old style with a slash separating the two styles. Hence, 10 February 1559 [old style]/1560 [new style].

IF I LOSE MINE HONOUR I LOSE MYSELF

Introduction: Approaching Honour

Honour and Its Import

William Gouge, the early modern English clergyman, moralist, and conduct book writer, noted in his 1622 treatise *Of Domesticall Duties*, "a good name is a most pretious thing."[1] Almost a hundred years later, Juba, a character in Joseph Addison's *Cato, A Tragedy*, exclaimed, "better to die ten thousand deaths than wound my honor." These sentiments, pointing to the importance attached to honour and reputation, would have resonated with both Gouge's wide readership and the theatre attendees of Addison's time. This work examines these concepts among the elite in early modern England and demonstrates that honour was so often invoked because its flexible nature made it a particularly effective representational technique.[2] The varied meanings of honour could be used in an array of interactions, and variously privileged, one over another, with fluidity depending upon the needs and objectives of an individual in a given situation.

While earlier scholarship often reified honour, discussing it as a static, overarching code of behaviour, recent work focuses instead on the many contradictions and ambiguities found in early modern understandings and expressions of honour. Indeed, this shift in focus has yielded such a range of diverse descriptions of honour that several historians have questioned its usefulness as an analytic category. For example, during a 1996 symposium, "grave doubts were expressed as to whether the term 'honour' had any practical utility as a historical category" owing to its "fluid and contradictory" nature.[3] This work embraces some of these recent insights with respect to honour's flexible nature. However, while demonstrating that honour was highly protean (yet bounded by broadly recognizable central tenets), it affirms its centrality as a category of analysis and stresses the profound sense of importance it had for people in the period. It was from its malleability that honour drew its strength.

One's honour and reputation were constantly articulated and referenced in early modern English society. Honour itself was a broadly constituted mode of conduct that bound social groups together; it likewise served as a frame of reference in reaching decisions about self-presentation and in reacting and responding to the behaviour of others. Simply put, honour was a key facet of people's daily lives. While all social orders in early modern England were concerned with issues of reputation and social credit, and recognized their importance and ubiquity in social interactions, the concept of honour played a particularly large role in the lives of elites. It was a key aspect of their social experience and self-fashioning. Elites cared a great deal about their honour, and issues of honour and reputation arose in almost every social interaction in which they participated.[4]

Yet, for all its importance, honour was not easily defined. Nathaniel Vincent, preaching a sermon before Charles II in 1674, articulated, "though there is not any thing in the world that hath been always more value and desired than honour, yet there is nothing that has been so little understood and explicated."[5] Honour has been insightfully and variously analysed as a value inherent in political discourse, personal and household display, constructions of self-identity, and notions of masculinity and femininity.[6] In contrast to much earlier work, analyses from the mid-1990s onwards have moved away from seeing honour in the period as linked most strongly to the expression of violence or a concern with sexual reputation.[7] Accordingly, they have eschewed a simplistic understanding of honour as rooted most prominently in chivalric displays and militaristic bravado in the case of men and as inseparable from sexual repute with respect to women. Scholars now recognize that honour was dynamic; something that took many different forms and was at play in a broad array of social interactions.[8] In re-evaluating the meanings attached to honour, recent work has thus overwhelmingly pointed to its plasticity and multi-vocality.[9] Honour is now described (much as it was in the early modern period) as both an interior and exterior quality, as a deeply personal value that had a role in understandings of self-identity and as a communal asset, and as something self-generated by birth whilst concomitantly bestowed through service and behaviour. With a complex set of interlocking and overlapping meanings, honour was nothing short of protean.

This study focuses on the multiple meanings associated with honour in the period, and specifically avoids smoothing the edges of honour as a concept. It highlights, rather, the inconsistent and occasionally competing understandings of honour as a social construct, while also connecting them and emphasizing the strength of honour as a concept, despite its ambiguous nature. By embracing these ambiguities, a three-dimensional understanding of early modern honour is achieved, one that considers its many pliable meanings and affirms its appeal as a rhetorical strategy with reference to the manner in which these multiple meanings could be used. As suggested, recent scholarship has provided numerous points of entry to connect the array of meanings attached to honour in early modern England, and the range of behaviours and venues of display associated with it. In particular, this analysis is indebted to work done by Linda Pollock. In a 2007 essay, which itself built upon earlier analyses that probed the contours of understandings of honour and reputation, Pollock drew attention to the role of honour in mediating settlements and mitigating (rather than sparking) violence, the active role of women in elite honour culture beyond a concern with sexual reputation, and the potency of family relationships as a source of honour and good reputation.[10] This project extends that analysis by further investigating some issues outlined by others and broadening the range of behaviours and attributes linked to honour.[11] More specifically, it attends to the manner in which early modern elite men and women interpreted honour and negotiated its various, sometimes competing, meanings and accorded them varying levels of precedence, often with a measure of fluidity, based upon their needs and objectives within a given interaction or social performance. In doing so, this work points to honour's utility as a representational strategy and also to the ways in which it can be employed as a lens through which to focus upon other elements, such as the quotidian experiences of elite women and men, the expansion of state apparatuses, the mechanics of family relationships, and constructions of masculinity and femininity, in the history of the early modern period.

In focusing on honour in this manner, I borrow an idea introduced in another essay by Pollock, that of the "cluster concept." As defined by her, a cluster concept is "an umbrella term that linked together a diverse array of related ideas, providing bridges between and connective pathways through the associated attributes."[12] Honour can be seen as a cluster concept, something that was deeply entangled in early modern life and that connected diverse elements of social behaviour together.[13] Because honour connected and encompassed such variable meanings and forms of articulation, it is deceptive to perceive too great an element of cohesion in early modern understandings of it. Honour cannot easily be described as a "code," something of which people possessed a unified and unitary understanding. Its meanings were often determined contextually in a purposeful way as individuals used the divergent understandings of honour present in order to realize their aims in a given moment.

This analysis also demonstrates the utility of honour as a category of analysis. Recognizing that honour was amorphous, this study focuses on how elite men and women used and understood honour in various ways, often deliberately depending upon the context, in the course of their daily lives. Far from rendering honour "empty" as a result of its abundant concurrent and occasionally contradictory meanings, it was this very malleability that made it such an enduring value. In essence, honour was so often appealed to and articulated because of, rather than in spite of, its flexible nature. Likewise, while honour as a social construct had multiple meanings and varied manifestations, this does not mean that it was devoid of tangible meaning. Honour as a culturally weighted, value-laden, yet flexible, term in the early modern period is not notably different from, for example, invocations of the terms "freedom" or "patriotism" in modern American society. Their precise meanings and varying connotations are difficult to pin down because they can be referenced in different ways, and to many diverse ends. And yet, to those articulating them, they are very meaningful.

While claims to honour were capable of generating an infinite variety of surface manifestations in the period, they cannot be dismissed as empty rhetoric. As Keith Thomas has noted, "without a good reputation, normal social existence became impossible" in the years considered here.[14] Advancement at court, the acquisition of prestige and wealth, the promotion to (and retention of) local office, credit relationships, and family reputation were entangled with honour. For elites, honour was deeply woven into the fabric of the everyday. This work, accordingly, addresses what early modern elite men and women understood honour to be in an array of contexts that were common in their daily lives and social interactions. Some of these, such as the importance attached to properly modest feminine behaviour and the role of honour in the political sphere, have been well studied; others, such as the place of the early modern household, and the relationships therein, as a potent site of honour, have been less explored. Likewise, while several scholars have pointed to various attributes and behaviours that could constitute honour aside from sexual reputation and a willingness to utilize violence to avenge slights, these disparate elements are joined here in a holistic analysis and also further elaborated upon.

Given the versatile character of honour as a social animator, we can gain a more complete awareness of how it was deployed in social life only when we examine the range of contexts and differing ways in which it was enacted. As Pollock asserts, "the only way to understand what concepts meant to early modern individuals is by uncovering the full network of associations" inherent within them.[15] Honour connected together numerous facets of social life, including personal and family reputation, economic credit, hospitality, friend, kin, and family relationships, household and marketplace behaviour, conflict resolution, political involvement, and others. It is in understanding how individuals and families enacted honour in these various spheres that one understands honour itself. Contemporaries recognized that "honour dependeth not onely of our will: but allso of theirs who are to allott it vnto vs according to our deserts," and so crafted social performances that were structured around broadly accepted models of honourable conduct even as they negotiated the boundaries of those models of behaviour based upon the circumstances of a given situation and their individual objectives.[16] Hence, at its core, honour was performative and its true nature can best be seen in its enactment. This work, therefore, looks at honour "not just as a system of meanings, but as a practical code informed by purposes and uses."[17]

Overarching Narratives

Alongside the notions that honour for men was encapsulated in a willingness to defend name and status by any means necessary, and that honour for women was rooted in sexual reputation (which will both be further considered in subsequent chapters), a major theme in earlier analyses of honour and reputation is that of a transition from honour to virtue and from collective to more personalized violence between the sixteenth and seventeenth centuries.[18] In these narratives, which bear similarities to the work of Norbert Elias on the civilizing process, a move from an untamed elite to a more "civilized" and governable one is postulated.[19] This line of argumentation is intertwined with other complex discussions surrounding the evolution of the early modern European state and its growing monopoly on violence and the regulation of social relations, as well as teleological notions of the development of modernity as related to the suppression of emotions.[20] With respect to understandings of honour among the early modern English aristocracy, this transition from honour to virtue/civility is argued to have been guided by a "moralization of politics" that stressed humanist education and learning, service to the state, and the cultivation of reformed piety as the true sources of honour in early modern English society.[21] These values are often characterized as being adopted most readily by relatively newly promoted, upwardly mobile individuals who lacked an ancient bloodline and were eager to cement their gains by achieving status through service.[22]

Yet, speaking to the multiple meanings associated with honour, most sixteenth- and seventeenth-century elites saw their reputations as tied to both a noble name and a reputation for good conduct. As Sir Francis Hastings expressed in a letter to the Earl of Essex,

> it hathe pleased God (my good lorde) that you shoulde be the sone of noble parents, and therfore honorable by birth; it hathe pleased him also that you shoulde be servant to a most noble Prince and thefore honorable by calling; and eyther these are sufficiente to make you honored of mere worldly men; but bothe these togeather must nedes encrease your accustomed affability and curtoisy joyned hearunto doeth not a little adde unto your honour and accounte amongst men … But (my lorde), I holde this not sufficiente for you to rest upon, for there is a God above that guideth the heavens, and governeth the earth, and without whom nothing is done … so he looketh to receave some use of them from you. In this can none be dispensed withall, and from this there is not anyone exempted; and the higher his place is in birth and calling, and the greater his guiftes are in wisdome and learning, the more is chalenged from him; for to whom muche is geven from him muche is required.[23]

To be truly accorded honourable then, *both* pedigree and behaviour mattered as "lineage created a propensity for honor, not the thing itself."[24]

Both "new" men (those whose families had only relatively recently been granted lands, titles, or positions, and who were sometimes labelled as upstarts by the members of the older nobility) and more established ones saw attributes such as Christian morality, sober behaviour, a veneer of education, and involvement in governance as markers of reputation and sources of honour, in conjunction with lineage.[25] These involvements and attributes, as much as bloodline, demarcated them from the lower social orders; although they were fully capable of according varying levels of value to these different elements of honour based upon their aims at a given time. Likewise, while it is certainly true that some closely associated their honour with displays of service and civility, these were not necessarily attributes that only mattered to recently established gentlemen, nor did these more newly elevated men disassociate their honour from their lineage.

Conversely, associating one's honour solely with a prestigious lineage could be problematic on a purely practical level, as failing lines of inheritance and the acts of attainder issued by various Tudor monarchs had done much to undercut the ancient authority of many noble houses by the early years of Elizabeth's reign. Thus, of the sixty-two living peers in 1560, only twenty-five held titles originating before 1509, and of the seventy-four peerages that existed under Elizabeth I, twenty-five had become extinct by 1640. This reality meant that an ancient birthright and genealogical entitlement to a peerage could not, per se, be held up as an undisputed claim to honour, as such birthrights could be stripped away. But the risks of a loss of title or the failing of a bloodline, or even of the advancement of "new" men (sometimes to the resentment of the more established aristocracy), were not entirely novel features of the Tudor period. Noble lines had always grappled with these threats and they did not necessarily lend themselves to a clear impetus in the early modern period for elites to develop new ways of thinking about honour. Thus, rather than seeing an early modern transition from a militaristic and violent form of honour rooted in noble status and lineage to one characterized by the cultivation of inner virtue expressed through service, it is more appropriate to see the two concepts as existing alongside one another.[26]

The view of honour as a single, unified concept that changed over time is further eschewed in this work, as it obscures the extent to which honour was actually a much more diffuse concept which could (and did) acquire different meanings based on context. Accordingly, this work focuses on the multiple meanings of honour that existed (and persisted) across the period and addresses the ways in which those meanings were negotiated and variously privileged. By investigating the diversity of both practice and understanding that characterized honour, this work addresses one of the problems associated with the perception of a cohesive code of honour and gets to the heart of honour's status as a multi-vocal cluster concept. Likewise, in demonstrating that honour could be invoked in many different settings and to many different ends, it points to some of the reasons underlying its durability and popularity as a concept. Social agents play a dynamic role in appropriating and remaking/redefining flexible and diffuse terms to both suit and legitimize their own agendas.[27] The individuals surveyed in this work, and the ease with which they employed the rhetoric of honour in seemingly conflicting ways dependent on context, are testament to this.

Defining Honour, Defining Elites

Asking what, precisely, "honour" as a term meant to people in early modern England generates a series of questions. Terms such as "quality," "honour," "credit," "name," and "fame" were often used interchangeably in the period, and yet they all described social and moral status in subtly different ways.[28] But what were the different connotations of these entangled terms? In what contexts was the usage of "honour" dominant, and not some other term? How were these labels used differently based on one's social rank? Was "honour" only applicable to social elites? Were terms such as "credit" or "reputation" more appropriate for those lower on the social scale? Were all these terms, and "honour" in particular, situational? To whom did people attribute honour, and in what contexts? Like "honour," its various associated terms are social constructs that have complex social and linguistic histories. In this sense, "honour" and its associated terms were concepts that were constantly "being encountered, slowly added to linguistic repertoires, gradually appropriated and turned to advantage as occasion offered."[29] While this makes it difficult to satisfactorily resolve the various questions posed earlier, some general assessments are possible. However, what is attempted here is a preliminary examination of the diverse meanings attached to these words, rather than an exhaustive analysis of their cultural complexities.

In its most basic sense, honour was about protocol and hierarchy. Commonplace books from the period show a keen interest in issues of protocol, such as "the Setting of Estates in order at the table," "the forme how that women should beare theire Armes," the procedures involved in the "disgrading of a Knight of the garter," "orders for placeing Lordes and Ladies according to their degrees," and in historical examples of honour conflict.[30] In addition to this interest in honour as an issue of social protocol and as an element of historical and fictional narratives, the idea of honour as social currency and a facet of self-identity surrounded contemporaries. Honour, despite its ambiguity, bred trust and confirmed social authority. It was a leading component of the moral system, an arrangement of ideas of right and wrong conduct, which informed the actions of individuals positioned within all levels of the early modern social hierarchy. Alongside, and intertwined with, the related concepts of "credit," "reputation," and "worth," honour structured social reality and interaction. Thus, attributions of honour and matters of reputation formed an integral part of even the most mundane social interactions and were referenced in things as simple yet fundamental as modes of address, interactions within the marketplace, and intellectual inquiry.[31]

It is also necessary to pay attention to the various terms used by those invoking the concept of honour and how they intersected with the social hierarchy of the period. For example, "honour" was a term applied more frequently to the upper ranks, while those of lower social standing typically used terms such as "honesty," "credit," "reputation," and "fame." An apt example of the manner in which members of the lower orders tended to employ terms such as "credit" or "honesty" more than "honour" can be found in Samuel Richardson's 1740 novel *Pamela,* in which the heroine uses the term "honesty" to reference her reputation because "I am poor and lowly and not entitled to call it honour."[32] While a review of the definitions of such terms gleaned from an array of early modern lexicons does not overtly reinforce the assertion that "honour" was a term most often claimed by elites, the usage of various associated terms in other documents, such as legal records, certainly does.[33] However, while "honour" as a term was thoroughly intertwined with the hierarchical social structure of the day, all members of the social order claimed variations of the concept for themselves using subtly different terms with overlapping meanings to do so.

The *Oxford English Dictionary* lists several meanings of "honour" prevalent in the early modern period. It is defined, for example, as a degree of high respect, esteem, or reverence accorded to one of exalted worth or rank. In this sense, honour was an attribute of birth. Yet a secondary meaning attached to the term was a quality that was received, gained, held, or enjoyed; a sense of renown, fame, credit, reputation, and good name that attached to oneself. Essentially, the honour one was born with was augmented by action. Also inherent in this definition was that one could lose honour or gain its opposite, dishonour, through poor behaviour. It is this meaning of honour that appears to have been the most prevalent in the period (the *OED* lists the most examples of usage and the oldest, dating from 1200, in association with this meaning).[34] Another definition, formulated in 1538 by Sir Thomas Elyot, characterized honour as something "gyuen or dewe to a man for his merites. sommetyme astate of nobilitie, or great authorytie. sommetyme beautie, proprely of a man, specially in gesture and communication."[35] John Baret formulated a primary meaning of honour as "due to ones merites."[36] In many instances, good conduct, just as much as blood and lineage, resulted in the accumulation of honour. In 1610, a treatise on *The Excellencie of Man* stated that all "errors doe proceede from perturbacion of reason and order" and "therfor meet it is th[a]t all … accions shoulde be performed according to moderacion, order, honesty, and comlynes."[37] Exhibiting moderate behaviour conferred good reputation in this context. Thus, as the author writes, "what can be more Noble, then emulation of vertue?" for "prayse is only the wordes pronounced by the Praysor but honor consisteth in the actions & signes of his vertue who is praysed."[38]

"Credit," "worth," and "honesty" were similarly defined as things one could accumulate and be entitled to through displays of proper conduct. Thus the *OED* describes "credit" as the quality or reputation of being worthy of belief or trust. According to Thomas Cooper, it was "supposall, an opinion or iudgement that one hath of a thing: Also: reputation, honour, estimation, credit or countenance."[39] Hence "credit," like honour, was understood to be an estimate of the character of a person, a measure of their reputation or repute based on behaviour. In 1598 John Florio defined it as "honóre, honor, worship, reputation, honestie, credit, estimation, the reward of vertue."[40] Writing after Florio in 1611, Randle Cotgrave offered a similar denotation, describing "credit" as "authoritie, sway, power … reputation, dignitie, estimation; also reuerance, grauitie."[41] Essentially, it was recognition of social status and character derived from behaviour and reputation. Behaving honourably entitled one to be treated with honour and so resulted in one's good credit. Tied to this was the notion of "honesty," the possession of which entitled one to credit from peers and deference from subordinates. Thomas Wilson, in 1612, defined it as "all kinde of duties, which men are mutually to practise one towards another, without doing any vncomely, filthy, or wicked thing."[42] The performance of proper Christian behaviours such as neighbourliness, kindness, and general good conduct marked one as honest and, in turn, as honourable.

The meanings attached to the terms "reputation" and "fame" also illustrates the extent to which they were linked, indeed entangled, with the concepts of "honour" and "credit." The primary definition of these terms was the common or general estimate of a person's character, although the *OED* shows that this usage was rare in the sixteenth century and only became prevalent in the seventeenth. The secondary meaning of "reputation," however, and one which was quite commonly used in the sixteenth century, was simply "to be." One was described, for example, as having a reputation for being learned in the same sense that one was spoken of as learned. Thus "reputation" itself was not necessarily a value judgment, but simply what one was thought to be by others. Reputation was attached to, and formed by, related concepts such as fame or *fama*. "Fame" was that which people said or told of another; it was public report and common talk. In his popular lexicon (reprinted three times between 1604 and 1620), Robert Cawdrey defined it as "report, common talke, credite."[43] The extent to which one was treated as honourable depended on one's fame, which strongly affected one's reputation and credit, as people observed behaviour and formed assessments of character based on these observations. To behave well gave rise to a good reputation, which was itself a source of honour, as possessing a good reputation resulted in "honour, glory, or reputation that one hath for doing a thing: comelines, honestie: worship, commendation."[44]

Another common understanding of honour among the elite was that based on Aristotle's *Nicomachean Ethics*; namely, "an externally bestowed quality that depended on the good opinion of one's peers" (although how one arrived at that good opinion was dependent on a range of shifting contexts).[45] For Aristotle, who ranked honour as the highest of external goods, true virtue was located between the extremes of virtue and vice – between zealously attempting to claim and retain honour through unacceptable behaviour and never attempting to seek honour at all.[46] True honour was conferred by temperance and personal mediation between these two poles. According to Aristotle, the moral virtues were courage, temperance, self-discipline, moderation, modesty, humility, generosity, friendliness, truthfulness, honesty, and justice, while the moral vices were cowardice, self-indulgence, recklessness, wastefulness, greed, vanity, untruthfulness, dishonesty, and injustice. In this scheme, acts of virtue brought honour to an individual and acts of vice brought dishonour. While some men were honoured for having power and wealth, or being born to it, the honour associated with wealth and position could be stripped away by a lack of virtue and good conduct. Having accrued an honourable status, this reputation for honour was then cyclically reinforced through social dealings; actions and conduct could alternately debit and credit one's store of personal honour, making it a potent form of social currency. Honour was reflected in action, but that action was also the outward projection of a virtuous mind and good character. Henry Peacham, in *The Compleat Gentleman*, instructed his readers that "nobilitie being inherent and Naturall, can haue (as the Diamond) the lustre but only from it selfe: Honors and Titles externally conferred, are but attendant vpon desert, and are but as apparell, and the Drapery to a beautifull body."[47] Essentially, individuals were honoured because they were honourable, and they knew they were honourable because they were so honoured.[48] By extension, being thought of as honourable augmented one's good standing and the desire to be regarded as honourable in turn motivated behaviour. Accordingly, Robert Ashley described honour in 1596 as a quality that, "giveth not onely a certaine grace & ornament to the dueties of this life, but is allso a great spurr vnto vertue."[49]

Honour was thus both an interior and an exterior virtue. It was a gauge by which elite men and women judged themselves and also by which they were judged in their communities.[50] As Thomas has noted, it was this "ambiguous combination of inner virtue and outward reputation which gave honour its distinctive quality."[51] Honour was both an internalized effort to adhere to the highest levels of virtuous conduct *and* reputation and credit, things that were more reflexive and dependent on one's estimation in the eyes of others. While the boundary between "honour" and "reputation" is thus rather imprecise, there is at least one important distinction between honour and reputation; namely that the valuation of honour is always positive. That is to say, one can have more or less of it, but it is always a positive attribute with a negative opposite (dishonour). Reputation, conversely, is an empty vessel and can take on all sorts of characteristics. One can have a bad reputation, but one cannot possess bad honour.

Also helpful for an analysis of honour is the framework developed by Frank Henderson Stewart focusing on vertical honour, or the honour owed to and expected by social superiors, and horizontal honour, which was extended to one's peers. This distinction can be useful in separating the terms "credit," "honour," and "reputation," and their intersections with the social hierarchy, from each other.[52] According to Stewart, members of the gentry and aristocratic classes used the terms "credit" and "honour" as they resonated with other members of their own station. In this sense, "credit" and "honour" were judged largely by peers, not inferiors, and elites were most concerned about their standing with each other and in each other's estimations. On the other hand, "reputation" was rooted in an estimation that anyone could hold about anyone else; it was more public and less easily controlled. All of this is to say that elites could have credit and honour with their peers but not their subordinates; however, they could have a reputation among both.

While it can perhaps be helpful to think of honour and reputation in these terms, on a practical level there were so many overlaps between the two categories that drawing such neat conclusions can be misleading. It is difficult to untangle honour and its associated concepts from one another. Most sixteenth- and seventeenth-century men and women do not appear to have developed clearly delineated definitions of each, but, rather, tended to use the various terms synonymously and with a notable lack of precision. Accordingly, within this work, the terms "honour" and "reputation" are often used interchangeably. This is not done without a proper understanding of the differences between the two, but, rather, to avoid over-using one term to the exclusion of the other, as they were deeply interrelated concepts.

The various attributes that collectively entitled one to an honourable reputation were daily expressed through social performance. Notwithstanding the awareness that individuals undoubtedly had a strong sense of their own internally held honour in the period, honour and reputation were fundamentally concepts that were projected and measured through social interaction and self-fashioning. As Pollock has defined it, honour was "the reputation of an individual, according to his or her peers, less derived from a person's internal virtue than from society's judgment of an individual's worth."[53] Investigating social performances, in which judgments about one's worth were made, allows one to see the divergent aspects of personal behaviour that contemporaries saw as constituting honour (even if they did not label them directly as such) and the varying ways in which they enacted them. Likewise, it allows one to come closer to understanding the complexities of how honour and reputation honour functioned in social life, and the ways in which elite men and women could privilege the various understandings of honour to varying degrees.

Because elite performers enacted honour in a reciprocal manner before audiences of their peers (displays or invocations of honour before members of the lesser social orders were, in contrast, not reciprocal, but, rather, rooted in deference), the contours of that audience must also be delineated. The great noble families of early modern England are relatively visible and easily pointed to by the historian, being defined by their heritable titles, right to sit in the House of Lords, and privileges before the law. The qualities that entitled one to gentry or gentlemanly status, however, are more difficult to discern. Thomas Smith distinguished between the *nobilitas maior* and the *nobilitas minor*, recognizing that elites were not a homogenous category.[54] Other contemporaries also grappled with the level of precision with which the various social orders could be delineated. For example, William Harrison further developed Smith's scheme for the ordering of society and noted the existence of four degrees of people.[55] The first degree consisted of gentlemen who, while divided internally into nobility, knights, esquires, and others, were taken by Smith and Harrison to represent a distinct social group, those whom birth, blood, and virtue made the preeminent citizens of the realm.[56] Harrison, importantly, also noted that living like a gentleman made one a gentleman. Smith more cynically noted that "as for gentlemen, they be made good cheape in England," and went on to state that anyone who studied in the universities, who had the ability to live without working, or who bore the countenance of a gentleman was entitled to be called such ("shall be taken for a gentleman").[57]

The possession of wealth, land, titles, and estates all played prominent roles in the construction of elite identity.[58] However, the categories of gentleman and gentility, often constructed to varying degrees on claims to resources and lineage, were fundamentally flexible ones and often disputed.[59] As Alexandra Shepard notes in a statement that holds true for all social orders in the period, it is clear "that different titles could be claimed by, or applied to, the same individuals in ways that suggest not only the mutability of social categories … but also the blurred boundaries between them."[60] While, ostensibly, the criteria for claiming gentle status were rooted in lineage and the possession of wealth, most people "generally agreed that gentlemanly identity in early modern England was not a simple matter of wealth or blood but involved complex considerations of style of life and social image."[61] It is also hard to precisely define the gentry as a social class because they possessed various levels of wealth and the group was further made porous by prosperous members of the middle ranks of society claiming the status of gentlemen.[62] As the social and cultural divide between the aristocracy and the gentry was not always an overly great one, it is best to think in terms similar to those outlined by Smith of a linked gentry and peerage, "presenting the one as a lesser, and the other as a higher, nobility."[63]

While, as discussed earlier, the ranks of the peerage were thinning in the period, the number of gentlemen was on the rise. For example, in 1524 there were approximately 200 knightly families and somewhere between 4,000 and 5,000 lesser esquires and gentlemen. By 1600, there were as many as 500 knightly families and 16,000 esquires and gentlemen. Even allowing for some inflation of the figures, it is clear that the number of those who felt themselves entitled to displays of honour suited to a gentleman was rapidly expanding.[64] And these men on the rise, despite their recently gained status, were just as proud of their bloodlines as the ancient aristocracy. They saw themselves as the "better sort" and claimed authority and honour by commissioning genealogies, building lavish houses, having a presence at court, and distributing largesse locally in the same manner as more established men. Many were, likewise, increasingly drawn into state structures via the holding of office, and came to see this as a mark of distinction that carried with it the potential to enhance their spheres of influence and importance, as well as play a role in the shaping of governance.[65]

In this study, most of the individuals examined can clearly be counted as members of the gentry or the lesser nobility. Members of these families held local magisterial offices, sometimes served at court, formed networks of sociability and patronage with other elites, and occasionally hosted monarchs on their progresses. They were entitled to deference within their communities. In identifying these families as elite, I have employed the inclusive definition of the term developed by Diana Newton, namely that "elites are the more privileged members of society exercising the greatest authority or enjoying the highest standing."[66] Some of the individuals considered in this study are also clearly identifiable as members of the aristocracy, individuals such as the Earl and Countess of Shrewsbury and the Countess of Bath, for example. Finally, there is a small sampling of clerics. While they were not members of the gentry strictly speaking, several came from gentry bloodlines and they can be classified as occupying positions of authority and elevated status within local society. They felt themselves deserving of deferential treatment, and often were treated in a manner that was, in many ways, comparable to the deference accorded to some members of the gentry.

All the ambiguity surrounding gentlemanly status can also be viewed as providing a further impetus for members of groups aspiring to gentle status to behave in ways that accrued honour. After all, as writers such as Ashley noted, behaving honourably was how one was known to possess honour, and that was how one was recognized as a gentleman. Behaving honourably and having a reputation as an honourable gentleman could make one an honourable gentleman.[67] In this sense, honour bound elites (both those whose status as vested in lineage was beyond question and those eager to claim such an established status for themselves via the expression of elite behaviour and the promotion of their lineage) together in a sort of "emotional community."[68] That is to say, elites can be identified as a group that adhered to a shared recognition of the importance of honour and a broad set of relatively stable, yet flexible, assumptions with respect to the manner in which honour was articulated. This was a cultural and social solidarity, of sorts.[69]

Sources and Methodology

As has been stressed thus far, honour was, above all, flexible. As with so many other social constructs, its highly pliable nature can best be seen in its performance. Elite men and women were highly attuned to the expectations of their social audiences when it came to behaviour that denoted an honourable reputation. As the many cases examined throughout this work attest, they employed a broad range of performative techniques to claim and maintain honour for themselves and for their families. These techniques, and the malleable nature of honour as revealed in its deployment, become more clearly visible in an examination of practice. As Brendan Kane has noted, "a more fruitful approach to studying honor is to think of it less as a reified code of behavior or ideology and more as a dynamic claim or right through which multiple takes on the subject could be negotiated."[70] Accordingly, this work concentrates neither on the prescriptive and popular literature associated with honour culture, nor on the litigation that resulted when elite honour broke down as a discourse and conflict became unavoidable (although a sampling of such sources are examined, as they tell us about the social expectations that existed and point to the ways in which articulations of honour were framed with reference to these expectations), but rather on the manner in which the rhetoric of honour was deployed within daily life and commonplace social interactions.[71] In so doing, it draws attention to the various tendrils of honour and sheds light on the diverse areas of social life in which it was referenced and articulated.

The documentation generated by dispute is an important set of sources for the examination of honour in early modern England. Such records reveal much about social attitudes because, in seeing how expectations associated with conduct were transgressed, we also see how people were normatively expected to behave. Legal records also indicate the pervasiveness of social expectations with respect to honour as people endeavoured to frame their actions, when recounting them in the courts, as being in accord with those expectations. However, as they tend to be reflective of moments of tension when individuals were concerned in a heightened way to present themselves and their actions as justified, legal records have limitations. In speaking to moments of conflict and even of crisis, an approach based solely upon adversarial court records can tend towards the presentation of a one-sided view of honour as a divisive social value that promoted litigiousness and even violence. Focusing on a one-sided interpretation of legal records can be, as one historian has aptly phrased it, "akin to trying to determine the health of a community by looking solely at the records of its hospitals."[72] Honour was certainly about the projection of one's worthiness and, among some, this could manifest itself as a willingness to avenge slights to one's reputation. But this analysis also considers the equally prevalent role of honour as a vehicle of consensus and communal harmony.[73] This is not so easily gleaned from legal proceedings. Legal disputes, lawsuits, and accusations of slander offer glimpses into moments in which the values of reciprocity, neighbourliness, good order, peacefulness, and deference (adherence to which were all sources of honour in their own right) broke down and situations became adversarial. Accordingly, in addition to using legal records, this work examines instances in which such values were upheld, albeit sometimes only following intense negotiation, and as such do not appear in the sources generated in instances of dispute.

Another set of often-used sources for the study of honour is the volumes of popular and prescriptive literature from the period.[74] The problematic division between prescription and practice has been the subject of much analysis by historians, especially with reference to the experiences of women in the period, and it is not necessary to revisit those discussions here. But it can be noted that, as prescriptive literature illustrates behavioural ideals, there are limitations in what it can tell us about practice and reality when used without appropriate critical analysis.[75] Prescriptive sources both reflected and influenced, to a degree, social practice and served as a means to regulate behaviour. In that sense they cannot be cleanly separated from practice, as they helped to both develop and support the mental structures within which behaviour was enacted.[76] Yet, while understandings of honour were shaped in part by such texts, people, then as now, had a complex relationship with such sources. Looking at a sampling of prescriptive sources aimed at a female readership in the period and at women's actions and speech, for example, reveals the divergent ways in which they absorbed, modified, and flouted the dictates of prescriptive literature when it came to translating those ideals into practice.[77] As Pollock has noted, "social practice was not a single, wholesale enactment of a set of principles: individuals formed social custom from a miscellany of texts and attitudes."[78] An understanding and appreciation of prescriptive literature nonetheless remains foundational because, in providing a set of behavioural ideals, such sources supplied individuals with both a base social script to follow in their own social performances and a vocabulary to use when attacking others whose behaviour contravened those ideals.[79]

Alongside a limited use of prescriptive sources and the records of litigation, the primary sources employed in this study are family paper collections. These collections include materials such as letters, commonplace books, diaries, and various forms of documentation generated within the context of the management of the household. These speak both to the prescriptive dimensions of honour and to the richness of lived experience and personal attitudes. Letters, in particular, provide a wealth of information on the social world of elites and their self-fashioning. The gentry of the period were involved in a complex web of interactions at the local level associated with their roles as householders, figures of authority, dispensers of hospitality, and in their work as local officeholders. These activities necessitated that gentry men and women interact regularly with each other, although often they lived at least a modest distance from one another. The realities of the distances that separated most landed elites from each other made this means of communication a practical necessity, and elites used letters to maintain social and business networks both locally and over long distances.[80] This results in a particularly rich source base for the study of routine social interactions.

Letters can, undeniably, be complex documents and present their own unique challenges when employed as sources."[81] Letter writing in the period was a mode of self-presentation that was structured by epistolary conventions and codes of deference which themselves shifted over time.[82] It would be naive to suppose that, in reading a letter, we are always getting a straightforward peek at someone's true and inner self, their *actual* thoughts or emotions. Yet the examination of such materials does provide a great deal of insight into how men and women in the early modern period constructed themselves and understood their social roles. Unsurprisingly, in their letters individuals typically represented themselves as acting in accordance with the values and norms of the day. As with the ways in which people presented themselves in legal disputes, social expectations structured their self-presentation. Regardless of the literal truth behind those representations, which were oftentimes mediated in some sense, whether through a clerk in the case of legal records or through a secretary or scribe in the case of letters, early modern men and women recognized the importance of constructing their actions as being in line with social expectations. A keen awareness of the so-called conduct book virtues was a component of this.[83] Because honour encompassed a range meanings under its umbrella, the ways in which people variously relied on prescriptive dictates, privileging some over others at various times and to various ends, can be glimpsed in their correspondence. Thus, in many ways, letters complement the prescriptive literature of the period. Letters also offer a particularly interesting source base in instances in which responses survive. In these cases, letter writing becomes a collaborative enterprise in a way in which sources such as commonplace books or diaries are not.[84] They have the potential to reveal portions of a conversation and shed further light on techniques of social performance and self-presentation.

This work uses the sources discussed above to analyse several issues with respect to honour. These include well-known themes such as honour and sexuality, and honour and violence, for example. These sources are also used to analyse other, more disparate, sources of honour, such as honour as associated with hospitality, household maintenance, and involvement in mediation. While some of these sources offer only fleeting glimpses of the larger issue of honour, such as an isolated letter or an entry in a diary, I have aimed to be as inclusive as possible with respect to sources and to present those isolated cases alongside others in order to tease out the connective pathways between the two. I have been similarly broad in my examination of the varied contexts in which honour was invoked. This approach allows for a more extensive understanding of honour than emerges when it is discussed in discrete and bounded contexts because, as a social value, honour was diffuse and intertwined with many different aspects of quotidian early modern thought and social life.

Discussing the manner in which elites used and understood the concept of honour can be complicated by the fact that honour and reputation were so socially ingrained that contemporaries often discussed matters relating to them without specifically referencing those terms. They were so much a part of elites' lives that it was self-evident when an issue touching their personal credit arose. While early modern men and women may have used the words "honour" and "reputation" sparingly and in restricted contexts, this should not be read as a lack of awareness of the broader range of meanings and definitions that were connected to them, nor as evidence that matters of reputation and self-identification as one who possessed honour and behaved honourably were not at play in many of their social interactions. Teasing out the manner in which elites thought about their honour, and used concepts of honour and reputation in their social interactions, requires an expansive and inclusive approach to the sources considered; such an approach is employed here.

This examination of honour covers roughly the years 1540–1640 (with most of the sources presented dating from the later half of the sixteenth century and the first two decades of the seventeenth century). However, in the interests of inclusivity I have not enforced those chronological boundaries with undue rigidity and readers will find several examples in this study from outside this date range. The rationale underpinning a focus on this time span has several components. In many senses, these years (and those immediately preceding and following them) saw a great measure of change related to, for example, the expansion of the state and of the use of the courts, the evolution and increasing polarization of religious attitudes occasioned by the confessional upheavals of the period, and the changing circumstances of many families as a result of economic expansion and increased opportunities for official involvement as figures of authority within the local community.

That this was a period of marked social change in many senses contrasts with honour's durability as a social value among the elite. This, in turn, speaks to the manner in which honour as a concept encompassed many diverse, sometimes contrasting, meanings under its umbrella. As a medley of values, its versatility meant that elites could emphasize and privilege its various meanings in accordance with their needs and objectives. Accordingly, while understandings of honour did not necessarily themselves undergo a transformation in the period (and arguably did not until well into eighteenth and nineteenth centuries – although even this is open to debate and may merely represent some meanings of honour gaining a more enduring precedence over others, rather than new meanings emerging), the ways in which they were referenced and deployed in the course of social interaction and in self-presentation were variable and affected by the changing social environment in which they were enmeshed. In other instances, some involvements that elites saw as foundational components of their reputation were subject to less variation across the period – for example, the sense of honour that they saw as vested in their positions as family and household heads remained largely static. There is thus an interesting interplay between social change and continuity with respect to understandings of honour that is brought out through a focus on these years.

Finally, on a more prosaic level, the reality that increased numbers of family paper collections (including letters by and to elite women, which allow for a focused examination of the elements of social life and behaviour that they associated with their reputations) survive from this period compared to earlier ones, coupled with the boom in the publication of prescriptive literature to meet the demands of an increasingly literate population and what such sources can tell us about contemporary understandings of honour, to say nothing of the rise in litigation and associated documentation in the period, has informed the choice of time span.[85]

In the next chapter I focus on the various meanings of honour among elite men and explore the connections between violence and understandings of honour. This section examines the ways in which honour could mitigate conflict, as well as the performative strategies using "honour" employed by men who did engage in violent and contentious behaviour. It also engages with the other involvements that elite men saw as affecting their reputations. A chapter on the diffuse sources and meanings of honour for gentlewomen follows. As in the preceding chapter, the ways in which these meanings were variously privileged by individuals dependent on the context of a given situation, and the manner in which conceptions of honour could be used as a weapon within the course of a quarrel, are explored. The following chapter focuses on a further range of attributes that both men and women perceived as connected to their honour and reputation with reference to the spaces of the community and the household. This section also examines conflicts that erupted in these areas and the role of honour as a legitimating technique therein.

In the final chapter, intertwined issues with respect to elite families and their honour are analysed. Examined through the lens of collective family honour, and the ways in which it was contravened, several manifold, yet connected, behaviours associated with understandings of honour are revealed. The ongoing nature of many intra-familial conflicts, and the sheer number of them which are to be found in family paper collections, also points to the manner in which elite men and women employed the shared discourse of honour in order to maintain their own reputation in a conflict with a family member while simultaneously refusing to end such a conflict. They often relied in such instances upon the flexibility of honour in order to pursue their objectives and justify their actions. This is followed by a brief conclusion that affirms the importance of honour as a representational strategy and considers shifts in understanding and enactment with respect to the meanings of honour across the period (and beyond).

Chapter One

Men and Honour

Honour, Anger, and Violence

In the popular imagination, though often without actually precisely delineating them as such, the medieval and early modern periods are often seen as replete with action-packed duels and pitched battles between rapacious villains and wronged heroes over matters of honour and reputation. Some earlier scholarly works likewise tend to characterize honour among elite men as realized predominantly in moments of conflict, and as primarily rooted in a concern for status and a willingness to use violence to avenge slights. Yet the linkage between honour and violence among gentlemen is not as direct or unfettered as may be supposed.[1] Elite men saw a range of behaviours as affecting their reputation, including both projecting an image of restrained maturity in the face of provocation and not allowing slights to their name to stand. Even within instances of conflict, as honour was a multi-vocal concept, understandings of it as linked to violence in the defence of name *and* as rooted in restraint existed alongside one another. This affected how gentlemen presented themselves when they initiated or were drawn into quarrels. It also influenced how those self-presentations were received as the varying understandings of honour jostled with each other for precedence in a given situation, often being used with fluidity and variously privileged, one over another, by individual gentlemen based on their objectives at the time.

Ideals of restraint and non-contentious behaviour served to smooth social relations and bolster good order, and it is perhaps unsurprising that an understanding of honour as rooted in the avoidance of violence would be frequently articulated in both prescriptive sources and governmental edicts. Likewise, alongside this prominently expressed understanding of honour as rooted in civil conduct, several other factors, including early modern ideas of the importance of self-mastery (connected to stages in the life cycle) and a wealth of prescriptive dictates concerning proper behaviour within social interactions were also entangled with understandings of honour and could mitigate potential impulses towards the use of physical force in its defence. These factors entailed that other meanings associated with honour, aside from a willingness to defend name and status at any cost, were often brought to the fore with greater frequency.

The powerful rhetoric of the desirability of peaceful relationships, settlement, and reconciliation that persisted across the medieval and early modern periods (remaining prevalent in the modern age as well) served to constrain, though not eradicate, honour-based violence.[2] Here, as the terminology will recur, it is worthwhile to draw a distinction between *reconciliation* and *settlement*. "Settlement" implies the restoration of peaceful relations and stasis within the community, while "reconciliation" implies the fostering of amiable relations. While reconciliation was certainly the social ideal, settlement and the ending of conflicts, or the restoration of neutral rather than amiable relations, was a far more common outcome when it came to the management of disputes, and the rhetoric of honour was often employed to effect such settlements.[3] In this sense, the range of contexts in which honour was displayed, and the diverse array of behaviours with which it was associated, can be extended with the recognition that honour was commonly appealed to as a tool to promote settlement (if not actual reconciliation), even as it could occasionally be used as a justification for violent behaviour or be translated into the restrictive code of duelling which a small proportion of the early modern male elite subscribed to. Accordingly, while honour could and did prompt quarrels, it is important to recognize that it was also often claimed in displays of restraint. In this sense, although the assertion that one was defending honour could occasionally effectively be used to justify quarrelsome behaviour, the importance attached to restraint as inherently honourable was a powerful force in the containment of violence. Unsurprisingly, in much prescriptive literature from the period, self-control was heralded as a more honourable form of behaviour than aggression. This was wholly in keeping with the definitions and Aristotelian understanding of honour discussed earlier, as well as with an understandable desire to maintain social stability. The values of mutuality and the importance attached to the preservation of order, which both occupied pivotal positions in the structure of early modern communities, were as crucial to the rhetoric associated with honour as a willingness to defend reputation at all costs. This ensured that, especially since threats to the social order were a constant bugbear of much early modern thought, the idea of true honour as vested in restraint was often cited as a mechanism to combat behaviour which threatened to upset that order, even as honour could also occasionally be invoked as a means to justify and even further a conflict.

The hierarchy of status and rank also had a prominent role to play in early modern conceptions of violence. While the state condemned private violence and contests of honour, and most moralists decried them, violence was more excusable when directed against those of inferior status. The use of violence as a social corrective could be a way of bolstering, rather than destabilizing, the social order. Yet, although contained, sanctioned violence towards subordinates had a role to play in relation to the preservation of stability, as private violence that did not respect the realities of the class hierarchy could be seen as destabilizing. While this did not mean that violence was absent from early modern social interactions between men, it did mean that the use of the rhetoric of honour in such incidents was complex and open to interpretation. Interpersonal violence was irrefutably a part of the landscape for elites, and early modern society was, generally speaking, a violent one.[4] It would be a mistake to view the early modern English social landscape through a rose-tinted lens: there was conflict, dissent, and violence between individuals.[5] This was a society in which disputes were common and several of the examples considered below illustrate this; anger had its place in early modern social life, and fraught interactions between male elites had the potential to become violent.[6]

Yet, while anger was and remained throughout the period an acceptable response in certain situations, and it is unwise to uncritically adopt the notion of a "tamed elite," a problem arises when it is assumed that early modern men inevitably coupled anger with violence.[7] Anger was permissible in certain circumstances, those circumstances often intersecting with the hierarchy of status, and violent behaviour could occasionally be endorsed as a necessary corrective to social disobedience.[8] However violence as the result of unbridled anger, anger taken too far, was not nearly as tolerated, especially when it unfolded among social equals. As Anthony Stafford, in his manual on honour, cautioned, "let not your Anger precede your judgement [*sic*], nor afford it leisure; for it quickly becomes master of the Place."[9] Early modern elite society was not one composed entirely of reckless and law-flouting rogues, prone to violence and duelling in the streets – although such individuals did, of course, exist. And here another distinction can be made, this time between *conflict* and *violence*. There was undeniably a great deal of conflict between elites in the period; however, the extent to which these conflicts ended in violence was more constricted. Likewise, when conflict did erupt, especially among peers, it was often perceived as constituting a breakdown in social relations. It was an undesirable situation that was seen as needing repair, not a normal and acceptable state of affairs. As such, conflict between gentlemen, though endemic at times, was less likely to lead to actual violence than might be suggested by focusing on isolated incidents of violent clashes. In addition, one should avoid seeing such violent clashes as did occur as inexorably tied to a culturally dominant understanding of honour that excused or endorsed violence; doing so obscures the many other facets of honour and the manner in which they interacted with each other, as well as the roles that Christian values, the rhetoric of community, and the bonds of neighbourliness played in placing constraints on the ways in which people expressed their anger and frustration with others.[10]

Early modern elite men perceived a range of attributes as connected to their honour, and they did not necessarily see violence as the best way to remedy a slight to their reputation, although the use of physical force was always a possible course of action and could be privileged as an expression of honour if needed. Recent work thus powerfully illustrates the complex meanings attached to violence in the period, and suggests that it is reductive to draw a clear line between honour and physical aggression.[11] As Linda Pollock notes, "honor, like passion, could be used to excuse violent behavior, but much of honor culture lay in preventing such outbursts and, when they occurred, in repairing the breaches if possible."[12] Far from being the norm, violent clashes were, more often than not, exceptional events that cannot be understood solely through the lens of honour. Likewise, appeals to honour often also served as a way to mitigate local conflicts and prevent them from becoming violent. Gentlemen often endeavoured to avoid the appearance that they were behaving "in a very quarrelynge" manner and look pains to present themselves as acting with restraint.[13] But honour as a multivocal concept also encompassed the idea that, as an essentially public commodity, reputation was something that needed to be defended at all costs, even when that entailed the employment of violence. This speaks to the many overlapping and occasionally contradictory ways in which honour was articulated; it could spark and justify conflicts in some instances (sometimes being deployed disingenuously as a cloak for otherwise transgressive behaviour) and serve to ameliorate them in others. These varied meanings of honour can be seen in an examination of several instances of conflict between gentlemen.

"Deale Cloaselie In This Business If Thow Be a Gentleman": Honour and the Gentlemanly Duel

For some early modern gentlemen, the idea that honour was a commodity to be defended at all costs translated most readily into participation in duelling, often problematically considered in modern popular imagination to be the embodiment of elite male honour. Consonant with this, some earlier analyses have portrayed the English male aristocracy as a violent group, easily goaded into conflict and lacking the self-control necessary to allow a slight to their honour to go unavenged. Perhaps the most important of these, aside from Mervyn James's *Society, Politics and Culture*, is Lawrence Stone's *Crisis of the Aristocracy*.[14] The image presented in these and other works of an elite, masculine society riven by interpersonal violence and prone to duelling has already undergone scholarly revision. Yet, and without wishing to unfairly focus on Stone's conclusions or press him into service as a straw man, his important insights on elites merit some dissection here.

For Stone, among an irascible nobility obsessed with status (as he saw it), the duel served a necessary social function. This form of single combat became, in the late sixteenth and early seventeenth centuries, a type of safety valve that allowed nobles to defend their honour in public while ensuring that collateral damage was minimal. This was in stark contrast to earlier conflicts over issues of honour that could resemble small battles with private armies composed of a lord's retainers engaging each other over their master's honour. Stone's work suggested a picture of an honour – and status – fixated nobility (an accurate depiction in some ways) resorting to violence with ease and enthusiasm (less accurate as a broad characterization, although certainly a fair description of some individuals). A number of Stone's characterizations are attributable to his interpretation of some of his data, as well as to the nature of the sources he used. For example, Stone pointed to a perceived increase in duelling in the seventeenth century as evidence of high levels of violence among the elite. However it is more probable that the slight increase of such instances beginning in the reign of James

I and reaching a pinnacle after 1660 with the emergence of the figure of the rake is attributable to the influx of French cultural influences at the English court, as duelling flourished at the French court in a manner in which it never did in England.[15] This aligns with scholarship that demonstrates that duelling was not tied to broader, historical practices and ideas of honour in England during the period but was, rather, the result of the importation of Continental concepts. While England certainly had a cultural tradition of elite men engaging in one-on-one combat, the ritual of the duel (and its associated choice of weapons) arrived only in the sixteenth century when Rocco Bonita established the first fencing school in England in 1576. Training in swordplay associated with duelling was understood to be an Italian innovation that was further popularized by the French nobility before its importation to England and moment of cultural vogue at the Restoration court.[16]

Even at the peak of its supposed popularity in England in the latter half of the seventeenth century, instances of duelling were not overly high, especially when one considers the numbers of elite men on the scene. The numbers of the peerage increased markedly in the years after 1660 and the gentry could be counted in the thousands; that there were approximately 356 reported duels in the years 1680–1750, or 100 reported contests in the 1790s, when viewed in the context of the numbers of the associated elite population, is not indicative of a widespread and pronounced surge in the activity (although there was a measured increase in instances of duelling, at least in Kent, between 1680 and 1700).[17] Likewise, while the ranks of the peerage were thinner in the sixteenth and early seventeenth centuries, gentry numbers were still high and the approximately sixty-two duels reported to have been fought between 1580 and 1620, a number offered by Peltonen, is not overwhelming evidence of an increase in duelling's popularity.[18]

There are, of course, some difficulties associated with gathering accurate statistics on the numbers of duels and thereby gauging the nature of its "popularity" across England. For example, many legal records, following the Jacobean regime's proscription of duelling, stopped referring to the practice specifically, although it was undoubtedly occurring.[19] Likewise, many such contests that did not result in death or serious injury likely escaped official attention. Finally, legal records provide evidence of the number of prosecutions associated with a particular offence, rather than the actual number of such offences committed. Yet, even if one assumes that a proportion of duels escaped attention and remained unrecorded, the numbers of gentlemen that were so lucky would be limited and the overall numbers would still remain low. The exception to this, perhaps, would be within London. While duelling appears never to have gained a truly significant foothold outside of the city, within the metropolis instances of duelling were certainly more numerous and the practice retained a limited popularity there after it fell out of fashion in other areas.[20] Notwithstanding, the evidence that can be gleaned from legal sources (critically used), coupled with the reaction to duelling of many elites as reflected in their correspondence, does not support the conclusion that it was an exceptionally widespread practice, a largely tolerated one, or even a straightforward one when it came to ameliorating feelings of dishonour.

With respect to Stone's interpretation of his selected evidence, some of his assertions can be viewed as the result of a few celebrated instances of elite violence being used to characterize a much broader segment of society. For example, Stone described the ongoing feud between Sir Thomas Knyvett and Edward de Vere, the seventeenth Earl of Oxford, in the 1580s as representative of the violent tendencies of the Tudor nobility as a whole, even likening the behaviour of the two men to that of Mafia bosses in the 1920s.[21] The nature of the creation and preservation of historical sources is such that honour disputes that were peaceably resolved were less likely to be remembered than those that led to violence; this means that such incidents as were recorded should not necessarily be read as representative of elite society more broadly. Multiple meanings were associated with honour, driving to its durability and effectiveness as a rhetorical strategy, but the experience of many elites across the period was with honour as vested in restraint and a reluctance to engage in violence, despite the willingness of a small number to do so. This broad-based privileging – and there were of course exceptions to this – of one understanding of honour (as rooted in sober behaviour and a reluctance to engage in violence) over another (honour as a willingness to defend name and status at all costs) was increasingly common as gentlemen saw their reputations intertwined with their roles as upholders of social order. This was not, however, a newly sprung conception of honour. It was the continuation, if perhaps with more prominence, of an already existing understanding of honour as tethered to serving as a figure of authority and a maintainer of order.

For all this, the idea that there was a profound upsurge in instances of duelling in early modern England is partially reinforced by sources such as the records of the Court of Chivalry (where gentlemen ostensibly pursued suits in order to avoid duels). The impression is tempered, however, when one looks beneath the surface of the cases brought before this court. In the early seventeenth century, the crown vested authority in Henry Howard, Earl of Northampton and Earl Marshal, to draft legislation to provide for the adjudication of competing claims of honour in the Court of Chivalry.[22] Under the regulations established by Northampton, the only ground needed to bring a case before the Court was testimony that slanderous words likely to provoke a duel had been spoken. As a result, the vast majority of the cases tried in the Court were rooted in allegations of defamation. Looking at the high volume of cases that went before this body (e.g., between 1634 and 1640, the Court heard more than 1,000 cases), one might be tempted to see it as proof of a rise in duelling. However, alternate explanations for the high caseload are possible. For example, the Court of Chivalry was attractive to those seeking quicker and relatively less expensive resolutions to their suits than was possible in other courts. In addition, only those considered to hold the rank of gentleman were permitted to press suits in the Court.[23] It is therefore likely that the high volume of cases occurring between 1634 and 1640 may not be the result of men engaging in honour disputes on an unprecedented scale (although the Jacobean regime was rather panicked that this was the case) but reflects, rather, individuals using the Court as a means of proving their status as gentlemen within the community, and also as a convenient and expedient way to get a judgment.

As the surviving records for the Court show, even before a case was tried there were sometimes protracted disputes as to whether or not an individual could actually claim the status of a gentleman and hence gain access to the Court. Numerous witnesses and documents were paraded through to try to prove whether one could justly call oneself a gentleman through claims to bloodline or land ownership.[24] The records suggest that, in a manner comparable to the use of church courts by women ostensibly to protect their sexual reputations, suing in the Court of Chivalry could be a way of asserting status and responding to (or furthering) a quarrel with a local rival that had its origins in matters not necessarily related to an honour dispute. While bringing a suit in the Court also served as a mechanism to potentially avoid the escalation of violence, or at least to be seen as attempting to do so, the threat of violence (while certainly present in some cases) was often of secondary importance in terms of accessing the Court.

Despite the impression gleaned from the high volume of suits that came before the Court of Chivalry, the anti-duelling campaigns of the

Jacobean, Caroline, and Restoration regimes, and the later printed criticisms of duelling in venues such as newspapers, disputes between elite men, even over matters of reputation and name, were far from always violent.[25] Likewise, although duelling enjoyed a period of brief popularity among some portions of the English elite and members of the middling and lower orders, instances of it quickly began to decrease in the eighteenth century.[26] By the mid-nineteenth century it had largely died out entirely.[27] There were, of course, some celebrated instances of duelling, such as the exploits of Charles Mohun, fourth Baron Mohun, especially in the post-Restoration period, that illustrated its enduring popularity among some segments of elite society, as well as governmental ineffectiveness in prosecuting such offensives among the aristocracy, leading to a measure of public outcry. Yet these were exceptional incidents, as evidenced by the level of attention and public condemnation they attracted, especially as a means to critique the regime for failing to adequately punish those involved.[28]

Some gentlemen in the sixteenth and earlier seventeenth centuries, associating honour with a willingness to use violence in defence of reputation (or at least claiming this reasoning as a way to justify an attack on a rival), did of course engage in duelling. But that does not mean that duelling was unambiguously perceived as appropriate behaviour. The limits of its acceptability were never settled and were constantly being probed and redefined.[29] Most treatises on the subject stressed that it was only permissible in specific, and limited, contexts. Involvement in quasi-violent activities (that could also be important facets of gentlemanly sociability and elite masculinity), such as the hunt and training in swordsmanship and in the structures of duelling and single combat, may have furthered an attachment to duelling among some. And this was no doubt furthered by the perception of some that, when the prescribed ritualized behaviour was adhered to, the code of duelling was itself a vehicle for the promotion of civility, as it offered instruction in courtesy and proper comportment. Yet the experience of most gentlemen was with the constraining, not unleashing, of violent tendencies.[30]

Notwithstanding, as suggested above, many perceived the duel as promoting ideals of civil and gentlemanly conduct.[31] When properly conducted it was a highly ritualized and stylized form of combat in which duellists were urged to remember their social positions as gentlemen and behave with equanimity. In order to distinguish the practice of duelling from the street fights and tavern brawls of those from the lower social orders, duels were meant to follow a set of rules that prized fair conduct and marked the combatants out as gentlemen. Ambushes were prohibited and the involvement of third parties was strictly forbidden. Even before a proper duel could begin, the participant's second had to attempt to elicit an apology from the other duellist in a final attempt to avoid the conflict.[32] This was a ritual aimed not at suppressing violence but at containing it. Participation in the ritual of the duel could also importantly serve as an affirmation of gentility, as both the rhetoric and practice of duelling were intertwined with the hierarchy of social status and served to demarcate gentlemen from their inferiors. Yet, while the duel's occasional ability to contain more scattershot violence and its potential usefulness as an articulation of status may have attracted some, the bulk of prescriptive literature, augmented by sermons and the law (even if not always consistently enforced), urged gentlemen to control their tempers and avoid violence – things detrimental to an ordered society and potentially, by extension, to their claims to be the governors of that society. Conflict, even when it occurred within the structure of the prescribed rituals of duelling, could be viewed harshly. This ensured that, even though honour was flexible enough to be co-opted into a duelling code which certainly did influence the behaviour of those who subscribed to this constrained understanding of honour, it was never particularly widespread and was rejected by many.

Nonetheless, as noted above, a small proportion of gentlemen undoubtedly did associate honour with a willingness to harness violence in its defence, and these individuals could be enthusiastic participants in the culture of duelling. Duelling offered them a type of behavioural "code," although a highly restrictive one that was only adopted by a relatively small segment of the elite male population. It was a model of behaviour that was not aimed at thinking about honour more broadly as a shared social value across communities or at considering the other meanings of honour aside from the importance of defending and advancing one's reputation by whatever means necessary, and, for most, was outside the realm of lived experience. It is indicative of honour's flexibility that, while a particular understanding of it was articulated as a foundational element in the code of duelling, most gentlemen typically emphasized alternate understandings of honour within social interactions. Likewise, while the idea that honour was most strongly associated with a willingness to defend name and status by any means necessary (including violence) was certainly a feature of the mental landscape for early modern gentlemen, the prevalence of such things as duelling was constrained by the equally prevalent view that honour for a mature elite man was rooted in impulse control and sober self-governance in furtherance of the maintenance of the social order more broadly. Other factors, such as the law and prescriptive dictates, also served to augment this perception of honour and limit instances of violent conflict among the gentry and aristocracy.

Constraints on Violence

While duelling never achieved notably widespread popularity in sixteenth- and seventeenth-century England, instances of it were also limited because many men subscribed to an understanding of violent action as potentially dangerous to personal honour because it pointed to a lack of self-control. It implied a rash and even irresponsible character and could be detrimental to personal reputation. The appearance of self-mastery mattered a great deal for men in the patriarchal social order of early modern England.[33] Accordingly, most gentlemen, desiring to be seen as masters of themselves and their emotions and conduct, did not subscribe to the rather narrow understanding of honour inherent in the practice of duelling. That, however, did not preclude an awareness of this view of honour, and some gentlemen were not averse to seeing it as a legitimate justification for the occasional violent actions of others – after all, most acknowledged that the defence of reputation was important, even if there was a degree of ambiguity surrounding the best way to achieve it. Yet an interconnected series of cultural assumptions and social pressures also served to limit the acceptability of violent conflict and involvement in duelling, contributing to its relative rarity among gentlemen.

Medical knowledge, for example, could serve as a check on such behaviour. The dominant medical discourse of the period, Galen's humoural model, dictated that men, as the hotter, drier sex, were more prone to anger, while women were more likely to become enraged over trivial matters and be unable to control that anger once roused.[34] Proper and complete men, in short, should have heightened impulse control, and men were encouraged to live up to this standard, often by the suggestion that to do otherwise was shameful. Accordingly, Helkiah Crooke wrote in his 1616 *Mikrokosmographia* that "anger is a disease of a weak mind which cannot moderate itself but is easily inflamed, such are women, children and weak and cowardly men."[35] An inability to control one's emotions could be perceived as a feminine characteristic; unbridled anger in a man could thus be regarded as effeminate and, accordingly, potentially socially destructive.[36] While Crooke believed that young men in particular (because their inner heat was all the greater by virtue of their youth) were prone to this type of behaviour, anger among all needed to be moderated, lest it become destructive and bring dishonour.

Unrestrained violence could merit condemnation. For example, in a letter to Lady Jane Cornwallis, Ambrose Randolph referred to an ongoing conflict between Sir John Suckling and Sir John Digby. The quarrel began when the two men clashed over a Derbyshire heiress and Digby attempted to use force to make Suckling sign a paper disavowing a matrimonial interest in her. In retaliation, Suckling assaulted Digby outside of the Blackfriars Theatre in London. As Randolph described it to Lady Cornwallis, "on Tuesday last he waie layed Mr Digby, that had formerly strook him, and, as he came from the play he, with many more, set upon Mr Digby; in which quarell Sir John Suckling had a man rune through, som say he is dead."[37] In instigating a violent and uncontained retaliation against Digby, Suckling had both forfeited a measure of his personal honour and put himself in a position to be arrested and prosecuted. Randolph believed that, in choosing to use force rather than attempting a settlement, "Sir John Suckling, in place of repairing his honour, hath lost his reputation for ever, and drawne himself in dainger of the law."[38]

Likewise, when Thomas Lunsford made an attempt on the life of a local rival, Sir Thomas Pelham, while he sat in a carriage with his wife and several others, his reputation suffered. Lunsford was practically ostracized from local politics, and, in 1635, more than three years later, he was still lamenting his "want of friends" in his own county.[39] A lack of self-control could be detrimental to honour and could also negatively affect opportunities for participation in networks of patronage and the holding of office that had the potential to advance a gentleman's career. By engaging in such behaviour, gentlemen ran the risk of being seen as incapable of governing themselves, perhaps even as effeminate. This could result in the perception that they were, by extension, ill suited to exercise authority effectively over others.

While the examples offered so far concern unbridled and careless violence (not the sort of violence typically associated with the gentlemanly duel), many nonetheless also condemned duels, and legal and prescriptive dictates further served as checks on violent behaviour. Characterizations of the duel and other violent clashes of honour as vices to be shunned are found in letters and an array of non-governmental sources from the period. Likewise, given that it had a vested interest in encouraging the rule of law and preserving its own monopoly on the use of violence, the government also strongly opposed duelling and other forms of interpersonal violence. That said, however, such prohibitions against duelling were not often consistently enforced. Many who engaged in such contests escaped punishment altogether, and others saw their contravention of the prohibition on duelling largely forgotten after what amounted to a judicial slap on the wrist.[40] In this sense, duelling, like some other crimes, was "much maligned in prescriptive literature, but more ambivalently received in daily life ... much decried, but little prosecuted, often vilified but rarely punished."[41] This, however, perhaps speaks more to the reality that the enforcement of the law was deeply entangled with the beliefs and attitudes of the individuals responsible for its enforcement (who might, perhaps, have personal relationships with those accused or be generally more tolerant of duelling and less likely to harshly prosecute people when injury or death resulted from what was perceived to be a fair fight) than it does to a widespread belief in the acceptability of the use of violence in defence of honour.[42] Many of those involved in duelling were able to take advantage of this and could defend themselves and mitigate the punishment they received by framing their actions as limited, necessary in a particular circumstance, and resulting from a conflict that was two-sided and, hence, honourable. In so doing they were sometimes able to evade punishment, often using the rhetoric of honour to do so. And the concept of honour was flexible enough to encompass such justifications for the use of violence.[43]

The doctrine of chancemedley also aided some gentlemen in evading the full rigors of the law. Edward Coke, in 1604, described a chancemedley homicide as one "done by chance (without premeditation) upon a sudden brawle, shuffling, or contention."[44] Those who committed such a crime were considered to act "in the Time of their Rage, Drunkenness, hidden Displeasure, or other Passion of Mind."[45] While such a defence was more difficult in the case of a pre-arranged duel, in which there was a measure of premeditation, it could sometimes be used effectively as a strategy of justification. Thus, "the law (as it had been doing since the late sixteenth century) took a much more lenient view of the hot-blooded and spontaneous combat or duel than it did of the premeditated one, categorizing the former as manslaughter only."[46]

However much the priority of the state may have been vested in the suppression of violence and the upholding of its own authority (trials and ensuing punishments often serving an exemplary purpose), the participatory nature of law enforcement "involved the continual renegotiation of the priorities of the state and the community."[47] The law was, in many senses, a discretionary instrument used in the preservation of social relations within the community and those involved with the enforcement of the law were influenced by personal relationships. Likewise, ideas of social justice and Christian conceptions of the value of forgiveness shaped legal responses.[48] That some gentlemen, enmeshed in both local and far-reaching alliances and patronage relationships, were unwilling to bring the full force of the law to bear on their peers who engaged in activities such as duelling need not be interpreted as broad-based tolerance of the practice or as an endorsement of the idea that honour was best associated with an unambiguous willingness to use violence in its defence. Early modern society was one in which the ideals of the state were "tempered by the political realities of local social relations," and this meant that instances of violence, while officially condemned, sometimes went under-punished or unpunished altogether.[49] The government was not equipped to effectively suppress and prosecute all forms of criminal activity and depended upon this participatory apparatus. Consequently, that individuals sometimes escaped punishment for crimes committed should not be read as indicating a widespread tolerance of their behaviour.

Finally, the relative rarity of duelling (even allowing for many instances that likely escaped official attention) meant that, while it was important for the regime to articulate a harsh stance towards it in the interests of asserting its authority and demarcating its position as the ultimate arbiter of social relations, stability did not depend on the government mercilessly cracking down on a phantom epidemic of duelling that threatened to subvert the entire social order. While the force of the rhetoric of the Jacobean regime's anti-duelling campaign was disproportionate to the actual level of punishment doled out to those who became embroiled in physical confrontations over matters of reputation, it was also disproportionate to the actual level of duelling. As with all forms of crime, it is to be expected that the government would condemn duelling, but the fevered tone of much governmental criticism of duelling should not be interpreted as evidence of a broader prevalence of such conflicts.

The Jacobean regime notably adopted a harsh stance towards duelling. And in its anti-duelling material, unsurprisingly and speaking to the recognition that some did subscribe to the restrictive idea of honour as contained within the code of duelling and privileged this idea of honour over other, competing understandings (or at least claimed to do so when it suited them, such as in the aftermath of an attack on a rival), the government denied duelling's role as a means to enhance or restore honour. For example, a proclamation against duelling issued by the Jacobean regime stated that those who duelled would be punished "for pretending aboue all things to regard Honour for a flourish, yet to satisfie their owne inordinate desires."[50] Duelling here was the antithesis of true honour. A smokescreen for people to indulge their own petty grievances, invocations of honour in the course of a duel became a mockery of true honour.[51] According to Sir Francis Bacon, in his anti-duelling tract, the elaborate ritual of the duel provided "a kind of satanicall illusion and apparition of honour; against religion, against lawe, against morall virtue."[52] It represented "a kind of sorcery, which enchanteth the spirits of young men." The duel sprang "only from the vnbrideled humors of priuate men" and was condemned as such.[53] In addition, it was not only duellists who were often condemned by writers, moralists, and the courts but also those who abetted duels because, "between an Actor therefore and an Abettor, the difference cannot bee great, howsoever malice may be masked vnder false couers."[54]

As noted, governmental hostility to the duel should not be read in isolation as proof that it was a largely condemned practice.[55] However the manner in which many individual gentlemen reacted to duelling serves as a further indication that attitudes towards such contests were ambiguous at best (if not negative), despite their appeal to a small segment of the elite population. In a commonplace book, possibly written by William Sandys between 1651 and 1653, a further example of the idea that duelling was a perversion/inversion of true honour can be found.[56] Within the text is found "A Discourse of Duelling according to ^the^ vniustiable Custome of this age by a true louer of honour," in which the author condemns what he sees as the foolish custom of young English braggarts engaging in duels and other violent behaviours in the name of honour.[57] The manuscript asserts that "the first Duell hapned betwixt the two first borne, Cain & Abel."[58] While, as noted, the actual number of duels fought in England was relatively low, the author nonetheless lamented that "the humour of Cain is too muche practised by the debauched youth of our nation."[59] In a piece of nationalist rhetoric the author then notes that, despite the reckless behaviour of certain wayward youths (in some senses this text is a diatribe against the troublesome nature of the young), the laws of England were far too advanced and sophisticated to tolerate the barbaric practice of duelling which featured prominently in other European states. He then indicted duelling as a contest which only occurs when a man is unable to conquer "his Tyrannical passions"; the practice is thus derided as the result of a lack of proper self-control and as the product of the kind of destructive anger that was socially damaging.[60] In contrast, those who behaved with virtue and possessed the ability to control their actions and their propensities for aggression were characterized as the true possessors of honour. In the same vein, William Martyn noted in his conduct book aimed at the rearing of the young, "he that soweth vertue shall reape honor."[61] For these authors, the duel was neither a ritual of honour nor a socially acceptable means of preserving one's reputation. For them, rather, the duel, "stripped starke naked is downe right murder."[62]

Among the aristocracy and gentry, the importance placed on an adult male's level of self-mastery also aided in mitigating resorts to violence when one's reputation was slighted. A similar situation with respect to adhering to notions of proper gentlemanly conduct (including the exercise of restraint) prevailed in urban spaces. Claims to corporate citizenship, as well as involvement in political discourse and the provision of good government, often revolved around the "discussion and debate and the adaptation of requisite conventions and attributes, most notably civility."[63] This was a concept with obvious links to contemporary thinking about honour and entailed a rejection of violent action, or at least a series of rhetorical maneuverings in order to justify it. A failure to show restraint and manifest the virtues associated with good lordship could be viewed as an impediment to the proper exercise of responsibility by those in positions of authority. During the early modern period there was a notable expansion in governmental infrastructure and a commensurate expansion in the structures of governance at the local level; linked to this expansion, "office-holding became a mark of status and distinction for county gentry, parish notables, and urban citizens alike."[64] Holding office, typically only open to the "better sort," served to demarcate the elite from their social inferiors, and this added a measure of impetus to acquire such positions.[65] The desire to attain associated influence, as well as potential financial benefits, added further motivation to adhere to broad-based standards of civil conduct in the interests of gaining promotion.[66] While some gentlemen on the rise, eager to cement their positions as figures of local authority, may have been more enthusiastic about acquiring such positions, in varying measure they mattered to all, as they could offer an affirmation of one's status as a man of means, station, and influence. There was a level of symmetry between social status and political power, and many gentlemen (although certainly not all) perceived that exercising political power through office-holding and associated governance responsibilities enhanced the level of honour and deference to which they were entitled from their neighbours, whether other elites or people situated at lower positions in the social hierarchy. In this respect, service confirmed and enhanced social status while simultaneously offering a means for gentlemen to augment their reputation at the local level through their involvement in a political space that, while serving the regime, in many senses also operated partially autonomously from state authority.[67] While such positions were, ostensibly, rooted in service to the state, the government depended in a meaningful way on men on the ground in the localities for the enforcement of policy. Thus the interests of the "the early modern state were mediated and filtered by the particular needs, perceptions and responses" of both local office holders and the communities in which they lived, and gentlemen serving as local officials were able to attain a measure of influence and autonomy in the shaping and maintenance of local governance.[68]

Some gentlemen perceived that rewards, such as gaining a role in governance, went more readily to those who were unimpressed by provocation (although there were, of course, exceptions to this, motivated, for example, by the demands of patronage or personal relationships and other factors), as they seemed best suited to maintain stability. This served to mitigate a willingness to use violence among some or, at the very least, spurred them to deploy carefully considered legitimating techniques if they did engage in socially breaching behaviour. Given the expansion of the number of governance positions at the local level throughout the sixteenth and seventeenth centuries, and the enhanced sense of importance attached to the holding of such positions (as noted above), many members of the social elite increasingly saw a measure of their honour as vested in their ability to acquire and hold such offices.[69] In addition to serving as an acknowledgment of status, many recognized that attaining such positions was a useful way of shaming local rivals who were passed over.[70] Better still would be to gain an office that a local rival had been stripped of; the loss of office could be more devastating than a failure to gain it in the first place.[71] Thus the Earl of Northumberland was launched into a state of anxiety when his appointment as custodian of Mary, Queen of Scots, when she first fled to England, was revoked. Worried about how the loss of this charge would be perceived, he pleaded unsuccessfully that "my credyt be not so much impared in the face of my contrey, as she shuld be taken from me."[72] Unfortunately for Northumberland, he already had reputational problems before charge of the recently abdicated Scottish queen was granted to him and then revoked. It was felt by those at the centre of the regime that "the lorde himselfe in his owne countrie [is] not regarded" and his tenants were "not so much in feare of his lordshipe … as of other gentlemen ther neighbours."[73] It was perhaps unsurprising that his commission was withdrawn.

Other gentlemen who consistently failed to adhere to standards of social courtesy and good lordship, aside from facing possible legal penalties if their actions ventured into criminal territory, could likewise potentially lose political influence within their counties and at court. While honour as a concept was broad enough to encompass divergent meanings, those who regularly failed to adhere to notions of proper gentlemanly conduct and who also served as ineffective governors of social subordinates, especially those who did not acknowledge that their authority and honour were bestowed by the higher authority of the state (the larger fault), often failed to gain the level of influence they felt appropriate to their station.[74] For example, when Gilbert Talbot succeeded his father as seventh Earl of Shrewsbury he proved such a negligent landlord that, in 1594 and 1595, he was banned from court for resisting the crown's attempts to relieve one of his distressed tenants. Gilbert blamed many of his reputational problems on rumours spread by local rivals. Ultimately, however, his own poor management of his estates and treatment of his tenants, combined with his contempt for crown authority, were to blame.[75] He also possessed a contentious personality and notably contended with his stepmother Elizabeth Talbot over the terms of his father's will, with Elizabeth eventually prevailing in 1592.[76] This dispute divided the family and, while Elizabeth was eventually reconciled with her daughter Mary (who, as Gilbert's wife, supported her husband in the matter), she never forgave Gilbert, who had, indeed, once been Elizabeth's ally in her drawn-out conflict with Gilbert's father, her husband. Gilbert's temper also led him to challenge his younger brother Edward to a duel in 1594 after a dispute over a lease (the challenge was refused) and later to accuse Edward of attempting to poison him.[77] While some elite men did not see their careers blemished by a propensity for quarrelsome conduct, others did pay a price for such behaviour.

Honour, Restraint, and the Life Cycle

Ideas related to the elite masculine life cycle also mediated expressions of honour associated with the deployment of violence in the defence of reputation. The importance of self-mastery as an integral component of mature elite male self-presentation influenced understandings of honour and reputation. Through the displays offered by jousting, sporting matches, hunting, military action (when directed at an appropriate party or in the spread or defence of Protestantism), and a wealth of prescriptive literature exhorting men to be the true masters of their wives, children, and servants, boys and men were socialized to link physical prowess, tempered by control, to honour and masculinity. While dramatic and literary representations of duelling and a more generalized revival of chivalric culture may have contributed in a meaningful way to some younger men seeing such involvements as a feature of their youthful masculine identity, the meanings presented in such sources could be ambiguous.[78] For example, while violence was glorified in some popular literature centring on chivalric romances, such pieces also included examples of violence as linked to cowardice, betrayal, and vice alongside depictions of violence associated with bravery, friendship, and virtue. They could, likewise, be inconsistent in their portrayal of violence and associate it variously with both honour and shame, allowing early modern elite readers to glean different messages and morals depending on the contexts in which they read such works. For example, the popular tales of the deeds of Guy of Warwick contained narrations both of his physical and military victories and of his later repentance for past violence and pilgrimage to the Holy Land in atonement.[79] Furthermore, in addition to these chivalric romances and dramatic representations, a wealth of prescriptive literature and the norms of social interaction as expressed from venues such as the pulpit emphasized that honour was vested in restraint and civility. This served, in part, to contain actual violence among men as they matured.

Excessive force in attempting to project a masculine self-image could also be detrimental to claims to effective self-control and, by extension, to authority, full masculinity, and honour.[80] This could be a powerful check on "youthful intemperance" when it came to violence. As Shepard has demonstrated, manhood in the patriarchal structure of early modern society was assessed based on age and social and financial status, alongside an ability to exert effective control over oneself and others. As such, many men, especially the young and financially insecure, with no household or resources to govern, as well as the old and poor, were not considered full men.[81] Likewise humoural theory also dictated that young men ran "hotter" than mature men and so, like women (who "will bark and brawl like mad dogs") had greater difficulty controlling their tempers.[82] These people of marginal masculinity may have attempted to find alternate, and transgressive, codes of manhood that united them, such as drinking, carousing, and womanizing, or engaging in various forms of violence, either in tavern brawls and street fights or in more socially accepted and structured forms, such as football matches.[83] Young men looking to assert alternate forms of masculinity because full, normative masculinity was denied to them, and seizing upon one understanding of honour which tolerated violence, while disregarding parallel messages of the virtue of restraint, could thus be more prone to actions such as duelling. Engaging in such behaviour was a way to deal with being denied the trappings of full manhood as "in its most extreme forms violence was deployed by men in ways which deliberately contravened prescriptive tenets of self-government."[84] Yet such behaviours remained on the periphery with respect to their social acceptability, and most pursued normative ideals of masculinity embodied in mature conduct and the exercise of authority.

Notwithstanding, breaching behaviour was more expected of younger men, and those who participated in violence often found that their youth afforded them a certain level of protection from severe punishment. After all, a certain level of reckless behaviour and flouting of societal conventions was to be expected from them.[85] Hence, when the cousin of the wife of Sir Francis Walsingham got into trouble in Surrey and was due to be presented at the Assizes, Walsingham wrote to Sir William More, the High Sheriff of Surrey, to plead for clemency, emphasizing that the young man's errors were the result of the willfulness of youth. Making special note of his personal repentance, Walsingham implored, "my wifes cosin confessed his fawlte, and promyssed amendment … I beseeche you therfor yf he may be dispensed *wi*th his personale appearance at your next assises."[86] He added that "he is yonge and this is [his] fyrst fawlte I beseeche you therfor let yt not receyve so [s]harpe a pvnyshement as open discredit in an open assemblye."[87] Walsingham's hope was that the young man's future would not be cast into jeopardy by questionable actions committed in his youth. Sir Thomas Egerton similarly advised Robert Devereux, Earl of Essex, to master his youthful passions when he fell out with the Queen. Egerton urged him to "conquer yo*u*rself which is the height of true valour."[88] To behave otherwise, he continued, was to "forsake yourself and ouerthrowe your fortunes and ruyn all your honor and reputation."[89] Earlier in his career Essex had seemed to temporarily heed advice of this ilk; after his elevation to the Privy Council, he studiously endeavoured to project an image of himself as a sober gentleman. As Anthony Bagot described it in a letter to his father:

> hys L*ordshi*p [Essex] is become a newe man cleane forsakinge all hys former youthfull tricks carringe hym sealf w*i*th very honorable gravyty and singulerly lyked of boath in p*ar*liam*en*t and at Counsayle table.[90]

Yet such displays of maturity by Essex were fleeting, prompting Egerton to offer his guidance. While such rash behaviour may have been more broadly acceptable among the young, that tolerance had limits, especially when appropriate displays of repentance and reform were not forthcoming.[91] Most gentlemen, as they matured, realized that elevation to adulthood and its associated responsibilities depended on their manifestation of appropriate respect for authority and social propriety. As Herrup puts it, "a man who could not control himself was not deemed a fit member of the commonwealth."[92]

Involvement in duelling and other violent clashes was, perhaps, slightly more socially acceptable among military men, as it could be interpreted as evidence of martial spirit. By the mid-seventeenth century, however, the military functions of the elite had declined considerably and most gentlemen had no military experience, and gained even less so as "soldier" increasingly became a separate and bounded occupation.[93] While some commentators in the period were actively hostile to military values, seeing them as at odds with Christian dictates and as contributing little to the social order, others bemoaned the lack of actual practice at arms that most elite men had, and most gentlemen, for their part, continued to perceive military prowess as a component of both their masculine and their elite identity.[94] Accordingly, rituals associated with the hunt and other displays of martial skill, including the erection of funeral monuments that emphasized military ability, held a high level of importance in early modern elite society; they provided regulated spaces in which to display appropriately masculine physical prowess.[95] And many gentlemen went a step further and sought to engage in actual military service, often either in Ireland or the Low Countries, where they could both play a martial role and aid in the spread and defence of Protestantism.[96] Gentlemen also maintained a keen interest in things such as chivalric texts and displays, other means of projecting both their masculinity and their elevated social status. But, by and large (the exception being those who signed up for military service), these were ways of acting out, in a contained way, the more martial aspects of masculinity rather than actually relying on one's physical prowess.

Likewise, though it might seem that duelling would be viewed more charitably among the military, event within military ranks it was not endorsed as acceptable behaviour (though a broader level of tolerance towards it tended to be present). Duelling likely did occur between those of military rank with more frequency as, by virtue of it being the essence of their profession, slights to personal courage or aptitude in battle could not be allowed to stand. Nevertheless, such quarrels were not accepted as proper behaviour. Disorder within the ranks remained an area of concern, linked as it was to issues of disobedience and the inability of commanders to effectively govern their subordinates. During the Civil War, for example, commentators bemoaned the rivalries that occurred among officers.[97] Such incidents risked being interpreted as compromising the discipline, leadership, and even righteousness of the respective forces.

Connected to the appearance of self-control and sober self-governance expected of mature men, preserving order among one's social subordinates was also a reputational matter for gentlemen. When a servant of the family died in a duel in 1570, Henry Cavendish wrote to his mother in horror, saying, "I thought yt good to let your La*dyship* vnderstande of a mysfortune that happened in my howse."[98] Henry went on to describe how two of his men "fell owt aboute some tryflynge woord*es*."[99] The next morning the two men fought each other, "to my great greyfe booth for the sodeyne deathe of the one and for the vtter dystructyon of the other whom I loved very well."[100] Cavendish's assessment was that involvement in a duel had thereby tarnished the honour of the actual victor of the contest. Henry was also concerned because the incident had occurred on his property and might tarnish his honour, as it spoke to his lack of control over his household. To this end he told his mother that it was to "my greattest greyffe … that yt shoulde happen in my howse."[101] Henry averred that the fault lay not with him, however: "alas mada*m* what coulde I dooe w*ith* yt, altogether not once suspectynge any thynge betwyxte them. I haue byn ryghte sorofull for yt, and yt hath trowbled and vexed me, more then in reason yt should haue donne a wyese ma*n*.[102] Henry concluded his missive by writing that "I would to God I could forget that theyr never had byn any shuch matter."[103]

While Henry desired to present an image of himself as an effective governor of servants and social subordinates, he proved unable to govern himself at times. Indeed, his mother, the redoubtable Elizabeth Talbot, Countess of Shrewsbury, referred to him as "my bad son Henry."[104] Alongside having a violent temper and being easily driven to quarrelsome behaviour, Henry accorded a higher degree of precedence to the notion that violence in defence of honour was acceptable than to the idea that honour was best articulated through sober conduct and self-restraint. In 1574, when he was twenty-four, this led to his involvement in an armed affray in Staffordshire in which a man was killed. As a result, Cavendish came to the attention of the Privy Council (who launched an inquiry) and his attempts at gaining a military commission were thwarted. Finally, in 1578, tired of waiting for advancement, Cavendish raised a regiment of several hundred of his own men and joined the army of William of Orange in the Netherlands. His desire for battle quickly slackened, however, and by 1579 he was back in England after abandoning his regiment on foreign soil. After travelling to Turkey in 1589, Cavendish returned to England and was once again involved in a violent quarrel in 1591. This time he brawled with William Agard, and both men employed armed retainers. The situation became so heated that Cavendish's brother-in-law and step-brother, Gilbert, seventh Earl of Shrewsbury, intervened by writing to the Privy Council and asking that the men's grievances be adjudicated before violence erupted, a request that was heeded.[105] While Henry was still a relatively young man in 1574 and could claim youthful willfulness for which he repented, he was over forty when he quarreled with Agard – there would be no tolerance for something that could not be explained away as a youthful indiscretion.

Also of interest in this incident was the conduct of Henry's brother-in-law and step-brother, Gilbert, who was at pains to both stop conflict from erupting, which would tarnish the collective honour of the family, and to assert his own authority as governor of the family's affairs. Gilbert, as discussed earlier, had experienced his own reputational difficulties, and Henry's behaviour offered him an opportunity to display himself as an effective settler of conflicts and as an upholder of social order. Gilbert recognized that violence and other disorderly behaviour without appropriate justification were contrary to the perception that a mature gentleman would retain mastery of himself and his social subordinates and junior family members, even though at other times in his life he flouted such behavioural conventions as much as Henry did. The fluidity with which early modern gentlemen such as Gilbert Talbot and Henry Cavendish adapted contrasting conceptions of honour dependent on the circumstances, and their individual objectives in a given interaction are indicative of honour's inherent flexibility as a social value. In addition, like Gilbert and Henry, most gentlemen who were unable to commit to manifesting the conduct book ideals of good behaviour nonetheless often paid them lip service and employed a range of techniques of legitimation (often cast in the language of honour) to explain their socially breaching activities or make amends for them. In such instances they relied, with varying degrees of efficacy, upon the flexibility of understandings of honour and good reputation to envelope and excuse their behaviour.

Negotiating Confrontation

Given the multiple interpretations of the meaning of honour possible and the existence of social norms, knowledge systems, and governmental edicts that served, at least partially, to mitigate the use of violence associated with honour and good reputation in early modern England, how were instances of duelling perceived and reacted to? In what ways did gentlemen accord precedence to the varying behaviours associated with honour (including the occasional use of violence in furtherance of a duel) in ways that best suited their circumstances and objectives in a given interaction? In the case of the early seventeenth-century dispute between the Earl of Northumberland and Sir Francis Vere, in which a challenge to duel was issued, the manner in which both parties negotiated the challenge speaks both to the limits of violent acts as a clear cut means of restoring honour, and to the manner in which honour's inherent flexibility could be used to pursue an objective. The incident also echoes Pollock's suggestion that, in contrast to the view presented by Stone, refusing a challenge to duel was not universally seen as damaging to honour; it implies that it was possible to avoid a challenge or simply to refuse to dignify it with a response without one's honour being lost.[106] Finally, the episode provides evidence of an array of tactics based in varying understandings of honour that Vere was able to deploy to avoid engaging with Northumberland, and which also factored in many other challenges to duel from the period.

As background, Vere served with distinction as a commander in the Netherlands during the reign of Elizabeth I, and Northumberland was under his command. An example of Stone's depiction of a status-obsessed noble and one who did subscribe, at least in this instance, to the restrictive idea of honour contained in the code of duelling, Northumberland felt that serving under a man who fell beneath him in station was a source of dishonour. In response, he was openly insubordinate, ultimately returning to England prematurely to avoid further serving under Vere. For his part, Vere viewed Northumberland as an inefficient soldier, and did not accord him the respect that Northumberland felt he was entitled as a peer. Vere went on to win a great victory at Ostend and returned to England in 1602. Northumberland, still resentful, challenged him to a duel. Vere refused to fight, and the quarrel reached the ears of the Queen, who forbade the parties from duelling. Northumberland, however, persisted in his challenge and wrote to Vere, asking him to appoint a time and a place "to your likeing that I may meete you; bring you a friend w*i*th you, and I will be accompanied w*i*th another, that shall be a wittnesse of the things I will lay to yo*ur* charge."[107] According to Northumberland, "if you satisfye me, we will returne good freindes, if not, we shall doe as God shall put in our mindes."[108]

While Northumberland attempted to goad Vere into a duel by claiming that Vere's refusal to fight would cause Vere to "batter [his] owne Reputation," Vere did not see meeting the challenge as necessary to preserve his honour.[109] Initially, he refused to respond to Northumberland and stated that he needed more time to consider possible courses of action. Northumberland sent a new messenger to Vere with a fresh challenge; this time Vere agreed to meet him but refused to nominate a second, as he desired that there should be no drawing of swords.[110] Presumably his goal in agreeing to meet Northumberland was to broker a settlement. After several more exchanges Vere finally agreed to meet in London to duel, but also informed Northumberland that he meant to bring several knights and gentlemen who were known at court with him. This was a tactic of avoidance on Vere's part. In threatening to make the matter public to figures at court, he knew that the Queen's attention would be drawn, and that this was likely to make Northumberland reconsider. Ultimately the tactic was successful, as it led Northumberland to express concern that the men in question "were men like enough to acquainte the Queene & Counsell."[111] He was fearful of the punishment he was sure to receive if it became known that he had defied the Queen's order not to fight with Vere.

In the event, Northumberland need not have feared that their contest would be brought to the Queen's attention, as Vere soon changed his mind about the entire matter. He communicated to Northumberland that he felt "it not reasonable to satisfy him after that manner he required, and therefore would not doe it."[112] In invoking the language of reason Vere levied a subtle swipe at Northumberland's honour by implying that his challenge was not a rational one. Despite Northumberland's public assertion (in a paper written in English, French, and Italian) that Vere was a "Knave, and a Coward … a Comon Buffoone," Vere avoided duelling with him and does not seem to have thought that his own honour would be called into question by his refusal to meet Northumberland in armed engagement.[113] Indeed, by recasting Northumberland's actions as unreasonable and irrational, Vere attempted to negate any pressure to meet the challenge while simultaneously providing himself with a means of levelling further insult. This was another tactic of avoidance on Vere's part, as well as a method of attacking Northumberland. This episode illustrates, then, that it was possible to refuse a challenge to duel without tarnishing one's honour, and that not all gentlemen felt duelling to be imperative in conflicts over reputation and good name. The varying understandings of honour held by Vere and Northumberland jostled with each other and illustrate that more than one response was possible with respect to the issuance of a challenge to duel.

It is also possible to see in this example what David Quint has referred to as the practice of "paper duelling" in Renaissance Italy. Quint's definition of the practice is worth quoting at length. According to Quint, "paper duelling" was:

> another ritual of the sixteenth century duel [that] allowed adversaries to fight virtually without violence at all; it was cheaper, too, if hardly less elaborate and ceremonial. These duellists fenced on paper and spilled ink rather than blood. It had been a long established practice, reaching back into the fifteenth century, for offended parties to issue challenges in the form of short written documents – "cartelli di sfida" – that they posted in public. Around the middle of the sixteenth century the *cartelli* began to be printed instead of handwritten and became more embellished, spelling out the causes for the duel and often provoking responses from the challenged parties in the form of other *cartelli*. The exchange of such

> documents, which since they were printed could have a wide distribution, might go on for some time, constituting a kind of publicity campaign before the duel or – as I suspect was most often the case – replacing the duel itself, since many of the *cartelli* accuse the other party of delay, of failing to live up to stipulated conditions, or simply of not showing up on the appointed day.[114]

In England, paper duelling did not typically include formally printed and circulated challenges and responses, although such things could and did become available to the public, as evidenced by the inclusion of correspondence exchanged between Vere and Northumberland in several commonplace books.[115] Yet the actual practice of fighting was often eschewed in favour of a series of elaborate rituals and formal declarations of honour and knavery that were akin to the posting of the *cartelli*, although modified in usage by the English elite. In the exchange between Vere and Northumberland (as well as in Northumberland's multilingual paper denouncing Vere), we can see a series of techniques concerned with containing violence whilst simultaneously constructing a platform from which to continue levelling nonviolent attacks at an opponent. The exchange of written and verbal barbs offered a space (often a relatively public one, depending on the level of circulation of such materials) to articulate competing claims to good conduct and honourable reputation, and to voice criticism of an opponent's behaviour in a way that stopped short of violence. Such exchanges could arguably be more effective both in the defence of one's own reputation and in diminishing the strength of the original attack than actual duelling.

In cases where such exchanges were not sufficient to contain conflict and a physical confrontation did result, it was usually accompanied by some recognition that such behaviour was considered questionable by many and could result in formal punishment and a measure of social shame. Even though prohibitions against duelling and associated punishments were somewhat patchily enforced, participants often made attempts to conceal their actions in order to avoid drawing attention; they were aware that the consequences of such involvements could be negative. Such was the case when Edward Bruce, second Baron Kinloss, and Edward Sackville arranged to duel in 1613.[116] Like the quarrel between Suckling and Digby, this conflict arose because both men wished to marry the same woman, Venetia Stanley. Bruce and Sackville resolved to duel over which man was worthy of her. To avoid detection and punishment, they travelled to Bergen op Zoom to duel. Copies of the correspondence between the two men, made over the course of arranging the duel and later circulated by Sackville to justify his conduct, reveal their awareness that secrecy was needed. While Sackville wrote to Bruce that "you shall finde me disposed to give you honorable satisfacc*i*on" he went on to caution Bruce to be covert: "in the meane tyme be as secret of the appoyntm*en*t as it seemes you are desirous of it."[117] In this instance, it served the interests (and likely accorded with the personalities of both men) to subscribe, at least in the moment, to the idea of honour as encapsulated in the code of duelling. Yet, though Bruce was killed in the affray and Sackville was seriously injured after being run through by Bruce and having his finger sliced off, the duel did not bring Venetia to Sackville. After lingering in the Netherlands for a time, afraid of the punishment for Bruce's death that James I might visit upon him (he was eventually forgiven, speaking again to the manner in which the enforcement of the law was mediated at all points by individual beliefs and interests), Sackville later discovered that Venetia had secretly wed Sir Kenelm Digby in 1625; the marriage became public in 1627.[118] As a means of definitively settling such disputes, duelling was ambivalent and this blunted its utility.

Duelling, and the injuries or death that could result, could also be held up as moral examples to dissuade others from following a similar course. Such was the case when a Master Thornnelles was killed in a duel and one observer noted that while "thes things are no dowt most grivous to there parence, god grawnt other maie marke proffit herby."[119] Challenges also often resulted in pleas from family members and friends that violence would not result in the recapture of honour but would, instead, result in its loss. Such arguments were grounded in conceptions of honour as vested in civil and peaceable behaviour. As an example, when Walter Ferrers fell out with Jermain Poole and threatened a duel, family members evinced concern to prevent a violent confrontation from happening and were explicit in stating that such an event would result in a loss of social credit and honour. As Walter's father, Humphrey (also the commentator on the above-noted duel involving Thornnelles), stated in a letter offering a narrative of events, he indicated that he had told Walter that a duel would be "greatly to the discredyte of my sonne" and, because of this, "I did com*m*ande him neu*er* to meddle w*i*th him [Poole]."[120] Walter was further cautioned by his father that he "sholde get no credyte by quarrellinge" with Poole.[121] While Humphrey was no doubt desirous to assert control over a wayward child as well as discourage him from socially divisive behaviour such as duelling, other family members also interjected. Hence, Ferrers's cousin, John Harpur, claimed that he advised his cousin that there were only two possible outcomes of a duel, "being only death or banishm*ent*."[122] He advised Ferrers that, if an actual duel should happen, it would be most grievous "to you and yo*ur* frends," a technique to further dissuade him.[123] While gentlemen often demonstrably endeavoured to avoid violent strife with their opponents, and deployed an array of tactics in doing so, physical conflict did, of course, erupt between some. In these instances, one can find examples of the highly malleable rhetoric of honour being invoked as a legitimating technique to both justify involvement in quarrels and, paradoxically, reaffirm the value attached to restraint. This serves as an illustration of the fluid nature of the various, sometimes contradictory, understandings of honour present.

The Limits of Honour as a Technique of Justification

The example provided by John Holles (1564–1637) is illustrative of the degree to which honour, as a flexible technique of legitimation, could encompass both a justification of violent behaviour and an emphasis on moderation in the navigation of disputes. Holles used the discourse of honour as a way to validate his violent conduct while also, conversely, stressing his normally sober and restrained nature, appealing to the value of a reputation for self-control as an element of one's honour. In contrast to the example offered by the small segment of gentlemen who unapologetically adhered to the restrictive view of honour embodied in the duel, Holles did not want to be seen as believing that honour was rooted in violence. To achieve this he used the rhetoric of honour as a way to justify his poor behaviour and occasional lack of restraint. The occasions leading to Holles articulating one understanding of honour through his actions while claiming simultaneously to adhere to another understanding in his written self-presentations were quarrels into which he was drawn by virtue of his marriage. Holles's father had spent a considerable amount of time arranging a match between his son and one of the nieces of George Talbot, Earl of Shrewsbury, but his efforts came to nothing: John repudiated the Talbots and instead married Ann Stanhope. The Stanhope and Talbot families, formerly friendly with each other, had developed an acrimonious relationship. For example, in the 1590s, when Shrewsbury's son Gilbert failed to secure promotion to his father's old office of the Lieutenancy of Nottinghamshire and Derby after inheriting the earldom, he blamed the Stanhopes for spreading rumours about his fitness to hold the post and retaliated by circulating libels about the family.[124] The Stanhopes similarly blamed the Talbots for slandering them within the local community and at court, prompting Holles to complain to Edmund Sheffield, the Vice-Admiral and later Lord Lieutenant of Yorkshire, that Gilbert (whom he referred to as "this dishonourable Earl") "hath malitiously menaced S*ir* Tho*mas*: Stanhope."[125] By rejecting the Talbot match and marrying into the Stanhope family, Holles exacerbated an inter-family quagmire and became irretrievably enmeshed in its politics.

Tension earlier erupted in 1593 when a neighbour and agent of the Talbots, Gervase Markham (1557–1637), challenged Holles to a duel. The local sheriff reacted immediately to this threat of violence by placing Holles under a bond of good behaviour. Nevertheless Holles was as eager as Markham to duel, and, in contrast to other men who seem to have been unconcerned that their refusal to duel could lead to dishonour, eschewed his bond of good behaviour. Each party nominated seconds and arranged a date to meet in London. This time the Privy Council caught wind of their plans and Holles and Markham were imprisoned in the Fleet. The two refused to give up their quarrel, however, and arranged to travel to the Low Countries and off English soil to fight. This time Markham did not show up at the appointed hour. Finally, in 1598, the two men did draw swords in Sherwood Forest, and Markham was seriously wounded. While both were eager to further their quarrel, it is significant that five years of challenges, counter challenges, and malicious talk, ensued before an actual duel. The manner and timing in which violence as a means to advance honour was used was negotiable for Holles and Markham.

Holles provided two justifications for his conduct, both of them aimed at finding some way to satisfactorily explain his use of violence and stress that it was limited and unlikely to be repeated. On the one hand, he alleged that Markham had ambushed him, in violation of all protocol governing duelling. Holles further maintained that Markham had the advantage in the affray, having twice as many men with him as Holles did, another violation of the code of duelling. He alleged that Markham had pressed this advantage to the fullest, leaving Holles with no choice but to defend himself.[126] He further claimed that Markham had levelled a series of insults at him to which he was obliged to respond, and that this also served to legitimate his attack. According to duelling manuals this was an acceptable reason for engaging in a duel, but those manuals were not to be confused with the law, and Holles's declaration of repentance for his role in the affray was decidedly lackluster. Even he was cognizant of this and, in a letter to the Lord Chief Justice of the Common Pleas, Holles wrote, "this ill accident I wishe with all my hart had not been," but then proceeded to negate his own responsibility by exclaiming: "seeing it was Gods will to have sumthing done, thus beeing done, your Lordship in your wisdom examining all the circumstances … I trust yow will not muche condemn me, though in rigour of law alltogether I can not be excused."[127]

While Holles was clearly aware of his legal culpability in the affray, he nonetheless attempted to justify his involvement in the duel by alleging that Markham had spread libels and slanders against him. To this end he attempted to refute Markham's allegation that he had behaved dishonourably in wounding Markham by authoring his own form of libel, the "Discourse on the Duel with Gervase Markham." In this declaration Holles claimed that Markham's earlier slanders were filled with the "most horrible venim in manner & matter yt euer was divested."[128] He further spoke of the

> untollerable and unheard of wrongs this Mr Markham sum years past offered me, how at all the market crosses in Nottinghamshire he sett up most infamous libells and proclamations against me … and that ever since in all places, uppon all occasions he hath reported most slanderously of me, allthough my self never deserved the least stroke of his toung, but was ever reddy in gentlemanly manner to acquit myself.[129]

If one were to analyse this episode with respect to an Anglicized form of Quint's *cartelli* (a technique to contain violence by offering a verbal or written substitute), the overall assessment must be that the circulation of such materials failed to perform the purpose of preventing confrontation. However, in authoring his own style of *cartelli* in the form of the "Discourse," Holles participated in this form of paper duelling as much as Markham did with his "most infamous libells and proclamations."[130]

In addition to serving as a technique to legitimate his behaviour in battling Markham, Holles's text cast aspersions on his opponent, most notably his social rank and standing. In this Holles appealed to the idea that honour was rooted in proper comportment, even as he himself violated such dictates. Holles claimed that in the quarrel, he had behaved like a gentleman, while Markham had acted little better than a thug who had attempted to viciously murder him. Holles alleged that

Markham had quit "all gentlemanlike courses" and was plotting a "villanous reuenge" against him.[131] Ultimately, Holles believed that he was the aggrieved party in the matter and Markham "with lyes & braggs would he pinn his shame vppon my shoulder."[132] In spite of his previous acknowledgment of legal culpability, Holles wrote to a member of the Stanhope family of his own supremely gentlemanly conduct in the matter, which he alleged was in stark contrast to Markham's behaviour. Holles noted that, "he [Markham] falling at my feete, I lett him rise without hurt: that I falling, he and his would have murdered me, passing uppon me many thrusts."[133] Holles was here able to use various aspects of the discourse of honour to legitimate his behaviour, as well as criticize Markham for breaching the conventions of gentility. Holles portrayed himself as desiring quiet, and yet as being bound by another's behaviour to defend his reputation; he then showed himself as willing to utilize violence but characterized his own behaviour in the ensuing battle as gentlemanly and equitable (even though he was as eager to destructively utilize violence as was his opponent), in contrast to Markham's disregard for the prescribed rituals of a fair duel. In his attempts to explain and justify his conduct, Holles placed these differing understandings of honour at the forefront.

Assigning culpability to Holles was complicated by the fact that Markham had issued the initial challenge. Other incidents in Holles's life, however, reveal that he possessed a trenchant personality that often led him to clash with others. For example, in addition to his conflict with Markham and the Talbots, Holles involved himself in the family disputes of others as a means of harassing people whom he felt had impugned his honour. Thus, as a result of a dispute with Sir Edward Coke related to the criminal activities of King James's former favourite Robert Carr, and his subsequent trial in 1615, Holles became a vocal supporter of Coke's estranged wife in her struggles with her husband. Holles was prominent in the attempts to clear Carr's name. For his audacity in refusing to accept Carr's guilt, Coke imprisoned Holles and levied a fine against him of £1,000. Coke delivered a stinging attack against Holles when he passed sentence and Holles was offended, feeling that the incident had done damage to his honour. Following this, Holles took to describing Coke as the author of most of his subsequent legal troubles, and alleged that Coke had exploited his position as Chief Justice in order to show malice. As Holles wrote to his son in a later recounting of events, "I was restored to my liberty fryday ... which the chief Justice of the Kings bench would gladly have contradicted:

Figure 1 John Holles, 1st Earl of Clare, by R. Clamp, 1792, © National Portrait Gallery, London

this gentleman grew so proud uppon his employment, as in his own imagination he had thrown all men under his feet."[134] In the meantime, Holles had come to be friends with Coke's wife Elizabeth and, when her strained marriage began to disintegrate and she quarreled with Coke over her property rights, maintenance, and the marriage of their daughter, he aggressively supported her interests as a means of exacting revenge against her husband.[135]

Similarly, Holles was delighted when Coke fell out of royal favour and lost his position on the bench. As he wrote jubilantly to his son, Coke's fall from grace would surely entail that his "peacocks feythers will be pulled."[136] Coke's fall did not abate Holles's hostility towards his old foe and, several months later, he was still derisively referring to Coke as "the vyper."[137] Contrary to ideals of proper behaviour, Holles was prone to holding grudges and mercilessly goading his opponents, even as he strove to articulate the importance he placed on sober behaviour and proper conduct. Holles's career was one of varied successes, and while he did secure some positions of local governance for himself, he failed to realize his desires for further promotion at court after the death in 1612 of Prince Henry, in whose household he had been employed.[138] He greatly lamented this inability to further advance, although it was, in part, the result of his own quarrelsome nature.[139] His defensiveness over perceived slights made him more likely to seek confrontation than to exercise restraint. This tendency, especially as he was not always able to offer satisfactory justifications for his conduct, likely dealt his hopes for office a blow as they contravened his attempts to present himself as a sober and self-contained gentleman.

As the example of Holles suggests, many quarrels over perceived honour were occasional and motivated by local competition and long-standing feuds, rather than by an adherence to the restrictive idea of honour as linked to an absolute imperative to avenge reputational slights by any means necessary. Yet, in these instances, the rhetoric of honour and its multi-vocality could sometimes serve as an effective technique of legitimation. One can examine the particularly bitter quarrel between the Earl of Huntingdon and Sir William Fawnt, a local JP, within this context. This conflict from the 1630s, analysed by Thomas Cogswell, culminated in Huntingdon launching a Star Chamber suit against Fawnt at a time when Huntingdon's reputation was especially vulnerable. However, the incident that formed the basis of the complaint had actually taken place over a decade earlier, when Huntingdon's local reputation was more secure. At the time, Huntingdon had been content to ignore Fawnt's alleged slanders, and stood to gain little or nothing from litigious aggression or confrontation. By the 1630s, however, Huntingdon was the target of public criticism and faced tenuous financial circumstances; indeed, he was dependent upon the crown to maintain solvency. He was now keenly attuned to the threat that Fawnt's slanders posed.

Realizing that he needed to recapture his honour (brought low by his failure to contribute to the Forced Loan and further tarnished by public criticisms of his local administrative abilities made at the 1627 Leicestershire quarter sessions by Sir Henry Shirley, which Huntingdon was summoned to Whitehall to address), Huntingdon exploited his earlier conflict with Fawnt.[140] Indeed, Huntingdon grossly exaggerated the extent of Fawnt's decade-old words against him in order to bring the matter before the Star Chamber and secure a verdict that would reaffirm his status in local society.[141] The case centred on three letters that Fawnt had written criticizing Huntingdon's administration: they suggested that Huntingdon had corrupted his position of responsibility by levying militia assessments to impose harsh financial measures against his local enemies while rewarding his supporters. At the time that the letters were written, Huntingdon privately indicated his disapproval of Fawnt, but made no attempt to disavow the charges. Years later, Huntingdon was under official scrutiny and Shirley had publicly accused him of corrupt administration. Shirley further called Huntingdon's honour into question when he slandered a follower of the Earl's, Philip Chetwynd. Chetwynd responded by confronting Shirley and pummeling him with a stick, shouting, "I will beat your honour out of your arse."[142] In the midst of all these slights to his honour, and frustrated by the government's refusal to punish Shirley, a recusant of lower social standing, Huntingdon reverted to his earlier conflict with Fawnt and sought to use the courts as a way to redeem his reputation. Huntingdon now described Fawnt as "a man of p*er*verse and factious disposic*i*on" who had "w*i*thout anie cause att all borne p*ar*ticular and p*er*sonall hatred and mallice" to him.[143] According to Huntingdon, Fawnt had "falsely & malitiously wrote a Libell in forme of a letter" against him.[144] His lawyers alleged that Fawnt's letters had only recently been written, and that they were intended for public circulation, neither of which was true.[145] Huntingdon won the lawsuit, and Fawnt was forced to make a humiliating public supplication before the Earl and pay a crippling financial penalty. A copy of Fawnt's submission survives, in which he states, "I S*i*r Willi*a*m

Fawnt knight doe humbly acknowledge that I haue much wronged the right hono*ra*ble henry Earle of huntingdon … in wrytinge and sendinge a false Libellous & seditious Letter."[146] Fawnt contritely added "I doe hereby acknowledge my fault and humbly Crave pardon and forgivenes of the said Earle for the same."[147] In order for the Earl of Huntingdon to re-establish his honour as a responsible local gentleman and governor of his social subordinates, he rather dishonourably forced Fawnt into making statements about himself which tarnished his own honour as a gentleman. Put another way, Huntingdon, seeing that he could not prevail against the critics who posed actual, current threats to his honour, chose instead to defend himself against an easier target. By impeaching Fawnt in Star Chamber – indeed, by making him look ridiculous – Huntingdon gambled that he could effect a public rehabilitation and immunize himself against further criticism.

Huntingdon's conflict with Fawnt points to some of the disparate elements of honour and illustrates the manner in which disagreements over local administration and the enforcement of government policies could be connected to personal reputation. Likewise, the fact that it took Huntingdon over a decade to respond to the slight to his name, and that he did so only at a time when he felt his reputation was under threat from other sources, suggests that his level of concern with his personal honour ebbed and flowed. He evaluated attacks on his honour carefully and based his responses on his objectives at the time, rather than responding immediately and with consistency regardless of the level of seriousness. Huntingdon waited until it was in his interest down the road to fully address the criticisms levied against him.

The manner in which duelling often failed to definitely settle quarrels (as several examples considered thus far suggest), and the manner in which such involvements were often negotiated over a period of years and motivated by longstanding rivalries that often had little to do with an isolated perceived affront to honour, can be further seen in the case of a duel that occurred in 1610 between Edward Morgan and John Egerton. In this encounter, Egerton, a kinsman of the Lord Chancellor, was slain. There was a long-standing feud in progress between the Egerton and Morgan families that Morgan's father may have initiated and, in August 1608, Edward Morgan openly insulted John Egerton. The relationship between the two men further declined when Edward Egerton (John's brother or cousin; the relationship is unclear) sent some servants to the Morgan family home at Goldgreave in order to recover a bird lost during hawking.[148] Morgan denied having any knowledge of the hawk's whereabouts, although it was suspected to be in his possession, and an acrimonious correspondence, a series of English-style *cartelli*, ensued between himself and Edward Egerton in which Edward attempted to induce Morgan to retract derogatory statements that he had made concerning John Egerton. Edward further insulted Morgan's own lineage (evidently after Morgan denigrated Egerton's):

> in termeinge mee to bee a base villainne thou dost lye in the throate for I was borne free and lyve vnder the Kinges ma*jes*tie a free Subiecte and a gentleman borne wheras thou art discended of a dunghill by thy father, what by thy Mother I knowe not belike of noe worthie race. And in thy disgracefull wordes vsed of Sir Iohn Egerton, whose name thou art not worthy to lock in thy mouth ... thou art an vnseemely groome ill bredd & worse taughte.[149]

Morgan refused to retract the statements he had made against Egerton and instead invited him to fight, saying "base Egerton lette vs multiplye woordes no more we muste now fight or we muste boathe be healde the Coward."[150] Morgan continued, "I challenge thee and defye thee for a Runnegate Rouge and for a damnde author & instrument of al detestable wickednes and this I will maintaine like a gentelman where when & with what weapons thou darest."[151] In another issuance of the challenge, Morgan alleged that Egerton's refusal to duel was a mark of cowardice, emphasizing that the honour of both parties was at stake: "lett vs multeplie wordes now more, wee must now fighte, or wee must bothe bee helde the cowardlyest of villainnes this day lyveinge."[152]

But, despite Morgan's provocations and suggestion that Egerton's honour was at stake should he ignore the challenge, Egerton refused to fight. Indeed, levelling his own insults at Morgan, he noted that he would not "then vouchsafe an ans›weare to one yt I heald was eather drunke or out of hys wyttes as yt seemed by hys writing."[153] As Vere had earlier done with respect to his quarrel with Northumberland, Egerton employed this language as a technique to both avoid violence and denigrate Morgan's reputation. While Egerton was initially uninterested in a violent confrontation, Morgan was keen to avoid drawing official attention to their dispute and warned Egerton that he should "deale cloaselie in this business if thow be a gentleman."[154] Morgan, as a member of the Inner Temple, presumably had at least more than a passing appreciation of the potential legal ramifications of engaging in a duel (and, in theory, should have possessed a heightened commitment to upholding the law) and, while he was not eager to openly advertise the impending duel, he was likely more than well aware that such involvements were often not strenuously prosecuted and heavy punishment was unlikely. As earlier examples have illustrated, the legal system was ill equipped to actively suppress most crimes, duelling included, in spite of having a hardline stance with respect to such activities.

There the matter lay for a time, with neither side pressing the issue. Nearly two years later, however, the quarrel was resumed in London, when the two men met accidentally at Whitehall. They quickly resumed their prior disagreement, and Morgan began a campaign of harassment against Egerton. Egerton wrote to his kinsman, Thomas Egerton, the Lord Chancellor, and Baron Ellesmere, seeking to have Morgan punished for harassing him. As he put it, Morgan was behaving "contray to law and Iustes."[155] He complained that "dyvers of my serveanes [servants] haue ben ... sett apon ... by M*aste*r Edward Morgans folowares" and asked Ellesmere to see that justice was done and Morgan punished.[156] In accordance with the idea that refusing to respond to a challenge did not necessarily entail a profound loss of honour, Ellesmere responded that Morgan's threats and slanders need not be detrimental to Egerton's honour or necessitate a duel as "credite or R*e*putac*i*on standes not vpon the waste wynde of the mouths of the multitude."[157] Ellesmere reminded Egerton that his reputation was tied to his deeds and conduct, which Morgan could not malign. Ellesmere went on to urge that Egerton endure the slights with a good face, as "tyme & longe expirience haue taught me to indure greatter matters."[158]

In the vitriolic correspondence that passed between the two men, we can see many of the characteristics of the *cartelli* as identified by Quint: slanders passed upon one's gentle status and birth, allegations of servile status, a willingness to utilize force in the defence of honour, and imputations of cowardice and irrationality juxtaposed with claims to courage and self-control. A multiplicity of varying understandings of honour coalesced in the conflict between the two men. In the end, despite Ellesmere's advice that honour was to be found in deeds, not bravado and slanders, and Egerton's own earlier refusal to fight, a further series of missives between Morgan and Egerton resulted in a duel being arranged for 21 April 1610. This time it was Egerton who issued the challenge, although he took care to ensure that the place chosen for the duel would not be widely publicized in an attempt to avoid intervention by the authorities.[159]

During the course of the affray Morgan was wounded and Egerton was killed. Egerton's family maintained that he had been murdered and that Morgan had inflicted the three wounds that had killed him while he was trapped in a hedge and unable to defend himself, thus attempting to negate any attempts Morgan might make to allege self-defence. In the ensuing legal action, a large number of statements were taken from Morgan and his brother William (who had served as Morgan's second), from William Robinson (Egerton's second), and other witnesses. Despite their own connections with people in power at the Jacobean court, the Egerton family maintained that Morgan was being protected by his friends through a series of actions designed to delay the administration of justice, such as continually putting off the trial date, packing the jury with supporters of Morgan, and intimidating witnesses. They made a full list of what they described as Morgan's "invetrate mallice and his base & most vylle behavior towards S*ir* Iohn Egerton."[160] As noted, Morgan was himself a member of the Inner Temple and this likely factored into the Egerton family's allegations that he was abusing his connections within the courts in order to evade punishment.

The Egerton family alleged that, not only had Morgan forfeited his honour by killing a defenceless man under the guise of a fair duel, but he had then further sullied his reputation by suborning the legal process and refusing to accept responsibility for his actions. As they phrased it, Morgan, with the help of friends, was "casting about to haue the said murder said but manslaughter."[161] The courts, like the *cartelli*, offered a means of using the language of honour as a weapon to assert one's honourable status and denigrate that of another, while containing actual violence. And while violence had not been contained in this instance, the Egerton family subsequently used the courts to further the conflict by contrasting Egerton's gentlemanly conduct throughout the affair with Morgan's dishonourable behaviour. To this end, Egerton's family endeavoured to paint a posthumous portrait of John as the model of an honourable gentleman. Accordingly, they enlisted several witnesses to swear to John's exemplary conduct. Sir Thomas Challenor, Sir Ralph Gray, Sir John Mallery, and Sir Basil Brooke, upon viewing Egerton's body and swearing that his wounds must have been received while his back was turned or he was lying prone upon the ground, also attested that "we haue not knowne or hearde that the saide M*aste*r Iohn Egerton was ever reputed to be quarrelous or contentious."[162] Rather, he was "of a very quiett, cyvell and honest carriage and behaviour, nor ever heard of an quarrell he had any hande in before this that hath lately happned."[163] The intent of such testimony is clear: Morgan was the contentious instigator and, in contrast, Egerton had conducted himself honourably. However, a major sticking point, which most likely served as the reason Morgan was able to successfully elude prosecution in spite of the Egerton family's court connections, was that, as with the duel between Holles and Markham, it had been Egerton who had issued the challenge to Morgan (although Morgan had issued an earlier challenge to Edward Egerton that was refused). This was acknowledged by all concerned, and made it difficult for the Egertons to allege that Morgan was entirely responsible for John's death.

Those involved in this episode attempted to use the rhetoric of honour and gentlemanly behaviour to legitimate their actions. Both Morgan and Egerton advanced personally, or had advanced for them posthumously by their surviving family members, presentations of themselves as honourable gentlemen who should not be faulted for their conduct. Thus Morgan framed his initial challenges to Edward Egerton in the language of honour and John Egerton's family found people willing to swear to John's peaceful and respectful disposition in contrast to Morgan's quarrelsome nature and dishonest attempts to avoid prosecution. Morgan's previous harassment of the Egerton family was also recounted to further legitimate Egerton's conduct. Perhaps more tenuously, the Egertons claimed that Morgan, in true cowardly and non-gentlemanly fashion, had plotted to murder Egerton. As they recounted, Morgan had "practised to stab S*i*r Iohn Egerton and his sonne in the Church."[164] Despite these invocations of honour, contested and appropriated by both parties, ultimately John Egerton invited his own death by issuing the final challenge to duel. The Jacobean regime appears to have been content to let the matter rest there: the exemplary lesson of the contest, that duelling and claims to honour through violence resulted in death and further potential legal troubles, was clear enough. The possibility of prosecuting Morgan was explored, evidenced by the crown's investigation of precedents concerning the prosecution for murder of men who killed someone in a duel even if the victors had not issued the initial challenge.[165] But an earlier pardon of Morgan issued on behalf of the King under the Great Seal was formally recognized by the Court of King's Bench in 1611. The pardon was based on the grounds (glossing over Morgan's earlier repeated challenges and Egerton's refusals) that it did appear "that the provocac*i*on to fight came not from Morgan but from Egerton, who having formerly given Morgan a Challenge w*hi*ch he refused … & more after, Egerton sent to Morgan a second Challenge, w*hi*ch Morgan (being hereby much provoked) did accept."[166]

As the example of Egerton and Morgan suggests, it was not uncommon in the aftermath of a duel for the friends and family members of those involved to use the courts to attempt to secure punishment against the victor. In 1584 George Best challenged Oliver St John to a duel in which Best was killed. St John was tried for the crime and a verdict of manslaughter was delivered against him (although, with benefit of clergy, St John's actual punishment was negligible, another example of the relatively minor punishments that most duellists received in spite of the law's harsh stance towards duelling). As with Morgan's killing of Egerton, Best's family was not content to let the matter rest and attempted to have St John charged with murder, prompting his family to mobilize their networks of local support against what they termed the "malicious p*ro*ceading by the enimies" of St John.[167] As with the Egerton-Morgan case, however, the difficulty in prosecuting St John to the fullest extent of the law was that Best had been the challenger and so it was argued that, in killing him, St John was acting in self-defence. St John's supporters invoked the language of honour against Best's supporters and the episode was described as one in which dishonourable men attempted to "prosecute one of good house reputid an honest gentillma*n*."[168] In these instances, not only was duelling relatively ineffective in ending quarrels and decisively putting an end to feuds, it also opened the way for those involved to use the courts in an attempt to settle disputes and seek revenge, thereby prolonging, rather than ending, quarrels. That these sorts of actions commonly occurred in the aftermath of a duel blunted its efficacy as a means of dispute resolution and point to the ways in which differing conceptions of the meaning of honour as vested in restraint and civil behaviour or as rooted in a willingness to defend name and position at all costs could continue to jostle with each other well after a conflict was ostensibly concluded through duelling.

Strife and Settlement

There certainly existed, both in prescriptive literature and in the core values of many early modern elite men, an understanding that honour was the most important commodity for a gentleman to possess, one that should be maintained at all costs even to the point of the use of violence. And a small portion of the elite male community doubtless subscribed (at least when it suited them) to a restrictive understanding of honour as expressed in the code of duelling. But there was a parallel discourse of restraint and Christian forgiveness that coexisted alongside and tempered the former. Cultural beliefs associated with the nature of gentlemanly conduct and masculinity also exerted a pull and there was a thin line between asserting control over a situation, a masculine and gentlemanly trait, and losing control through lack of sober self-government. It was both dangerous and emasculating to allow emotion to rule; effeminacy itself was a source of destabilization.[169] This was tethered to the sense of paternalism that was so powerful a force among the elite during the period. Claims to honour among gentlemen, both well-established and more newly minted, were in part tied to claims to being worthy governors of the lower social orders and, hence, entitled to displays of deference and a recognition of social status. Established gentlemen with houses of their own and all the attendant responsibilities of adulthood were careful to use the language of honour to emphasize their restraint and respect for social stability. If they engaged in acts of violence and otherwise quarrelsome behaviour, many gentlemen nonetheless often simultaneously articulated a desire for peaceful relations and suggested that their use of violence was both aimed at restoring the peace and limited to an isolated incident. That so many gentlemen who did find themselves involved in violent confrontations employed this understanding of honour that emphasized civil conduct as a means to stress their usually restrained and sober natures speaks to the prevalence of this conception of honour, as well as to the reality that alternate meanings could be privileged when it accorded with one's needs.

While violence did erupt between gentlemen in early modern England, the peaceful settlement of disputes was nonetheless held up as more desirable, Christian, and effective with respect to preserving communal good relations and maintaining the bonds of local society. Honour could and did encompass both sources of tension and the imperative to settle them, and the differing levels of importance accorded to these varied understandings dependent on situational dynamics and objectives are often visible in examinations of conflict. However, as violence could lead to social instability, honour as linked to the cementing of settlements without the use of violence was typically accorded a higher value in daily practice. The activities associated with peacemaking and the restoration of serviceable relations was a part of the deeply ingrained "moral tradition" of early modern Europe and played an important role in understandings of honour.[170] While full reconciliation was the ideal, the settling of conflicts, even if it did not entail the restoration of fully amiable relations, was sought. Accordingly, settlements and the healing of breaches were typically perceived to be more honourable than recourse to aggression. Even as this understanding of honour as rooted in settlement and the patient toleration of slights could be violated in practice, as men did occasionally allow their tempers to get the better of them, they nonetheless vowed to adhere to it as they attempted to explain their breaching behaviour.

In addition, while honour-based violence could be broadly acceptable in certain circumstances (and several notable incidents of elite violence went unpunished), if it was seen as socially destabilizing or as threatening to the hierarchical order it was typically condemned. Thus there was a greater level of tolerance at play when elites used violence against their inferiors, or even when it was employed in isolation against a peer, as this did not necessarily entail a subversion of the social order. Most sought to avoid a poor local reputation for subverting the peace by resorting with frequency to contentious behaviour, even if they did from time to time allow their anger to get the better of them. It was important to avoid – as someone like Holles was unable to – a reputation for being a barrator, one who stirred up strife and pursued perceived enemies spitefully, either privately or through the courts. Reputation could be damaged if one were labelled as engaging in "sondry misbehauio*rs*, some of them tendinge to barratinge and stirringe of quarrells."[171] Many gentlemen acknowledged that gentle society was bound together by a web of mutualities and obligations that, while perhaps subject to reconfiguration and redefinition as a result of economic and religious changes affecting the structure of communities, still occupied a key position within daily life.[172] In this sense, Christian passivity, forgiveness, restraint, and peacefulness were constantly upheld as the foundation of social relations and were powerfully intertwined with honour. In this sense, honour could be invoked coercively to pressure people into attempting to settle an argument, or at least into behaving properly, with backsliders risking social disapproval.[173]

In their exposition on the Ten Commandments, John Dod and Robert Cleaver wrote that "everie man is bound to have a charitable opinion and good conceit of his neighbour, with a desire of his good name and credit," a sentiment also expressed in numerous conduct books, sermons, and moral commentaries.[174] While it is arguable that this describes the ideal, rather than the experienced reality of social interaction, such an attitude (a foundational element in religious moralizing and with deep roots in popular mentality) was highly internalized. Hence, most members of the elite only entered into conflicts with their peers reluctantly, and typically sought to avoid violence or to characterize their use of it as exceptional and limited when it did occur. From the context of local communities up to the highest levels of the state, order and the restraint of violence were encouraged. Thus, the Stuart gentleman Sir Richard Grosvenor advised that forbearance was to be used in interactions with hostile people. Rather than aggressively reacting to slanders, Grosvenor advised the rejection of idle gossip and counseled,

> you ought not to receive easily every idle tale that such pickthanks or itt may bee flattering servants will bring unto you: for (besides the discomfort to live att a distance with your neighbours) if you beleive & receive them, beinge false, you make your selfe as guilty of the rounge as the informer is.[175]

While believing that scurrilous tales were being told about oneself and then resorting to violent retaliation was certainly not unheard of, people recognized that such conduct could be viewed as unbecoming in a gentleman and, as such, could potentially impeach claims to authority vested in gentle status. Many sixteenth- and seventeenth-century men and women saw a willingness to reach settlement and restore stasis within the community as more honourable than engaging in conflict. Likewise, asserting a desire for settlement and quiet also served as a way to denigrate the honour of an opponent. Earlier examples have touched upon this tendency and it can also be clearly seen in a quarrel that occurred between Edward Willoughby and Thomas Darby, a local cleric and clerk of the Council for the West Country. The source of the tension was Darby's support of one of Willoughby's tenants, Robert Walton, who was at odds with Willoughby. Following Darby's initial complaints against Willoughby in support of Walton, Willoughby drafted a letter of response and alluded to slanders made to his name, saying, "wheras you have sene and herd divers pers*on*s afor you redy to averre Robert Waltons sklanders [by] hym spoken and utered to my wyfis dishonestye & myn wyche sklanders they wer redy to justefye afor Waltons face."[176] Willoughby next moved to sue Walton in the Court of Arches for slander and Walton countersued, with support from Darby. The dispute dragged on in the courts for some time. Despite Willoughby's statements to Darby that, since Willoughby regarded his own reputation as free of stain, "I had thought that ... ze wold have surcesed in any further medlyng with the said Walton or in beryng hym in his lewdness," Darby continued to support Walton and further slandered Willoughby.[177] Willoughby persisted in his accusations that Darby was a disturber of the peace and "a mentenor of the said Robert Walton contrary to the Kings lawes."[178] For his part, Darby defended his actions by suggesting that Willoughby had an extant reputation within the county as a poor landlord and that he (Darby) was trying to restore the peace on a local level, in keeping with his role and associated expectations as a cleric. He said that, "beyng desirous of quietnes and right sory that any suche contraversie shuld be amonges my neybours, beying moeved with love and charitie," he was attempting to mediate between the two parties.[179]

Representing himself as a Christian peacemaker, dedicated to amiable relations within the parish, Darby cast Willoughby as the villain who was behaving dishonourably. In the conflict between the two men, understandings of honour were employed by both parties to denigrate the other and defend their own actions. In a passage which nicely sums up many of the constitutive elements of honour, including blood and lineage, service to the local community, quietness, the expectations of neighbourliness, and a desire to be seen to be acting without malice in conflicts, Darby claimed

> and pitie it is that a gentleman of so auncient a blodd and house beying by his prince called to honour, namely, to sett rest and quyet amonges his neybours and tenauntes shuld, in my opynyon, utter suche cruell wordes, to make all men see his inquietnes and malice, that shuld be a light and example to others of quyet and gentleness ... it is not mete to suche a gentleman called to honour, to execute all his power for the undowying of suche a pore wreche beyng his tenau*nt*.[180]

Darby here invoked honour as a means of pressuring his opponent into a settlement. Refusing to be so pressured, Willoughby maintained his claim to an honourable reputation and wrote that "I dar well say that I have the holl love and universall love of all the people in the cuntree aslargely as any man within the schyre non expected, specially of the comen people, wyche love I set most by."[181] The interactions between Darby and Willoughby, although they were unfriendly and openly abusive at times, suggest the premium both men placed on their reputations as local keepers of the peace even as they broke it, thus illustrating the degree of tension that could be present between representation and actual action with respect to understandings of honour.

While violence was unsurprisingly condemned by most, the perhaps more socially accepted tactic of seeking vindication through the courts was also discouraged unless other means of settlement had failed. While litigation was itself a form of dispute settlement, arbitration outside the courts was often more desirable than legal action, as there was a widespread recognition that litigation was a breach of proper neighbourly relations.[182] Most were united in condemning vexatious litigation that was entered into with no ostensible intention of effecting a settlement. Thus, even while involved in a legal suit over matters of reputation (which were filed readily enough), people were aware that their actions were being viewed within the context of community social values and attempted to ensure that they were broadly perceived to be acting in accordance with those values. They took care to ensure they were not seen as spiteful or overly eager in their suits. Indeed, the act of filing suit itself was often sufficient to make one's point, regardless of whether a formal judgment was ever received. As Bernard Capp argues with respect to slander litigation initiated by women, a statement that holds true for men filing suits as well, many suits were filed as "a public declaration and warning shot, a device to trigger an informal settlement involving an apology and some financial compensation," rather than with the intent of securing a formal judgment.[183] People were thus not necessarily concerned with preventing conflict; their concern was with how to contain it while simultaneously asserting the justness of their position. Tactics of avoidance in reaction to challenges issued, such as relying on verbal and written exchanges or recourse to the courts, were aimed at this containment. In addition, a desire to cast themselves as peacemakers worthy of honour could serve as a powerful motivator for disputing parties to seek a settlement and thus contain conflict.[184]

Gentlemen and Mediation

In the interest of cementing local reputations as just governors of their subordinates and sources of sober advice to their peers, gentlemen were often pleased to be called upon to mediate local conflicts. In 1569, Sir William More was asked to mediate between Thomas Copley and William Richbell because it was stressed that, without his intervention, "blowes may happe to followe, w*hi*ch I woold be sory for. Y*our* wisdoome may p*re*vent the worst."[185] As is widely recognized, early modern England was a litigious society: at the beginning of the reign of Elizabeth I there were 781 cases in the Court of King's Bench and 4,497 in Common Pleas, and by the end of her reign those numbers had risen to 6,639 and 23,147, respectively. However, the majority of suits brought before the courts never reached formal judgment, suggesting that settlements were negotiated outside of the court.[186] While the cost of seeing a court case pass to sentence could be a barrier for some, for most (and certainly for gentlemen) the courts were not prohibitively expensive. The relative rarity of such cases reaching a legal conclusion suggests, as previously noted, that formal judgments were less important than being able to employ the courts as a public platform from which to refute slanders and mar the reputation of an opponent. The mediation of out-of-court settlements to restore social order and the status quo, if not fully amiable relations, was a common occurrence. Accordingly, gentlemen often employed mediators to settle differences between them and their peers. George More, for example, after exclaiming "I haue long sustained and yet doe suffer much wrong at the handes of S*ir* William Elyott of whome I haue deserued better," was happy to employ an arbiter to settle their differences, noting that he had made "overtures vnto hym of a peaceable course, wherby to determyne all matters of differens betweene vs."[187] Accepting a submission which resulted from an out-of-court mediation likewise did not necessarily deprive disputants of the ability to affirm the rightness of their cause. The act of voluntary submission outside of a formal pronouncement to do so could attribute fault clearly enough and also allow the aggrieved party the opportunity to be seen as humbly desiring the restoration of agreeable relations without recourse to the courts, a marker of honour. As Alice Stanley, Viscountess Brackley, wrote to her brother, the Earl of Huntingdon,

> I haue had conference w*i*th our best frendes about your cause … it is thought your aduersarys humble submyssyon wyll be better for you to accept then to follow on your intended course against him … if my aduise maie preuayle, I would wish you to take his submission, w*hi*ch I perswade my self will be the best way for you, and to the world a sufficient testymony of his disgrace.[188]

In addition to using mediators, being called upon to act as a mediator was a source of honour for gentlemen. William More was often asked to mediate local conflicts, and he appears to have been regarded as a man with enough patience and wisdom to fairly settle disputes, as in 1596 when he was asked alongside several other men to act collectively to end "all controversies betweene the parties w*it*h asmuche speede as may bee."[189] Earlier, More was asked to mediate another dispute because "there is a quarrell evell begonne allreadye and lykely to growe … yf good order be not speedlye taken in it."[190] More's intervention, it was hoped, would result in "avoyding the hurte that may ensue thereof, aswell amongst the gentlemen the*m* selves as aomongst suche others as are lykely to take parte w*it*h the*m*."[191] Walter Bagot echoed a similar sentiment in 1597 when he offered his services as mediator between his brother Anthony and an unnamed party. Walter noted that he "thought good to intrude my selfe as a mediator betwixt you that those things w*hi*ch are begoone with s*o*me vnkyndnes maye in frendship and amitie bee ended" and wrote of his hope that

> both^ this occasion allredie sprung and some others lyke to aryse hereafter maye bee rooted out. ^for as^ A ^little^ breache by a violent streame at the first maye safely bee stopped ~~where~~ which yf w*it*h that force it continew afterwards can hardly bee stayed. ^so^ These matters I hope are not ^so^ growen to that p*ro*portion of vnkyndnes but that they maye safely bee drawen by frends to a frendly reconsiliac*io*n yf with some speed the same maye [be] p*er*fected w*hi*ch for my p*ar*te I earnestly desier and will vndertake my brother shall not refuse.[192]

In 1610 Walter likewise worked to persuade a man and his brother-in-law to avail themselves of a mediator to stay a pending legal action, so that "the excessive charge of a suite bee spared" and to "bringe great contentment vnto your wiffes," who were upset about the fighting between their husbands.[193] Walter noted that he was happy to recommend a suitably wise and sober man to arbitrate the conflict, someone who "maye bee chosen to heare and determin all controversies and differenses betywt you."[194] He then expressed the hope that matters were "not so fare passed but by the motion of your good frends they maye bee reduced to good conformitie" and noted that he had an "earnest desier to ~~make~~ p*ro*cure a frendly reconciliac*io*n betwyxt you."[195] He stated in closing that, via mediation, he believed that "all matters in frendship bee ended and your naturall good opinions of eche other restored."[196] The destabilizing element of such conflicts can be inferred here by Walter's invocation of the term "conformitie." More and Bagot's services as mediators and the arrangers of arbitration, and the reputation for fairness this involved, contributed to their honour in a more effective way than, for example, a willingness to tolerate violence in the settling of disputes. It also had obvious links to the rhetoric of paternalism and benevolent lordship that was a source of honour for many gentlemen. A reputation for both restraint and sober mediation was further linked to the Aristotelian understanding of *general justice*. In this rubric, just as an honourable reputation could be secured by honourable behaviour, the just man was seen and known to be just by dealing equitably with others. His internal virtue, his justness, was expressed through his actions and social involvements. Contemporaries saw it as "a deede of charitie to doe good and to end strifes that may be," and involvement in dispute settlement could augment one's reputation as a man of honour within local society and among one's peers.[197]

Flexible Honour, Limited Violence

Honour was a nebulous concept and was associated with a range of behaviours and attributes among early modern elite men. Under the umbrella of "honour," gentlemen were concerned with the attainment of office and associated influence, the performance of duty, and a reputation for charitable and neighbourly behaviour – all of which denoted both gentle status and the possession of full, mature masculinity. Likewise, there was a marked expansion in local governmental posts throughout the period and many gentlemen saw a measure of their honour and influence as connected to their exercise of authority in these positions within their localities. This understanding of honour was not a new development of the early modern period, although it likely assumed an enhanced level of importance commensurate with the enhanced level of authority attached to such positions, only open to the "better sort."[198] Running parallel to this conception of honour as based in service and duty was the connection of honour to competition in an aggressively hierarchical society, coupled with a refusal to tolerate perceived insults, which also persisted across the period. These ideas were not mutually exclusive: for example, a desire to accrue honour through office-holding and the exercise of local authority could generate intense competition for available positions. In addition, while claims to honour could spark quarrels and be used to legitimate confrontation, such claims were just as frequently invoked to stop the escalation of strife and were also used as a weapon to critique the behaviour of others. Varying conceptions of honour ran parallel to each other within the mental landscape of many elite men, and they could be used with fluidity based upon their objectives in a given situation.

While conflict was common and anger had its place within early modern elite society, actual violence was relatively less common among the elite. When strife did erupt, many gentlemen sought to present themselves as beleaguered peacemakers, attempting to effect a settlement with those who had acted against them. In doing so they often relied upon the discourse of honour. Likewise, when a fissure did occur and pursing it accorded with their interests at the time, gentlemen often used tactics of avoidance and containment, such as the courts, or written or verbal engagements, rather then resort to physical aggression. Such strategies allowed them to continue to pursue a quarrel and articulate their own honourable behaviour and denigrate that of others without engaging in actual violence. They also often invoked the language of honour to shame their opponents into a settlement, illustrating the manner in which the language of honour could serve as a means to limit conflict and also be used as a verbal/conceptual sword within a quarrel.

That honour could be put to so many uses ensured it was a value that was often appealed to. In those instances when relations broke down completely or individual obstreperous personalities commanded the situation and violence ensued, gentlemen employed a range of techniques, some more successful than others but often framed in the rhetoric of honour or appealing to other cultural beliefs such as the impetuousness of youth or an awareness of the importance of stability, to justify their actions or to distance themselves from the incidents. Although, in theory, the common law prescribed severe penalties and punishments for duelling (especially those which resulted in death), in practice common law courts were often subverted by various understandings of honour and permeated by social relationships that could render the appropriate punishment of offenders rare. But legal ramifications were only one of the potential consequences of such involvements; reputation among peers, among those with influence, could also be damaged by the perception of recklessness, irresponsibility, and a tendency to allow pride and anger to rule. While most adhered to the idea that honour should be defended when attacked, that duelling or other forms of physical confrontation were the most effective means to do so was far from clear or agreed upon by all. There were limits to honour's effectiveness as an excuse for rash and ill-considered behaviour, although many who were involved in such confrontations probed these limits. Established and mature gentlemen were expected to show mastery and self-governance, of which restraint was a signal characteristic, in accordance with the expectations of adulthood, true masculinity, and the behaviour of the "better sort." Failing to do so risked the loss of honour. As Henry Peacham told his readers, by "vice and basenesse" a man might lose his nobility.[199] There was a connection to be drawn between conduct and status and, as surely as "he that is ignoble and inglorious, may acquire Nobilitie by Vertue; the other may very well lose it by his Vice."[200] This perception served to limit the popularity of the restrictive view (nonetheless held by some) that honour was properly and most prominently vested in a willingness to unapologetically utilize violence.

Chapter Two

Women and Honour

Honour and Sexual Reputation

In a letter to her nephew about a legal conflict over property she was engaged in, Lady Elizabeth Russell exclaimed with exasperation, "I howld my Honowre more dere then my life."[1] It was not an uncommon statement for an early modern elite woman to make. While the link between honour and sexual reputation among early modern women is prominent in many earlier analyses, in this instance Lady Russell saw her honour touched by matters not connected in the slightest to her sexual behaviour.[2] In recent years, the preponderance of complaints like Lady Russell's (concerned as they are with honour despite a lack of sexual circumstances) have led scholars to look beyond sexual reputation to form a broader composite sketch of the early modern woman's sense of honour. Female honour has, accordingly, been conceptually broadened, and is now understood as constituted by a broad set of characteristics enacted in a diverse range of social interactions, although sexual reputation did nonetheless play a role in the construction of reputation.[3]

Focusing exclusively on a passive concern with retaining a good sexual reputation does not illuminate the other, active areas of involvement that women associated with their honour, such as displays of proper motherhood, efficient housewifery and domestic management, economic honesty, and involvement in networks of sociability. Women's sense of personal reputation as connected to these involvements persisted across the medieval and early modern periods, and has arguably endured into the modern age. While recent work has drawn attention to these attributes and involvements, analysis can be extended through an examination of materials relating to elite women. Such an examination also demonstrates, as was the case with elite men when it came to honour, the ways in which these elements were often emphasized to varying degrees depending upon an elite woman's individual objectives and the context of the situation in which she found herself.

Many now recognize that, while sexual conduct was undoubtedly important in constructions of honour and reputation among early modern women, it was less of a practical measure of honour and more of a cornerstone of female behaviour – a standard of behavioural acceptability expected of women – and arguably of men as well.[4] As such, while sexual reputation was an important part of many elite women's constructions of honour, it was one part alongside many others, rather than the *sine qua non* of their personal reputation. But where can we locate the origins of the idea that women's honour was rooted primarily in sexual conduct (both real and perceived)? Many earlier examinations of women's honour and its links to sexual reputation (to say nothing of aspects of modern popular culture) have, whether consciously or not, been influenced by social anthropological ideas. This interdisciplinary perspective has resulted in a now widely challenged set of characterizations with respect to the gendered dimension of honour. Focusing on the study of honour in Mediterranean cultures, numerous anthropological works have depicted it as having radically different meanings for men (who have honour) and women (who have shame). For men, honour was represented as essentially a public matter, something that was not entirely lost until it was seen to be lost, and which could then be restored through deeds. In contrast, women were concerned solely with the preservation of their chastity before marriage and with a reputation for sexual circumspection afterwards. One of the most influential proponents of this set of characterizations, Julian Pitt-Rivers, further posited that, within the family, honour was vested solely in the male head, and women played little or no role in maintaining family reputation aside from preserving their sexual good names.[5] For men, honour was an active value, something to be gained or re-gained through conduct, while for women it was thoroughly passive, a thing to be guarded and preserved rather than gained. Women had no means of restoring lost honour.

As historians began to appreciate decades ago, there are several impediments to fitting early modern England into the honour and shame templates developed in the anthropological literature.[6] There has also been a concomitant questioning of the appropriateness of this model by anthropologists. Critics have noted that not only is this sexually-based scheme not consonant with the field experiences of many anthropologists, but it also ignores the array of other mechanisms, aside from assertiveness, by which men accrued and maintained honour in their communities, such as "generosity, honesty, and personal probity, which are by all accounts also vigorous masculine ideals in Mediterranean lands."[7] Ken Stone makes the point that ideas of honour in these studies were often formed by the fact that earlier anthropologists spoke to male informants within the Mediterranean societies they analysed, and this resulted in a somewhat distorted view of female realities within these cultures.[8] As Michael Herzfeld has noted with respect to the binary relationship between honour and shame so forcefully argued by earlier anthropologists, "these polarities are symbolic oppositions ... it makes no sense to argue that ... women 'have shame' while men 'have honor'."[9] Herzfeld has also, more seriously, asserted that previous anthropologists constructed Greek and Hellenistic societies as "other" and in cultural opposition to more "sophisticated" northern European states.[10] This ethnocentric divide was achieved by labelling Mediterranean societies as ones of honour and shame, in which people were ruled by sexuality, violence, and their passions, and lacked the rationality, civility, and culture of northern Europeans. According to Herzfeld, these studies implied that inferiority and cultural backwardness were the essence of Mediterranean culture.[11]

While the anthropological model is a flawed one that is now wisely set aside in most works on women's honour in early modern England, a reading of contemporary prescriptive, popular, and moralizing literature can, on the surface, bolster the impression that sexual purity was the foundational component of a woman's reputation. Sexual reputation did, of course, play a role in constructions of honour for women, but the idea of women's honour as being *inseparable* from their sexual reputation driven by prescriptive literature was not adopted unilaterally by most in the course of daily life. The readers of prescriptive texts and sermon literature had complex interactions with what they read, and both appropriated and flouted the dictates of conduct literature as individual personalities and situations demanded.[12] While such sources provided women with a script to utilize in their social performances, it was not a rigidly circumscribed one, as many have demonstrated. Likewise, even within these sources, women were presented with an array of other elements of personal behaviour aside from sexual reputation that were linked to honour. Thus, while honour for women was undoubtedly tied to sexual purity in some foundational sense, it nonetheless encompassed many other elements of social behaviour. That elite women saw a wealth of other attributes as contributing meaningfully to their personal honour (even when they did not explicitly describe them as such) can be further demonstrated through an examination of the ways in which they presented themselves and represented their reputations.

Notwithstanding, in addition to what one finds in prescriptive and moralizing sources, the ostensible importance of sexual reputation is, on the surface, largely reinforced by the examination of defamation litigation in ecclesiastical court records that seems to strongly link women's honour to their sexuality. For example, in the church courts at York, 90 per cent of the cases presented involving women dealt with sexual slander in some form.[13] Indeed, the high levels of such cases and their utilization by historians led one scholar to note:

> the evidence of the church courts is so luridly compelling that it has led many historians to focus unduly on the sexual components of female honour and to give far too little weight to the other qualities and actions which gained or lost women the respect of their neighbours.[14]

In her influential work on women, honour, slander, and the courts in early modern London, Gowing noted that, on the surface, women's honour and reputation were perceived through their sexual conduct, while these same attributes among men were judged according to a much broader range of values.[15] However, this is supplemented by the significant argument that women's honour was not solely to be located in examples of their dishonour, despite the interpretation suggested by court records.[16] The numerous examples of women suing over sexual slander can, of course, be read as proof that sexual purity was the main basis for female honour; and many earlier analyses have done just that. Likewise, the fact that women deployed sexual insults in the course of conflicts is telling of the social pervasiveness of the gender hierarchy which prized female passivity and circumspection and which most women had, no doubt, internalized to some degree.[17] Yet recent scholarship has persuasively shown that such conflicts were not necessarily always about sexual behaviour. Rather, they could have their origins in any number of local conflicts. The terminology of sexual insult, which appears so frequently in church court cases, was often expressed as a set of standardized slurs hurled in the course of larger hostilities that were not specifically rooted in sexual transgression – they were a way to heighten a conflict and strike a blow.[18] Hence, the use of the language of sexual insult may not be as transparent and straightforward as one would assume.

The use of the church courts in these conflicts is also significant. Women, denied access to most political and legal arenas, were more inclined to make use of this venue, where slander litigation could be pursued, as a space to display agency and stake specific claims to moral authority within their communities, quite apart from any concerns they may have had about their own or their neighbours' sexual behaviour or reputation.[19] Early modern women were able to make use of the courts to contest a variety of matters, such as conflicts over economic transactions or other neighbourhood hostilities, which they often cloaked in the language of sexual slander. So, while the fact that sexual slurs could be employed as a means of levelling insults about other issues is indeed indicative of the importance attached to sexual purity as an element of female reputation, the use of such terms was also often shorthand for indicting women's honour in matters unrelated to chastity or personal purity. Labels "such as 'whore,' 'rogue,' or 'knave' were often used indiscriminately, sometimes serving merely to mark the seriousness of a quarrel or to raise the stakes of a conflict."[20] And so we must be wary of seeing such records as unambiguously illustrating women's sense of honour by interpreting the slurs noted above solely as examples of a persistent and cohesive understanding of honour among women as rooted in chastity, something which can be limiting.[21] Likewise, that the level of legal allegations of slander related to sexual reputation eventually declined may have more to do with women's increasingly enhanced access over time to other public venues for expressing their opinions than a perceptible shift in the importance, never exclusively pronounced, attached to sexual reputation as a source of honour.

In addition, while sexual slurs were a very common form of insult, many other slurs that had nothing to do with sexual behaviour abound in litigation from the period. For example, in the university courts of Cambridge, Shepard found that, of the slander allegations brought to the courts by women, while roughly half involved terms of sexual slander, the remainder were allegations of theft, drunkenness, lying, or cheating.[22] Such words spoken by an enemy were clearly viewed as actionable by women, who were concerned with more than just a reputation for sexual purity. Likewise, as Shepard's most recent study has concluded, "the most common slur deployed against women and men alike, and especially those of limited means, was that they were poor."[23] While it is undeniable that women could be damaged by allegations of sexual impropriety, a host of other factors also informed estimations of their honour, and many of these variables were applicable to men as well as women. For example, honesty, fairness, and equitable dealing with others were values that women as well as men were expected to espouse and, in this sense, male and female codes of honour overlapped in many ways. Sexual behaviour also factored in masculine conceptions of honour and the appearance of sexual constancy was of importance to men, especially among men judged to have reached maturity.[24] Sexual license represented a loss of self-control and maturity that could disrupt household order and social order more broadly. It was often seen as corrupting and feminizing and, while women undeniably sued over such instances in higher numbers and their credibility within the courts was more frequently questioned based on their reputation for sexual honesty, such insults were also of concern to men.[25]

Alongside the urgings of moralists and prescriptive sources, court cases brought by men over issues of sexual slander and instances of men being ridiculed within their communities on sexual grounds likewise demonstrate that intemperate sexual behaviour on the part of a man could threaten his honour.[26] While the emergence of libertinism and shifting views of female sexuality after 1660 may have contributed to many of our modern notions of male sexual rapaciousness and restrained female sexual appetites, most men in the early modern period were aware that a poor sexual reputation, which violated Christian principles and prescriptive codes of conduct, could be damaging to one's good name.[27] Men were expected to cultivate just as many of the conduct book virtues of forbearance, self-control, and mature conduct associated with sexual probity as women and, when they failed to display these attributes without just cause, they risked forfeiting the respect of their peers. Young men especially were counseled to overcome impetuous and profligate behaviour as they moved into manhood and were urged to display self-restraint and cultivate a reputation for sexual honesty.[28]

Because proper sexual behaviour was expected from men as well as women, the Earl of Essex took umbrage when Lady Anne Bacon, the widow of the Lord Keeper, chastised him for a carnal dalliance she believed he had engaged in, allegedly with Elizabeth Stanley.[29] Essex wrote a letter of protest, noting, "this charge which is newlie laide upon me is false and unjust."[30] He went on to inform Lady Bacon, "since my departure from England towardes Spaine I have been free from taxation of Incontinency with any woman that lives I never sawe or spake with the Lady you meane."[31] Essex's main concern was ensuring that the rumour did not reach the ears of the Queen (and possibly Stanley's husband). He was certainly no stranger to illicit sexual encounters, having a number of mistresses throughout his life, but he was also keenly aware that circumspection was expected. This was not only because his standing with the Queen might be damaged by a reputation for sexual prolificacy, but also because such licentious behaviour denoted a lack of maturity and responsibility. He was, accordingly, anxious to defend himself.

Sexual Transgressions

During the Elizabethan and Jacobean periods, while sexual indiscretions could be potentially highly damaging to women, actual responses to illicit sex were bound up with other factors, such as the existing perception of the character of the person involved and his or her social rank; the importance of sexual purity among women was also powerfully connected to and affected by the social hierarchy. There was thus an element of fluidity to the significance of sexual probity, and its boundaries were negotiable. While sexual standing was only one of the factors that determined a woman's reputation, for elite women it was of even less importance as they were not, by and large, exposed to allegations of actual sexual impropriety (in contrast to such allegations being a stand in for criticism about other matters) in the same ways as women positioned lower on the social scale. This is attributable to several factors, including elite women's reduced levels of private, casual contact with men that could lead to rumoured or actual sexual relationships (compared to women from the lower orders), their not occupying the sometimes claustrophobic atmosphere of (often urban) local communities where conflict had the potential to erupt more frequently with greater levels of contact, and their not typically being victims of the type of poverty which could lead to sexual bartering in order to survive. In addition, while elite women were less vulnerable to charges against their chastity than non-elite women, those who did engage in sexually-transgressive behaviour often found that an illicit sexual encounter "was neither a mere 'fashionable vice' nor a moral death."[32] Rather it fell somewhere between these two poles: a matter of seriousness but not an end of all honour in itself. Lineage, wealth, and social position often mattered a great deal more than sexual reputation and tempered the associated threat to honour faced by an elite woman. Social hierarchy cut across and could contradict, even subvert, gendered sexual norms in a palpable way.[33] This ensured that alleged sexual indiscretions were often not enough per se to rob elite women entirely of their good names, although many undoubtedly felt the consequences of such relationships in other ways, such as husbands withholding support or turning them out of the home (if they were married) and censure from parents and other family members.[34] Notwithstanding, there was a great measure of flexibility present with respect to women's reputations as connected to their sexual conduct, in spite of the existence of a restrictive rhetoric that implied that sexual probity was all important.

That involvement in an unsanctioned sexual liaison was not enough on its own to cost an elite woman her reputation is evidenced by the relationship between Anne Vavasour and Edward de Vere, the seventeenth Earl of Oxford. Anne was sworn as a Lady of the Bedchamber to Queen Elizabeth in 1580.[35] Shortly thereafter she became one of the Queen's six maids of honour and de Vere's mistress. On 23 March 1581, Anne gave birth to a bastard son sired by de Vere in the maidens' chamber at court. As one contemporary described the event, there was "a great mischeaunce at court yeasterdaye beinge tewsdaye that one of the mayds of Honor ... was delyvered of a goodly boy begotten by my L. of Oxford."[36] While the affair sparked a feud between Anne's relative Sir Thomas Knyvett and de Vere, Anne does not appear to have suffered overly for her indiscretion. After a brief stint in the Tower (Elizabeth I also sent de Vere there), she was released, and by 1590 she had married John Finch and begun an affair with the Queen's champion at the tilt, Sir Henry Lee.[37] Finch appears to have been relatively tolerant of the liaison and was later to receive a pension of £20 per year from Lee, suggesting that any outrage he may have felt over his wife's indiscretion had been easily soothed. Anne lived openly with Lee and the couple had a son, Thomas Vavasour. When Lee died in 1611, Anne inherited a jointure worth £700, and by 1618 she was married again, this time to John Richardson. At the time Finch was still living, making the union with Richardson bigamous. Lee's heir accordingly sued her for bigamy in the Court of High Commission in 1621 and she was fined £2,000. In this case, Lee's heir was not so much interested in censuring Anne's sexual behaviour as in depriving her of what he saw as a portion of his inheritance. Despite her later legal troubles, Anne Vavasour does not appear to have ever been seriously censured for her lack of sexual honesty (indeed, she and Sir Henry even hosted the Queen at Ditchley during one of her progresses). Her 1581 pregnancy did result in her expulsion from court and the loss of her position as maid of honour, but this seems to have been more of a temporary inconvenience rather than a life-shattering occurrence.

One can find a parallel situation in the marriage of William Parr, Marquis of Northampton (brother to Henry VIII's last queen), and Anne Bourchier. Their marriage was a disastrous one and Anne lived openly with another man (John Lyngfield, alias Huntley or Hunt) while William took up with Elizabeth Brooke, whom he later married. In 1543 he secured a separation from his wife and an Act of Parliament that debarred any of Anne's children from inheriting his lands. While Anne appears to have endured a brief period of impoverished exile at Little Wakering manor in Essex, her honour was not permanently tarnished by her sexual transgressions. Neither was Elizabeth Brooke's reputation irreparably damaged by her open relationship with Parr, nor by the vicissitudes of her marriage to him (which he had entered into bigamously in 1547: the union was declared valid in 1548, invalidated in 1553, and then made valid again in 1558, which meant that she was not officially recognized as Parr's wife at the court of Mary I).[38] She was later to find great favour with Elizabeth I.

Lady Mary Darcy offers a further example. In 1583, Mary, the youngest daughter of Thomas and Elizabeth Kitson, married Thomas Darcy, third Baron Darcy of Chiche. Darcy was often away on official business, and it was reported to him that Mary had made some cutting remarks at his expense in his absence. At this juncture, Lord Darcy also suspected his wife of engaging in flirtations, if not outright adultery. The marriage broke down shortly thereafter and, in 1594, a deed of separation was executed whereby Lady Darcy received a settlement of £350 per annum. Perceiving that her social status and position as a well-born gentlewoman largely negated the attacks levelled at her by her husband, Mary relished her new position as a wealthy, independent woman. Indeed, she commissioned a portrait of herself in which she is pictured clutching the deed of separation in her hand with the inscribed motto "If not, I care not" (presumably dismissing any suggestion of reconciliation with her husband). Honour encompassed multiple meanings and behavioural standards and, depending on their needs and objectives at any given time, individuals could privilege one meaning over others. For Mary, rank and wealth mattered more than allegations of sexual inconstancy, and she unapologetically attached little importance to her husband's suspicions of her.

While Mary's husband served as her main detractor in the matter, she also had her defenders and admirers. One of them was Sir George Carew, who wrote to Mary to inform her of her husband's allegations against her and also to affirm his intention to defend her character. He told her that, "your Innosenssy for me is an vnspotted virginnetty" and proclaimed that he had always "honored your fayrenes fayrely and with noe foulle affection."[39] While allegations of sexual misconduct could perhaps have been damaging to Mary, she appears to have rebounded from the dissolution of her marriage nicely. She wrote to Carew that, while she was alarmed at her husband's accusations, "yet haue I digested them w*ith* patience."[40] She also denied that she had acted "in any vnlawfull or vnmodest sort whatsoeuer."[41] However she did take care to safeguard her honour in the future by instructing Carew not to write to her again, enjoining him, "as you ar a gentellman so regard my honer & neether writ nor send no more to me."[42] Mary ended her missive by telling Carew that, if he did write to her again, she would make it known that he was pursuing her and it would be "small to your credet."[43] While Mary undoubtedly recognized that sexual indiscretions could adversely affect her reputation, she was able to effectively and easily deal with rumours of her alleged promiscuity. She took care to ensure that she was perceived as behaving with all due decorum, without troubling much over her husband's allegations against her. There the matter rested; Mary's reputation was not overly adversely affected by rumours surrounding her constancy as a wife.

In contrast to her relatively tame reaction to allegations of promiscuity, when accusations that Mary had behaved contentiously and slandered another woman reached her mother shortly after the deed of separation was granted in 1594, she experienced a good deal of anxiety. On hearing that her mother, Lady Elizabeth Kitson, had heard rumours that she had slandered another woman, Mary wrote to Elizabeth imploring that it not be believed. Mary wrote that she was aware "that your La*dyship* meeting her at the corte she shold tell your La*dyship* I had much wronged her in report saying whersoeuer she becam she rayled of her owlde husband."[44] Mary denied that she had spoken such words and, of her alleged detractor's taunts, she proclaimed, "how true it is god only knowse & myself" but she hoped that no one would believe "this gret a slander of me."[45] Mary theorized that these reports of her poor conduct were being circulated as a plot against her. As she told her mother, "I wonder not at thys because I haue & dow fynd it a vissiacc tric [a vicious trick] of sume to gette my best frends loue frome me."[46] She then accused those who spoke against her of having lying tongues and lamented, "trewly madam I neuer lawke to liue so long as to be free from mallisius tonges I besich god geue me grase to take no worse carse then I dowe & I hope I shall make them a shame frust."[47] Mary was desirous that her mother not think she had behaved badly and seems, in this instance, to have viewed this negative perception of her as more damaging than allegations that she was overly flirtatious with other men or unfaithful to her husband. Her reaction demonstrates that allegations of contentious behaviour could be a matter of concern for elite women when it came to their reputations, and they could accord precedence to this element of honour over sensitivities to accusations of sexual misconduct.

The experiences of Lady Penelope Rich, sister of Elizabeth I's favourite the Earl of Essex and wife of Robert, Lord Rich, demonstrates that some elite women were not persuaded to modify their engagement in illicit sexual conduct even when it did threaten palpable damage to their reputation. Aware that factors such as honourable birth, social standing, and previous favour at court would, in time, likely compensate for breaching behaviour, coupled with the fact that continuing an illicit relationship outweighed a desire to immediately recapture the small measure of her honour that had been damaged, Penelope did not feel compelled to repent of her actions when, in 1590, she embarked on an adulterous relationship with Sir Charles Blount.[48] For fifteen years Lord Rich ignored his wife's infidelity (and the children she bore Blount), but in 1605 he sued her for divorce in the ecclesiastical courts and cast her and Blount's illegitimate children out of the family home. During the ensuing proceedings Penelope openly admitted her adultery and the divorce was granted; Penelope's request to marry Blount and legitimize their children was not.

This, however, did not stop the couple. Late in 1605, William Laud, Blount's chaplain, married them. Until this point the couple had been high in royal favour. Penelope was one of the ladies chosen to escort James I's wife, Anna of Denmark, into London in 1603, and she also served as a Lady of the Bedchamber, while James made Blount the Earl of Devonshire. Despite these successes at the Jacobean court, the couple were banished when news of their defiance of canon law became public. In a statement addressed to King James attempting to explain his actions, Blount wrote that Penelope had suffered greatly in her marriage to Rich and had been joined to him despite her strong objections to the match. He described her case as that "of a poor lost sheep; a Lady of great Birth and virtue being in the power of her frends was by them married ag*ain*st her will unto one ag*ain*st whom she did protest at the very solemnity and everafter."[49] For good measure he added that the couple had not been intimate ("the chiefest duty of a husband") for the past twelve years.[50] He also told James that, throughout their union, Rich "instead of a Comforter he did study in all things to torment Her, and by fear and fraud did practise to deceive her of her Dowry," which drove her into Blount's arms.[51] According to Blount, the mistreatment that Penelope endured from her husband was enough to convince him that "in some cases to dissolve the Bond of Marriage is neither ag*ain*st the Civil Institution, the Law of Nature, not the Law of the Gospel."[52] Blount's protests were to no avail, however, and the couple was not forgiven. However, it is arguable that they would eventually have been allowed back into royal favour had they not both died shortly after the marriage, Blount in 1606 and Penelope in 1607. In this instance, it was not so much Penelope's adultery with Blount which affected her reputation as their marriage in defiance of the law; and this affected his reputation as much as hers. Despite this, it is significant that the pair did not waiver in their course of action and continued to cohabit even after their banishment from court. They accorded their desire to remain together more weight than any compulsion they may have felt to rehabilitate their slightly tarnished honour by separating. Honour was not a static concept for Penelope and the varying levels of importance she could accord to its disparate meanings made it a negotiable one, rather than something she wholly associated with a reputation for sexual probity.

This is not to say that elite women did not care at all about their sexual honour. There were instances in which elite women reacted immediately and angrily to accusations of sexual impropriety. For example, when King Christian IV of Denmark visited the court of King James and his sister Anna, a series of rather drunken entertainments designed for the Danish king ensued, and during one of these Christian made a joking reference to the Earl of Nottingham being a cuckold. It was reported that he waggled his fingers at the side of his head as if to suggest horns. Dudley Carleton, rather improbably, alleged that the whole affair was a misunderstanding and that Christian had been gesturing with his fingers to indicate that it was two o'clock but that the Countess of Nottingham, "she being now with child and jealous of her credit would not so put it up."[53] While, in all likelihood, this was simply a drunken jest in poor taste, a report of it reached Nottingham's wife and she reacted very angrily. It is probable that the Countess was also sensitive because she was roughly just less than fifty years her husband's junior (Margaret was around twelve or thirteen when she was married). This marriage to a much older man, and the associated sexual innuendo and the potentially salacious gossip it lent itself to, may have made Margaret more sensitive to her reputation in this area than she might otherwise have been and this enhanced sensitivity guided her response to the Danish king's "jest." Upon hearing of the incident, she wrote to one of Christian's agents, the Scotsman Andrew Sinclair, "yt is reported to me by men of hono*r*: the greate wrong the king of the Danes hath done me when I was not by to answere for my selfe."[54] According to Margaret, "if I had bin present I would haue letten him knowe how much I scorne to receiue that wrong at his hands, I neede not write the perticuler of it, for the King him selfe knoweth best."[55]

In words analogous to those of men who took to print to defend themselves against gossip and/or accusations, the Countess cast aspersions on the reputation of the man who had slandered her. To achieve this she implied that, by virtue of Christian's inherent baseness (a rather loaded accusation to lob at a monarch and an example of the perceived link between personal behaviour and social status), his ill words would surely not be countenanced. As she wrote to Sinclair, "I did think hono:*ra*ble of the King your M*aste*r: as I did of any one Prince, but now I perswade my selfe there is as much basenes in him as can be in any man."[56] She added, "for although he be a prince by birth, it seemes not to me that there harbereth any princely thoughts in his brest, for either in prince or subject it is the basest parte that can be to wrong any woman of ho:*nor*."[57] Margaret closed her letter forcefully by noting what she would do if ever she discovered who had whispered such slanders about her to Christian IV. She claimed,

> if euer I come to knowe what man hath informed yo*u*r M*aste*r so wrongfully of me, I shall doe my best to put him from doing the lyke to any other, but if it hath come by the tongue of any woman, I dare say she would be glad to haue companyons.[58]

Implying a threat to employ violence if the rumour monger should prove to be a woman, this statement served to slightly soften her earlier attack on Christian and his status by suggesting that she believed him to have been duped by the false reports of others, rather than inventing the scurrilous words himself. Despite this attempt to temper her expression of rage, the Countess's actions turned out badly for her and she was temporarily banished from court on the orders of Christian's sister, Queen Anna, with the support of James I. While her complaints about Christian's behaviour did not result in the public rebuking of the Danish king for which she likely hoped, the Countess nonetheless saw it as important to defend her honour from what she perceived to be a direct attack. In this situation, the honour she saw as attached to her reputation for circumspect sexual behaviour mattered more than the competing measure of honour she might accrue through a deferential demeanour towards King Christian.

Despite this incident, the sexual reputations of most elite women were infrequently commented upon, and those who did engage in illicit sexual relationships often did not see their honour irretrievably lost, as earlier examples demonstrate. Conversely, one action that could cause damage to an elite woman's reputation, and which was connected, in a sense, to sexual reputation, was the making of an illicit marriage. What appears to have caused the most damage to a woman's honour in these cases was not transgressive sexuality but the display of a lack of proper obedience to parental wishes. This was serious breaching behaviour. The unsanctioned match made by Margaret Bagot can be pointed to as an example of the deleterious effects that such action could have on the honour of an elite woman. The Bagot family was one of the oldest Staffordshire gentry families, having established themselves at Blithfield Hall in 1362. During the reign of Elizabeth I, Richard Bagot consolidated the family's position in local society by holding multiple positions over the years, including those of sheriff, justice of the peace, and local Deputy Lieutenant. Richard sired several children: Walter, Anthony, Margaret, Ann (who married Richard Broughton), Dorothy (who married Ralph Okeover), and Lettice (who married Francis Kynnersley). The Bagot family had strong connections with the Devereux family and, in 1587, Margaret (Richard Bagot's eldest daughter) married William Trew, a member of the Devereux household, without the knowledge or permission of her parents.[59]

An elite woman's reputation for obedience and submissiveness to her family mattered a great deal and was often a foundational element in how she was seen by others.[60] To this end, it formed a key part of the education and socialization of girls.[61] It would undoubtedly have been deeply troubling to Margaret to know that her father, upon discovery of the match, wrote to his son-in-law, Richard Broughton, that "my daughters lewde dealinge in this her match hath not a litle trobled me and her mother."[62] In deliberately flouting the authority of her parents and showing herself to be an undutiful daughter, Margaret damaged her honour. Bagot doubted that the marriage would be deemed lawful (in the event it was) and declared that his daughter's dealing in the affair was so dishonest that it was bound to blemish her reputation. He told Broughton, "w*hi*ch if it be a mariage (as I rest doubtfull) I way it not so much as the maner of yt the practyes wherof are so dishonest to her selfe as hardly wilbe recouered besydes dishonest to others."[63] He was so angered by Margaret's conduct that "apon knowledge of yt I torned her away to him to Chartley."[64] William Trew wrote to his new, and reluctant, father-in-law in an attempt to secure forgiveness and Bagot also noted that he had received several other letters requesting him "to p*ar*don th*ei*r offence and not to cast her of."[65]

Margaret's damaged reputation in the eyes of her parents resulted less from her actual relationship with Trew and more from her failure to consult them about the match (just as Lady Penelope Rich's reputation was damaged when she illicitly wed Charles Blount); it was Margaret's self-presentation as an obedient daughter, and not as a chaste virgin, that was injured by her actions. Yet, as was the case with other elite women involved in sexual scandals, the cultivation of a chaste reputation was not the only attribute that constituted Margaret's honour, and she privileged her illicit pursuit of her position as Trew's wife above the understanding that her honour was connected to her deference to her parents or her maintenance of purity. That this was a tenable position for her to adopt was likely informed by her awareness that it was possible to recapture any lost credit in these alternate areas associated with honour by seeking forgiveness in a dutiful way for her transgression. This she must have achieved, for her father, after his initial expression of displeasure, was able to note, "I am contented to forgive the fault."[66] For elite women, honour was accrued and maintained through many variable social behaviours, and while lapses within one of these often overlapping spheres – involvement in an illicit sexual liaison, the contraction of an unsanctioned marriage, or the refusal to exhibit proper obedience to a parent – could be damaging, it was often not enough to ensure that they entirely forfeited their honourable reputation, especially if they appropriately expressed remorse and sought forgiveness (much as was the case when young men were involved in socially breaching behaviour). Rehabilitation was achievable and an awareness of this likely informed the choices of many with respect to which of the varying conceptions of honour they privileged over others at a given time.

Servants and Sexual Indiscretions

While direct challenges to their sexual honesty were rather rare occurrences for elite women, this did not mean that they were not involved in the monitoring of the sexual conduct of others. In particular, elite women often evinced concern for the sexual reputations of those in their employ. Women took pride in their successful running of a household and their ability to manage affairs for their husbands.[67] Desirous to maintain the appearance of a well-ordered household space, elite women understood that the behaviour of their servants reflected on themselves. With the need to maintain control over servants in mind, when Elizabeth Clinton, Countess of Lincoln, was having problems with one of her maidservants (with whose parents she was on friendly terms) she mobilized her local network of friends to reform the girl's behaviour. The maid, Mary Tyrrell, engaged in an illicit relationship with a man named William Porter, another servant of the family, that was frowned upon by the girl's parents.[68] Her role as mistress entailed that Elizabeth act *in loco parentis* and there was a need for her to take a firm hand to ensure that the proper training of the girl under her roof continued, and that her future marriage prospects were preserved. A failure to ensure that the girl behaved with obedience to her parents and others in positions of authority could negatively affect Elizabeth's honour as the conduct of servants affected the reputations of their employers.

In order to punish the girl and separate her from Porter, Lady Clinton sent her for a time to the household of her friends Sir William and Lady Margaret More in Surrey. At first Porter and Mary refused to end their relationship and Elizabeth wrote to Margaret More to warn her that "I am gyven to vnderstand by a frynd of porters that he … seeke the meanes to steale awaye the gearle."[69] Elizabeth advised keeping her close, saying "therefore I praye yow to haue the more care that she haue no lybertye abroade."[70] Eventually, however, the importance of obedience was taught to the girl. The methods by which the lesson was imparted do not survive, but Elizabeth was soon writing to thank More for reforming the maid. She wrote, "I thanke yow for your good kare had of thos matters consernynge my lytell meyd."[71]

Elizabeth was, however, cautious to ensure that Mary did not revert to poor behaviour. To that end, she kept Mary under surveillance and read the letters that she composed to ensure they were not directed at anyone deemed inappropriate. Accordingly, Elizabeth read one that the girl had written to her father and noted approvingly that it was "dutyfully wryten in promysynge obedyens to hyr father and mother and denyenge the sendynge of any letter to wylyam porter."[72] She was concerned, however, that the letter perhaps did not reflect Mary's true feelings but rather the influence of the Mores and added, "I dout wither thys letter be wryten by hyr owne dyrectyon or by sum better aduyse had in your house."[73]

Nevertheless, the maidservant, having promised obedience, even if disingenuously, to her mother and father and denied any further contact with William Porter, could now be safely readmitted to the Countess's household, provided her behaviour be monitored in order to ensure that any additional transgressive acts would not bring the reputation of her mistress into question (although it appears Mary remained with the Mores for a significant period of time, temporarily in their service). While apprehensive as to whether Mary had truly and completely been reformed, both Elizabeth and her husband were grateful to the Mores for assisting them in reasserting control over the situation. Edward Clinton wrote to them in 1570 to thank them for their involvement:

> my wyf dothe thynke her selfe moche beholding vnto yow, For that yow and M*istres*s Moore have bene contente to have the young mayde so long with yow where in my wif thynke herselfe moche beholding vnto yow and dothe geve yow her most harty thanks for the same.[74]

Elizabeth also wrote sometime later to express her thanks "for yo*ur* frendeshepe showed vnto my yonge mayde mary Tyrryll."[75] In this instance, sexual reputation did indeed play a role in the honour of an elite woman, but in a more complex way than would initially be supposed. Elizabeth Clinton was concerned with the sexual reputations of the servants in her household, not her own, because the servants were in her charge and their indiscretions reflected on her ability and discretion as a governor of the home. Her focus centred on the control and proper ordering of her household as a public space whose internal discipline would have been visible to many people. A failure to keep things in line within this sphere could have been perceived as a failure to fully meet the expectations of her social role as a household manager.

As part of this role, elite women were expected to tend to the care of their servants and, especially in the case of female servants, to behave in an often *quasi* maternal way to them. Fulfilment of this role was observed by other members of the elite with whom they interacted as partially indicative of their effectiveness as the governors of estates and the arbiters and enforcers of proper behaviour within the household. In this regard, many of Queen Elizabeth's rages over the illicit marriages and sexual encounters of her servants, so often interpreted as evidence of the Queen's innately jealous character, can likewise be linked to a more mundane desire to ensure that proper order was maintained in her privy chamber. The Queen, like other elite women, was aware she had a responsibility to be a conscientious guardian of those in her charge.[76]

In addition to having a duty to properly care for and discipline servants, in isolated cases where elite women were concerned about their sexual reputations servants could also be valuable allies in their attempts to refute allegations of impropriety.[77] Thus, when Bridget Eyre became aware that rumours of illicit sexual conduct on her part had reached her father, she acknowledged that such behaviour, if true, would be "to the ottar ovarthrowe of my selfe the gret descreder of yov my cheldren and all the reast of my freandes" while also affirming that she was blameless of any misdeeds.[78] She beseeched him "for god sake bare a beattar openyon of me vntell svch tyme as I prove othar wease then A honest woman," but also defended herself by noting that the household servants could vouch for the truth of her assertions.[79] As she told him, "I can brenge forth all the sarvants In the house to be sowrne for the oneste vssenge of my selfe In all repectes."[80] Her alliance with the family's household servants took on a new level of importance in this instance as Bridget depended on them for more than just material aid. Yet Bridget Eyre's experience, with respect to the aspersions cast upon her sexual reputation, was not a typical one. Most elite women were rarely confronted with such challenges. They were more likely to be concerned, on a practical basis, with the other values encompassed under the umbrella of honour.

Piety and Circumspection

As was the case among men, a reputation for honesty and kindness within the local community was also of great importance to women as a marker of honour.[81] Thus, when seeking to discredit a woman and damage her honour, it could be just as damning to state that "she seemeth scarse honest" in her business and social dealings as to allege that she was promiscuous.[82] Likewise, while contemporary conduct books all emphasized the importance of sexual reputation, they also indicated that women's honour was equally vested in an array of other qualities and behaviours. Among these, religious observance and the display of circumspect behaviour in realms aside from sexual conduct were accorded considerable weight with respect to women's honour. Thus, in his manual detailing the proper behaviours of "good women," Barnabe Rich wrote of "the zeale of vertue and the desire of good name which to euery honest woman is more precious than gold or siluer or any other gemme."[83]

In addition to virtue and sexual purity, Rich listed a host of other attributes that a proper, honest woman and wife should possess. He stated,

> a man that wanteth a friend for pleasure, a seruant for profit, a counsellour to aduise him, a comforter to cherish him, a companion to solace him, a helper to assist him, or a spirituall instructer to informe him, a good & vertuous wife doth supply all these occasions.[84]

As Rich's use of the term "spirituall instructer" suggests, faith and displays of piety could also be very potent sources of honour for women. And while the religious differences wrought by the English reformations appear to have played a relatively insignificant role in perceptions of honour (especially when one considers the many other potent social and cultural changes they occasioned), the display of particular forms of piety in accordance with the dictates of reformed religion did become important as a marker of honour for some, as it served as a means to articulate their religious identity. Hence, in his final letter to his daughters (Deliverance, Comfort, Safety, and Sure Hope), the religious controversialist and non-conformist John Penry, hanged in 1593 on charges of sedition, highlighted, from prison, the honour for women to be found in learning and the cultivation of true piety. Penry's letter is based on biblical excerpts, and considers the pursuit of true honour. It illustrates how he valued the acquisition and application of godly, reformed learning as a component of female honour. Accordingly, he instructed his daughters to learn to read and write through their mother's teaching, and advised them to learn humility and not to "delight in any vanitie."[85] He closed his missive by enjoining them to "praye muche and often."[86]

Penry also wrote a letter to his wife close to his execution in which it is clear that he valued her piety and intellect, and saw these as contributing to her personal honour. He entrusted her with the further spreading of the gospel to their children, whom he requested she educate in both temporal and spiritual matters. He also entrusted her with educating a wider audience by asking that she collect his papers on religious affairs and make them available to like-minded friends so that they might be published.[87] Penry trusted that, because his wife was an honourable, honest, and pious woman, she would "continue a member of that holy socyetye" after his death and allow nothing to "be dearer vnto yow then Godes service."[88]

The evidence of published funeral sermons preached in remembrance of elite women also points to the role of duty in religious observance as a marker of honour. While this genre should not be used uncritically, surviving sermons suggest that active piety among women was highly praised, and undoubtedly contributed to their reputations.[89] Prior to the 1640s, this genre was rare, and even more rarely published. David Cressy's search of the *English Short Title Catalogue* reveals that three sermons were published in the 1560s, three in the 1570s, seven in the 1580s, eleven in the 1590s, twenty-nine from the 1600s, fifty-six from the 1610s, and forty-nine from the 1620s. After this the number grew steadily, a development, Cressy argues, that reflects the expansion of printing and literacy in the decades before and after the Civil Wars.[90] Those who patronized the writing of such sermons wished to draw attention to the deceased woman's proper piety and social behaviour and, as with conduct books, they reveal sources of female honour beyond sexual probity, such as sober conduct and moral gravity. Although sexual incontinence naturally compromised an individual's claim to either virtue, it was not the single determinant of the verdict, nor even the most important one.[91] It was an indicator of her honourable reputation, as surely as any mention of her sexual purity, when Elizabeth Machell, who died aged twenty-three, was described by Stephen Geree in his offered funeral sermon as "so growne in grace, that shee might seeme rather three-score and three, for gravity sobriety and modesty, matching the eldest matrons."[92]

Tied to this emphasis on religious dedication as a marker of honour were other behaviours associated with decorum, circumspection, obedience, and humility. A combination of these virtues made for an ideal woman, and this is reflected in the advice given to sons regarding the choosing of a "good & vertuous wife."[93] When an unnamed gentleman in Derbyshire left a set of instructions to his newly married son he included, among a plethora of advice on finances, husbandry, the choice of friends, and domestic economy, guidance on his relationship with his wife. The son was warned not to permit his wife to "come to London to tary there past one weeke for I *per*ceave that she is much disposed to play at Cardes and all other games," suggesting that a woman's honour could be negatively affected by these activities.[94] He was also exhorted to ensure that his wife was "discrete" and sober in her behaviour.[95] Likewise, when John Holles penned a series of counsels for his son to assist him in his future life (Holles termed it "a legacie at his death"), he advised him to "vse greate prouidence and circumspection in ye choise of thy wife: for from thence may springe all thy future good or ill. For ye choise of a wife is like ^to^ a stratageme in warre."[96] Holles advised his son not to choose a "base or vncomely creature" for that would breed contempt in others and loathing in oneself.[97] He then extolled the virtues of a good wife, few of which were based solely in sexual circumspection.[98]

Honour in Housewifery

As all this advice of the choosing of a wife suggests, wifehood was an important social role with respect to women's honour – this was a facet of female reputation that extended into the deep past and remained relatively static until the sexual revolution of the modern era, where it became a rather more contested value. Within marriage elite women were expected to be proficient in a range of activities associated with the running of the household. They gained honour through their industry in these areas. They were also expected to project the attributes of genteel femininity, such as proficiency with needlework and musical ability. Some husbands, Nathaniel Bacon for example, had some initial misgivings about their wives' abilities to serve as model gentry spouses. Nathaniel's first wife, Anne, who was married to Bacon from 1569 until her death in 1597, was the illegitimate (but acknowledged) child of Sir Thomas Gresham. As a result of her illegitimate birth, she had not been as well educated as other elite brides in the standard skills taught to early modern gentry women. Anne saw this as detrimental to her reputation, and wrote often to her father concerning her efforts to improve herself, in particular in the realm of ornamental pursuits, such as vocal performance and playing the virginal.[99] It was not uncommon for new brides to be anxious about establishing their role within a family and proving their worth as domestic partners.[100] Feeling that her training as a gentlewoman was lacking, Anne accordingly endeavoured to acquire such skills as would garner her honour as a wife. As for Nathaniel, he wrote to his mother in the early years of the couple's marriage to inform her that he was attempting to "bring up" and educate his bride, as was expected of him as the family head. He wrote to Lady Bacon, "y*our* La*dyship* knoweth how beinge matched in mariage as I am, it stode me vpon to haue some care of ye well bringinge vp of my wife."[101] He continued,

> these wordes of Erasmus are very trewe, plus est bene instrui quam bene nasci [it is better to have been well instructed than well born]. yf she sholde haue had ye want of both I had iust cause to feare what might befall herevpon beinge not able to rememdie ye one I did as mutch as in me lay to p*ro*vide for the other & therfore I sought by all ye meanes I colde to haue her placed w*ith* y*our* La*dyship*.[102]

Anne was anxious to rise to early modern social expectations of womanly and wifely accomplishment, and assiduously attempted to improve herself. Her husband helped her in this respect, as he felt he had a duty to properly educate her.

It was important for Anne Bacon to master the skills associated with household management and wifely conduct because, as an early modern elite wife, she would be expected to effectively aid in the oversight of domestic affairs. While final oversight when it came to household management remained the purview of husbands, the prudent running of a household and the managing of their husbands' affairs were key ways for women to gain and maintain social capital. Women's involvement in these activities constituted a powerful source of honour for them across historical periods and most early modern women were educated from a young age in the intricacies of household management in anticipation of their later careers as wives.[103]

While a cursory examination of the rhetoric of submissive femininity as described in sources such as sermons and prescriptive literature suggests that women's exercise of authority within the household was heavily circumscribed, elite women undoubtedly played prominent roles in this space, often negotiated the terms of their marriages, and had the ability to "reshape a repressive system of principles" in the course of daily life.[104] Likewise, while wives were subject to the ultimate authority of husbands, prescriptive literature did place some elements of the running of the household under the oversight of a wife. According to Gouge, "the wife is by Gods prouidence appointed a ioynt gouernour with the husband of the familie."[105] While men had charge of the "great and weighty affairs" of a household, women were tasked with the "some less, but verie needful matters as nourishing and instructing children when they are young, adorning the house, ordering the provision brought into the house, ruling maid-seruants, with the like."[106] Dod and Cleaver similarly wrote that the duty of a wife was "to oversee and give order for all things within the house."[107] Gouge further enjoined husbands and wives to respect each other's authority within the household, as failing to do so could lead to the collapse of proper hierarchy. He advised,

> let an husband be churlish to his wife, and despise her, he ministreth an occasion to children and seruants to contemne her likewise, and to be disobedient vnto her, yea to be churlish and forward one to another, especially to their vnderlings.[108]

As Thomas Kitson wrote to his half-sister Susan with respect to his wife, "I have accepted her for my wyef so likewise to be a partaker in the governement of my howse."[109]

Given the importance attached to the administration of the household as a source of honour and a sign of coming into full adulthood for women, it was no surprise that Anne Bacon was desirous of assuming her position as a householder, and the associated authority, in the years immediately following her marriage – perhaps spurred along by her husband's early lack of confidence in her abilities. While marriage typically resulted in an elite couple, provided they were of an age to do so, establishing themselves in their own household, the Bacons were financially constrained in their initial years of marriage and unable to establish themselves independently; they leased a property rather than acquiring it for themselves. It was a situation that caused Anne a considerable amount of anxiety and she wrote both to her birth mother, Winifred Dutton, and her stepmother, Lady Anne Gresham, to seek their assistance and express her frustration. She wrote to both women once in the same letter, saying simply "yowr dawghter wisseth her self in a house of her owne."[110] She then implored them to approach her father so that he might offer her and Nathaniel financial assistance.[111] She told them, "my husbande hetherto hath provided nothinge towardes our goinge to house. I thinke the let be because he is not able."[112] She asked again that the women assist her and said that "vnlesse my father be good vnto we are like to remaine sojorners more than one yeare or two."[113] Fortunately Nathaniel was able to acquire a house for them and by September of 1573 Anne was able to write happily to her father that she was now "in a house of myne owne, w*hi*ch I am glad I am come vnto."[114]

Once in possession of a household, early modern elite women took its successful running very seriously. At times, they could approach household maintenance with a level of enthusiasm bordering on the domineering, which was perhaps to the chagrin of their husbands at times. While playing an active role in the sphere of the household was expected of women, deference to husbands was also required. Nathaniel Bacon's sister, Elizabeth, the second wife of Sir Henry Neville, offers one example of an early modern elite woman rigorously controlling household affairs and occasioning the censure of her spouse. Sir Henry wrote to his brother-in-law Nathaniel about a lease held by the couple and confessed that, in their relationship and the running of their household affairs, Elizabeth was very much in charge. Neville compared her to another woman whom he reports was recently censured by Star Chamber "for that she wore the bryches" when it came to her interactions with her husband.[115] While Neville may have been slightly exaggerating his wife's strong attitude, perhaps for comic relief, it is clear that she took a leading, even controlling, role in household affairs in defiance of prescriptive literature which emphasized the obedience she was obliged to offer to her husband. Katie Barclay has noted that "the ambiguous relationship between men as head of the home and women as managers meant that lines of power were not always clear" in the period and, while some elite women negotiated these ambiguities in ways that allowed them to exert authority and control, even over a spouse, others grappled with the limitations this placed upon their power within the household.[116]

While elite women had authority over some within the household (such as servants and junior members of the family), this was mitigated by the deference that they, in turn, owed to their husbands. In this sense, when we focus on the hierarchy of authority within the household, we are, in fact, looking at a series of overlapping and interlocking hierarchies involving husbands, wives, children, and those related to servants. The bedrock of these overlapping hierarchies was the relationship between a husband and wife. As noted, while prescriptive literature and the practical necessities of daily life dictated that women participate actively in this sphere and be figures of authority, recognizing the constraints upon their power in this area and the manner in which they were negotiated, often referencing the language of honour, is key. The household was an area in which women's authority was "legitimate in theory but often not treated as such in practice," and many men undermined the positions of their wives as *quasi*-household heads and questioned their abilities.[117] Conflicts between spouses about the management of the household and other matters were, as might be expected, a common occurrence.

The perception that she was an inefficient household manager could be damaging to an elite woman's sense of personal reputation, especially as they expected to be accorded a certain respect in this area. It is unsurprising that gentry and aristocratic wives often reacted angrily when their abilities were questioned. In some instances women could use these moments of tension as opportunities to reformulate unsatisfactory relationships; they could offer a chance to declare to their spouses that their judgment in these areas was sound and deserving of respect, emphasizing the importance of their activities within marriage and the household as a means to apply pressure and negotiate a particular outcome.[118] Ideas about the importance of honour and reputation and the dictates of prescriptive literature aided in this as they offered women a means of critiquing their husbands' questioning of their authority by asserting that the exercise of that authority was an element of their honour and so their husbands' actions dishonoured them. Yet elite women were also aware that the pronouncements of prescriptive literature and medical wisdom that women were affective beings, and not as in control of their emotions as men, could be used to trivialize their expressions of anger towards a spouse and that this could do further reputational damage. Most expected that women would be less self-possessed and more inclined to fits of emotion, including anger over trivial matters, than men. Indeed, an angry woman was almost a caricature of herself and, as Nicholas Breton vividly described in 1615, "an unquiet woman is the misery of man, whose demeanour is not to be described but in extremities. Her voice is the screeching of an owl, her eye the poison of a cockatrice, her hand the claw of a crocodile, and her heart a cabinet of horror."[119] While men, as hotter and drier in the Galenic model of the humours that structured much medical knowledge in the period, were seen as more prone to anger, women, who were believed to be colder and wetter due to their possession of greater quantities of phlegm and black bile, were perceived to be more inclined to both unrestrained anger and as having a greater propensity to become angry over inconsequential matters – a symptom of their heightened irrationality.[120] The Dutch physician Levinus Lemnius believed that "a woman is quickly angry and flaming hot ... upon every small occasion she casts off the bridle of reason, and like a mad dog, forgetting all decency, and her self ... she sets upon all."[121] Richard Baxter further commented on women's perceived temperamental nature and propensity for anger over mere "fantasies" when he wrote, "women are commonly of potent fantasies, and tender, passionate, impatient spirits, easily cast into anger, or jealousy, or discontent."[122]

This ability to discount women's anger as irrational and trivial ensured that displays of irritation, even if justly founded and related to a slight involving some form of behaviour or social involvement that was seen as connected to honour, had to be carefully constructed or they risked being delegitimized and treated as evidence of the lack of self-control expected of the weaker, less rational sex, rather than proof of a matter worthy of redress. The venting of antagonism against a spouse thus needed to be presented as reasonable and rightful and connected to honourable and appropriate behaviour within a given setting. This reality often informed the ways in which women negotiated relationships with their spouses and sought redress when they felt their husbands' actions had affected their reputation. They often relied upon framing/legitimating techniques that echoed the accepted rhetoric of gendered honour and proper behaviour as a means to ensure they did not forfeit their standing in a quarrel, even as they asserted themselves. Likewise, while the perception that they were not as in control of their emotions as men could hamper female authority and their ability to gain honour through its exercise, many women could judiciously employ the language of emotion as a way to assert themselves by making an impassioned plea that was, nonetheless, rooted in an acceptance of their deferential positions in relation to their spouses. In this sense, elite women played with gender expectations of honourable conduct and demeanor within matrimony in order to achieve their ends, and it is not uncommon to find correspondence from gentlewomen detailing complaints that are peppered with references to their various affective states. They characterized themselves as "sory & ashamed," "much disquyetted," "troublesome," and made gestures towards their obedient and loving dispositions.[123] Thus, even as they took an active role in criticizing the behaviour of their spouses when they felt an issue touched upon their honour, elite women often projected a gendered construction of themselves as individuals whose power remained limited by conventional norms that dictated that honourable women behave deferentially towards their husbands.

For example, Maria Thynne adopted framing devices that referenced how honourable married women were meant to conduct themselves when she complained about her husband's encroachment upon her authority within the household. She expressed her irritation in such a way as to emphasize her submissiveness to his will (affirming her altogether appropriate belief in her inferiority within her marriage as befitted an honourable married woman).[124] Employing this rhetoric was a way to both soften her message and pre-empt the suggestion that she was behaving dishonourably by advancing concerns that were without basis and reflected only the physiological tendency of women to be carried away with the illusory and not be in full control of their emotions. As she wrote to Thomas, "I am both sory & ashamed that any Creature should see that you hold such a contempte of my poore wyttes, that beinge y*ou*r wyfe, you should not thinke me of discreation to order (accordinge to y*ou*r apoyntment) y*ou*r affayers in y*ou*r absince."[125] While careful to adhere to social expectations with respect to honourable wifely submissiveness by noting that she only exercised her household managerial responsibilities "accordinge to y*ou*r apoyntment," Maria nonetheless clearly expressed her anger that Thomas did not think her able to order their affairs.[126] As she expressed it, her anger arose because her input and advice "should in no cawse be taken, no not so much as in choseinge of Servants."[127] Given the urging of writers that women be involved in the maintenance of the household and its servants (and, in particular, be charged with the oversight of female servants), Maria was demonstrating that her irritation was rooted in a legitimate matter, in this instance the questioning of her rightful authority in an area which she saw as connected to her honour as a householder.[128]

Maria also invoked, subtly, the understanding that honourable wives should be the limited domestic partners of their husbands when she noted that Thomas should have more confidence in her, "beinge y*ou*r wife."[129] Maria raised this point again, in stronger terms, when she wrote that Thomas's actions gave her "a very much disquyetted minde, for I can*n*ot greeve a lyttle to finde that I, w*hi*ch haue binn a wyllinge Companion & partaker in y*ou*r harde fortuns, should now be made so greate a stranger to *you*r proceedings."[130] In another letter from around the same time she again affirmed her commitment to serving her husband faithfully and obediently, stating, "I wyll promyse to be inferyor to none of my Deverill neighbors in playeinge the good huswyfe, though they stryve tyll thay stinke."[131] Maria then reminded Thomas "I haue never yett craved anye thinge of such greate Importance as hath ever binn preiudicill to *you*r reputation or profite ... no, in good fayth thys age wyll not helpe you to an equall, I meane for a wife."[132] In doing so she emphasized that her intention, even while expressing her displeasure, was to satisfy him and that, should he truly judge her abilities as wanting, even then she would "contentedlye beare the disgrace."[133] However, she also suggested to Thomas that, in denying her a fuller role in the management of the household, his honour as well as hers was touched. As she told him, "yf you be perswaded that ytt is most for *you*r creadytte to leaue me lyke an Inocent foole here," she would accept such a "disgrace." Yet she also noted that such a state of affairs was abnormal and might result in the wagging of tongue for "others (excepting *you*r cownsellors) can wonder (as thay well maye) that my aduise & consent (beinge in ryght to be m*ist*res ther [within the household]) should in no cawse be taken.[134] Likewise, in her other pointed reminder to her husband that she was as much a partaker of his fortunes as he, she again utilized a shaming technique in the hope that his reputation would be touched enough to alter his behaviour.[135] Thomas, like most elite men, took as much interest in the proper running of his household as his wife did, however. It was this concern for effective maintenance of his estate that likely led him to challenge Maria, regardless of her protestations concerning her own effectiveness as a household manager. He may also have believed that, as a woman, her abilities in this regard were more limited than his.

Elizabeth Hastings, Countess of Huntingdon, reacted in a comparable manner to Maria Thynne when her husband questioned her decision to remove a particular wet nurse and employ another woman instead on the grounds that the turnover in employment was a waste of money. While angry that her authority in this realm had been questioned, Elizabeth articulated a response that made it clear both that her original decision was legitimate and that the impression that she would do anything detrimental to her husband and his estate was a mistaken one that touched her honour. She curtly responded to her husband with an affirmation that she was a prudent steward of the family's resources and noted "I haue giuen you no cause to thinke I spende you any thinge vnfittingly nether doo I increase your expences."[136] She then defended her decision to terminate the wet nurse because she was "altogether vnexperienced how to dress or tende a chylde."[137] As a woman and mother, Elizabeth claimed for herself a specialist's knowledge about such matters and rooted her expression of discontent over her husband's questioning of her in this claim while simultaneously emphasizing her frugality and care for the family's finances – things ordered at the discretion of her spouse and of which the successful stewardship brought her honour.

While some elite women expressed indignation when their role in household matters was challenged, and used framing techniques to articulate their anger at these slights to their reputation, others reacted with embarrassment and reached out to their families in an attempt to set things right. Such was the case when Francis Kynnersley undermined the authority of his wife Lettice Bagot (Walter Bagot's sister). In the fall of 1608 the marriage took a strong downturn when Francis, who strikes one as a rather prickly personality, quarreled with his wife after she had failed to provide an adequate amount of beer. The fight must have been particularly bad as it prompted Lettice to write to her brother, pleading with him to intervene. She wrote, "good brother upon satter day last my husband fel out with me. for not haueing provistion of beare: I told him of my want of mault. abute three wickes agove. but he wold nether prouid it him selfe. nor alow me money."[138] Lettice continued, "I borowed of my neghtbores as much as I cold. yet for all that. The falt was layd all upon me: with money bitter corsses. and the charge of the house takenn from me. and commanded to medle with nothing: but keepe my chamber."[139] In this instance, Lettice was deprived of her authority within the household and denied her role as co-manager of the family's estate. Her husband's actions forced her to turn to neighbourhood acquaintances in order to secure household provisions and this must have been embarrassing for her. Given the importance that elite women attached to their roles as household managers, Francis's actions towards his wife dishonoured her.

A similar set of issues relating to the authority in the household, although operating at a more fevered pitch, was at play in the marital relationship between Sir Francis and Lady Elizabeth Willoughby. The marriage was a tense one and the disputes between the couple were well known. In one particularly fraught incident, Lady Willoughby appeared before the Court of Star Chamber and appealed to several members of the Privy Council to censure her husband for what she described as his cruelty to her. Lady Willoughby alleged that her enemies, whom she believed to be members of her husband's natal family, had slandered her and that her husband had cut her off from her position of household authority because of her perceived disobedience to him. As discussed, while women were expected to play leadership roles within the household, they had to do so within a framework of deference to their husbands that Francis alleged his wife had contravened. For her part, Elizabeth felt her husband had been tricked into believing rumours of her purported disobedience; and there may have been some truth to her allegations that members of her husband's family were conspiring against her. The couple had married in their teens and their families sanctioned the match, but Francis's sister, Margaret Arundel, bore a great measure of resentment towards her sister-in-law and engaged in repeated attempts to block the marriage. The underlying reasons for her animosity are unknown.[140]

Lady Willoughby was adamant that, in removing her from her rightful position of albeit limited authority within the household, Lord Willoughby was damaging her reputation. She also dismissed the allegations against her and declared to her husband, "I say agayne as I sayd before and will say whilst I lyve, that I defye any villeyn or parson that shall go about to impeache me."[141] As other gentry women frequently did when they felt their reputation within their marital family to be under attack, Elizabeth Willoughby turned to her natal family for support and was dismayed to find that her father appeared unwilling to assist her in rectifying the "discomforts of my lyfe."[142] She wrote that nothing that had happened to her troubled her more than "the alienation of yor good opynion & fatherly affection towardes me."[143] She went on to entreat him to "take pitie of me … encrease not the reioycing of my yll wishers, w*i*th the encrease of my sorrowes."[144] As these examples suggest, being deprived of a role within the household and the affairs of a family touched in a meaningful way upon the honour of elite women. Therefore, when challenged, they used a series of techniques to voice their objections, often hinting at the link they perceived between their positions as figures of authority within the household and their honour, and sometimes looking to other family members for aid. Elite women navigated these situations of domestic discord with care in order to ensure the security of their positions and authority within the household, indicative of the importance that they attached to these matters.

The Making of Marriages

Alongside the importance of wifehood as a source of honour, the reputations of elite women were also affected by their involvement in the business of matchmaking, an important element of both household and family governance.[145] Gentlemen were also closely involved in such negotiations and recognized the role that their wives played therein. When the Earl of Dorset concluded a match between his grandson and Lady Anne Clifford (whose family had earlier been in negotiations to marry her to the heir of the Earl of Exeter), he was chastised by several people for ostensibly corrupting the Clifford family's negotiations with Exeter in order to snatch away the wealthy heiress for his grandson. Dorset expressed concern that such perceived dishonesty would also negatively affect his wife's reputation, as she had been as involved in the making of the match as he. Dorset wrote to his friends to ensure that they understood that there had been "an absolute breaking" in negotiations for a match between Lady Anne and Exeter's son and that he had not "secretly concluded" between Anne and his own grandson.[146] Dorset went on to note that if people were to believe this allegation, it would be dishonourable for all those involved and he prayed the reader to consider "how dishonorable it shalbe to my lady & to my lady anne & to my wife & me self."[147]

When the ward of Walter Bagot, who was contracted to marry Bagot's daughter, instead illicitly wed the daughter of Oliver Cheney, Bagot's immediate response was to blame Cheney's mother, who he saw as orchestrating the match. Bagot wrote that "S*ir* Olliver p*ro*tested hee was ignorant in the matter which I belive because I account him a worthie gent*leman* and take this for a stratagem or trick contrived ^by^ ~~betwixt~~ the La*dy*" and her chaplain Gibbon (who performed the ceremony).[148] Bagot also referred to her as "his wicked mother" and "his wicked La*dy* the mother" and it is clear that he saw her as forfeiting a measure of her honour by her actions.[149] Walter was eventually pacified (after threatening legal action) with a payment of £2,000 as compensation for what he termed "the wronge doone vnto my Child."[150] In these cases, dishonour could come to elite women through their involvement in marriage negotiations if others believed that potential suitors had been fraudulently dealt with. The matrimonial marketplace was very like the economic one: personal credit was vulnerable to the perceptions of others, and accordingly had to be managed with care.

While women's involvement in the making of matches could provide opportunities for challenges to their reputations, they could also gain honour and augment their reputations when they were involved in the making of marriages that satisfied all the parties involved. Here as well one's reputation for upright and trustworthy dealing had a role to play. Thus, Anne Bacon was trusted enough by one of her acquaintances to dispense advice on the choosing of a marriage partner. Because she herself was deemed honest, her assertion to a Mistress Billingford that a prospective suitor was a similarly honest man ("I my self do knowe to be a man very honest") carried weight.[151] Anne added,

> yf yo*u*r mind be not otherwise settled, I praie yow for my sake lett him be ye the more welcome vnto yow ... yf yow can frame yo*u*r self to like of this man yow shall haue no worse match of him than yow haue had of yo*u*r two oth*er* husbandes. His yeares be sutch as maie well agre w*i*th yowrs, & I dare speake it, yow shall live a quiet life w*i*th him.[152]

Women's involvement in the negotiation of a match could be extensive. Once a pairing was arranged, women often worked to ensure that the new extended family member was brought into their social orbit as a way of boosting the collective honour of the entire family. For example, after her daughter had married Henry, heir to the earldom of Huntingdon, Alice, dowager Countess of Derby and wife of Thomas Egerton, wrote often to her new son-in-law's father to ensure that Henry's education proceeded at a certain pace. She also declared her preference that it be furthered at Oxford rather than Cambridge, saying "Oxforde I could wish the place to be."[153] As Henry's future conduct would bear upon the honour of her daughter and the collective honour of the family, Alice felt justified in intervening in this manner. In later letters, written after Henry had become the fifth Earl, Alice further enquired as to the progress of his studies to ensure that he was acquitting himself fittingly. Alice wrote of her hope that,

> you haue gayned your selfe a good report of the wyse and lerned, for soe I heare you haue, and I hope euer wyll, yf the directions of those that take comfort in your well doing be imbraced and followed, which out of my loue I desier you to doe, no lesse for your owne good then for the great Contentm*ent* yt will geue your frends.[154]

Her input was heeded, as it was recognized that she had a legitimate stake in moderating the education and behaviour of her son-in-law. This role in governing the behaviour of the young men of the family was an activity in which women routinely involved themselves, linked as it was to the broader honour of the family collective.[155] By offering guidance in conduct to family members and matchmaking advice to kin and friends, elite women not only reaffirmed their roles as co-heads of households and governors of the young, an expected exercise of authority on their part, but also staked out a position for themselves in the maintenance of honour associated with sociability and alliance-building with other families.

Honour in Influence, Lineage, and Property

At a more elevated level, women could also acquire honour by assisting in the political advancement of both their marital and natal families, as in the case of John Scudamore (1542–1623), who secretly married Mary Shelton (c. 1550–1603) in 1574. Mary was a member of Elizabeth's Privy Chamber and was her second cousin via her mother, Margaret Shelton, a kinswoman of Elizabeth's mother, Anne Boleyn. It was reported that when the Queen became aware of the union, and the commensurate defiance of her right to involvement with respect to the marriages of not only her ladies but also her family members, she became so enraged that she attacked Mary with a candlestick and broke her finger.[156] Despite this rocky start to the marriage, Mary proved an invaluable asset to her husband after she was restored to the Queen's favour. Mary eventually became Mistress of the Robes and her husband's chief political ally at court, as she had the ear of the Queen. Indeed, Mary was so successful at advancing her husband and his interests that, alongside Blanche Parry and the Countess of Warwick, she was described as one of "a Trinity of Ladies able to worke miracles."[157] As a political player, she was enough of a threat for her enemies to describe her as "a barbarous brazen-faced woman."[158]

Other women also helped their male relatives and friends secure favours from influential individuals. When John Thynne was at a loss to secure favour at court, his wife, Joan, suggested that if his male contacts were unable to secure advancement for him, perhaps his female friends would be able to get the job done. Lady Thynne wrote to her husband: "if all your courtely frendeis can not proqure you that tytell I thinke the will do very letell for you. if men can not procure it yett my thinkeis som of your greate Ladeis might do so much for you," and she was clearly aware of the ability of well-placed women at court to acquire advancements for their family and friends.[159] Elizabeth Wolley offers another example of this when she mentioned, in a letter to her father, Sir William More, her efforts on his behalf with the Queen, which included presenting her with a gown which prompted Elizabeth I to tell her that she would be like a mother to her except she feared that More's wife "could be angry with her for it."[160] Elizabeth went on to tell her father that the Queen had also said "that she would give ten thousand pounds you were twenty years younger, for that she hath but few such servants."[161] Having his daughter in the Queen's confidence was clearly a boon to More, as it was to so many other elite families who were anxious to see a daughter in service to the Queen, especially given her noted devotion and attachment to several of her ladies.[162] Elizabeth also commented to her father on her brother George's progress at court and noted that he was much beholden to another woman, the Countess of Warwick, a great favourite of the Queen's and another example of a woman serving as a power broker for her family and friends.[163] The past successes of a woman at court could also be long treasured by her family as markers of honour. Thus, within the Seymour family, a bed reputed to have belonged to Jane Seymour (1509–37), consort of Henry VIII, was treasured and passed down between generations. This piece of furniture, which appears in the inventory of goods made on the death of Frances Seymour, Duchess of Somerset, in 1674 (137 years after the death of Jane) as "the bedd which was Queene Jane's," provided a reminder of the family's earlier successes and relationship to the centre of political power; it was obviously a highly regarded item.[164]

Even removed from the realm of influence that could be gained by proximity to royal favour, some elite women became political figures in their own right. Dorothy, one of the daughters of Margaret, Countess of Bath (from her earlier marriage to Sir Thomas Kitson), married Sir Thomas Pakington of Buckinghamshire and, following his death in 1571, became an influential parliamentary patron in Aylesbury and commanded a great degree of influence within the community. She even issued a writ in her own name as "lord and owner of the town of Aylesbury," and appointed burgesses for the constituency.[165] While this type of direct political involvement was not generally expected of elite women (or necessarily encouraged), their ability to successfully play a role in local politics also contributed to their personal honour, tied as it was to benevolent service to their communities.

Connected to the honour they associated with their roles as wives, elite women could further garner honour from their roles in the birthing of children and the begetting of heirs: the Seymours, for example, would have been far less likely to emphasize their relationship to Queen Jane and treasure her bed had she not been the only one of Henry VIII's wives to produce a son who survived infancy. Bearing children was, provided they were of an age to do so, one of the most basic expectations of elite wives and they took considerable pride in their production of offspring.[166] Extending the range of contexts in which this sense of honour was enacted, we can examine the decision of some women to have portraits painted while heavily pregnant.

Pregnancy portraits were relatively uncommon in Europe (aside from a few Italian and Hapsburg examples), "but in English art of the sixteenth and early seventeenth centuries, women were sometimes portrayed – quite unambiguously – as pregnant."[167] For example, Mildred Cooke, Lady Burghley, had her portrait painted while pregnant in 1563 before giving birth to her son (and William Cecil's political heir), Robert. Lady Katherine Knollys posed for her portrait when she was pregnant with her fourteenth child. There is also evidence that Sir Arthur Throckmorton paid for a portrait of his wife four days before he recorded her delivery of their child.[168] Another earlier example can perhaps be seen in a sketch by Hans Holbein the Younger of Cicely Heron dating to 1526–7.[169] In addition, there are two portraits in the Tate collection, both by Marcus Gheeraerts II, depicting heavily pregnant women. One, dated 1620, shows an unnamed woman, possibly a member of the Constable family, in a deep red–coloured gown, her hand resting on her swollen, clearly pregnant, stomach. The other, dated c. 1595, portrays a pregnant woman wearing a gown covered with pearls – a widely recognized symbol of purity and a visual indicator of her status as both an elite woman and a loyal wife – and smiling, a rare facial expression in portraits from the period. Maria Thynne likewise had a portrait painted of herself while heavily pregnant with her husband Thomas's third child. Maria was to die in childbed, and so the portrait serves as a sad reminder of the danger in which pregnant women stood.[170] While it is certainly true that a desire to have a current portrait because of fears that they might die in childbirth may have motivated elite women and their husbands to have these pregnancy portraits painted, such images were also a way for them to visually articulate their fecundity and thus their fulfilment of their role as wives, something which gained them honour.[171]

Figure 2 Portrait of an Unknown Lady, attributed to Marcus Gheeraerts II, c. 1595, © Tate, London

Figure 3 Portrait of a Woman in Red, by Marcus Gheeraerts II, 1620, © Tate, London

Another area of visual culture that women as well as men linked to the affirmation of an honourable reputation, similar to the genre of funeral sermons discussed earlier, were funeral monuments. The erection of such memorials served both to consolidate one's reputation in life and to make an enduring architectural and symbolic statement about one's status. Many women were closely involved with the erection of such monuments and, "in general, funeral monuments supported the principle that an honorable reputation was legitimately an ambition for noble women."[172] Like elite men, women also cared a great deal about the honour attached to their lineage, family history, and acquired titles: many examples survive of elite women commissioning heraldic images and genealogical tables.[173] The possession and successful management of titles and lands (either ancestral or acquired by marriage) was a prominent source of honour for women. The example offered by Anne Clifford's ongoing dispute with the crown, her husband, and other family members over her right to hold her ancestral lands, which has been analysed in detail by others, is evidence of this.[174] In the period, being a property owner was a social office carrying a unique set of responsibilities for the owner; it also conferred honour. Anne Clifford's dogged determination to preserve her ancestral claims to her property suggests that she saw her role as a landowner as a part of her social identity (and, of course, elite women cared just as much as elite men about their rightful claims to titles and land).[175] In the aftermath of Anne's prolonged struggle over her disputed inheritance, she vested much of her sense of personal honour in her position as a landowner – perhaps because this source of reputation was made all the more potent for her as a result of her efforts to preserve it. For example, in 1649 she commissioned a remarkable triptych known as the Great Picture to celebrate her final success in her inheritance dispute. The painting represents various biographical moments in Anne's life. In the central panel she is portrayed as a child still in her mother's womb, which serves to celebrate her parentage; in the left panel she is shown aged fifteen, the age at which her father died and her inheritance battle began; and in the right panel she is shown as a somber woman of fifty-six, working hard to repair her various estates and serve as an honourable landlord to her tenants. As a whole, the picture exalts both her lineage and marriages and her personal honourable qualities. Once she had prevailed in her assertion of her property rights, Anne worked tirelessly to rebuild the various houses and castles on her lands (many of which were in a ramshackle state after years of absentee landlordship), and to reassert her

Figure 4 Lady Anne Clifford, Countess of Pembroke, by William Larkin, c. 1618, © National Portrait Gallery, London

authority as a great landowner within the region, embarking on ambitious rebuilding schemes that often involved erecting plaques bearing her coat of arms, and striving to ensure that tenants accorded her full deference and respect.[176] Anne's determination to assert her rights over her estates caused conflict with her family and led to extended legal confrontations, things which could cause one's reputation to suffer. Honour, however, was composed of a medley of values, and an emphasis on her social position, bloodline, and land rights took precedence for Anne over contrasting meanings of honour as vested in deferential behaviour that aimed to smooth over conflicts. Accordingly, she pursued her claims, regardless of the conflict it engendered.

Elizabeth Talbot (née Leche), Countess of Shrewsbury, also saw her possession of family and marital property as a key aspect of her honourable social identity. During her fourth marriage to the Earl of Shrewsbury she acquired from her brother, James, the Leche family's manor house of Hardwick and embarked on what became a legendary rebuilding and refurbishment process. When Shrewsbury died in 1590 and left Elizabeth with a sizeable inheritance, she lavished funds upon the project, which she had begun shortly before her husband's death.[177] Elizabeth transformed the house into a magnificent showpiece and, in effect, a grandiose monument to the lofty social level she had achieved. Hardwick was an unapologetic pleasure house and Elizabeth laid out an impressive amount to finish it. Architecturally, the house was self-referential and Elizabeth decorated the interior and exterior with her arms and initials. She saw the construction of her elaborate and majestic house as something that highlighted her honour; it was an external manifestation of her social station and the high regard in which she held her reputation. In this sense, elite estates (like funeral monuments) can be viewed as frozen instantiations of social performances and their architecture and design as forms of self-presentation.[178] For Elizabeth Talbot and other early modern elite landowners of both sexes, "the house was not only the scene where ideals of gentility and manners could be realized: it provided an essential display of gentility in itself."[179]

Like Anne Clifford, the Countess of Shrewsbury saw a measure of her honour as tied to her rights to certain titles and lands. Hence, the Countess quarreled with her husband the Earl of Shrewsbury over his right to her property of Chatsworth House, which she held by virtue of a former marriage to Sir William Cavendish, after having convinced him to buy the property in 1549 from Sir Francis Agard, to whom it had been sold by her natal family.[180] Elizabeth Russell also evinced great concern to safeguard her rightful title to properties. Accordingly, when she became embroiled in a legal tussle regarding her ownership of some lands (by virtue of her late husband, the heir of the Earl of Bedford) and she felt that the justice hearing the case had overstepped his bounds in overturning an earlier judgment in her favour, she reacted immediately. Taking advantage of her family connections, she wrote to her nephew Robert Cecil asking that Justice Warburton be reprimanded and instructed in his "Duty sins He knoweth not Honesty nor iustice."[181] When Cecil did not act quickly enough, in her estimation, to redress the wrong, she appealed to the Privy Council and turned her abuse on her nephew. Lady Russell used shaming techniques directed at Cecil's honour in order to assert her own, which she saw as connected to her rightful ownership of her lands. As she told Cecil, "it toucheth yow in honowre in the face of the world to see *your* aunt, a noblewoman that hath made peticyon in a most iust cawse to ye Cownsell table to have redress agaynst so Flatt a wronge."[182] She closed her letter by asserting that it was imperative that the judgment against her be overturned and her proper authority on her lands restored as it threatened her honour, and "I howld my Honowre more dere then my life" (words quoted at the outset of this chapter).[183] The denial of ancestral claims to titles and property could motivate elite women to be very aggressive in what were disputes over their honour. And in these disputes, elite women's sense of personal honour as attached to these claims (and right to exercise authority based on their status and property ownership) were more important to them than their sense that their reputation might be damaged by acting fractiously or not exhibiting gentleness in their dealings with others.

A defence of honour rooted in social status and associated claims to authority was again employed by Elizabeth Russell in another conflict that was also tied to what she perceived to be a violation of her authority as a land owner and governor of an estate. In this instance a writ was issued against her for preventing a bailiff from arresting one of her servants, likely on charges of recusancy, given Elizabeth's subsequent reaction to the attempt in a letter to the Lord Keeper. As Elizabeth phrased it, she was being prosecuted and her authority within her "Liberties" was usurped for "deteyning a Baylif in my Howse yt arrested a man of myne w*ith* a fals warrant w*i*thin my owne Liberties; not in ye Bayliffs iurisdiction as was proved after in the Starr Chamber and there punished and Fyned."[184] Having a writ issued against her was a potential threat to Russell's reputation as the legitimate governor of her estate. She reacted to this slight by asserting her status, and stated that "great Ladies persons [are] no more pretiows in Law then to be attached by a Base vndershrive or Hygh shreve."[185] Rather than offering an explicit defence of her actions, Russell invoked the honour associated with her social status and exercise of legitimate authority on her lands as a means to discredit those who had issued the writ. She also countered by denigrating the reputations of those who had attacked her, in particular the Lord Keeper, who had held Catholic beliefs earlier in his life. Elizabeth perceived it as rank hypocrisy that he would seek to prosecute one of her men for recusancy and bluntly said so to Egerton, writing "I have cowrse to deme *your* self an arrant Ipocritt and a Depe Dissembler."[186]

Likewise, elite women, as much as men, saw their statuses and bloodlines as an element of their honour. An episode recounted by Clive Holmes provides an interesting case of female honour, lineage, and social place and focuses on Elizabeth Grimes, the second wife of Thomas, first Earl of Coventry.[187] Elizabeth was from a much lower social station than her husband. In fact, she was one of his domestic servants and the niece of his housekeeper. She was also forty years younger than her husband, who began his courtship of her while his estranged wife was still alive. While Elizabeth inherited a great deal of wealth from her husband, she wanted to fully cement her reputation among aristocratic circles by claiming honour not just as Coventry's wife and then widow but as a person of gentle blood in her own right. So when the Earl died in 1699 she convinced Gregory King, the Lancaster Herald, to produce false arms that connected her to the Grahams, a gentry family in Yorkshire. These dubious heraldic devices were displayed in the Earl's funeral procession and later featured in a monument that Elizabeth designed to honour her deceased spouse (here though the Graham family was suspiciously listed as coming from Norfolk). Women, as much as men, were concerned with their families' genealogical connections, and Elizabeth Grimes was not above resorting to fraud in order to secure a honourable lineage for herself, even if it was of dubious veracity – the honour associated with name and status took precedence for her over the honour associated with honest conduct. Unfortunately, her attempt at deception did not go smoothly and resulted in her stepson, the new Earl, bringing suit against both King and Elizabeth's second husband. In this legal action, the second Earl was concerned with protecting his family name and inheritance. He suspected Elizabeth's claims of being exaggerated, if not outright false. His ire was further raised when Elizabeth quickly remarried, this time to Thomas Savage, another of the first Earl's servants and an individual who had supported her in her efforts to claim gentility. She also arranged for King to marry her sister, providing the £2,000 dowry herself in an attempt to close the loop on her fraudulent claims by binding King to her still further. It also later emerged in the ensuing court case that the second Earl had courted Elizabeth before her marriage to his father. Having been spurned may, in part, have contributed towards his animosity. While this was a rather sordid episode, it nonetheless reveals the stock that early modern elite women attached to their bloodline and status as a source of honour and the privilege they could accord to this understanding of honour.

Defending Their Honour

When an elite woman's honour was challenged they, like men, were capable of engaging in displays of aggressive behaviour in attempting to defend their good names, as the example of the Countess of Nottingham's conflict with Christian IV illustrates.[188] While prescriptive dictates certainly argued that honourable women should behave with decorum, kindness, and a desire to maintain good relations, honour was also associated, as we have seen, with a willingness to defend name, reputation, and position. Depending upon the circumstances of a given situation, this understanding of honour could matter more to an elite woman than that of honour as characterized by forbearance and gentle conduct. Indeed, the defence of honour could motivate women to be downright nasty.

Accordingly, in some letters, one can see glimpses of elite women engaging in the "type of vituperative personal battles characteristic of oral street culture … though without the emphasis on female sexual honour, and importantly not in the street."[189] Such a glimpse can be seen in the lengths to which Margaret, Countess of Bath, went in defending her honour against the slights of a Master Savage. As she relates in a letter to Savage, one of the Countess's servants, who later reported back to her, had overheard him casting aspersions. Within the missive, while maintaining a thin veneer of civility, Margaret made a series of puns on Savage's name that served as an indictment of his behaviour and of his status as a gentleman. She began by stating (with a pronounced note of sarcasm) the dishonour that Savage had done to her, saying, "wheras not longe syns a seruant of myne beying in your company at your comynge ffrom London and my selfe repayryng … ye beyng th*erewith* in no smalle rage gaue me … your gentle blessinge prayinge god the plage and pestilence to lyght on me."[190] The Countess averred that "in good fayth to my knowledge I neuer offendid you in my lyffe wherfor the mor is your shame so to vse me."[191] Margaret charged that his conduct was also in keeping with his character, which was "more ruffyanlyke than gentlemanlike."[192] In a carefully crafted piece of invective that linked his poor behaviour to low status, she continued, "when I remember your name Savage I ffind it not moch dissenting from your natural disposition."[193] She added, "for indede if I might so grossly terme it. this beastly blessinge of yours declare you to be more savage or brutish than discrete or reasonable in so cruelly cursinge me yt nev*er* harmyd you."[194]

Margaret not only denied being deserving of such treatment but also indicted Savage's character and status as a way of delegitimizing his complaints against her. She also accused Savage of being the instigator of the conflict, as he ("beyng th*erewith* in no smalle rage") had angrily attacked her first as a way to justify her own angry reaction to him.[195] She resolved to punish him by making others aware of his behaviour and publicly humiliating him. She threatened that, after she had

> adv*er*tisyd my betters and yours of this your unhonest behavior ye shall haue no great cause to pleasure in your so doyng and in malisynge me ye feel yo*ur* owne harme for none can ye do to me and then are ye in worse case than the serpent for the serpent kepithe his poyson w*i*thout his owen perill and so cannot the malicious man which hurtithe himself most w*i*th his owne malice or poyson.[196]

Margaret's final thoughts were exacting: "thus leave I you, praying god in the stead of your plage and pestilence wished me to send you instead of a malycious mind an honest one whereof ye have nede as it appareth."[197] In threatening to advertise Savage's conduct to "my betters and yours," coupled with her attack on his status, Margaret used the understanding of honour as associated with social position and correspondingly proper civil behaviour as a weapon, a means to make a potent attack on the reputation of another.[198]

When she felt her reputation was adversely effected by "my Auncient enemye Percivall Willoughby," Dorothy, Lady Wharton, reacted in a similar manner to the Countess of Bath.[199] She wrote to Robert Cecil to complain of Willoughby's "matchaviliam practizes and enchantinge tongue," which he used to persecute her through "so many vexac*i*ous sutes trobles and molestacions as were odyous to declare" and which struck at her reputation.[200] She countered by calling Willoughby's honour into question and stated that "hee hadd nev*er* yett anye good matter or couller or shaddowe of truth or honesty [or] ryght, conscyence or equity" with which to justify his attacks on her.[201] In other instances, accusations of dishonourable behaviour elicited curiosity, rather than righteous indignation, on the part of gentlewomen. Mary, Lady Rogers, upon hearing that her reputation was being attacked "in wrytyng the quantytie of seven sheates of paper contaynyng many moste odyous & slanderous matters agaynst me, deapely touchyng me in honour," was interested in knowing what the specifics of the allegations were, no doubt with an eye to mounting a defence.[202] The papers had been produced in the course of a legal conflict between her brother and father-in-law and she noted that the counsel of the two parties "wyll not permytt any for me to peruse or have syght of them … beyng so skandalous."[203] As a result of this prohibition she wrote to Cecil that she had "greate marveyl & long to se" the list of her reputed dishonourable actions and hoped that the Secretary would be willing to order that they be released to her, so that she could confront the vague slanders head on.[204]

Another member of the Bagot family experienced a similar questioning of her local reputation in the second decade of the seventeenth century. Dorothy Okeover, the sister of Walter Bagot, discovered to her chagrin in 1617/1618 that rumours about her were circulating in the community. She turned to her brother for support and asserted that her reputation was sound enough to weather such insults. She wrote: "faulchud [falsehood] may: and doth many tymes: make abetter shewe than truth: there fore to cleare my selfe: and to ashure you how much I haue bin wronged: my innosency shall pleade for mee," and steadfastly maintained that there was no truth to the rumours being spread about her.[205] While Dorothy was anxious to deny the truth of any rumours, her defence of her own good name consisted not in denying the accusations made about her but in asserting her honourable reputation to counter whatever lies were being spread. She was confident that her self-presentation was unassailable and stated, "I ashur my selfe you doe: and will thinke of mee: as I euer shall: and will deserue: then lett them spitt there poysonne at mee and spare not."[206] Crafting an honourable image anchored in proper conduct and good name was important for early modern women; such an edifice was a ready-built defence against future indictments, and could be advanced as an effective argument against allegations of misconduct.

Women who failed to develop honourable self-presentations in an array of spheres were often unable to defend themselves in the face of accusations of contentious and dishonourable conduct. Past reputation mattered. An incident chronicled in the More family papers provides an example of this. A woman, unnamed in the correspondence related to her, was charged with beating her daughter nearly to death. It was alleged that she had claimed that the girl was infected with the plague and used this as an excuse to prevent friends and neighbours from entering the house to offer assistance to the girl. It was also rumoured that, five years previously, she had so misused one of her maids that the girl committed suicide.[207] The incidents in question were described as follows: "amongest sondree her lewde condic*i*ons, she hathe at this po*in*t so cruellie beaten a dawghter of her owne that yt lyeth in greate dawnger of deathe."[208] In an attempt to conceal her actions "because she wolde haue no bodie to see her … she tells them yt ys the plague."[209] In addition, "she hadd a mayde servant abowte v yeares agoe whow she so mysvsed that the mayde hanged her self."[210] The woman's behaviour was described as "disorderid, or rather lewde."[211] Her previous poor behaviour with respect to her treatment of her maid made it almost impossible for her to assert that she was blameless in the mistreatment of her daughter. Prior bad acts, especially without defence, contrition, or reform, counted for a great deal. The same was true of a woman in Staffordshire who, as the wife of the local parson, was entitled to a measure of deference had she not forfeited her reputation in the community through her contentious behaviour to such an extent that she was described simply as "that lewde woman the person's wife."[212] She was alleged to have an "ill behaviour & cariage" and "a most outrageous scold" who had "accused her owne brother of felonye and hyered false wittnesses who is a very sufficient man she p*er*secuted the matter vehemently to hange hym that she might haue ^had^ his land."[213] This woman suffered from a poor reputation because she subverted the social order both in attacking a family member and because "she neither cares what she sayes nor sweares she is also a com*m*on slanderer of her neighbours."[214]

Unlike gentlewomen, who – by leveraging their elevated positions to safeguard their reputations and attack their enemies – were often able to continue with breaching behaviour in certain areas as long as they exhibited proper conduct in others, such a course was often denied to their non-elite counterparts. In addition, more frequent and unregulated contact with other members of the community brought more opportunities to make enemies, and for perceived poor behaviour to be noted, and later used against them. Status mattered. When Morgan Benyon was accused of being in a physical altercation with a local woman beneath him in social station (the wife of a man named Beamon), he defended himself by alleging that she attacked him first. He backed up this allegation by calling her reputation into question much as the Countess of Bath had done in her conflict with Savage. Noting that her low social status was proof of correspondingly low morals was a way for Benyon to lend credibility to his assertion that "I did not stryke her but I strok at the axe wher w*i*th she purposed to have brayned me, & I did not stryke twysse."[215] He continued by alleging that she was "a como*n* whore, & standeth excom*m*unicated ... the vilest in Cranly in respect of povertie & estimatio*n*: & I thinck in respect of my place & calling at this tyme no ma*n* in Cranly is above me."[216] In his string of "proofs" against the character of Beamon's wife, Benyon discussed not only her sexual reputation but also her impiety, her poor local reputation, and her low social standing. One's place in the social hierarchy was important when it came to articulating claims to a good reputation. This was to an elite woman's advantage and they accordingly often emphasized their status, which underscored their honour, when attacking another's reputation.

The Importance and Permeability of Honour

While a reputation for circumspect sexual behaviour mattered to elite women in early modern England, it was but one source, among many others, of their personal reputation and honour. For the elite women considered here, honour was constituted by a series of overlapping social expectations and roles, including piety, circumspect social behaviour, their positions as wives and household heads, and their roles as potential channels to political influence. Likewise, matters of reputation diffusely underscored a range of interactions and behaviours beyond sexual conduct. Accordingly, contemporary conduct books and moralizing literature, as well as the surviving letters of women themselves, suggest that honour was to be found in a collection of complex and often interconnected factors that were interwoven with the expectations of the audiences in front of whom (and with whom) elite women daily performed their social roles. Many of these interconnected factors, such as the expression of piety, the activities associated with wifehood and household governance, the role of women in the making of marriages, and the importance attached to status remained relatively static across the period and retained a high level of importance as markers of honour and contributing factors to good reputation for elite women by the end of the period considered here. The reconfiguration of both social and gender relationships, coupled with significant changes to the structure of the family and conceptions of social class over time, led eventually, however, to a waning in importance of these sources of honour, with the possible exception of the weight attached to wifehood as a contributing factor to reputation (and possibly also sexual conduct, at least among some), to which many still accord a certain primacy of place.

Ultimately, as was the case with elite men, the relative weight attached to all these sources of women's honour were essentially permeable and negotiable. These elements of reputation also intersected meaningfully with elite women's relative positions in the social hierarchy and the stage in the early modern life cycle in which they found themselves. These realities could colour the manner in which gentlewomen presented themselves and employed the various ideas associated with honour with fluidity in pursuit of their objectives. For instance, the ways in which a young, unmarried woman referenced or defended her reputation could be different than the manner in which honour was articulated and enacted by a more mature, married householder; honour was not a unified and clearly bounded behavioural code for these individuals. In investigating the varied levels of meaning that individual elite women attached to the constitutive elements of their personal honour in a given setting or interaction, and the ways in which they used the language of honour, reputation, and credit as a means to justify or explain behaviour (often with reference to gendered expectations surrounding proper female conduct), we glimpse not only the broad range of meanings attached to honour, but also their relative flexibility with respect to actual behaviour.

Chapter Three

Honour in the Community and at Home

Reputation In Local Society

Cicero, the idol of many early modern humanists, remarked that, "honor is the reward of virtue." Statements such as this, as well as the Aristotelian idea that honour was bestowed based on the display of virtuous behaviour, were crucial to how honour was conceptualized among early modern gentlewomen and gentlemen. Central to appreciating the manner in which honour was understood in the period is the recognition that it operated in a circular fashion: one was accorded honour because one was perceived to be honourable. Outward performances of the perceived attributes of gentility (such as those associated with upright conduct, judicious involvement in the community, and displays of civility and largesse) served to cement and augment a reputation for honour. Two primary spheres of social engagement and self-presentation that played a prominent role in elites' sense of honour in the early modern period were the household and the local community. A permeable boundary separated these arenas, and matters of both personal and family reputation were present in a diverse array of interactions in these spaces. Within them, elite men and women negotiated the multiple meanings of honour in their roles as householders, officeholders, hosts, guests, and estate managers. They likewise engaged in representations of themselves aimed at bolstering their reputations and defending them when necessary, sometimes using the multiple meanings associated with honour to attack their opponents and advance their own interests, a tactic familiar from earlier chapters.

The structures of local governance in the community, and the associated exercise of authority therein, could be an especially important venue with respect to engagement in involvements that touched upon one's reputation. For example, among gentlemen, administrative and governance positions could be key indicators of their prominence, and level of honour, within local society. This was not necessarily a new feature in the years considered here. Yet this element of reputation perhaps took on greater significance during this period as the number of positions and the level of local authority and autonomy associated with them took on enhanced importance within the larger process of the expansion of the participatory apparatuses of governance associated with the early modern state. Most government was essentially local in nature during the period and the regime depended, with varying degrees of success, upon the involvement of gentlemen at the local level to enforce edicts, uphold and administer the law, and oversee a range of economic matters.[1] As the infrastructure of local government expanded, many gentlemen increasingly associated the attainment of positions of local governance with a level of influence and an acknowledgment of their status. Such involvements were also expressive of a certain cultural solidarity (and sometimes a political solidarity) that, while not necessarily a novel development, was further "forged and sustained through the daily round of sociability, hospitality, and mutuality" in which elites engaged during the sixteenth and seventeenth centuries.[2] Of course not all gentlemen were invested in the pursuit of local office but, for many, such posts offered recognition of status and a potentially enhanced measure of influence within the community, and so contributed to reputation. Because the capacity to attain a position of authority within the apparatus of governance (either at the local level or in a more elevated way) could reinforce their standing in the local hierarchy and contribute to wealth and influence, being deprived of responsibilities in these areas could be a reputational blow to an early modern gentleman, as was considered in an earlier chapter. Likewise, just as an elite man's engagement in violent conduct could call into question his fitness to govern others, so too could his employment of malefactors who violated conventions of social propriety. Such behaviour could negatively affect a gentleman's claims to the rightful exercise of authority.

Thus Charles Howard, Earl of Nottingham, was anxious when he discovered that a man whom he labelled a "lewd and disordered fellowe" was wearing his livery and passing himself off as one of the Earl's followers.[3] The behaviour of servants and retainers had the power to reflect back upon their employers, and householders typically endeavoured to distance themselves from those who acted inappropriately, even as they attempted to enforce discipline. According to Nottingham, in addition to several other offences, the man pretending to be his follower abused "his poore wife by violence dailye offered vnto her."[4] Nottingham recognized the potential damage that having such a miscreant associated with him could do to his reputation. He wrote to all the JPs in the area to inform them of the situation and avowed that "I haue noe knowledge of any such man and would be loath to shroud soe lewd a lyver vnder my cloth."[5] He asked that, should the man be apprehended, he be told "I doe not onlye mislike his lewde caryage but doe herforth vtterly discharge him from wearing my cloth."[6]

Gentlemen were also concerned with the honour that attached itself to them in their roles as overseers of various community projects, an extension of their responsibilities with respect to local governance, as these involvements contributed to their reputations as figures of authority within their localities and so touched upon their honour. Thus, when Thomas Smethwick countered accusations from Walter Bagot that Smethwick had poorly managed work on Tutbury Bridge, he did so by claiming not only that Walter had spread false rumours, but also that it was this, and not Smethwick's management of the project, that had hindered the work. Walter was quick to respond, aware that this questioning of his legitimate exercise of authority (and the allegation that he had spoken falsely of others) was injurious to his reputation. Bagot's letter of response to Smethwick appears to have been written in anger, with many lines hurriedly penned and then crossed out, which was not in keeping with his usual restrained style. In response to Smethwick's allegations that "I haue bin a great hinderanse to the repayers at Tutbury," Bagot stressed somewhat indignantly, "I haue hetherto lyved that nether you nor any man else can iniustly chardge mee to haue hindered the com*m*en good of my Contrie."[7] Bagot objected to the suggestion that he had not acted in the best interests of his county and its proper governing. He added that "except you geve mee good satisfacc*i*on wher vpon ^or on whome^ your reportes are grownded I shall hold my selfe much wronged."[8]

While gentlemen were often concerned with their roles as local administrators and the recognition of status that this implied, both elite men and women saw their honour augmented through participation in the conventions of elite sociability expressed through their interactions with each other. Manners and displays of civility had deep cultural roots and were felt to be the external markers of elite standing, an understanding of reputation that remains a factor in assessments of relative social status to this day. Performances of civility were, in essence, a way of acting out elevated status in daily life, and such involvements drew elites together and bound them to each other.

Connected to this emphasis on civility was the expectation that elite men and women would exhibit politeness to others and contain their anger unless its display was appropriate and justifiable, such as when it was directed towards a social subordinate as a corrective for poor behaviour (here as well the realities of status played a role). Failure to adhere to these social expectations, or not being able to lend a veneer of legitimacy to social breaching behaviour, could call one's gentility itself into question. Hence, when one of Walter Bagot's sons became involved in a dispute over gaming with Richard Draycote and reported to his father that Draycote had lost his temper and spoken harshly to him, Walter wasted little time in writing to Draycote to reproach him for breaching the conventions of gentle society in his rough behaviour. Just as Margaret, Countess of Nottingham, had earlier criticized Christian IV's actions as indicative of an inner absence of honour and gentility, Bagot alleged that Draycote had contravened the tenets of status and honourable behaviour that bound the elite community together. In doing so, Bagot also used the rhetoric of status and associated honour in a coercive manner as a shaming technique in order to force Draycote to admit to a fault and amend his behaviour. In response to Bagot's allegations, Draycote denied that he had used "hearde words" or that he had acted "not lyke a gentleman."[9] He felt stung by the accusation and closed his letter by affirming that he had not "broken the boundes of gentilitie" in his anger.[10]

The early modern English state also used the language of honour and status as a means to coercively shame fractious individuals into reaching settlements that might restore peace between competing interests. Such was the case when Joan and John Thynne quarreled angrily with Edward Stafford over ownership of Caus Castle. The property had been part of Joan's dowry when she married John Thynne, but Stafford, the former owner, refused to cede his claim to the estate and conflict erupted. The Thynnes pursued their claim through the courts and eventually took possession of the property by force. The quarrel was highly acrimonious. When the Thynnes, for example, obtained the assistance of Joan's brother-in-law, Henry Townshend, a Justice in Chester, Stafford lashed out against both parties. He wrote angrily to Townshend to say that he regarded him as "my open cankard enymy."[11] He also threatened violence against both Townshend and Thynne, saying it would "haue eased my stomacke rather to have met y*our* peevishe brother Thyn & you a myle out of town w*i*th my sword in my hand."[12] Stafford's threats caused the Privy Council to become involved, recognizing that such confrontations between elites could threaten social stability. Accordingly, both Thynne and Stafford were summoned to London and commanded to settle their dispute. Thynne then compromised his reputation by refusing to heed the summons and thus showing contempt for governmental authority. While this course of action obviously seemed less important to Thynne at the time than continuing his quarrel with Stafford, it did cause him to forfeit a measure of his credibility with the regime and the Council wrote to him to complain of his frivolous and "contemptuouse answeare so made."[13] The letter then indicted his conduct in the affair and cast aspersions on his status and personal honour by noting that "yt becometh yow, and a man of much better qualitie then y*our* selfe, to haue obeyed o*ur* comandem*en*t vpon sight of o*ur* le*tt*re."[14]

Claims to elevated social standing and the ability to reference a prior reputation for honourable conduct were of particular use when it came to gaining the upper hand in conflicts with other community members, as was the case, for example, in the Countess of Bath's dispute with Master Savage. For instance, when he was having a dispute with a local man named Chetwynd, Edward Aston appealed to Richard Bagot for assistance and cited Chetwynd's own poor local reputation as evidence that he was at fault in the matter. Aston wrote that he was aware that Chetwynd "dothe beare a most ca*n*kered and malitious mynde towarde me" but that he "litle regarde it" because Chetwynd was a "base and du*n*ghill fallow in co*m*parison to me."[15] Likewise, Sir Thomas Fitzherbert appealed to Bagot when he felt slandered by Thomas Cawarden. He accused Cawarden (along with "that vnreasonable woman his wife") of spreading the "moste false and slanderous reportes" which for "seven yeres space and more haue bine verie rife againste me and are likely so to continewe."[16] He also feared that such reports and rumours would be used against him by Cawarden in a financial dispute that the two men were having.[17] Invoking the discourses of both gentlemanly behaviour and neighbourliness, Fitzherbert stated that "I trust y*our* wisdom will consider of the p*ro*misses and of myne estate as one neighbor or gent*leman* should do vnto another" in an attempt to assert his own reputation for past honourable conduct as a defence against Cawarden.[18]

When Robert Cole, the vicar of Epsom, entered into a particularly nasty quarrel with Nicholas Saunder, he appealed to Sir William More in his role as High Sheriff of Surrey and Sussex to help him restore his good name. The strife arose because Saunder continually refused to take communion and was reported by Cole. In retaliation Saunder began a campaign of slander against Cole, alleging that he was a barrator who was stirring up trouble in the community and abusing his position as vicar to pursue his enemies. As was the case with gentlemen, it was expected of Cole as an ecclesiastical figure that he would be a source of unity rather than division within the community and so Saunder's allegations were damaging to his reputation. They could also result in Cole being deprived of his living, adding economic consequences to the effects that such words could have. As Cole noted, Saunder's accusations would be "to my great impoverishinge and vndoinge."[19] Cole then appealed to his already established reputation for civil and peaceable conduct and his role as a godly figure as a means of asserting his honour. He also decried Saunder's behaviour as uncharitable and prayed for More's

> favourable ayde and furderaunce in easinge and realisinge of my molestations by M*aste*r Nicolas Saunder and other vngodly people through his procurme*n*t vncharitably practises againest me, in causinge me and my wife to be indighted for barators and troublesome people.[20]

Cole noted that these allegations were "to my great disfamigne and cost to travis the same for as knoweth god I would very gladly live in peace with all people" and added that "neither man nor woman cann iustlye saye that I at any time caulled or reviled sithens I came to that parishe any man or women."[21] Responding to Saunder's allegations that he had initiated brawls and used force against others, Cole averred that "neither haue I smitten any maner of person, excepting children the whiche I haue taught in learninge and those of my owne household."[22] To the contrary, and attempting to represent himself as acting in accordance with his role as a religious authority who was at least partially responsible for the unity and quietness of the parish community, Cole asserted that he had "bin glad alwaiese to make peace and agreement between any of my neighbours which haue bin at any discorde."[23] In advancing his own past reputation for peaceful and fair dealings with his neighbours, and establishing himself as having the moral authority that accompanied his status as a clergyman,

Cole was providing what he believed to be an effective counter to Saunder's slanders – it also served as a means on which to base his attacks on Saunder.

For his part, Saunder also relied upon the language of honour and uncivil behaviour in order to discredit Cole. He claimed authority for his accusations by presenting himself as an honest man who was true to his word, in contrast to Cole, whom he labelled as corrupt, a sin in anyone but markedly so in a clergyman. Saunder claimed that Cole was "owr deformyd vicar, w*hi*ch like a madde man tossed Firebrands And shotte deadly Arrows ag*ains*t vs his owne parishoners."[24] He added a reference to Cole's "detestable lyes, brawlinge, and practises" and closed his missive by indignantly adding, "S*ir* Will*ia*m More, yff Nicholas Saunder tell yow that Rob*er*t Cole ys A knave, yow may beleve him, the better because his testymony is so generally ratifyed trew, & by so many records."[25] In this conflict, both parties relied upon the behavioural norms associated with honour and a good reputation to attack each other and defend themselves. It is not without a touch of irony that both relied on assertions that they assiduously conducted themselves with civility, even as they openly insulted one another.

When the parson of Ockley was similarly accused of dishonourable behaviour, he defended himself not by invoking his own claims to status but those of his family connections, in this case the Buckhursts. Thomas Sackville, Lord Buckhurst, thus wrote to the local JPs to complain that the parson's "good name & honest reputac*i*on is (as he alledgeth) by practise & combinac*i*on of evell parsons called in question."[26] Buckhurst testified "I may truly say that he hath ben long knowen vnto me more then 40 yeres yet did I never vnderstand that he was suspected of any such loose & in continent sort of life."[27] On the contrary, Buckhurst stated, he "hath alwaies lived w*i*th good estimac*i*on born of lief & maners preaching & teaching in his vocac*i*on w*i*th good comendac*i*on to him self & godly exhortac*i*on to others."[28] Buckhurst further drove his point home by casting aspersions on the social status of the parson's accusers (a familiar tactic when it came to attacking someone's reputation), writing of the "basenes & beggerlines of his acusers and the malice covetice and envy of some that seke & gape after his living."[29] In another, private, letter to More he further added that all the evidence against the parson came from "some lewd persons of the parish ... that live upon the common in cabins covered with earth," thus using the connection between poor behaviour and low status as a way to dismiss the accusations.[30] While

Buckhurst believed that his kinsman had been falsely accused, he also noted, should the charges be proven true, "I protest before god I wish him no favour but shame and confusion to fall vpon him although I could not but be much sorofull for the same considering that he is of my blood & name."[31] While Buckhurst was willing to defend his kinsman's honour, it was within limits and he refused to risk the honour of his family by defending a man guilty of uncivil and disreputable behaviour.

Claims to honour in the community rested partially on a reputation for good conduct and, as many of the examples considered thus far have suggested, were also buttressed by an elevated position in the social hierarchy. Given the importance of social status with respect to honour, gentlemen and gentlewomen reacted quickly when they perceived that that status was being questioned, thus illustrating the level of importance they accorded to name and status when it came to their personal honour. Richard Bagot, accordingly, quarreled angrily with Edward Stafford in 1590 over allegations that Stafford had made slurs upon the family's origins, including claiming that the name Bagot meant a "bagge of oates" and that the family was lowborn in comparison to the Staffords.[32] Bagot reacted indignantly over the questioning of his house and expressed disdain that Stafford should so "contenned and deface the name Bagot w*ith* so bad terms and base speches as you do."[33] He also noted that Stafford's conduct was ungentlemanly and his attack was "more dishonorable to yo*ur* self then any blemishe or reproache to me."[34]

While claims to lineage and name undoubtedly formed the cornerstone of elite honour for many, a host of other factors and associated behaviours also contributed to the respect and good opinion a gentleman or gentlewoman could gain among their peers, and the level of deference they could acquire from their subordinates. To this end, elites recognized the importance of having a reputation for honourable conduct characterized by civil behaviour, as this served as both an outward expression and reinforcement of their inner, honourable status. For example, and similar to the concern of Richard Draycote that he should not be thought of as breaking the conventions of gentility in his anger, when Thomas Thynne was involved in a dispute that had the potential to result in accusations of behaviour unbecoming in a gentleman, his mother Joan urged "I pray yow in regard of yo*ur* worth make some speedy end w*ith* them [the disputants], that the mouthes of clamorous people in this Country may be stopped and yo*ur* owne reputation carefully p*re*serued."[35] A reputation for past fractious behaviour could be detrimental to an elite in a future conflict as it could provide a basis for criticism.

Household and Financial Management

While the honour of elites was often meaningfully located in their social interactions in the wider community, a large measure of their reputation was also tethered to their roles and responsibilities within their households and on their estates. Thus, in an observation applicable to women as well as men, "it was in his home that a gentleman's enactment of honour found its most consistent daily expression through the standards of behaviour that he set and the leadership that he imposed."[36] The permeable nature of the boundary between the "private" world of the household and the "public" realm of the local community meant that behaviour within the home – including issues of financial management, the treatment of servants (with which elite women, in particular, were often involved), and one's role in the provision of hospitality – contributed to one's public reputation for honourable conduct. Accordingly, early modern gentlemen and gentlewomen strove to represent themselves as capable estate managers who oversaw well-ordered households while also maintaining involvement in the elaborate and symbolic economies of early modern gift-giving and hospitality. These practices reinforced their honourable reputations within their communities and endured as sources of honour across the period. Likewise, as was the case in other spheres of interaction, when tensions and fissures erupted within the household and in association with things such as the extension of hospitality and household management, people strove to present themselves as behaving correctly and honourably, sometimes negotiating the variable understandings of honourable conduct that coexisted alongside one another in order to do so.

The vital matter of maintaining the integrity of one's estate was intimately connected to elites' sense of honour. The most foundational aspect of this was the holding and defending of property if it was in dispute. Sometimes this could be downright dangerous and elite men and women rose to the challenge. The example of the protracted dispute between the Thynnes and Lord Stafford over Caus Castle serves as an illustration. As noted, John and Joan had procured the property as a part of the dowry settled upon Joan when they wed and Stafford refused to cede ownership of the already decaying castle. The dispute was acrimonious enough to draw the attention of the Privy Council and the couple was eventually successful in expelling Stafford by force when attempts at settlement failed. After his expulsion from Caus, Stafford brought a series of legal actions against the couple and Joan was especially active in the pursuit of these. At one point Stafford threatened to enter the couple's lands by force and impound their cattle and Joan vowed to personally guard the estate against this. As she told her husband, "the Lorde Stafford makes greate bragges what he will do the next asises and hath geuen out that he meanes to driue and to pounde your cattell but I trost he shall com short of that he brages."[37] Joan referred to him as "that wicked Lorde" and clearly stated her intentions to use whatever means necessary to keep him from infringing upon the Thynnes' rights as estate holders.[38]

After they took the property by force Joan had to occupy and defend the castle while her husband resided mostly at their seat at Longleat or in London. As Alison Wall notes in her examination of a selection of letters by the Thynne women, Joan's repeated requests to her husband to send gunpowder suggest that she was prepared to employ violence in defence of Caus.[39] Joan also played an active role in repairing and refurbishing Caus, which had been rarely used by Stafford. She employed masons and plumbers and redecorated the interior with yellow and white silk hangings and matching window curtains.[40] Having gone to great lengths to obtain the property, Joan was invested in making it truly her own.

Once established in an estate, the prudent administration of it revolved around dutiful attention to financial management and the procuring of adequate provisions. These were often activities with which elite women were highly involved.[41] Related to the honour that they gained through the effective stewardship of family fortunes, gentlewomen were also often engaged in a variety of business transactions in the context of the household – doing business in an expanding marketplace where trustworthiness and character were essential to economic relationships.[42] While the principle of coverture, in theory, prevented married women from business involvements, in practice they frequently engaged in such activities under the "law of necessities."[43] These economic transactions were often done on a credit basis.[44] As a result of the expansion of economic networks over the period, relationships "were increasingly interpreted in terms of judgment about trustworthiness and credit," and good character, alongside a respectable reputation in the marketplace, counted for a great deal.[45] Women's honest economic behaviour contributed to their honour (and, of course, dishonest behaviour could be damaging).

Elizabeth Bradborne, at the end of the sixteenth century, offers an example of this.[46] When Elizabeth became involved in a financial dispute with her son Francis, his ensuing allegations that she was dishonest in the affair affected her honour because it suggested that she was duplicitous and not to be trusted, a damaging accusation. Elizabeth had told her daughters that their brother would pay her debts to them out of the rent money he had collected from her tenants. Francis, however, insisted that Elizabeth had given this money to him, and that she had pledged to repay her debts herself. He claimed that he had witnesses to the agreement and suggested that she was behaving dishonestly and with a lack of proper maternal affection, especially after a blistering letter to him in which she decried his behaviour and accused him of speaking "false othes."[47] Francis bluntly told her that "these uniuste dealinge maketh frendes to fall out & doth noe good & maketh ther is noe credet to yor worde."[48] He insisted she acknowledge her error and focus on trying to "gett the good will of yor neyghbours."[49] He then further chastised her by noting his wish that "I would have you to lyve in charyty wth yor neyghbours & governe yor chyldren in peace yt you maye be well spoken of when god shall call you out of this worlde."[50] According to Francis, her behaviour as a mother and as a neighbour was causing her to forfeit her honour.

Lucy Touchet, Lady Audley, likewise dealt with challenges to her honour in economic affairs when, in the early months of 1610, she was involved in the acquisition of some land for her daughter and son-in-law, Maria and Thomas Thynne. The couple was attempting to purchase Warminster Abbey for £3,650 from Maria's brother, Mervin, and enlisted Lucy's assistance in the transaction. Thomas suspected his mother-in-law of not negotiating fairly, and this prompted Lucy to write a letter to her daughter in which she defended her reputation as an honest woman who dealt fairly in economic transactions such as this one. She wrote to "Mall," as she affectionately referred to Maria, "sopposinge that you know mee a louinge moother, and not a cunnyng shifter, to putt a trycke vppon my sonn Thynne and your selfe for servinge any turne, and the trouth ys enoughe on that."[51] In defence of her honesty, Lucy bluntly informed her daughter that she ought by now to know her own mother's reputation well enough to not suspect her of any untoward dealings. She stated that "bargaynnes w*i*th mee doothe so vsuallye take my word for matters of good worthe, as I forgett to thynke what shulde bee donn accordinge to the ordinary course of Dealynge *with* others."[52] Lucy defended herself by pointing to her proven track record for fair dealing, and expressed her displeasure over being challenged by her daughter and son-in-law as a "cunning shifter." She closed her letter by stating indignantly that, "theare was never man yett abused in hys truste by mee."[53] Such incidents demonstrate how a reputation for economic dishonesty could cast a shadow over the honour of an elite woman. They also illustrate the manner in which the rhetoric of past honour accrued through previous fair dealing could be marshalled as a defence to accusations of fiscal impropriety.

Occurring outside an atmosphere of conflict, the degree to which women viewed effective management of finances and credit as underscoring a personal reputation for honour can be seen clearly in the activities of Margaret, Countess of Bath (born Margaret Donnington and later the wife, first, of Sir Thomas Kitson, then of Richard Long, and finally of the Earl of Bath). Margaret, like so many other elite women, served as a keen estate manager for her husbands, beginning with Sir Thomas Kitson, who was frequently away from the family's seat of Hengrave Hall due to his civic duties and mercantile responsibilities.[54] She then served as an adept household manager to her other husbands and numerous examples of her management of affairs survive.[55] She also continued to manage her husbands' affairs after they died and left property and associated responsibilities to her. For example, for years following the death of her second husband, Richard Long, Margaret continued to manage his affairs and strove to settle any remaining debts that he had, as was expected of her as his widow.[56]

Margaret kept her husbands well informed of her dealings on their behalf and, as one might expect, several examples of her writing to her spouses and apprising them of local and household affairs survive.[57] In offering regular reports to her husband, Margaret both asserted herself as a competent manager of their affairs and conformed to gendered codes of deferential behaviour by maintaining that her husband was the final authority regarding all things connected to their estates and business interests. In her letters, she offered advice to her husbands on the management of their affairs and paid close attention to the issue of finances. Desirous in a time of financial constraint to avoid a reputation as someone who did not settle her debts, she urged her third husband, the Earl of Bath, to give consideration to "the communicacyon that hathe of latte bene betwyxt yow and me co*n*cernyng o*u*r detts bothe at london and in other places w*hi*ch of necessetye at lengthe must neddes be payde."[58] Margaret prayed that he would "talke *wi*th yo*u*r counsel at london" about their finances and advised him that selling a piece of land to pay their debts would be the best solution to their current problems.[59] She also added that she was desirous that the matter be resolved so that "we maye bie the grace of god lyve the more at rest and quyett."[60]

When she and the Earl of Bath again stood in some debt, she was anxious to ensure that all sums were promptly repaid. As a letter she wrote to him indicates, she feared that their financial situation would provoke malicious gossip and gladden the "hartes of them that nether lovethe me nor yet greattly favor yow how be yt I do nott so greatly waye the sayngs of suche forward p*er*sons."[61] She also urged her husband to study how "ye may be able accordyng to your honour hereafter to mayntayne yo*u*r estate."[62] While the Earl valued his wife's advice, he was sometimes reluctant to take it (and, as the final authority within the marriage, was under no obligation to always accept her guidance), such as when he expressed to her that he was loath to sell a parcel of land in order to repay a debt, writing, "but to be dryven to selle a peice of land … I wold be very sorry & lothe to doo."[63] In other instances she acted as an agent for her husband, collecting debts and engaging in other business on his behalf. Like other elite mothers, she also encouraged her children to keep accurate accounts and behave responsibly with the family's funds. When he found himself short of funds, her son (with Sir Thomas Kitson) was forced to write assurances to his mother that, even though "I haue not the suffycyet mony for the bying of suche necassaries as I intend to haue," he was a judicious manager of his funds.[64] As he told his mother, he was "a good housband" of his finances and would be able to repay a loan she had provided shortly.[65] A reputation for fiscal responsibility, even among other family members, could be of the utmost importance in securing aid, as Kitson recognized.

Likewise, when Margaret felt that the family had a financial obligation to meet, she evinced a great concern to settle such affairs promptly. She was aware that the perception of financial irresponsibility or negligence could diminish the family's standing, while a reputation for fiscal honesty was a boon. Often, her management of finances was connected to her management of servants, another area in which she exercised authority within the household. While not all mistress-servant relationships were necessarily characterized by kindness, Margaret took seriously the responsibilities that she bore to those in her employ. Thus, when a certain Jane Hawsley, the mother of a deceased servant of Margaret's named Rebecca, wrote to the Countess asking that some back wages be paid, Margaret quickly settled the debt. Hawsley praised her, writing that she hoped that the Countess would be "longe to lyve in honor."[66] In this instance, by no means an exceptional one, Margaret's proper show of responsibility and care for her servants resulted in expected expressions of deferential praise.

When, in 1556/7, Margaret found herself dealing with a local famine, she gave generously to those in need and, in so doing, augmented her reputation within the community. It was expected of elites that they care for their tenants and not behave graspingly towards them, although many elite landlords were, nonetheless, unscrupulous in the period and faced censure for it.[67] The ideal, however, is fittingly expressed in Stow's *Chronicle*, where he praised the deceased Elizabethan Earl of Derby for "his godly disposition to his Tenants, neuer forcing any seruice at their hands, but due paiment of their rent."[68] In the face of the famine Margaret set a similar standard and extended largesse and displayed benevolence. As she told her husband, had he "hard the greatt lamentac*i*on that is made here of bothe poore & riche for the lacke of bred and drynk yt woolde pytty yo*ur* harte or any manse."[69] Margaret was generously charitable and doubtless understood that this cultivated display of communal good will was to her credit, as it augmented her honourable reputation.

Like Margaret Donnington, Elizabeth Talbot also spent a considerable amount of time cultivating a reputation as a fiscally responsible woman, as this was a source of honour for her. Elizabeth, although one of the richest people in England by the time she died in 1608, owing to her brilliant matrimonial career that culminated with an ultimately unhappy union with the Earl of Shrewsbury, was no stranger to monetary problems. As a child, following the death of her father, John Hardwick, in 1528, her family's fortunes suffered a setback and the crown seized their lands until her brother James came of age. The remarriage of Elizabeth's mother to Ralph Leche brought three more daughters into the family and did not help their financial circumstances. Indeed, Leche served a six-year term in a debtors' prison. Elizabeth Talbot also encountered some financial problems as an adult. In 1557, her second husband, Sir William Cavendish, died owing £5,237 to the crown.[70] This motivated her to marshal her social networks, including the Thynne family, to assist her in lobbying the Queen in parliament against a proposed bill aimed at debtors.[71] Once her financial affairs were settled, however, Elizabeth was in a position to offer aid to her natal family. Thus, when her mother was fearful that some debt in which she stood might damage her reputation and implored her daughter, "I hertilie preye you good doghtter sum what to streayne your selfe for my sake," Elizabeth was able to provide her with a much needed loan.[72] This ability and willingness to offer financial aid was a boon to her reputation and it underscored her position as a woman of prominence and status, which enhanced her personal level of honour.

Elizabeth likewise felt compelled to defend her reputation for sound and honest financial management when it was challenged, indicative of the importance that she attached to such things as touching upon her honour. During her third marriage (to William St Loe), she began extensive renovations on her natal family's home of Chatsworth, a property that she had earlier convinced her second husband, Cavendish, to purchase. Elizabeth wanted to refurbish the house on a grand scale and spent a great deal of her time interacting with builders at the estate. Negotiations did not always go smoothly, as in 1560, when Elizabeth was caught up in a dispute with one of the builders she had hired. Elizabeth was angered over the man's assertion that he had discharged his responsibilities to her and that she was withholding funds from him under false pretenses. She claimed that "he doth Lye Lyke a false knave for I am moste sure he ded never make any thynge for me."[73] In 1594 she was again in conflict with another workman whom she alleged had not fulfilled his obligations to her. This time she referred the matter of "that lewde workman Tuft" to Sir Richard Bagot and his fellow local justices, noting that he "hath delt very badly and lewdly w*i*th me" after "he vndertoke and covenannted to doe great worke for me and to fynishe the same long since."[74] According to Elizabeth, even though she had compensated Tuft more than fairly, he had "greatly disappoynted me and hindred my worke."[75] For someone like Elizabeth, involved as she was in extensive building projects that necessitated the forging of ongoing credit relationships with an array of people and the settling of numerous bills and obligations, her word (and her reputation, both as a fair employer and as one who could keep control over those in her employ) counted for a great deal. As Lucy Touchet had, Elizabeth reacted strongly when it was suggested that she had behaved less than honestly. The criticism was also linked to what she saw as the rightful exercise of her authority with respect to the ordering of her estate – something else that touched her honour.

Figure 5 Elizabeth Talbot, Countess of Shrewsbury, by an unknown artist, c. 1590, © National Portrait Gallery, London

Despite the modest-to-high levels of debt that many early modern gentlemen racked up, men were equally concerned about their reputation for financial responsibility. When Sir Christopher Standish was involved in negotiations to acquire some lands that necessitated that he borrow a large sum of money, he was anxious that word of his borrowing not become public lest people think he was unable to cover his purchase. As he wrote to his brother James, he would "rather spende an hundreth pounde" than hear his "name in slander" with respect to his financial management.[76] Thomas Shirley, desiring to rent a property from Sir George More, was also desirous to advance a reputation for economic honesty. In this instance he had his sister, Elizabeth Onslow, vouch for him and she wrote to More that "yow shalle be faythfully & honourably dealt with for your rent by this brother of myne."[77] According to her, "I know my brother doth more regarde his owne reputation … then to break his word in such a matter."[78] Accusations of financial impropriety could also be used to impeach one's character more broadly. When, for example, Walter Bagot entered into an agreement in 1611 to purchase supplies and felt that the seller had not kept his word in terms of selling him quality merchandise, he wrote to him about the matter and used the language of honour and social worth, suggesting he was being cavalier with his reputation, coercively as a way to pressure him into resolving the affair in Bagot's favour. As Bagot told him, "I can not but marvell a man of your worth shold so little regard" of their agreement.[79]

Miles Temple, somewhat of a spendthrift and frequently in financial straits, was nonetheless as concerned about the negative effects that his mismanagement would have on his reputation as the gentlemen discussed above and, like Thomas Kitson, he turned to family members for assistance when it came to financial matters. In one instance he lamented that one of his creditors was calling in a debt and wrote to his mother to plead for her help because "hee [his creditor, a man referred to as "Sir Peter"] tolde mee I must looke to my selfe for I should bee arrested … I am become his enemy."[80] Temple was highly apprehensive about the damage that would be done to his name and reputation were he to be arrested. A few years earlier Miles and his wife were heavily in debt and borrowed from his wife's mother in order to solve the problem, but now, finding themselves unable to repay her, Miles was forced to approach his mother for assistance. He claimed that her help was urgently needed "for my wifes credit is els vtterly broke w*ith* her mother."[81] Even among family members, one's economic reputation could be fragile.

Given the importance of a reputation for effective financial management as a source of honour, Henry Hastings, the third Earl of Huntingdon, was assiduous in his management of his credit and his papers are filled with examples of his close attention to his financial affairs.[82] However, his efforts at fiscal responsibility were sometimes less than totally successful and, by the 1590s, the Earl found the fortunes of his family at a pronounced low. The Hastings family had seen ebbs in their prosperity and reputation before. Henry's father, Francis, the second Earl, was in favour during the reigns of Henry VIII and Edward VI, but his support of John Dudley, Duke of Northumberland, and Lady Jane Grey in 1553, resulted in Henry being briefly incarcerated in the Tower. The family was soon reconciled to Mary I, however, and swore an oath of loyalty to the new regime, which they upheld. Under the rule of Elizabeth I, the family's political fortunes again took a slight downturn. While Henry acquired a number of offices, including being named a Knight of the Garter and President of the Council of the North, his claim to the throne through his Plantagenet ancestors and his hotter Protestant sympathies led the Queen to view him with a measure of distrust. This was particularly so in the aftermath of the Succession Crisis of the 1560s, when his name was advanced by a number of Puritan politicians as a possible successor to the Queen. The financial fortunes of the Hastings family likewise suffered under Elizabeth. Huntingdon had good reason to closely monitor his financial affairs as he was forced to sell or mortgage many of his land holdings, as his debts grew rapidly. By 1595 very few of the family's holdings outside their core lands in Leicestershire remained in their possession.

It was with this recognition of the link between good reputation and prudent financial management in mind that Henry and his brother, Sir Francis Hastings, exchanged missives related to the family's declining fortunes and alienation of lands, and the commensurate diminishing of their reputation. Francis was then acting as his brother's estate manager and, in that capacity, he wrote frequently to Henry. Francis drew a clear connection between financial and estate mismanagement and the Hastings' broader level of honour. Thus, he noted with concern that "the honour and credite of your self dependeth upon your leaving the heyre of the house in the ... ability to live in his place & calling as an

Figure 6 Henry Hastings, 3rd Earl of Huntingdon, by an unknown artist, late sixteenth–early seventeenth century, © National Portrait Gallery, London

Earl."[83] As Francis reminded his brother, it was Henry's responsibility to play the role of a judicious and effective financial manager for the sake of his heirs and a failure to do so would bring dishonour. In response, Henry thanked his sibling for "your greate care of my selfe and ye hole howse ... for ye honor and safetye whereof [of the family's good name]" which he had carefully guarded.[84]

For their part, much of the downturn in the family's fortune Huntingdon and his successors, the fourth and fifth Earls, attributed to rising families in the area, who they alleged had robbed their more established house of its rightful dignities and honours within the community. The fifth Earl was overly eager to maintain a reputation as a man of great dignity and ancient honour as a result.[85] In advice written to his son Ferdinando in 1613, when the Earl believed himself to be on his deathbed, he condemned the rising gentry and exhorted his son, "let not thy speech be loud and gaping for that will show thee to be but a country gentleman."[86] Huntingdon's advice was centred upon the behaviour he desired his heir to display in order to avoid diminishing the ancient honour of the family. However, if it could be of economic benefit, he was not adverse to his heir marrying into a rising gentry family. While he maintained that his preference was for Ferdinando to "marry with one of thy own rank," he advised him to "match with one of the gentry where thou mayest have a great portion, for there is a satiety of all things, and without means thy honour will look as naked as trees that are cropped."[87] Without the monetary resources to buttress its reputation both locally and at court, an ancient name or a reputation for financial circumspection was not of much use.

Honour, Servants, and the Household

As the previous chapter argued, women saw their role in the successful running of a household and their ability to manage affairs for their husbands as partially constituting their honour. Even though elite women might not always have directly stated as much, it is apparent through the ways in which they represented their activities in these areas (and reacted when their work was challenged) that they saw these involvements as contributing meaningfully to their reputation. A considerable portion of the effective management of an early modern elite household was rooted in the successful oversight of servants. This integral part of household management was one with which elite women (and, though oftentimes to a lesser extent, elite men) were closely involved, as the example offered earlier of the Countess of Lincoln and her "little maid" illustrates. Desirous to maintain the appearance of a well-ordered household space, elite women understood that the behaviour of servants reflected on them. Indeed, issues associated with the employ, care, and discipline of servants occur with pronounced frequency in many elite women's letters to others involved with the upkeep of the household. Joan Thynne, for example, was careful to only allow access to the household to servants whom she felt were both circumspect and effective in their duties. Hence, she wrote to her husband that she refused to further employ George Halliwell because she perceived him to be negligent with respect to the performance of his responsibilities. She wrote, "for gorge halywill I will nether medell nor sett him in any offeis vnles I se him more carfuller then he is."[88] Similarly, Lady Mary Jollife wrote to her brother, Theophilus, the seventh Earl of Huntingdon, about the poor behaviour of one of his valets and reminded him that the servant's actions had the potential to tarnish their "good and honrable reputations."[89]

Both elite women and men were concerned with both providing properly for their servants, as conduct literature and household manuals enjoined them to do, and with properly disciplining them for transgressive acts and uncivil forms of behaviour. The way that servants conducted themselves mattered and, as Cleaver noted, good employees were expected to obediently perform their duties "with fear and trembling in singlenesse of heart" and only do that which would be to the "honestie, credite and profite" of their employers.[90] Likewise, as Richard Braithwaite remarked in his conduct book *The English Gentleman*, "as a good servant is a precious jewell, tendring the profit and credit of him he serveth; so an evill servant ... is a scatterer of his substance whom he serveth; aiming only at his owne private profit without least respect had to his Masters benefit."[91] When servants failed to live up to these high standards, discipline was warranted.[92]

As Naomi Tadmor has observed, family units in the period were constituted less by a nuclear family grouping than by a set of individuals (not necessarily related and including servants) living under the shared authority of a household head. Thus, "the boundaries of these household-families are not those of blood and marriage; they are the boundaries of authority and of household management."[93] While women's success as household managers, something that contributed to their honour, often depended on their forging domestic partnerships with servants in order to facilitate their labour, the household-family was also held together in a very meaningful way by the firm governance of women as household heads.[94] Thus, although bonds of collaborative friendship could form between elite women and their helpers, gentlewomen also needed to assert their authority over servants within the household, and sometimes their relations with servants could be strained.

In addition, the potential for illicit and possibly abusive sexual relationships between masters and servants that could undermine an elite woman's standing within her own home was ever-present, and this necessitated that mistresses closely monitor their servants.[95] Even aside from concerns such as this, as servants knew a great deal about the inner workings of the household and had the potential to slander their employers or even testify against them in the courts, regulating their behaviour and actions was important. As Richard, Earl of Carbery, advised his son, "let your servants be temperate, diligent and true … take special heed of familiarity with them and suspect them humouring of your vices."[96] In closed and occasionally cramped quarters, it was difficult to keep anything truly private, and contemporaries were aware of the need to employ servants who could be trusted to hold things in confidence and behave with circumspection. There was, however, a fair degree of scepticism as to whether such a thing was truly possible and, as one moralist noted, servants were "running vessels that can keep nothing."[97] Many were convinced that servants revelled in gossiping about the foibles of their masters and mistresses. Servants, simply put, needed to be carefully managed in order to preserve a household's good reputation, even if that sometimes meant employing coercive tactics. Insufficient levels of obedience and loyalty were not to be treated lightly.

The management of servants, and its intersections with understandings of women's roles as figures of limited authority within the household and the practical reality that women could have complex emotional and working relationships with their servants, often offered particular challenges for early modern elite wives. Guides to conduct and household management from the period clearly show that women were expected to play a leading role in the management of servants (recall Gouge's injunction that women were to have oversight of the "some less, but verie needful" matter of "ruling maid-seruants").[98] Yet many works also implied that women, by virtue of humoural compositions that made them primarily affective beings who were driven by emotion, were not always as up to the task of dispensing and enforcing effective, detached discipline as were men.[99] As Dod and Cleaver cautioned, a mistress should not be overly familiar with subordinates but, rather, display modesty and wisdom so that her subordinates would "feare, reuerence, and so stand in awe of her, as the Mistresse and mother of the house."[100] On a practical level, some men complained about their wives' tendencies to allow emotions such as anger and feelings of friendship to cloud their judgment when it came to interactions with the servants.[101] Relationships with their female servants were further mediated by the practical reality that some of them, such as personal attendants, could be closely positioned in the social hierarchy to a mistress herself and were occasionally placed in the service of an elite woman in pursuit of local networks of patronage and sociability, thus making it more likely that closer, informal bonds would be nurtured.[102] This could lead to situations that reinforced the suggestions of some that women were prone to the sort of overly familiar relations with servants that impeded their ability to effectively govern the household.

As with their involvement in other spheres of household management, this gendered conception contributed to the perception that women's conduct needed to be closely monitored and potentially corrected. Thus, while women were monitoring their servants, their behaviour was, in turn, also often being scrutinized. As Gouge and other authors warned their readers, women could be more lax when it came to discipline, and were more susceptible to forming inappropriate bonds with their servants, making "themselves thereby slaves to their servants" and blunting their effectiveness as household managers.[103] William Jones likewise lamented that such behaviour could threaten the structure of the family, as it encouraged members of the household to not "keep their rank."[104] While the reality was that female employers were sometimes more likely to be accused of excessive discipline (often bordering on physical cruelty) than male employers, the perception persisted that they were less able to establish themselves as authorities within the household and dispense proper discipline.[105] This could draw husbands and wives into conflict with each other and elite women could react angrily, much as they did in other instances in which their roles in the management of other aspects of the household were questioned, when they felt their authority in an area that they saw as connected to their honour and contributing meaningfully to their reputation had been encroached upon. Accordingly, Elizabeth Hastings (as discussed earlier) challenged her husband when he questioned her choice of wet nurses, and Maria Thynne scolded her husband when her input was not heeded, "no not so much as in choseinge of Servants."[106] Likewise, when Joan Thynne felt that a servant had conducted himself admirably, she was adamant that he should remain in her service, even while her husband disagreed. This servant, John Whitbroke, had earlier committed some unspecified offence against John Thynne, who ordered his removal from his position, yet Joan found a way to re-employ Whitbroke and defended her decision in the face of criticism from John by emphasizing that her motivation lay in ensuring the overall prosperity of the household. She wrote, "as for Iohn Whitbroke I am sory that you showld take yt so vnkindly for my sendeinge for him, it was your pleasher that he should make vp my bocks which bisnes did consarne you as well as my selfe."[107] As Joan implied, the business of proper household management, in this instance bookkeeping, concerned her as much as it did her husband, and servants who were able to effectively assist in such matters were not to be dismissed out of hand. Her support for Whitbroke was in the best interests of the household.

Joan also reminded John that Whitbroke had apologized for offending him and that, in order to appear as a fair employer and just household manager, things which touched her husband's honour, it was proper to forgive Whitbroke's transgression and re-employ him. She noted, "for his offence all thought it ware vaery greate vnto you yett consideringe his submisshon I thinke it parddenable and I dowbt not but his carredge here after will be both towardes you and yours as shallbe fittinge."[108] Joan closed her missive by appealing to the rhetoric of female subordination, perhaps mindful that the rest of her letter had been very assertive and she needed to temper this with protestations of obedience in order to fully persuade her husband. She stated that she had "thoughit my selfe a hapy woman but seinge that I neuer haue nor shall contente you I am and will be contented to do my beste endeveris if it plese you to esteme of them."[109] While she employed recognizable tropes of deference in her letter to her husband (although tacked on at the end like an afterthought), Joan clearly had a strong opinion concerning the employ and discipline of household servants and saw her ability to exercise authority in this area as something that contributed to her reputation as a householder.

Elite women were typically more involved with the day-to-day administration of household affairs, such as the oversight of servants, than their husbands, especially when their spouses were absent for significant periods, such as when they had duties at court or administrative business on behalf of the regime. But men were also careful to observe closely the conduct of those in their service, sometimes bringing them in conflict with their wives, as the examples above demonstrate. When it was perceived that some infraction had been committed which had the potential to be damaging to their honour as a householder, elite men stepped in to dismiss the servant in question. So it was that Anthony Browne, Viscount Montague, wrote to his neighbour in Surrey, Sir William More, that, as so many local residents believed an individual named Richard Covert in Browne's employ to be one the worst men in the area, Browne felt he could no longer keep him in his service "with honor or creditt."[110] Browne was also concerned about having tenants on his property whose behaviour reflected negatively upon him. For example, when two of his tenants were engaged in a dispute, after one of the men was harassed by the other for following orders given to him by Browne, he wrote to More that the matter touched upon his honour and asked More to assist him in settling the matter.[111] Browne wanted to ensure that his proper and rightful authority was asserted among his tenants. The effective management of the household was an integral site of honour for both men and women, and elite householders had a keen interest in ensuring that their estates were properly administered (both in terms of economic involvements and with respect to their servants), as such involvements contributed to their reputations.

The Extension and Reception of Hospitality

Another important area of intersection between the honour that elites accrued within the wider community and the honour that attached itself to them via the management of their households was the offering and acceptance of hospitality. With a long cultural history, this is an aspect of early modern elite social life that has been analysed in great detail by scholars.[112] Hospitality in the period was a marker of honour among the elite and served as one of the underpinnings of the moral economy. Although hospitality's relative importance in conceptions of elite social identity, while remaining in a position of some primacy, has declined, within the period considered here hospitality was of great significance. The extension of hospitality was praised while avarice and a failure to provide appropriate levels of hospitality could be harshly condemned and taken as evidence of a lack of standing and interior virtue. The elite were obliged to present themselves as inclined to largesse, for "the larger the number of guests and the display of generosity, the greater the honor and reputation of the host among peers and dependents alike."[113] While it was recognized that financial mismanagement in the name of providing good hospitality would be foolish, contemporaries clearly saw the value to their honour of being a generous host. Thus, John Holles advised his son to "lett thy hospitality bee moderate, according to ye measure of thy reuenues: rather plentifull than sparing but not too costly."[114] Hospitality could also play a role in a family's financial strategy, as it forged links that could lead to patronage relationships and other potentially lucrative opportunities, and nourished such networks as already existed. Accordingly, failing to provide proper hospitality could have financial and social repercussions, and the dictates of what constituted fittingly hospitable behaviour (despite being open to contestation, as many of the cases investigated below suggest) were a matter of import for elites.

In the demonstration of hospitality women often had an especially large part to play, and such displays were connected to their sense of personal and family reputation. Elite women, like Elizabeth Kitson and Joan Thynne, took special care to ensure that their halls were well stocked with an array of meats and other provisions (not to mention delicacies) which were used to feed and entertain both local visitors and more exalted guests.[115] Many women saw such activities as intertwined with their honour, and they were instrumental in the upkeep of a family's local reputation as they cultivated local friendships, visited kin, and used networks of sociability to further relationships.[116] In this sense such relationships were connected to the complex social alliances that women constructed and participated in.[117] These alliances both provided emotional (and sometimes physical and financial support) to women and served to bolster their reputations when they were properly managed. The successful provision of hospitality in keeping with one's social station, and its role in the maintenance of alliances with all the associated potential benefits, was further connected to family honour. For example, when Elizabeth, the daughter of Alice Stanley, Viscountess Brackley, married the grandson and heir of the fourth Earl of Huntingdon, she was entertained for a time at their estate and wrote to her mother in glowing terms of the reception that she had been accorded. Alice then told the Earl, "I vnderstande by my daughter, howe honorably it pleased your Lo*rdshi*p and your La*dy*: to shewe your selues, not onlely to her, and those her frendes she brought w*i*th her in theire entertaynemente."[118] For their "honorable giftes to her selfe for w*hi*ch as also sondrey other your honorable kindnesses I must acknowledge my selfe depely ingagedd vnto you; and in trewe affection most firmely bounde."[119] Alice also asserted that "you shall never finde me backwarde in yealdinge a free consent" in any matter which would profit the Earl and his wife.[120]

Men similarly constructed such networks and alliances and cemented them through the provision of hospitality. As one anonymous author advised his newly married son, establishing a reputation for hospitality was an effective way "to gett the good will & favor of all yo*u*r neighbours."[121] As both gentlemen and gentlewomen were aware, the extension of hospitality in such situations was a way to build, cement, and maintain alliances. And, as one never knew when such alliances would need to be invoked for support or advancement, hospitality (both in terms of how it was offered and how it was received) was a social obligation that they took very seriously. For example, Margaret Cave Knollys was quick to not only thank a Master Lee (possibly Sir Henry Lee) for the "great Intertaynment when I was with you," but also to ask for his assistance in another matter, noting "for the doing I shall think my selfe greatly beholdyng vnto you And will god willing be redy to requyte yt any way that I may."[122] Alongside serving as a means to build alliances and seek favours, the provision of hospitality provided another sphere in which distinctions of status could be displayed, and in which claims to gentility connected with proper social behaviour could be advanced.[123] The "quality" of one's hospitality, glimpsed through the richness of the goods provided for guests and the ease and pleasantness with which they were offered, was yet another component of the display of elite social identity.

Hospitality was also bound up with intricate rituals of gift exchange that characterized so much of elite social life.[124] Indeed, the desire to accrue honour through gestures, such as distributing venison, could lead to conflict over access to forest and park areas as elite men jockeyed for position with respect to the winning of friends through the giving of gifts.[125] They saw their ability to provide such things as contributing to their reputation and the level of honour in which they were held and, accordingly, vigorously pursued gift giving. Marcel Mauss has characterized the gift as something that was never truly given for free but, rather, always carried the unspoken obligation to reciprocate in some way. Accordingly, gifts are not just material objects. They transcend the divide between the material and the less tangible, as the givers of a gift are not just giving an object but something that is tied to themselves and their selfhood. Thus, "objects are never completely separated from the men who exchange them."[126] To give a gift is to draw someone into a social arrangement and cement a bond between giver and recipient, and this complex understanding of the importance of gifts and hospitality was ingrained in elites.[127]

Furthermore, failure to acknowledge a gift with a similar token could negatively affect one's honourable reputation.[128] Because both the giving and accepting of gifts and the extension and reception of hospitality "articulated shared identity and friendship, as well as deference," the failure to both properly accept and properly offer things could make for edgy social interactions.[129] Thus, when William Cole, the tutor to George More at Corpus Christi College, Oxford, refused a gift of venison from George's father Sir William More, he strove to ensure that his refusal was not frowned upon or interpreted as a negative action on his part. In rejecting the gift, Cole wrote that it was only refused "till I be worthy of it," and then went on to assure More that he would be a conscientious master to George.[130] He wrote that "I wil take vpon me to be his corrector alone, and you shal know that I wil be no harde maister to him."[131]

As was the case with the provision of hospitality, exchanges of gifts, in addition to being a feature of the maintenance of social networks, were also bound up with the complex webs of patronage that abounded within political culture.[132] This played a role in how gifts were received and reciprocated, or rejected. The great houses of the period, for example, prided themselves on their roles as patrons to particular towns and saw changes in those relationships as detrimental to their honour. Hence, the Earls of Huntingdon had a prominent position as the patrons of the town of Leicester and played an influential role in the governance of the town. But this relationship was not always smooth or conflict free.[133]

When the fifth Earl became embroiled in a conflict with the corporation of Leicester in the early seventeenth century and a lawsuit was threatened, the townspeople showed their disproval by declining to send the Earl a New Year's gift in 1606.[134] There was a long tradition of the town sending New Years' remembrances to the Earls of Huntingdon, and they were an important component of the local political culture. The current Earl thought it highly impudent that a gift was not sent in that year. The town then tried to make amends by making an end run around the Earl and approaching his wife, Elizabeth, with a gift of "a very fayre gelding abowte fowre yeere olde and dapple graye" early in 1607.[135] The people of Leicester hoped thereby to draw her husband, through her, back into the bonds of a reciprocal relationship to the town. Huntingdon, angered by what he perceived to be the lack of deference shown by the town, and unwilling to be drawn into an arrangement that he saw as detrimental to his honour, urged his wife to refuse the gift. While the Countess acquiesced, she wanted to adhere to conventional norms surrounding gift exchange and not appear rude or ungrateful in her refusal. As the Countess told her husband, she took care to communicate that "I did not refuse him owte of prowde disposition not to accepte of there gifte butt that I had not dissarued it and knew no means how to requite them in any other matter."[136] The townspeople attempted, to no avail, on several other occasions to persuade her to accept the horse, an indication of both the level of seriousness that Huntingdon attached to the incident as touching his honour and the complex relationship between towns and patrons in the period. The better part of a year passed before a compromise was reached.[137]

As this incident demonstrates, despite the fact that gift giving and hospitality "sustained connections among friends, neighbors, kin, and co-workers at all levels of society," such exchanges and displays did not always go smoothly. The meanings associated with hospitality were open to contestation and negotiation, much as the meanings associated with honour were.[138] Another example of this can be seen in the quarrel that occurred between the Hoby and Eure families, analysed in detail by Heal, during the reign of Elizabeth I as a result of the perception of hospitality both improperly offered and then abused.[139] In brief, it was alleged that the Eures arrived unannounced at the Hoby household and, after being, as they saw it, improperly welcomed and entertained, they refused to leave and so abused the hospitality of the Hobys. It was over this incident that the Hobys sued in Star Chamber.

While in the Hoby household, the Eures engaged in deliberate mocking of their hosts' Puritan faith. The Hobys, in turn, saw their conflict with the Catholic Eure family as bound up, in part, with their self-image as godly inhabitants of the heavily recusant North Yorkshire area. This was a conflict in which religious tensions clearly played a role, underpinning much of the dialogue surrounding the alleged breaches of hospitality that both parties hurled at each other. Neither the Hobys nor the Eures were prepared to cede the moral high ground in this contest of reputation. Indeed, the Hobys pressed their Star Chamber suit against the Eures for twenty-one months in order to secure a judgment in their favour. For their part, the Eures alleged that, as the Hobys had previously lost their honour through their failure to provide adequate hospitality, the Hobys' claim that their honour had been violated was baseless.[140] Both Sir Thomas and Lady Hoby saw the Eures' actions in not behaving as proper guests as damaging to the Eures' honour and to their own reputation as both godly people and proper hosts. They opted to press forward until they were vindicated, despite the urgings of some that they should withdraw the suit. Thus, in an entry in her diary, Lady Hoby wrote that "both Mr. Hoby and my selfe was solicited, by my Lord presedent and my Lord of Limbricke and others, to take vp our sute ["take vp" meaning here to end the suit] w*it*h my Lord Eure in Star Chamber which in regard of christia*n* peace we were inclined vnto."[141] However, seeing the episode as something that affected their honour, "perciauinge our selves to be wrong*ed* in regard that an end was sought which would haue tended much to our discredets, and that the truth of our Iniuries would not be Considered, we Came away."[142] Even though they could not get the redress of their grievances that they sought, the pair was unwilling to let the matter rest, as they saw it as intertwined with their reputation. As Sir Thomas "Posthumous" Hoby expressed it in a letter to Sir Robert Cecil, "for justice' sake I cannot swallow" the misconduct of the Eures.[143] While one understanding of honour dictated that breaches in relationships such as this be speedily mended in the interests of restoring order, the Hobys instead privileged their sense of honour as proper hosts with reputations for sober and godly conduct whose hospitality had been violated by recusant ruffians.

In the case of the Hobys, hospitality represented a key component of their local reputation. While they were not swayed by pressure to settle their differences with the Eures, even when such pressure was cast as the Christian, charitable thing to do, they did still strive to maintain their local alliances, even when the conflict with the Eures was at its height. As is reflected in her diary, Lady Hoby worked to preserve good relations with Lady Eure. For example, in May 1600, Lady Hoby's diary referenced her paying a visit in her coach to Lady Eure for a sociable afternoon: "to se my lady Eure wher I staied tell almost night."[144] By visiting Lady Eure and publically exchanging polite sentiments with her, Lady Hoby cultivated the appearance of maintaining a good social relationship with the Eures, despite the legal action between the two families. When conflicts did occur, powerful social norms about what it meant to behave properly as a member of the social elite often compelled individuals to be polite and friendly to one another, even as they battled on other fronts.

Manifesting a concern for hospitable and civil behaviour in the course of a conflict also served as a way to gesture towards the lack of honour by an opponent – further justifying one's own conduct. Thus, when Anthony Browne, Viscount Montague, opened his house to a young kinsman of Sir William More, George Elliott, Browne reacted indignantly when Elliott did not behave as he thought fitting, but was also careful to not appear inhospitable in his reaction to Elliott. Browne wrote to More of "the incorrigible insolencye of yo*u*r kinsman George Elyott."[145] According to Browne, Elliott had been as well treated in his home as any of Browne's own kin but had never reciprocated or been appropriately grateful for his good treatment. Browne rebuked him for "his loose manner of life," after which Elliott had stormed out, not reappearing until after one o'clock in the morning by Browne's reckoning. He then answered Browne insolently when Browne criticized him and began asking Browne to "recommend him for marriage."[146] Later, Elliott confessed to Browne that he had shot a deer in Browne's park, despite having been given a buck by Browne not ten days earlier. Browne was also incensed that Elliott had gotten a dismissed servant of Browne's to enter the park with him. This was a deliberate flouting of his authority over his own estate, and yet Browne, in his letter to More, was at pains to justify his removal of Elliott. He did not wish to be thought inhospitable by More and told him that he was compelled to do so because of "his insufferable pride," and because, if he had allowed Elliott to stay, "all my family may be encouraged to the like presumption."[147] While Browne was reluctant to be seen as violating the dictates of hospitality, his concerns over threats to the proper ordering of his household served as a means to legitimate his actions, thus illustrating the varying degrees of importance he accorded to different ideas of honourable conduct.

Most people endeavoured to maintain an honourable reputation in the course of a conflict over hospitality by using the language of politeness and presenting themselves as aiming to correct a fault in another by complaining about their behaviour – and there was, of course, a measure of irony in suggesting that one was preserving honour and civility by denigrating the behaviour of another. However, it some instances, such pretenses were abandoned when anger was sufficiently aroused. An example of this, as well as of the fallout that could occur from a failure to conform to contemporary notions of hospitality (both in terms of being a proper host and being a proper guest), can be seen in the conflict that erupted between Sir Thomas Kitson the younger and his younger half-sister, Lady Susan Bourchier. Kitson took great offence at Susan's behaviour in leaving early while a guest at his house over Christmas in

1567 and this led him to believe that she esteemed neither his friendship nor his goodwill. Kitson banned Susan from further visits to Hengrave, prompting her to write to him asking to be readmitted to the house while also chastising him for his anger towards her.

Susan's response suggests that she accorded a higher degree of precedence in this situation to her conviction that she had behaved honourably and that an attack of her reputation was unjustified, than to the idea that honour was rooted in preserving good family relationships and, for a woman, behaving deferentially to an older male relative.[148] Susan was more interested in defending her conviction in her display of proper conduct than making peace with her half-brother, and she refused to admit a fault. Susan's response to Kitson, while offering that she was "sory good brother Kytson that yow shoulde so moche mislyke of my departure from yow this Christmas tyme," snappily defended her actions by noting "that yow have not onely conceaved that opynion of my not to esteme of yo*u*r frendshipp and good will but also w*i*thowt any iuste cause to condemne me as gyltye in that w*hi*ch I proteste vnto you for thought I never offended in."[149] She went on to write "vnlesse yow will accompte the naturall affection and desire in me to see my longe absent Frendes a fautle w*hi*ch yow yo*u*r self I thanke yow to pleasure me were as willinge at my departure to grant as I to desire."[150]

According to Susan, "as my meaninge therein was honeste and voyde of any synister dealinge," her half-brother's anger was misplaced.[151] While Susan lamented the "losse of yo*u*r good will," she curtly maintained that she had "not deserved to be condemned amonge those vnthanckfull ons that neyther deserve feythe nor frendly favor."[152] Kitson reacted with rage to Susan's letter and retorted angrily:

> and this I must further saye vnto you that I doe not only thincke but verely beleve that yf yo*u*r wrytinge to me and yo*u*r desire to enter that you might retorne to my house had procedid rather for love then that yo*u*r other frends are nowe become weary of you, you wolde then have made request vnto my wief (whome I fynde more naturally & better enclyned towardes you in the furtherance of yo*u*r desire then ever I noted you to be towards her) to become a suter to me on yo*u*r behalf knowing that as I have accepted her for my wyef so likewise to be a partaker in the governement of my howse.[153]

Kitson continued, stingingly, that even though his wife Elizabeth may have been deceived by Susan's apologies, he remained unconvinced.

He told her, "perceyving hereby that the woontyd frett of your mynde & vnkynde disposicion in you towards her still festereth in you" and he still refused to forgive her.[154] He also refused "to grant my goodwill therin least therby I might seeme rather to feede your yonge and vayne ymagynacion."[155] Susan, however, refused to budge in her assertion that she had behaved honourably and done nothing wrong. Competing notions of what constituted proper, honourable conduct with respect to the display and reception of hospitality was a catalyst in the conflict between these half-siblings, and neither was prepared to cede the behavioural high ground to the other, ensuring that poor relations persisted for some time.[156]

While most individuals endeavoured to maintain friendly social relationships even in the face of conflicts (and tried to avoid the total collapse of social networks and alliances), sometimes relationships broke down. Thus breached, the re-establishment of hospitable relations could be difficult to achieve. Hospitality was meant to draw people into reciprocal relationships of kindness with one another, but sometimes it failed to do so. Like honour, there was an element of fluidity to understandings of what constituted appropriate hospitality and this could lead to conflict. Likewise, in a manner similar to situations in which violence erupted and the concept of honour was pressed into service as a means of justification, parties to an interpersonal conflict could use the rhetoric of politeness and hospitality as a way to critique their opponents and legitimate their own behaviour.

Such was the case when Anne Spring (née Kitson), married to Sir William Spring, became embroiled in a conflict with Anne, Lady Jermyn, the wife of Sir Ambrose Jermyn. This conflict erupted when Anne Spring and her mother, Margaret, Countess of Bath, were involved in a legal dispute with Sir Ambrose and allegedly spoke malicious words about him to which Lady Jermyn took exception. Anne had formerly been a guest in the Jermyn home and Lady Jermyn felt a sense of betrayal because she considered her husband's treatment of Anne Spring to have been extremely good "durynge your tyme in my howse."[157] As she told Anne, during that time he did not make more "of hys dowghterrs as he dyd of you and yours."[158] With her past offering of hospitality now adversely commented upon and with her husband maligned, Lady Jermyn wrote angrily to Anne. She alleged that Anne and her mother had undertaken to "deprave my husband in his doings an in dysdaynyng and mysnamyng of hym, calling hym toade & other evyll names whyche I ensuer you can not be well taken on my behalffe."[159] Lady Jermyn then scolded her for mistreating her husband after his former good treatment of her and wrote, "I assuer you I thynk scorne that my husband and I shold so be lawghed and scorned at for o*ur* good wylls towards you, and so to be abusyd for yo*ur* sake."[160] Lady Jermyn not only decried Anne Spring's behaviour but also countered that she had violated the obligation to reciprocate the hospitality offered by Lady Jermyn and her husband.

Indeed, Lady Jermyn was so incensed that she decided to end the quarrel by simply refusing to ever have anything to do with Spring again. She ended her letter by writing "wherfore troble yo*ur* selffe no more in wryghttyng vnto me of yo*ur* doyngs, ffor you shalbe well assuryd I wyll neuer speak, nor doo in yo*ur* behalff yf I maye speke or doo to the contrary."[161] However, the matter did not rest there. The Countess of Bath, whom Lady Jermyn had accused of defaming her alongside her daughter, wrote an equally angry letter to Lady Jermyn charging that her allegations were damaging to her reputation. Margaret blasted that she was "not a lytle offended" that "so ingrate and vnthankefull a one as you" should criticize her and her daughter.[162] The Countess denied having ever spoken ill of Sir Ambrose Jermyn or violating the conventions of hospitality and politeness: "I am right well assured that I and my saide daughter hathe not hitherto nether abused her said husband in eny pointe ... as you have touched us in your said *let*tres. Wherefore yt ill besemethe youe so vntrulye to reporte and wrighte of me."[163] The Countess continued by writing that her daughter regretted ever having come into the Jermyns' house given their treatment of her and called Lady Jermyn's allegations the product of "yo*ur* vaine ymagac*i*on."[164] She then closed her letter with a carefully crafted piece of invective, avowing "and for bytinge and etinge of youe I thinke nobodye myndithe the same for youe are to olde and to tough to be eten or bytten. I shall finde better meate your tauntes be to muche."[165]

In other instances, in which anger was not so keenly aroused, elite householders tried to mend breaches in hospitality, especially those committed by individuals under their authority, such as children. Thus, when reports reached them that family members had behaved poorly in the houses of others, elite householders were typically quick to offer apologies and to try to mend fences. When, for example, Humphrey Adderley's daughter was a guest within the household of Walter Bagot, Humphrey was quick to apologize for any poor behaviour on the girl's part. He told Walter that he was afraid Mary "hath binne I muche feare a rude gearle and a troble some geaiste a longe while," and made sure to emphasize how indebted he was to Walter and his wife for being so hospitable to her.[166] The headiness of youth was often invoked as an explanation for violation of the conventions of hospitality, much as it was invoked as a mitigating factor when it came to displays of violence or contentious behaviour within the broader community. When Walter Bagot's son and a young lady were the guests of Walter's sister Dorothy Okeover, it was judged that their "Cariadge might iustly haue deserued your displeasure" ... with respect to "theire dep*ar*ture of your howst in that manner."[167] Walter attempted to smooth things over and recapture his son's honour by placing the blame upon the young lady while also diminishing her responsibility by casting her behaviour as a youthful mistake.[168] He told his sister that he hoped she would "charitably impute to her vnbrideley youth whose want of experience" had made her breach proper etiquette.[169] As had been discussed earlier, however much the discourse of youthful indiscretions may have been deployed as a technique to legitimate socially breaching behaviour, it was only acceptable for a finite period. Once one was perceived to be in a position to control one's youthful passions, tolerance for such behaviour ended.

Honour at Home and Beyond

Behaviour within the household and within the context of the local community was of great importance to elite men and women in terms of their reputations, the prosperity of their houses, and their political fortunes. They viewed the household and the local community, and the roles they played within these spheres, as connected to their honour. Within the physical space of the household, elite householders upheld and enhanced their reputations through diverse activities such as the oversight of finances, the management of servants, and the extension and acceptance of hospitality, among others. And, as the household had permeable boundaries, much of this activity was intertwined with their self-presentations in the community and among their peers. That breaching behaviour connected to one's conduct as a householder, an estate manager, a local administrator, a host, and a guest could have such a detrimental effect on one's reputation, and was reacted to so strongly, is a telling indication of the extent to which these social roles were intimately bound up with the early modern discourse of elite honour. Even though they only infrequently directly described them as such, it is apparent from the energy expended in interactions within the community and the household, and in the level of defensiveness exhibited when their behaviour and actions were challenged in these spheres, that elite men and women perceived their roles within these realms of interaction as connected to their honour.

In their roles as figures of local and household of authority, through the efficient and prudent management of their lands and estates, and in their participation in local networks of sociability and the moral economy of gift giving and hospitality, elite men and women engaged in behaviour and self-presentations that they saw as augmenting and reinforcing their reputations as honourable individuals. These activities were an aspect of elite reputation that remained relatively static across the period, although the importance attached to hospitality and gift giving as markers of honour was eventually to decline in importance relative to the other facets of honour that persisted (yet such a development was not to occur until well after the period considered here). In navigating such conflicts as could arise in connection with their involvements in these areas, gentlemen and gentlewomen often employed reference to the various elements which they saw as constituting their honour and sense of personal reputation, alongside using these understandings to critique the behaviour of others and attack their enemies.

Gentlemen and gentlewomen could, likewise, risk compromising their honour and increasing their potential to be drawn into conflicts if they flouted social expectations associated with civil behaviour. The language of politeness and honourable behaviour, and the multi-vocal nature of their constitutive elements, were frequently invoked in such instances as legitimating techniques to avoid the loss of honour associated with breaching behaviour. In addition, young men and women who were involved in disruptive action were further able to achieve rehabilitation, and partially justify their behaviour, through reference to their youth and by submitting themselves to the authority of their elders and evincing repentance for their prior bad acts. As much as proper behaviour and acting honourably mattered to early modern elite men and women, and as much as they objected when it was alleged that they had behaved poorly, the contours of what constituted honourable, civil behaviour could be fuzzy and open to both contestation and negotiation – although within limits. Thus, when conflicts did erupt, elite men and women availed themselves of the multiple meanings associated with honour in order to legitimate their behaviour (although sometimes not with ease and with only varying levels of success).

Chapter Four

Honour and the Family

Honour as a Collective Value

Near the end of his life, Sir William More sat down to write a series of autobiographical notes and recorded that he was especially thankful that he had had a good relationship with his parents, including his stepmother, and all of his children.[1] More understood that these close ties resulted in a family that was perceived by others as unified and characterized by the appropriate relationships of deference and authority; this brought honour both to himself as the head of the household and also to his family. Elite men and women, as evidenced in their representations of themselves and their actions, perceived their honour as being based on an array of interconnected attributes and behaviours that were displayed in a similarly broad range of activities. As More's reminiscences on his life suggest, some of the most pivotal of these revolved around relationships within the family and the maintenance of family unity, an element of personal and dynastic reputation with deep cultural resonances.[2]

The ideal of a united family featured prominently in early modern moralizing literature; predictably, then, the perception of a divided family could be detrimental for all involved. Sir Thomas Cornwallis, writing to his daughter Lady Elizabeth Kitson, perhaps best framed the negative effect that intra-familial conflicts could have on a family's honour: "consider what a Crosse yt ys to me to se the vnkyndnes betwene my Chyldren in my life … what a dysgrace were yt to me & them also."[3] Despite this expression of frustration over family disunity and the statements to be found in prescriptive literature, and as some of the examples offered thus far with respect to interactions between family members and spouses suggest, many elite families often found it hard to negotiate competing interests when it came to familial bonds. While preserving both the peace and one's honour within the context of family relationships could be difficult to achieve and a unified collective could be problematic to maintain, through an examination of a series of rifts in familial relationships, and the tactics employed to handle them, the manner in which elites' concern with honour inflected both is brought out. The core familial bonds considered here could be especially difficult to maintain; relationships between husbands and wives and between parents and children had the potential to become particularly fraught. In assessing how those involved in conflicts within these relationships saw that strife as affecting their honour and how they simultaneously invoked the language of honour and reputation as a way to justify their behaviour (a legitimating technique common from earlier chapters), the fluid, and sometimes contested, meanings of honour can be glimpsed. Likewise, in considering these various episodes it can be seen that perceived subversion of proper order was at the heart of many quarrels and could have a polarizing effect on those involved.

Honour in the period was, importantly, more of a collective than an individual value. Ultimately, while temporarily held in trust by an individual, honour belonged to the family, to the house.[4] Contemporaries accordingly took pains to correct the behaviour of family members who were felt to be jeopardizing the collective honour of the house. Hence, in a letter to his brother, Alexander Temple made it clear that Thomas's actions reflected not just on his individual reputation but also on the honour of the entire Temple family. Alexander reminded Thomas "howe tender I have beene to defend my selfe much lesse to doe any thinge against *you* whereby *our* reputations should bee brought upon the stage."[5] Individuals attached a great deal of importance to the reputation of their families and, as Pollock has noted, a measure of a family's good reputation was tied to its level of internal unity.[6] A breakdown in the family collectivity was potentially damaging to both the individuals involved and to the dynasty.[7] Conflicts among family members were perceived to affect a family's honour because they pointed to disorder within the household and the failure of the individual members to perform their social as roles as fathers, mothers, spouses, and children. The analogous relationship between the household and the state, so frequently referenced by conduct book writers in the period, in addition to appearing in state-issued documents such as the *Book of Homilies*, ensured that "events within the family were never without a social significance," and the energy that elites expended in the management of their families clearly suggests that they saw it as an integral component of their reputation.[8]

With respect to the nurturing and upkeep of family bonds, elite women were intimately connected with the maintenance of the early modern family. Accordingly, they often positioned themselves as the arbiters of proper behaviour, offering instruction, praise, and occasionally rebukes to other family members when they felt it warranted.[9] However, the demands associated with the maintenance of family honour also fell strongly upon the patriarch of the family. The primary responsibility for the management of a family's wealth and estates typically rested upon his shoulders, and other members of the family unit turned to him for guidance in the management of their affairs. Elite male household heads, like their wives, recognized that the behaviour of other members of the family affected a dynastic unit's collective honour and, much as they did with servants, carefully monitored the conduct of their siblings, offspring, and other relatives. With this in mind, Francis Hastings wrote to his brother, the Earl of Huntingdon, of his hope that, as the public face of the family, Henry would not engage in any behaviour "whereby slanderous tongues may be set on worke to speake broadly & badly of your person & profession."[10]

Francis, as discussed in the previous chapter, was serving as the manager of his brother's estates and, in that capacity, engaged in many interactions within the community on Henry's behalf. He had a good sense of the family's reputation within this sphere and wanted to ensure that the honour of the house was upheld. To that end, Francis wrote of his desire that his brother, to ensure that the whole family was regarded as honourable, would free "your conscience from burthen, your honour from touché, your profession from slander, & your honorable house from ruine, that you may liue with contentation, dye with comforte, passe & ende your dayes with honour."[11] According to Francis, "the honour & credite of the whole house dependeth upon" Henry's example.[12] A failure to do so would ensure "that the honour of the house must fall, & the credite therof in that shiere quite ouerthrowne."[13] Years later, Henry's great-nephew, the fifth Earl, was also aware that a failure to maintain proper discipline within his house would affect his reputation. According to him, in a set of household regulations, his noble house "in proportion doth nearest resemble the government in publicke offices which men of my rancke are very often called unto … if I faile in the lesser, then the which ther can be no greater dishoner, it followeth of necessitie I shall never be capable of the greater."[14] Here a clear link is made between the "private" world of the household and the "public" world of local governance and community involvement.

Frances More was also aware of the wider consequences of the poor behaviour of family members and advised her son Poynings "to be warri what company you keep" while he was away from home.[15] She remarked with disdain that she had heard that "you were scars sobber which trobuls me much that you should liue so besly [basely] a life that the countrie should hear of it."[16] Nor was it only the immediate members of a family who could be chided for their disruptive behaviour. For example, William More took a hard line with his nephew, Francis Carew, when he committed an offence. While Francis did attempt an apology, his actions were serious enough that William was unwilling to easily forgive him. Writing on the reverse of a letter of apology that Francis had sent, William called him "a disgrace" for believing "you were so far elevated above our sphere."[17] He then reproached him for having "delte very vnfaithfully with a family that hath euer ^constantly^ wisht well vnto yours" and noted "in this action you haue more wronged your self then any other."[18] William felt it was important to correct the behaviour of a member of another branch of the family, as it had the potential to reflect negatively on the Mores, especially since Francis seemed to think he was above the family.

Despite the existence of a powerful cultural discourse revolving around settlement and the healing of breaches, especially between family members, some early modern elites found grudges and a sense of wounded reputation hard to let go of. Such was the case with respect to the quarrel over hospitality between Sir Thomas Kitson and his half-sister, Lady Susan Bourchier, in 1567 that was discussed in the preceding chapter. A year after the initial rift, Susan was writing to Thomas asking to be readmitted to his household, noting that she was "mystrustinge ^not^ of your brotherlie friendeshipp."[19] In a slightly later letter, Susan was still asking for forgiveness but was also still unwilling to acknowledge a fault on her part, as she had refused to do ever since the quarrel initially broke out. While striving to appear as though she wanted nothing more than a settlement with her half-brother, she refused to actually effect such an outcome by making a display of repentance. She noted, "yt hath bene no small grief to me that your pleasure or leisure hath not bene to sende for me according to my onlie desyer," but then stated "I neyther knowst or can coniecture any mysdemeanour (god is my iudge) towardes yow."[20] She lamented that his low opinion of her made her "thincke my self the moste vnfortunate woman that maye be" but concurrently maintained that she had done nothing wrong.[21] Susan, in essence, simultaneously articulated two competing behaviours associated with honour: a desire to behave with gentleness and seek peace alongside a spirited defence of her own conduct rooted in her conviction that her reputation was above reproach, and a refusal to admit that her actions may partially have been at fault.

Not only did Thomas refuse to forgive Susan's perceived indiscretion, he also exhibited a measure of pettiness and spite in his future dealings with her, behaviour potentially detrimental to his reputation. For example, when she fell ill in 1571, he wrote to her,

> I am right sorie Sister Susan to heare of your sicklye estate, but sithe the visitac*i*on semeth to agree with the pleasure of almightie god his blessid will be done I wishe you to take the same eyther as a iuste deservid ponyshment for your offences paste, wherof by this meanes he seeketh to move you to hartie repentance & intent never in the like againe to offende, or ells as a favorable warnynge and remembrance (or bothe) to you to serve & daylie to call vpon hym for his grace, wherby you maye avoyde suche perels as (otherwise perhapps) he seeyth you might fall into through frayltie, and overmoche forgetfulnes of your selfe.[22]

While Thomas couched his remark about Susan's "sicklye estate" being "a iuste deservid ponyshment for your offences paste" in the common religious trope of suffering as deserving punishment for prior bad acts, it was, nonetheless, a pointed thing to say and informed by his quarrel with her. Thomas also told Susan that he had earlier received word of further ill behaviour on her part but, now that it was reported she was behaving better, he was prepared to extend some forgiveness to her. He revealed that he had been monitoring her conduct via her servants and, as he had heard from them that she now feared God and was conducting herself with more propriety, he had "soche an assured trust of your Innocency that maye, as I am resolvid not to believe any reporte I shall heare againste you therin."[23] The pair's quarrel over Susan's behaviour during the holidays in 1567 had ended in a standstill and Susan likely bristled that Thomas now adopted such a moralizing tone. While no record of her repenting to her half-brother survives, Kitson evidently had warmed again to Susan by 1571. However, he still felt compelled to rather condescendingly write to her that he was content now to forgive her only because he believed she had reformed (and her servants confirmed as much), not because he felt himself to have been in the wrong initially. As he phrased it, he was happy to mend their relationship because he had seen "yowr good inclinac*i*on now toward me & my wife," a reference to the earlier falling out that he still held to have been Susan's fault.[24]

Other families also found settlements sometimes difficult to negotiate – especially when competing interests were at play and the parties involved refused to acquiesce and modify their behaviour, or even to seek forgiveness. In particular, strife between husbands and wives could become highly troubled and difficult to mediate, as earlier chapters have suggested. Often sparked by competing claims to authority within a given area that both parties saw as affecting their reputation, they were, as are all interpersonal clashes, worsened when cantankerous personalities were involved. In some cases, husbands felt that their wives had subverted the natural order of the family and the household by not exhibiting a proper level of obedience. In others, wives clashed with their spouses when they felt their rightful authority in a given area was needlessly challenged and the honour that they attached to their activities in that sphere was compromised. Whatever the root cause of tension, quarrels between husbands and wives had the potential to be highly acrimonious.

Husbands and Wives

Women had a pronounced role to play in the upkeep of a family's reputation and in keeping the peace among its members, an obvious extension of their roles as the junior partners in household governance and financial management.[25] While women were often actively involved in the preservation of peace within the family, the defence of impugned personal and family honour could mobilize them to be very assertive, even towards other family members.[26] But, at times, their behaviour within the family was itself the source of conflict and a fracturing of family bonds, especially in instances in which they were in open discord with their husbands. As Sir Edward Aston wrote to Richard Bagot about his own unpleasant marriage, "ther is no crosse lyke to haue an enemy in a mans owne house in his owne chamber in his owne bedd."[27] In the interest of both adhering to social expectations and preventing possible conflicts which could result in a fractured home, the fifth Earl of Huntingdon advised his son that he should "deny thy wife no necessary nor fitting things" while also moderating her behaviour by not permitting her to "have all things she would."[28] Like many other early modern elite parents, Huntingdon stressed that the choice of a wife and the relationship between spouses were public acts that had the power to affect one's reputation. For this reason, among other things, the Earl urged his son not to marry a woman of a different religious persuasion, "for thou wilt agree no better with her than an ox and an ass that draw together," a situation that could spark conflict and compromise the honour of the house.[29] In order to keep tongues from wagging and household relationships from becoming public fodder, there was a balance to be struck with respect to relations with one's spouse.

Thomas Egerton and his third wife, Alice Spencer, the dowager Countess of Derby, were unable to strike such a balance. The couple had married in 1600 and by 1610 had fallen out so spectacularly that Egerton was bitterly railing against his wife, who, perhaps owing to her previous matrimonial experiences, maturity, and dynastic status, did not feel obliged to frame her ill-feeling towards her spouse with reference to conventions of wifely submissiveness. In a set of instructions to his son John, born of his first marriage and, in a dynastic alliance, wed to Alice's daughter Frances, entitled "an vnpleasant declaracion of thinges pased betwene the Countesse of Derby and me since our Mariage," Egerton instructed his son to beware of his stepmother's machinations after his death lest she try to cheat him out of his inheritance.[30] Egerton took particular issue with what he saw as his wife's extravagant spending. Women's presumed excessive spending was a thorny subject with respect to the honour they saw as connected to their roles in household management, and allegations of careless spending on unnecessary vanities were more commonly hurled at women than at men in the period. Such behaviour accorded with gendered assumptions with respect to women's deficiencies and flaws in relation to the management of the household – recall the accusations of excessive spending levelled at the Countess of Huntingdon by her husband – and many conduct writers likewise implied that women's proclivities for spending had to be guarded against. For example, Dod and Cleaver noted that "the duty of the husband is to get money: and of the wives not vainly to spend it."[31]

Notwithstanding these gendered presumptions, Alice truly was a lavish spender. She was a patron of writers and artists, fond of elaborate entertainments and displays of hospitality, while Egerton was much more fiscally conservative. While she spoke negatively of his thriftiness, he complained of her "cursed railing and bytter tongue" to his son.[32] He closed his instructions by indignantly stating, "I thanke God I neuer desired longe lyfe not neuer had lesse cause desire it then synce this my last marriage for before I was neuer acquaynted with such tempests and stormes."[33] In this quarrel, two strands of honour clashed with one another. Alice saw it as honourable to spend funds on display and the provision of hospitality, while Egerton saw tight management of the family's finances as the more honourable course of action and was hostile towards his wife's perceived extravagances. These differing interpretations over proper conduct and financial management, often alongside other things, caused conflict to erupt.

Elizabeth Talbot and her last husband, the Earl of Shrewsbury, were similarly unable to reconcile their competing personalities and interests in the name of maintaining agreeable relations and a united family.[34] When Elizabeth's third husband, William St Loe, died, she embarked on her last and most illustrious marriage, to George Talbot, sixth Earl of Shrewsbury and one of the richest men in England. Letters exchanged by the couple near the beginning of their match suggest that a measure of affection was present and their union was further cemented by the subsequent joining of their houses through the marriages of their children.[35] Thus, George's son Gilbert married Elizabeth's daughter Mary Cavendish and Elizabeth's son Henry Cavendish married George's daughter Grace. The marriage between Shrewsbury and Elizabeth was, however, far from happy. As fully mature householders in their own right, with previous marital experience, both Shrewsbury and Elizabeth came to their marriage with set ideas regarding married life and an unwillingness to bend to the demands of their new spouses. Elizabeth, already well established as a lady of status, wealth, and matrimonial experience, was, like Alice Spencer, not inclined to offer displays of deference to her husband and their personalities clashed dramatically. During the time that Shrewsbury served as jailer to Mary, Queen of Scots (from February 1569 and for the next fifteen years – the financial stresses of which may have been a key contributing factor to the erosion of matrimonial bonds between the pair), relations between Elizabeth and her husband steadily deteriorated to the point where Elizabeth alleged that George was overly close to the captive queen.[36] Whether Elizabeth seriously believed this to be the case or hurled the accusation as a means of damaging her husband's reputation, it was a serious charge and further complicated by the dissolution of the once friendly relationship between her and Mary Stuart (Mary was also to make her own accusations against Elizabeth to the Queen). The couple also

Figure 7 George Talbot, 6th Earl of Shrewsbury, by an unknown artist, c. 1582, © National Portrait Gallery, London

battled over a range of other issues. For example, in 1575 they quarreled over building projects that they were respectively involved in. In that instance, Shrewsbury grumbled that Elizabeth was squandering time and resources on her works with little care for his engagements, and he wrote to his wife to complain that she did "hyndar me & my workes" by keeping so many men working on her projects.[37]

By 1584 things between them had soured so greatly that Elizabeth separated from her husband and retired to Chatsworth to live on her own. Shrewsbury claimed that Chatsworth was his personal property, coming to him by virtue of his marriage to Elizabeth under the terms of coverture, even though she had previously brokered a deal for her second husband, William Cavendish, to purchase the property, and his will had granted her possession of it during her lifetime. Shrewsbury, however, pocketed the rents associated with the property, rather than directing them to Elizabeth for her maintenance, and insisted that his wife had no right of ownership. He also accused her of buying up lands in Derbyshire in her sons' names to keep them out of his hands and selling other lands without his permission.[38] He lamented after a 1586 attempt at mediation that did result in a brief reconciliation, even though "it was promised that I should finde yow obedient vnto me in all pointes … what greater dysobedience could yow shewe vnto me than denye me that ys myne owne?"[39] The couple continued to battle across the decade. Occasionally it looked as though violence might erupt, such as in 1584, when the Earl arrived with forty men at Chatsworth in an attempt to assert his ownership and was repelled by an armed William Cavendish, who was committed to the Fleet for his role in this breaching of good order. Things were not resolved until 1587 when they separated again (after the brief "reconciliation" noted above and which was effected with the involvement of the Queen as mediator) and Elizabeth's right to Chatsworth was confirmed.[40] During their protracted conflict, Shrewsbury complained relentlessly about his wife's conduct towards him, such as in one letter to Francis Walsingham in which he referred to her "devilish disposition" and stated that she had "called him knave, fool, and beast to his face, and had mocked and mowed at him."[41] In a letter to Elizabeth, he alleged that, had it not been for their marriage, her reputation would have been forever tarnished, for "where yow were deffamed & to the worlde a byworde, when yow were seynt lowes widdowe, I covered those imp*er*fections (by my entermarriage w*i*th yow) & brought yow to all the honor yow haue and to the moste of that welth yow nowe enioye."[42] Accordingly, Shrewsbury felt it only fitting that

Elizabeth acknowledge that "yow haue cause to thinke yo*u*r self happier then others, for I knowe not what she ys w*i*thin this realme that maie compare w*i*th yow eyther in livinge or goods."[43] Yet he believed "yow can not be contented" and, in Shrewsbury's estimation, Elizabeth could still "doe me greater dishonour."[44]

In their conflicts with each other, both Elizabeth and her husband failed to adhere to the urgings of moralists such as Gouge that "the prouident care of husbands and wiues ought further to extend it selfe to the credit and good name of one another."[45] With respect to husbands and wives who railed against each other, as both the Earl and Countess did, Gouge stressed that, "as they impaire the credit and honour of one another, so they monstrously discredit and dishonor themselues."[46] Indeed, the couple's marital problems were no secret. Both Elizabeth and Shrewsbury approached the Queen and the Privy Council in order to gain the upper hand in their dispute. This resulted in several attempts at mediation, such as in 1580 when Nicholas Booth strove to effect a settlement but ultimately had to admit defeat, saying, "as yet I can not parseue that his Lo*rdship* wyl be by any parswasions reconsiled w*i*th her La*dyship*."[47] In 1586, as discussed above, the Queen intervened as mediator and issued a series of "orders sette downe by the Quenes moste excellent maiestie to be observed by the Earle of Shrewsburie and the Countesse his wife ... to the extent that concorde and amitie maye contenewe and be nourished betwyxt theyme and that the ympedimentes and hyndrances thereof maye be rooted vppe."[48] The orders clearly attempted to broker a settlement. They confirmed Elizabeth's rights to Chatsworth and her living and admonished her husband to "honourablie and curteouslie entreate and vse her and shall beare and defraye all her charges and suffer her not to wante anye thinge that shall be fitte and expedient for her degre and callinge as well in sickenes as in healthe."[49] Yet they also permitted Shrewsbury to disassociate himself from her after a year "yf he finde her forgetfull of her dewtie vnto him."[50] It is of some significance that the Queen herself served as a mediator and arbiter between the pair; alongside a concern to preserve order, she was cognizant of the honour that one could accrue through such involvements. After this year, which was intended to serve as a "probac*i*on of her [Elizabeth's] obedience," Shrewsbury still found his wife forgetful of her duty and the couple separated. Elizabeth took up residence at Chatsworth, where she was able to "enioye all her lyvinge so assigned," as per the Queen's instructions.[51]

The couple also vented against each other to their children. For example, after one particularly tense meeting with his father, Gilbert Talbot wrote to his stepmother to tell her that he had told his father all the things that she and Gilbert had discussed together, including Elizabeth's belief that "all his [Shrewsbury] wonted love & affection is cleane turned to the contrary," from her.[52] Gilbert also repeated to his father Elizabeth's feeling that he "thoughte him selfe moste happye when you [Elizabeth] were absente from him, and moste vnhappye when you were w*it*h him."[53] For his part, Shrewsbury complained to Gilbert (who reported the remarks to his stepmother, promising her that, in anticipation of an upcoming meeting with his father, he would "wryte agayne to yo*u*r La*dyship* what I fynde by him this day") that "if he [the Earl] lysted ... he cold remember cruell speches yo*u*r La*dyship* vsed to him, w*hi*ch weare such as, quothe he, I was forced to ~~say~~ tell her, she scolded lyke one yt came from the banke."[54] Shrewsbury's quoted use of the more authoritative "tell her" rather than the softer "say" reads here as an attempt to regain control from his wife. Similarly, his imputation that her expressions of anger made her seem as one "from the banke" (read here as meaning the south side of the Thames where the brothel quarter and its cadre of low status female workers existed prior to its 1546 suppression) read as a technique to trivialize her expressions of discontent by attacking her status and morality.[55] The strife within the family was to outlast the Earl and, after his death in 1590, Elizabeth and her erstwhile ally Gilbert, her step-son and the husband of her daughter Mary, were to fall out of the terms of the late Earl's will.

Lettice Kynnersley and her husband found it similarly difficult to maintain a united family. In a case of a disjointed family involving quarrels between both a husband and wife, and parents and children, Lettice's marriage to Francis Kynnersley proved to be less than happy, and a series of conflicts erupted both between Lettice and her husband and between Francis and his parents that made things between the couple worse. While some early modern gentlewomen, like Elizabeth Talbot, seemed uninterested in making peace with their spouses and children, others actively played the role of peacemaker in family conflicts and attempted to mediate between competing interests, sometimes invoking the assistance of others in order to do so.[56] Thus, throughout the quarrels that plagued her marriage, Lettice frequently turned to her brother Walter Bagot for assistance, asking him to both help and support her, and serve as a mediator. As James Daybell has observed in an examination of one of her letters, but which also characterizes the others, emotional and practical matters are intertwined in Lettice's missives to her brother.[57] As techniques to ensure her brother's assistance, she appealed to Walter's fraternal love and used emotive language, casting herself as "your louing sister euer" or "yore troublesome sister," while also suggesting that he had a duty, as family head, to aid in the restoration of order within the household.[58]

The stresses of the various intergenerational familial conflicts between Lettice's husband and his father, which first erupted in 1605 and are investigated more fully in the next section, took their toll on Francis and Lettice's marriage. By the fall of 1608, the couple had fallen out. Francis quarreled with his wife when she failed to provide an adequate amount of beer and the fight must have been particularly bad, as it prompted Lettice to once again write to her brother, pleading with him to intervene.[59] In this earlier discussed instance, Lettice's husband deprived her of her authority within the household and denied her the capacity to perform her role as co-manager of the family's estate. In part, Lettice blamed her husband's actions on his mother, saying that, "he wold neuer be halfe so ile. but for his mother."[60] Lettice derisively noted that Isabel Kynnersley "must haue the ouer seete of all."[61] She also accused Isabel of using one of her servants to spy on her – an example of the darker side of alliances between mistresses and maids. Invoking the assistance of a maid to aid in the surveillance of the household may have been a fairly common occurrence. Writers of conduct books encouraged female householders to keep a close watch on others. For example, Gouge urged that "the wife by her help causeth many things to be espied, and so redressed, which otherwise might never have been found out: for two eyes see more than one, especially when one of those is more at hand, and in presence, as the wife is in the house."[62] The potential normalcy of this did, however, prevent Lettice from complaining to her brother. The maid, as Lettice wrote, "useth ^to^ stand at my dore to heare what I say and then tels my mother in law."[63] Isabel also appears to also have had a similarly poor relationship with her husband Anthony, Francis's father. Interestingly, and perhaps because he was already involved in the family's troubles, Isabel likewise turned to Walter Bagot for assistance. She lamented in a letter to him that she and Anthony no longer lived as husband and wife and expressed a desire to leave. Isabel fretted that their estranged marriage was an affront to the almighty and wrote of "this vngodly lyffe contray to al mankynde besides it is a great greeffe to me and a greater daunger to our soules beinge that we made our promysses before the most almighty god to the contrary and for to liue this vngodly lyffe it is the gretest greeffe to my sowle."[64] She was even placed under *de facto* house arrest by her husband at one juncture, lamenting "I ame kept as a poore prisnor heere in my chamber and cannot goe abraude."[65]

Like Isabel, Lettice worried at times that her poor relationship with her husband might force her to leave the household. She was anxious about how she would be able to maintain herself should such a thing occur. As she told her brother, she was "yore troublesome sister" and very much needed his assistance in order to repair her relationship with Francis and resume her household responsibilities, the able performance of which brought her honour. Some years later, in 1619, the couple was at odds again and Lettice again blamed many of their troubles on Francis's mother. She spoke again of leaving her husband and wrote, "I lieu a pore and discontentted life" and that "maybe now he is freinds with his mother it will be worse."[66] She confessed that she disliked living with Francis but, even so, noted that leaving him "wold be the greatest crosse that euer came vnto me."[67]

Francis also made enemies in the community. He fought with his neighbours and incurred debts, which further strained relations with Lettice. In one sad episode, Lettice wrote to her sister-in-law, Walter's wife, to inform her that her sister Dorothy Okeover had sent a diamond ring that she must now sell to pay her debts. She noted that Francis did not know that she was selling the ring and offered Elizabeth the first chance to buy it.[68] Lettice was dismayed at the way that her husband's actions caused the family's reputation to suffer and wrote to Walter that Francis seemed not to care about his behaviour even "if it utterly undo me and all my children."[69] In another letter Lettice lamented to Walter that several warrants had been issued against her husband and described her fears that their property would become forfeit.[70] She asked her brother to help her ensure that her husband provided "mentenance of me and my poore children."[71]

The above are just a few instances of contentious marriages in the period, and there are certainly more that could be offered. These examples provide a glimpse of the stresses that such fractured bonds could induce as couples battled each other and sometimes refused to admit a fault in the interests of ending a quarrel (thereby showing by that, in these instances, they privileged their own reputation as an individual over their honour as associated with a properly ordered and functioning family) – coupled with fears that they would elicit negative reactions from observers. Poor relationships and strained bonds between husbands and wives were seen as subverting the proper ordering of the family as a social institution and affected the collective honour of a house. Breaches between parents and children could have the same result. Yet, while some early modern elites, like Lettice Bagot, openly fretted about how the poor behaviour of a spouse would affect their children, other elite parents openly battled their offspring.

Parents and Children

The family was an institution in which the structures of status, power, and subordination were regularly enacted – often in dynamic ways as embedded hierarchies of authority and obedience overlapped and intersected with each other. The perceived subversion of these structures could take a heavy toll and family bonds could be subject to frequent strain, as the examples offered above suggest. Yet, oftentimes, especially in instances of strife between parents and children, sober repentance and the affirmation of a commitment to offer proper deference was the key to ending a conflict. A certain level of tolerance with respect to dishonourable and breaching behaviour within a family was accorded to the young and, provided they were prepared to repent, their transgressions were often quickly forgiven. Thus when Nathaniel Bacon's wife Anne found herself in a skirmish with her mother-in-law, another Lady Anne Bacon, she quickly set pen to paper to craft a deferential missive that aimed to effect a settlement. She wrote of her hope that Lady Bacon "conceiveth no ill of me."[72] Continuing on, she noted that she would freely "acknowledg my self greatly bounden to yow for ye for the great ^care^ yow alwaies had of my well doinge."[73] Anne ended the letter by expressing hope that Lady Bacon would "take in good part this token of my goodwill vntill I shalbe better able to shewe my self thankfull."[74] Further conflict with her mother-in-law was avoided because Anne offered submission and, in so doing, reaffirmed the authority of Lady Bacon as a family head who was entitled to a level of deference and obedience from both her natural children and those by marriage.

Elizabeth, Countess of Lennox, employed similar tactics when she fell out with her mother the Countess of Shrewsbury, and another Elizabeth. Daughter Elizabeth told her mother that "I haue not so euell deserued as your La*dyship* hath made shewe" and expressed her hope that, because she "hath ben infoormed som great vntruth of me," she would not believe "shuch falce bruts."[75] She also stressed that she was an obedient child who, despite the false accusations against her, remembered her "humbl duty" and implored the Countess of Shrewsbury to remember "your mother like affeccyon towards me your childe."[76] In order to mend the rift, Elizabeth relied on the articulation of submissive and deferential behaviour.

Likewise, when Margaret Kitson, already wed and established in a household of her own, committed an unspecified offence that initiated gossip and the circulation of rumours among her family circle, she was able to make amends by employing two rhetorical strategies. First she denied that her transgression was as serious as it was made out to be (a tactic also employed by the Countess of Lennox), describing it a fantasy of those who wished her ill. As she wrote to her mother, "such blastes are blown a brode of my only behavoure (whith I feare hath sounded to my fathers vnderstandinge and yours) that I tremble and quake for euery worde when I heare from you leaste I showlde be blamed."[77] After attempting to thus dismiss the rumours, most importantly Margaret prostrated herself. Using techniques of submissiveness she cast herself as a repentant and dutiful daughter and continued: "I therfor withe trickelinge teares and most sorrowfull mynde (acknowledginge my faulte) do most humbly craue pardon and forgyuenesse at your handes assur*in*ge you by the grace of god that I wyll never com*m*itte the like againe."[78] She implored her mother not to hold her transgression against her but, rather, forgive her impetuousness and "remitte and forgette that w*hi*ch is past."[79] Margaret was also eager to secure her father's forgiveness and asked her mother to "be a meane vnto my father to pacifie his displeasure ... I greatly feare [he] is highly displeased w*i*th me."[80] While Margaret had to plea for forgiveness more than once before it was granted, her repentance and show of deference to her parents ensured that she was reconciled with her family.[81] In these instances in which strife was sparked by actions that did not adhere to social expectations of authority, obedience, and deference, particularly on the part of the young, unity could often be restored by the act of acquiescing and admitting a fault.

While forgiveness and the restoration of family bonds could be secured provided repentance was forthcoming, quarrels could spiral out of control when such behaviour was not manifested. The misbehaviour of children, even those who had struck out on their own, and the potential associated degradation of the entire house if the behaviour persisted, was a source of deep anxiety for many. As Henry Peacham wrote, it was of great disgrace when the offspring of those who "are nobly borne ... staine their stocke with vice, and all base behauiour, relying and vaunting of their long pedigrees, and exploits of their Fathers, (themselues liuing in sloath and idlenesse)."[82] Owen Feltham echoed this statement when he noted with horror, "earth has not any thing more than ancient nobility, when it is found with virtue. [But] a debauched son of a noble family is one of the most intolerable burdens of the earth, and as hateful as hell."[83] While some degree of rash and less-than-responsible behaviour could be tolerated among the young (but often only if the acknowledgment of wrongs done and a pledge of future obedience followed), forgiveness became more difficult to secure the more one moved into adulthood.

Recognizing the intemperance of the young and its role in breaching behaviour, Ralph Adderley was concerned that members of the Bagot clan in the liminal space between adolescence and adulthood begin to conduct themselves with the gravity and circumspection now expected of them. With this in mind, Adderley wrote to Sir Nicholas Bagnal, serving as a marshal in Ireland, asking him to ensure that John Bagot, who was soon to arrive there and had aroused concern about his youthful impetuousness, behaved properly. Adderley wrote, "where as my Brother in lawe ... John Bagott haith a vnconstant hedd and is more youthfull and wilfull then sober wittyd haithe vowed a voyage into Ireland to go sowe his wild oats god send them good keypinge."[84] He asked whether

> it might pleyse you att this my instannce nott only to Bestowe your good advise and counncell vppon hym Butt also to helpe to place hym in suche sorte as to your wisdome shall come good so that he maye be stayed from licencyuos boldnes and the Reign of lib*er*tie for feare he fall into owtragyuos folly or wilfullnes to the discomfort of his frends.[85]

Adderley also took care to stress that, even though John had earned himself a reputation as a somewhat troublesome youth, "I do assure yow he is vnsusspected of any vntruithe or oder notable crime excepte a white lye."[86]

Conversely, children who refused to offer such apologies and statements of repentance, or who lacked proxies willing to speak on their behalf (as John Bagot had in Ralph Adderley), could produce deep fissures within a family that could last for years. For example, when Sir Richard Newdigate had a falling out with his children over their attempts to have him declared insane and thereby gain control of his lands and property, he was understandably aggrieved and authored an accusatory pamphlet in a retaliatory attempt to indict the behaviour of his children and assert his own position. Following the death of his wife, Newdigate's relationship with his seven daughters and four sons deteriorated rapidly and in 1701 they petitioned to have him declared insane. The petition was eventually withdrawn following arbitration but Newdigate excluded his eldest son from his will in retribution. In the pamphlet which he produced to decry the actions of his children, Newdigate alleged that they "have lacerated their Father's Reputation although thereby they ruin'd their own."[87] Newdigate wrote that he desired to end the quarrel and extend forgiveness to his children, but they had "made him so infamous, as to be the By-word of all Taverns and Coffee-Houses about Town."[88]

As they moved from youth to adulthood, established themselves in households of their own, and began to grow their families, it was expected that elite men and women would behave with circumspection and soberness, and encourage a like example from their family members. When such behaviour was not forthcoming, and as the example offered by Newdigate demonstrates, conflict could ensue. Because they spoke to an inversion of the proper order, conflicts with children were painful occurrences. And, like skirmishes between spouses, they also had the potential to become very contentious. The poor behaviour of a child could initiate a conflict between them and a parent, with accusations of unnaturalness being alleged by both. When Elizabeth Slifield's son, for instance, attempted to enlist his mother's help in seeking to press a suit for some land currently held by the Viscount Montague and she refused him, he embarked upon a campaign of harassment against her. In a petition to the Lord Keeper, Elizabeth alleged that her son was "seeking therefore by all meanes to vexe, molest, and trouble her."[89] Elizabeth reported that Henry had succeeded in having two of her servants arrested on spurious charges. She claimed he had struck against her as both a mother and an honest woman and,

> began diversly to quarrell w*i*th his said Mother and did daylie vexe her w*i*th vnreverent speeches, calling her oftentimes Iew and Monster and telling her to her face that there was no truthe nor honestie in her more then in a dogge, to her greate greif & contynuall vnquietnes.[90]

According to Elizabeth, Henry's actions were all the more heinous and dishonourable because "I alwayes from tyme to tyme shewed my self most carefull of the advancement & well doing of my oldest sonne henrye Slifeld above the rest of my children, in hope of the more comfort by hym in these my old dayes."[91] In her petition, Elizabeth constructed a narrative that used the sense of social anxiety that accompanied the actions of a disobedient child, speaking as it did to threats to the social order through the inversion of proper social roles, in order to press her case. Other parents were prepared to be more patient with the disobedience of their children, depending, no doubt, on the extent to which their offspring were behaving problematically. In 1626, for example, Elizabeth Knyvett was having problems with her son and she wrote to her sister of her intention to suffer the matter with patience. She noted that, "as for my Eldest Sonn, I will beare his vnnaturall Courses towardes me, with as much Patience and Silence as I Can."[92] While Elizabeth was prepared to be more tolerant of her son's poor treatment, she nonetheless indicted it as unnatural, an inversion of the proper order.

Conversely, Lady Margaret Wotton, the widow of the Marquis of Dorset, faced censure from her neighbours and the crown because of her refusal to grant proper maintenance to Dorset's heir. While Margaret was financially constrained because her son had renounced a betrothal and incurred a hefty fine for breach of contract, and this forced her to place limits on the level of support she was able to offer to Henry, her conduct nonetheless resulted in whisperings that she was behaving like an unnatural mother. When allegations concerning her conduct in the matter that impugned her honour as a mother and family head came to the attention of the crown, she denied the "untrue and light reports of my unnatural and unkind dealings toward my son marquis."[93] Simultaneously, she made efforts to increase the funds she gave to him, realizing it would be beneficial to her reputation to attend to the issue. Denouncing a woman as "unnatural" in her treatment of her children was a cutting accusation and contemporary moralists and writers, in an array of venues ranging from the pulpit to the press, expounded on the idea that women should serve as nurturers of the young; elite mothers often accordingly reacted strongly when they were rumoured to have behaved in such a way.[94] Elizabeth Slifield and Elizabeth Knyvett deployed linguistic strategies that emphasized the unnaturalness of their children, and here they were making an effort to contrast and reaffirm their own proper behaviour while denying that they were the ones behaving unnaturally. Margaret Wotton refuted accusations of her unnaturalness by allowing her son more access to the family's resources.

One powerful technique deployed by elites to restore family unity by curbing the actions of wayward children was the threat of disinheritance. Thus, when the son of the Earl of Lincoln made a series of allegations that the Earl had neglected his parental responsibilities to the children of his earlier marriage at the instigation of his new wife, Lincoln enlisted the help of his friend William More to draft a new will in which he took pains to defend his spouse. As a way to further refute the claims of his son, the Earl also included a note saying that his daughters, Lady Chandos, Lady Willoughby, Lady Burgh, and Lady Bridget Dymock, had similarly rejected Lord Clinton's accusations.[95] Lincoln went on to say that his wife had proved a good mother to all of his children and that he had, likewise, provided handsomely for them in his lifetime, given his daughters marriage portions, and increased the value of his estates, a thing which would eventually be to their benefit. He added that, as a result of his breaching behaviour in casting aspersions on his father and stepmother's honour, Lord Clinton would now get nothing by his will.

Similarly, when the Earl of Shrewsbury took umbrage over his son's support for his estranged wife, Elizabeth Talbot, in one of their quarrels, he wrote in reproachful tones to Gilbert. Angered, as so many other elite mothers and fathers were, by a child's failure to show proper deference, Shrewsbury wrote that he would no longer provide his son with funds. Gilbert's financial mismanagement was another source of perpetual conflict between father and son and it now served as a method by which Shrewsbury could coerce his son into obedience via monetary threats. As he bitterly told his son,

> willing you either to provide for yourself as you may, or else be disappointed, for during my life I would not have you expect any more at my hands than I have already allowed you, whereof I know you might live well, and clear from danger of any, as I did, if you had that government over your wife, as her pomp and courtlike manner of life, was some deal assuaged. And, for mine own part, and your good, I do wish you had but half so much to relieve your necessities as she and her mother have spent in seeking, through malice, mine overthrow and dishonour, and I in defending my just cause against them.[96]

Later that same summer, Sir Henry Lee wrote to Gilbert to inform him that he had recently had a meeting with Shrewsbury in which he had again complained about Gilbert's behaviour as a son. Lee reported that Shrewsbury had said angrily of Gilbert, "you had been long a disobedient child unto him; that you joined and practiced against him, and with such as sought his overthrow."[97]

As Pollock has observed, elite women were "perennially concerned about the manners and conduct of their sons," as their behaviour had the potential to affect the entire honour of their house.[98] Thus, while Shrewsbury quarreled with his son Gilbert over his lack of obedience, his estranged wife also battled with her son, Henry Cavendish, over his poor behaviour. Relations between mother and son had always been somewhat uneasy (as noted in an earlier chapter, Elizabeth referred to him as "my bad son Henry"), but in 1602 open conflict erupted.[99] The incident that sparked the rift occurred when Henry attempted to free his niece, Arbella Stuart, from the custody of her grandmother where, as an orphan, she was being raised and, as a potential claimant to the throne, being kept under close surveillance. Cavendish had arrived at Hardwick with several armed men and demanded that Arbella be released. When Elizabeth flatly refused her son's demand, he and his fellow conspirators melted away. Elizabeth realized just how damaging such an incident could be to her own reputation, especially since she had earlier aroused the ire of both Queen Elizabeth and the Earl of Shrewsbury in 1574 in hastily arranging a match between her daughter Elizabeth and Charles Stuart, the son of the Countess of Lennox (and a niece of Henry VIII). Arbella, with her royal blood, was the product of that union and, as punishment, the Countess of Lennox had wound up in the Tower for a period and Elizabeth was threatened with equally harsh penalties.[100] By 1603, she was justifiably wary of meddling in the affairs of potential claimants to the throne. She was also deeply chagrinned by her son's overall dishonourable behaviour and failure to obey, and denounced him in the strongest terms to the Privy Council and to Robert Cecil. As she wrote to the Secretary about her son, "I wishe he had lived so that he were cleyre of all faults imputed to him … that then I might have taken less greif and care for his and others' vndutifull and vnnaturall dealings."[101] Elizabeth appears, overall, to have been singularly unimpressed by her son. Years earlier she had heard rumours that he was spending his time in London gambling and confronted him, prompting Henry to deny, "I am gonne onely up to Londo*n* to playe at Dyse" and not for "dallyance or for any other vayne delight"; Elizabeth's opinion of him was doubtless affected.[102] Later he incurred large debts, displayed a noted inability to take a leadership role within the family, and sired at least four illegitimate sons and daughters. Henry's finances became so bad at one point that Elizabeth's stepson, Edward Talbot, wrote to her in 1604 to inform her of her son's problems because Henry's mismanagement was affecting the fortunes of Edward's sister Grace, Henry's wife.[103] In addition, Henry was exceptionally poor at managing the affairs of his own family and openly spoke against his wife, calling her honour into question by derisively referring to her as a harlot. He equally disliked his mother and, in her numerous quarrels with her Talbot stepchildren, Henry took the side of his in-laws. Offering another instance of a family head invoking financial threats in an attempt to correct the behaviour of a wayward child, Elizabeth eventually added a codicil to her will that revoked all bequests to her son. Henry was, however, not cowed by parental pressure and he and his mother remained un-reconciled at her death in 1608. Cavendish outlived her by less than a decade and died in 1616, heavily in debt.[104]

For the Bagot family, the perceived disobedience of a child, especially when it jeopardized the patrimony, likewise served as a major point of fracture within the family. In a theme that has recurred throughout this book with respect to the behaviour of the young, while a measure of tolerance was extended to those who misbehaved in their youth, it ended if they refused to repent and conform. Some of the adolescents discussed thus far recognized that forgiveness (and sometimes inheritance) was dependent on their submission and such was the case when Lewis Bagot contravened the expectations of his father, Walter.[105] When Lewis was reported to be carousing and otherwise behaving like a rebellious youth while away from home (it was rumoured that he had sired a bastard while in London), Walter wrote to chastise his son. As had occurred when Margaret Kitson prostrated herself to her parents, Walter's letter of fatherly indignation prompted Lewis to write abjectly,

> if hitherto I haue spent the beginni*n*g of my tyme in that vncivill kinde of behaviour that I haue beene a d*i*sparagem*ent* to my house & a disgrace to my selfe yet I hope you will out of your fatherly love bee as willinge to forgiue and forgett as I vnfaynedly will be most dutifull to yow & by gods grace to am*en*d my misspent tyme & lead the rest of my life in such a civill manner that shall bee bothe pleasinge to God & noe thinge att all distastfull to yow, or any of my frendes.[106]

Emphasizing that he would behave in a civil way in the future and acknowledging the justness of his father's anger towards him, Lewis further pleaded:

> though your iust displeashure att mee, may bee a motive against my submission yet I beseech yow to p*ar*don this my bouldnes and the follies of my ill spent tyme & the too little acknowledgement, & p*er*formance of my duty, (I hu*m*bly beseeche yow for Gods sake) to forgiue & take once againe *your* loste son*ne* to mercy and thincke vppon mee with ^the eye of pitty and^ co*m*passion and not accordinge to my desert.[107]

Lewis, however, died shortly thereafter and, following his death, Walter was alarmed to learn there may have been some truth to the allegation that he had left behind a bastard son.

Walter asked his London agents John Chadwick and Thomas Docksie to investigate the rumours surrounding his son's misbehaviour. They dutifully did and sent Walter a lengthy report that exposed a sordid fraud that must have been of great concern to Walter.[108] The investigation revealed that a woman, Mary, was calling herself Lewis Bagot's wife and had "tolde that shee had marryed one M*aste*r Bagott sonne of a greate gent*leman* in Staff*ordshire* and a neere kinsman to the Lorde Treasurer & that the said M*aste*r Bagott & her frendes alsoe did keepe all thinges secrete for feare of his fathers displeasure."[109] Mary also "sayed she was w*i*th childe by M*aste*r Bagott" but Lewis had denied both a sexual relationship and a marriage to Mary, and the agents noted "but M*aste*r Bagott vtterlye denyed that there was anye suche matter."[110] The agents concluded that Mary was faking the pregnancy by padding her belly and that the whole affair "was but a plot to have made M*aste*r Bagott to have marryed her."[111]

Despite the fact that Lewis, like many other youths who contravened social expectations, pledged that "it is neuer too late to doe well," his reputation in the eyes of his father and other family members was further injured when it emerged that he had also been consorting with his cousin, Jane Skipwith, and had contracted himself to her without parental permission.[112] The episode lends some support to the accusations that he had engaged in similar behaviour in London. As an earlier chapter has discussed, the making of an unsanctioned marriage was regarded as high level breaching behaviour, as it called into question a parent's role as household head and as the arbiter of their children's marriage partners. Accordingly, upon hearing rumours of Lewis's exploit, an angry

Walter started to investigate. He wrote to Thomas Skipwith, Jane's brother (and Walter's nephew), to enquire "whether there were ether mairadge or contract passed betwixt my disobedient sonne and my neece your sister or not."[113] He further noted that he greatly suspected that a contract did exist.[114] In an expression of parental frustration, Walter lamented, "my gracelesse sonne … hath withdrawen his obediense from mee."[115] Walter's references to Lewis's lack of obedience are telling indications of what, precisely, about the situation concerned him. Referring to Lewis's other indiscretions, Walter lamented that his son, since his dalliance with Jane Skipwith, "hath continewed in a base infamouse place in Godwins howse ^in London^."[116] He informed Thomas Skipwith, lest he be under any misapprehensions about Lewis's character, that he was "chardged to bee the father of a bastard child begotten on a base Strumpet seruant vnto a gentlewoman of this Contrie."[117] Walter then informed Thomas that "for this his wicked lyfe his obstinate disobediense and infinite others lewde condic*i*ons I haue reiected him ~~and~~ purpose~~d~~inge (god willinge) to disinherit him."[118] Walter closed his missive with the threat that, "whilest I liue meane to withdrawe ~~my~~ ^all my^ maynteanance from him [Lewis]."[119] As we have seen, threats to financial security could be a powerful motivating factor in a wayward youth's decision to conform to the wishes of his or her parents, and Lewis was, a few months later and shortly before his death, sufficiently cowed by his father's threats to disinherit him to promise to do better, because "it is my duty to hon*n*or & obeye yow my parents."[120] The Skipwith family had earlier also moved to chastise their daughter. Jane's mother, Lady Skipwith, was shortly able to write to Walter, "I am fully perswaded of my daughter that she will never speake w*i*th your sonne agayne of that matter."[121]

Anxious to repair the family's reputation in Bagot's eyes, Lady Skipwith further wrote, "I beseeche you pardon that w*hi*ch is paste" and attributed the incident to "theyre younge yeares and want of experience."[122] She closed her letter by trying to downplay the incident and assuring Walter that neither youth "were never minded to make a matche without your good will."[123] She also encouraged Jane to write a letter of apology to Walter. Jane obediently did so and told Walter, "since I heare that it dothe discontent you: I am very sory that it was euer mosshoned: and am fully resaulefed neuer to here more of that matter."[124] She expressed regret for her actions and prayed "good vnckel I hope you haue not soe harde a concette of mee" as not to forgive her.[125] As she phrased it, "I should thinke my selfe very happy if

I might bee ansuered of your frendsheepe againe; which I feare I haue hassarded with this rashe bussines."[126] Jane was able to successfully deploy the discourse of the perceived rashness of youth as a strategy of repentance for her behaviour and was more successful in doing so than Lewis because, unlike him, she actually did reform herself.

Walter Bagot's sister Lettice, in addition to her poor relationship with her husband Francis, discussed earlier, also had to contend with Francis's equally fractured relationship with his father, Anthony Kynnersley. Perceiving the open discord between them to be having an injurious effect on the whole family, Lettice often invoked the assistance of her brother as a way to mediate between Francis and Anthony and mend their bonds. The relationship between the two was very fraught and, in 1605, they became engulfed in an episode of discord that was to last until 1607. The issue at the heart of the quarrel was Anthony's insistence on felling trees on property allocated to his son. As per Francis and Lettice's marriage settlement, Anthony was permitted to do this but it remained a source of contention for Francis ("my wicked sonne," as Anthony referred to him).[127] The dispute only grew and Lettice convinced her brother to step in, both of them perceiving that the open rift between father and son was injurious to the family's honour and potentially harmful to Lettice. Some years later, when Walter Bagot became involved in a legal proceeding between a mother and her son, he was alarmed that members of the same family should openly vie with each other in the courts and wrote to the unidentified man seeking to bring a writ of *suplicavit* for dishonest conversation against his mother, questioning why he would so risk endangering his own and his mother's reputation. He wrote,

> yf your mother were defamed by another man that shee were of vnhonest conversation a malefactor and a Common p*er*turber of the peace doe you not thinke (as you are her sonne borne of her bodie & a gentleman) you are bounden to defend her reputation?[128]

Walter then informed the recipient that the reputation of his mother was directly tied to his own, reaffirming the potent link between family and individual honour. As he noted, "you endeavor to laye such disgrace vpon her wherin you can not but receaue the lyke beeinge discended of her."[129]

Walter displayed a similar attitude to the conflict between the Kynnersleys. He wrote to Anthony asking him to refrain from felling trees or committing other acts injurious to his son, and stressed that such actions would result in Francis seeking to further resist his father. Walter informed Anthony that he had heard reports of "your vnkynd and vnnaturall ^vse^ towards" Francis which "euery daye more & more increastinge that hee is p*er*swaded you haue quite resolued to w*i*thdraw all fatherly affec*ion* from him." He also noted that the intemperance of both of them would be laid bare to other local families, potentially to the detriment of their honour in a society which valued harmonious family relationships, if they continued to "expose your selves in acc*i*on agaynst ech other."[130]

There was also some concern that Anthony was taking his anger at Francis out on his grandson, Francis and Lettice's young son. In allowing his anger at his son to so influence his behaviour towards others, Anthony had done that which Anthony Stafford cautioned against: he had placed his anger before his judgment so that it "quickly becomes master of the Place."[131] Walter felt compelled to write to Anthony regarding the matter and noted that, "I am sorie the offence of the father should w*i*thdraw yo*u*r affecc*i*on from the poore innocent Child."[132] Ideas about proper conduct among family members and about the damage to reputation that could be done by the perception that one was not behaving properly and with due deference were at stake in this conflict between father and son. Walter, as the senior representative of the Bagot family and a local figure of some importance, also had a measure of his reputation vested in keeping order among the various branches of the family. He was concerned about putting an end to the conflict and effecting a settlement as rapidly as possible, and therefore spoke to Francis as well as Anthony with respect to their conduct. When approached by Francis and asked to be a party in a suit he intended to file against his father in Chancery, Walter refused and told Francis that his goal was to avoid legal action and a furtherance of the quarrel, so he would serve instead as a neutral mediator. Walter wrote, "I thought I could doe you more good as a mediator betwixt you and your father then to isyue w*i*th you as a complaynant."[133] Accordingly, he refused to assist either Francis or Anthony in pursuing a case against the other.

During the same period that Walter was writing to Anthony Kynnersley and urging him to cease antagonizing his son, he also wrote to Francis to inform him that he was aware that he was resisting his father's attempts to cut timber on the property. He noted that this was "taken in verie displeasinge manner by yo*u*r father," and urged him to yield to his father as a means of preventing further strife.[134]

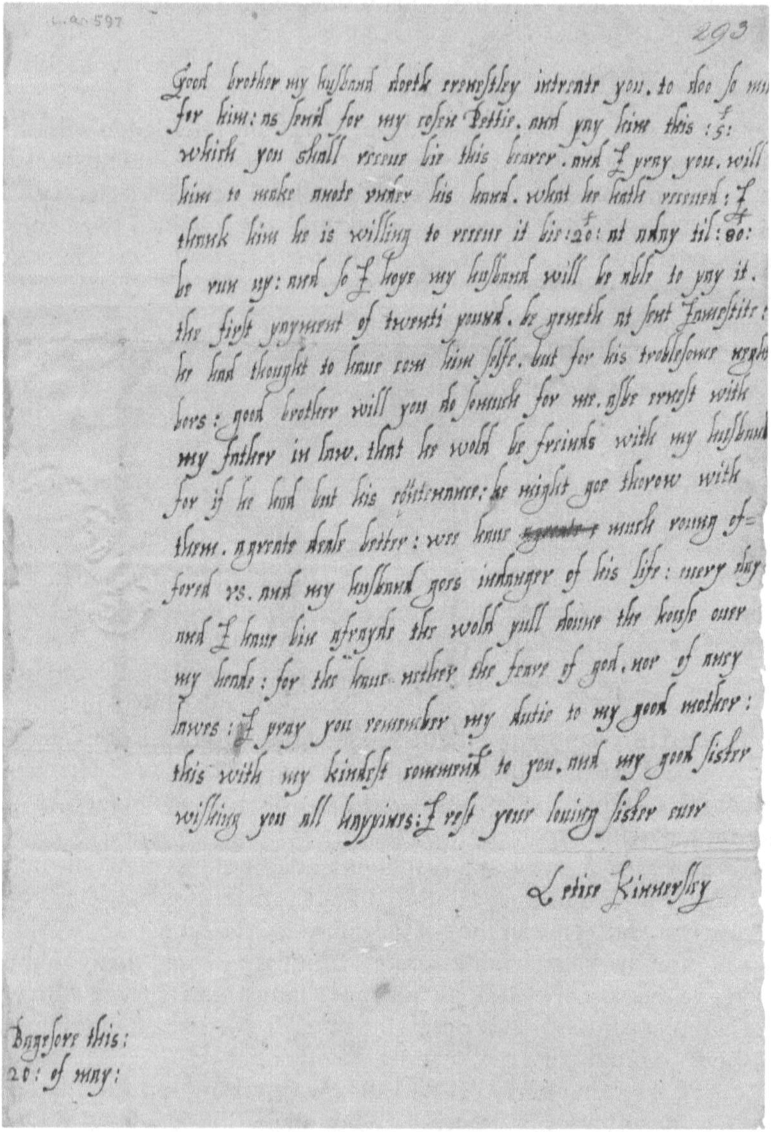

293

Good brother my husband doeth earnestley intreate you. to doe so mu
for him: as send for my cosen Pettie. and pay him this :5li:
which you shall receue bie this bearer. and I pray you. will
him to make anote vnder his hand. what he hath receued: I
thank him he is willing to receue it bie :20li: at aday til :80li:
be run up: and so I hope my husband will be able to pay it.
the first payment of twenti pound. be payeth at sent Jamestide:
he had thought to haue com him selfe. but for his troblesome neigh
bors: good brother will you do somuch for me. as be earnest with
my father in law. that he wold be friends with my husband
for if he had but his cotenance: he might goe therow with
them. agreate deale better: wee haue ~~agreate~~ much wrong of=
fered vs. and my husband goes indanger of his life: euery day
and I haue bin afrayde the wold pull downe the house ouer
my heade: for the haue nether the feare of god. nor of any
lawes: I pray you remember my dutie to my good mother:
this with my kindest commend to you. and my good sister
wishing you all happines: I rest your louing sister euer

Letice Kinnersley

Bagesore this:
20: of may:

Figure 8 Letter from Lettice Bagot, Folger Shakespeare Library, L.a.597, Lettice Kynnersley to Walter Bagot, 20 May 1608 [?], used by permission of the Folger Shakespeare Library

Walter wrote that, "I doubte not but you will quyetlie & with patience suffer your father to take that which of righte belongeth vnto him" and enjoined Francis not to let "the world take notice" of the falling out between father and son because it would surely be to the family's detriment.[135] Walter also told Francis that it would lead to his shame if it became publicly known "that you doe give him the first & iuste cause to deale hardlie & vnnaturallie by you, as you will if [you] denie vnto him his righte," thus reaffirming the notion that, as a son, Francis owed a measure of obedience to Anthony.[136] In order to further encourage Francis to mend the rift, Walter (perhaps drawing on information supplied by either Lettice or Isabel) assured him that his father's "affeccion is not soe much drawen from you as you thinke it is, for not withstandinge his new conceaved displeasure all his threatininge are conditionall (if you persist in your wilfulnes)."[137] Ultimately, Walter told Francis, the conflict was fast becoming a public affair and continued strife and legal action would be "to the great disgrace of you both."[138] Walter commandingly told Francis that he did "hartelie require you will write vnto your father, or if you rather soe desire vnto me to be a meanes for your reconsiliacion, vnto his favoure, and acknowledge your errorre therein with submission to his pleasure."[139] He followed this by sternly noting, in an attempt to shame Francis, that submitting was "not vnfittinge the person of a sonne" and would be "moste pleasinge to God and the world."[140]

While Francis and Anthony appear to have briefly patched up their rift, by 1608 they were quarreling again. The dispute was again a fairly public one. It also appears that Anthony was inciting Lettice's neighbours to riot against her and Francis, as she makes reference to her husband fearing for his life because of the local community's perception of him. She wrote again to Walter, pleading with him to assist her in ending the conflict. She implored him, "good brother will you do somuch for me asbe ernest with my father in law that he wold be freinds with my husband … my husband goes indanger of his life: euery day and I haue bin afrayde the wold pull doune the house ouer my heade."[141] Anthony further increased the visibility of the family's poor relationship in the public eye by refusing to deal with or socialize with members of local society who were friends of his son and daughter-in-law. Such was the case when he revoked the license to sell ale of a local brewer named Thomas Cowper. Lettice wrote to Walter asking him to provide a license for Cowper because "my father in law put him downe for no cause but for finding him so readie to pleasure my husband."[142]

Such incidents must have been embarrassing for Lettice and they were detrimental to the Kynnersley family's reputation. They showcased to the local community the extent of the internal fissures within the family and thus affected the individual honour of those involved, as well as the reputation of the family.

By 1610 Francis was again at odds with his father. Again, Lettice implored her brother to assist her in her efforts to settle the trouble between the two men. She told Walter, "I am afreade there is some disagreement between my husband and his father" and urged, "let him haue your counsel what is best to be done."[143] Eventually relations between Anthony and Francis became so poor that, in 1619, Anthony was commanded by the Lord Chancellor to appear so that the differences between him and his son could be resolved.[144] No further evidence of the conflict can be found in the Bagot papers. One hopes that, for Lettice's sake, they were able to repair their relationship, but, given their contentious personalities and refusal to lay aside their sense of personal honour attached to being justified in their actions in the interests of achieving settlement or even reconciliation, such an outcome seems unlikely.

The Making of Marriages and the Fracturing of Families

Issues rooted in a perceived subversion of proper order, and the effect that had on the honour and reputation of family heads, were often at the heart of many conflicts between parents and their children. Alongside other forms of breaching behaviour, the unsanctioned making of marriages by children could often serve as a point of fracture in relations with parents. When a child, whose behaviour could perhaps have been otherwise forgiven as the product of youthful intemperance, made an unauthorized match and refused to repent, even in the face of coercive threats from parents, early modern elite householders and family heads found themselves between a rock and a hard place. While wanting to at least maintain the appearance of a united family, their individual sense of honour as governors of that collective was wounded.[145] In some cases, they fought for the collective unity of the family by excluding the "interlopers" (as they perceived them to be) that their offspring had tried to bring in. In doing so, they asserted their authority as family heads and privileged the honour connected to this role over that associated with a united family. They also made it plain that they preferred a fractured family over one in which their authority was subverted and "undesirables" were allowed membership.

As earlier examples have suggested, oftentimes it was parents who reacted angrily to the inappropriate matrimonial choices of their children, but sometimes children objected to what they perceived to be ill treatment by their parents. While the involvement of parents was certainly expected when it came to the making of elite marriages – indeed this was expected among all levels of the social hierarchy – perceived meddling could cause conflict to erupt. Richard Broughton, for example, lamented a long-standing conflict he had with his father after a disagreement over Richard's marriage turned to "irreuocable cholerik speches & all turned vpside Downe."[146] Likewise, when Benett Joye opposed the marriage of his son and provoked an open conflict within the family, Anthony Browne, Viscount Montague, took up the cause of Joye's "poore sonne" against the "horrible and vnnaturall doinge of that old [man] (rather monster than man)."[147] In both of these instances, other family members on both sides were in favour of the union and parental involvement was perceived as being taken to extremes. Typically, however, elite parents were accorded a large role in the selection of their children's marriage partners. And, as the making of marriages was understood to be a serious business that affected the collective honour of the house, gentry and aristocratic family heads invested a great deal of effort and consideration in arranging matches for their offspring.

Securing an advantageous match was also an effective way to gain wealth and acquire an elevated social position. Like many other elite women, Margaret, Countess of Bath, used marriage as a way to elevate herself.[148] Born in 1509, the only child of the London merchant John Donnington, her first marriage was to the successful London-based merchant Thomas Kitson. After his death, Margaret furthered her ambitious matrimonial career by wedding Sir Richard Long, a gentleman of Henry VIII's Privy Chamber. Following Long's death in 1546, Margaret, having risen to the level of landed gentry through her first two marriages, married John Bourchier, Earl of Bath, and became a member of the aristocracy. Like the Countess of Shrewsbury and other women who climbed the matrimonial ladder into the aristocracy, Margaret was very proud of her achievements. The children of Margaret's first marriage to Thomas Kitson all followed the example set by their mother and made advantageous matches, with Margaret closely involved in the arrangement of the unions. While Margaret used matrimony strategically and reaped the benefits of it, the forging of matrimonial bonds to augment a family's honour did not always go so smoothly among her descendants. This proved especially true in instances where parents were denied the opportunity to engage in what Martin Ingram has described as the process of gaining "multilateral consent" to matches.[149] Thus, when Margaret's son Thomas attempted to orchestrate a marriage that would have greatly improved the Kitsons' social status, what resulted was an episode of intra-familial strife over a lack of parental consultation that further reveals just how fragile a family's unity could be.

In 1577 Kitson took advantage of a visit from his young nephew William, the third Earl of Bath and a student at Cambridge, and arranged for his marriage to Mary Cornwallis, the younger sister of his wife Elizabeth.[150] The ceremony was performed late at night and the couple duly bedded. While the late-night ceremony may be seen surreptitious, initially the marriage was accepted and legally recognized. However, things went sideways in fairly short order. William soon returned to Cambridge and declared to his tutor his delight in his new bride. The tutor promptly summoned the young man's mother, as he was aware that she had not been consulted when the match was made. When Thomas Kitson's sister Frances arrived, the tutor shut her and her son in a chamber and they argued extensively. By the end of the row Frances had banished William from her presence and her home. She doubtless felt that, despite her obvious connection to her brother and the family of his wife, the Cornwallises, the match was beneath her son as a peer. Elite women sometimes had to juggle the interests of their marital and natal families in the course of their careers as wives. In this instance, Frances identified more strongly with her marital family than with her natal family and saw her honour as vested in her position as a Countess – she did not wish to see the bloodline associated with the Bourchier house intermingled with that of the gentry, especially when her son could be matched with a great lady who would bring a large dowry and potential political connections to the family. Frances was also of the opinion that Thomas and Mary had conspired to trick her young son into marriage, behaviour that, if true, was most dishonourable with respect to the making of marriage and could be grounds for an annulment.

Initially the marriage was upheld but, in 1581, it was overturned after a further inquest into its validity was launched, possibly as a result of incompatibility arising from Mary Cornwallis's Catholicism and Frances Kitson's ongoing objections. Mary, however, steadfastly refused to accept the dissolution of the marriage and fractured the family by maintaining her claim to the title of Countess of Bath. Sir Thomas Kitson was never reconciled to his sister with respect to the marriage and, in his will, he made a generous bequest to Mary and included a statement of his belief that she was the rightful Countess of Bath. Shortly after the repudiation of his union to Mary, William Bourchier wed, in 1582, Elizabeth Russell, daughter of the Earl of Bedford. Mary refused to accept the validity of this new match and continued to style herself Countess of Bath for the rest of her life. Her intractability led her or her supporters to circulate a libel about Elizabeth Russell. This resulted, in 1600, in the poet Francis Davison, a connection of the Russell family, authoring an "Answer to Mrs. Mary Cornwallis," a response that appears in draft form in a collection of manuscripts. In the text, Davison denied the validity of the marriage in no uncertain terms and ascribed it to trickery on the part of Thomas Kitson and Mary Cornwallis. Davison also condemned the libel against Elizabeth Russell and created his own against Mary. He alleged that she had lived lewdly and incontinently, and bore a child by her lover Francis Southwell, before her marriage to Bourchier.[151] Whether this particular rumour ever reached Mary's ears cannot be determined, but it is likely that it was in circulation before Davison recorded it. Mary, however, refused to acquiesce in the face of the rumours concerning her dishonourable personal reputation, and doggedly maintained the validity of her marriage. In this instance, Thomas Kitson was instrumental in Mary Cornwallis's unsanctioned marriage to the Earl of Bath and she was not thus herself in the position of needing to disavow her matrimonial behaviour to gain the forgiveness of her family. Conversely, the Thynne family found themselves dealing with an heir who had not only not consulted them with respect to his marriage and then refused to repent, but who had also married into the family of their local enemies. In this case, wounded pride and competing notions over just who should be considered a member of this early modern elite family in the aftermath of an unsanctioned match intensified the conflict.

In 1594, at an inn in Beaconsfield, Thomas Thynne and Maria Touchet wed clandestinely.[152] Thomas was on a sojourn from his studies at Oxford and Maria was in service to Elizabeth I and temporarily away from court. When the marriage became known to Thomas's parents an intense family conflict was ignited, with both John and Joan Thynne steadfastly refusing, over many years, to agree to any settlement with their son that fell short of Thomas setting aside his wife. How did they arrive at this point? While their pride and sense of propriety bristled at having been excluded from the process of arranging the match – they undoubtedly had other plans for their heir – it was a longstanding political rivalry that most served to arouse the ire of the Thynnes.[153] As the enemies of the rival Wiltshire family into which Thomas had married, Joan and her husband John believed the Thynne family's reputation would be irrevocably damaged by the match, much as Frances Bouchier was determined that allowing Mary Cornwallis into her family would be to its collective dishonour. In the ensuing and drawn out dispute, in which the Thynnes sought to persuade their son to disavow his clandestine marriage and participated vigorously in legal proceedings in the Court of Arches to invalidate it (initiated by the Touchets in an attempt to force Thomas to acknowledge the match), Maria endeavoured repeatedly to reconcile with them but was met with an unrelenting John and Joan. Two conceptions of family unity were clashing with each other. Both Joan and Maria wanted a united family, but they disagreed as to whether the Marvin/Touchets were to be included in that family. Multi-generational strife ensued.[154] As Wall has discussed in her analyses of this clandestine marriage and ensuing fallout, which is examined here in the context of early modern understandings of honour, Maria herself was anxious to secure the approval or at least forgiveness of Thomas's parents for the match. To that end she composed many heart-rending letters to Joan pleading for acceptance. She wrote to her mother-in-law of her hope that God "wyll exercyse that power, to the turninge of y*ou*r harte towardes me" and also employed her own mother, Lucy, Lady Audley, to write to Joan Thynne on her behalf.[155] Because the making of a marriage between elite families was "the weightiest business," the Thynnes strongly objected to their son's exclusion of them from the process, not to mention his refusal to offer them a fitting level of obedience. Joan and John were deeply wounded that they had not been consulted and, as Joan complained to a kinsman of hers, "I haue all waise dislykeid my sonn to mach in this sorte."[156] Both were unwilling to compromise, even if it resulted in an irrevocable estrangement with their son and daughter-in-law.[157]

As the quarrel dragged on, Joan and John showed themselves to be exceptionally angry with their son. At one juncture Joan was so afraid of her husband's wrath that she implored him "lett not the desobedense of one be the ouerthrow of your other children" and begged him to remember his paternal responsibilities to his other children, no matter how angry he was with Thomas.[158] Initially, Joan was prepared to give her son at least a measure of the benefit of the doubt. She believed that the headstrong youth had been duped by the Marvin/Touchet family into marrying Maria. According to Joan, they had used all manner of deceit "to deseve a sily childe which is moste soryfull for his falte."[159] She further accused them, with Lady Audley as ringleader, of taking measures to ensure that the match was indissoluble, such as publically bedding the couple. Hence, Joan alleged of Lady Audley that "she caseid [caused] a pare of sheteis [a pair of sheets] to be lade on a beid and her datter to lydon [lay down] in her clotheis and the boye by her boteid and spored ["booted and spurred"] for a letell while that it myght be saide the [they] ware abeid together."[160] She shared this belief with her servants and, as her agent Thomas Higgins, describing the marriage to Richard Halliwell, informed him, if one were to consider "every circu*m*stance that ^was^ vsed by them for the effecting thereof, it will prove at the issue rather a matter of constraynt, wherevnto he was enforced, then a matter of choyse wich affection p*er*suaded."[161] Thomas initially also bolstered this view of things and seemed willing to repent for his youthful folly. Thus, Higgins also wrote that Thomas was dutifully sorrowful for his actions and that "his vowed resolution hereafter in all conformitye wholy to submytt himself to his parents direction, together w*i*th a voluntary renunciation of all their p*re*tended frendship, doth make me beleue that this action was wholy theirs [the Marvins and Touchets]."[162]

Joan partially blamed herself for her son's headstrong behaviour and confessed to her husband that she now had to "beare this his hevei cros confeissinge my falte in louinge him to wel aboue the reste for which I fere I haue offended all mite god."[163] As noted, Thomas initially played into his parent's perception that his actions were simply those of a headstrong youth who had temporarily disobeyed, rather than a more serious willing contravention of the proper respect and deference owed to his parents. He told his parents that he was "verie sorifull for his vnaduised deisobedences" and beseeched them "to parden his vndutiefullnes in this his childeish doinge which they [the Marvin/Touchet family] parsuaideid him was with your consente."[164] Joan appears to have wholeheartedly believed her son's protestations of regret, eager as she was to believe that their nefarious local rivals had tricked him. She advised her husband that Thomas was "hartely sory and hath voweid to me to be ruled by vs both hereafter."[165] She continued, "he hath voweid neuer whiles he lyueis to ofende you in this sorte and therefore

I hope you will the soner forgeue him whose childeish deide hath throly brout him to a hartye repentanceis of his former falt which I beseich you to excepte."[166] She remained concerned, however, that the Marvins and Touchets would attempt what Joan saw as illicit contact with her son via the Thynne's cook, Patrick, or one of the other kitchen servants (yet another reason for policing the conduct of servants).[167]

John Thynne was much warier of his son's repentance. Thus, several weeks after her initial attempts to persuade John to forgive Thomas, Joan was still trying to mend the rift. At the end of May she wrote to her husband "and so I pray you to execip of his true repentainceis which I hope you will reseue him in to your fauer agane and to haue that fatherly care which here to fore you haue had of him all."[168] Joan was, however, careful to note, "he hath Iustely desarueid your desiplesher."[169] John's frustration with his son was not lessened by the passing of the years and, during the height of the suit in the Court of Arches, John described Thomas with bitterness and anguish as "my proude and vndutyfull sonne whome after all these my trobells will be nowe a counterfoyle and revollte & hathe to me most vndutyfullye demeaned him selfe to my noe smale grefe."[170] Similar to Walter Bagot, John's main concern revolved around his son's lack of respect for the proper order of things and his refusal to offer obedience to his parents. In frustration, John exclaimed in a letter to his wife that "for to my face he vsed me vndutyfully & is suche case of contempt of me as I nether cane nor will endure."[171]

In spite of John's apprehensiveness, Joan was hopeful that her son would disavow his actions and admit that he had been tricked, which would result in the marriage being ruled invalid. She wrote of her belief that "he [Thomas] is contented to leve her seinge nether I nor his father am contented with the mach."[172] Thomas was still, rather duplicitously, encouraging such hope and, eight months after his illicit marriage to Maria, he wrote to his father to pledge "all dutie and obedience to you my good father and also to my mother."[173] He noted "for all other things concernyng my selfe I comyt them to youer wisedome that best knoweth what is expedyent for me."[174] However, beyond these early submissions, Thomas ultimately refused to conform to his parents' wishes concerning his choice of a bride. The match's legality was eventually upheld in the Court of Arches after four years of legal wrangling. Despite Joan and John Thynne's allegations that their son had been tricked and plied with alcohol just prior to his wedding, which he initially confirmed,

Maria was able to produce various love tokens (including a waistcoat and a pair of gloves) and letters that Thomas has written to her immediately after he returned to Oxford which pledged his love for her and referred to her as his wife – an indication that he, at the time, wholly embraced the marriage and considered it a real and binding one. Thomas, ultimately, had no desire to be separated from his bride. Despite what he allowed his parents to believe early on about his disobedience being the result of youth and the shady dealings of their local rivals, Thomas's interests clearly lay in joining himself to Maria. While, initially, he feared parental censure and refused to admit to the match (to this end, the suit in the Court of Arches was actually initiated by Maria and her mother as a tactic to force Thomas to acknowledge the union), he folded under questioning and the weight of Maria's evidence and the case was settled.[175] For their part, John and Joan Thynne remained infuriated by their son's conduct, which they felt had fractured the family and brought them dishonour. This was especially so as it involved Thomas's rebellion against their authority in so important an area as marriage. In their anger, they ceased to care how acrimonious or public their conflict became. Even when things became so fraught that family members felt compelled to intervene, neither Joan nor John was willing to forgive their son. Thus, when Elizabeth Hayward (Joan's sister) wrote to Sir John imploring that he not "bitterly in displeasure condemne as an vnpardonable offence" Thomas's actions, her letters had no effect on John and Joan.[176]

Despite their well-known objections to the marriage, however, the appearance of being desirous of a settlement and of adhering to accepted standards of civility and good conduct still mattered to John and Joan Thynne. Thus, when it was alleged that they had spoken ill of the rival family and impugned their honour, Joan was loath to have such things said of her. She protested angrily and wrote, "my greatest enimies could neuer tuch my credite" in such "indisgracefull manar."[177] Joan sprang to the defence of her personal honour, and by extension, that of her family, notwithstanding that she did, of course, regularly speak ill of the Marvins and the Touchets (and, as will be touched on, this was not the first time that Joan was accused of such rumour mongering). The outward appearance of circumspect behaviour was what mattered. Maria expressed a similar concern with her own personal honour in her dispute with the Thynnes. Writing once again to her mother-in-law to express her desire to be acknowledged as a part of the family, and to underscore the love and friendship she felt for her husband's family, Maria said "yf you finde my words and actions differ, let me be punished w*i*th the loss of my creaditt both w*i*th you, and the worlde, w*hi*ch god best knowes woulde be no smalle greefe vnto me."[178] As Joan had earlier been, Maria was upset that her sincerity, a source of personal honour, was called into question. She told Joan that she was greatly perturbed "that you shoulde not wronge me so much, as to holde the senceritye of my affection Susspected, esspeciallye since ther is not any pollityke respectes to cawse desemulation."[179]

Maria also enlisted the assistance of her mother, Lucy Touchet, Lady Audley, in an attempt to befriend her in-laws. Joan brushed off such advances and attributed Lucy Touchet's attempts to win her over as mere dissimulation. Lady Audley, similarly, took offence to this as she saw a measure of her honour connected to her reputation for honesty. She wrote to Joan to refute the charge, saying "good M*istres*s thynne, lett not mee be wronged in thease lynes, by a harde construction, for I protest that seruill feare, and base flattery, my harte ys not acquaynted w*i*th all."[180] She continued by protesting "yf I desier your Loue, or seeke to Imbrase your freendship (as vnfaynedly in all treuthe I do and wyshed yt long since) beleeue yt to proceed from suche a mynde, as wyllingly makes offer of the owner."[181] Lucy asserted that others "hath wronged mee by misreporting" her intentions to Joan. She maintained that she was an honest woman. It appears she suspected John Thynne of maligning her as well, likely by asserting that she and her husband had used trickery in order to convince Thomas to marry Maria. Thus, she told Joan,

> so haue I hard, and so do I confidentelye beleeue, but myne owne consiense who ys my best wyttnes, can not accise mee of giuing breathe to any thoughte, w*hi*ch myghte euer sound your leaste disgrace, no not when myne owne honor, was tuched in the highest degree, by a scandelus reporte of your husbands whearfore.[182]

Despite her displeasure over the malicious things said about her by the Thynnes, Lucy tried to end her missive on a hopeful note by saying "lastely, since your sonny ys myne, and so beloued as my deerest owne, lett mee obtayne thys request, my daughter may bee yours."[183] In response, Joan angrily stated that "my sone was not longe mine, but rongfully detained from me before he had ether yeares or expedience."[184] She further vented that the Audleys had profoundly disrespected her:

> I confes your Daughters berthe far aboue my sonnes desertes or degree, but sence you weare pleased not to scorne my sonne to be yours, me thinkes you shoulde not haue scorned to haue acknowledged me to be his mother, in respecktinge me as was my due.[185]

Maria continued to attempt to convince Joan and John to accept her into the Thynne family in the wake of her mother's failed attempt in the summer of 1601; but she was not willing to admit a fault, however much she endeavoured to present herself as a dutiful daughter-in-law. As she told Joan, she was confident in "the knowledg of my vnspotted Inocencye" that she had not tricked Thomas into marriage.[186] She was sure that Joan would come to regret her actions and that "one daye you wyll saye that I haue vndeservedlye borne the punishment of *you*r displeasure."[187] Maria employed an array of framing techniques and "politeness strategies" in her letters to Joan in an effort to show herself as deferential to her husband's family.[188] For example, she referred to Joan as "my deare mothere" and promised "yf euer ytt be my greate good fortune to gayne *you*r fauor, there shall neuer want a wyll in me to deserue the contynnuance of ytt w*i*th my greatest affection, and best servyse."[189] Five months later Maria again entreated her mother-in-law with the utmost courtesy to bestow her favour upon her. She told her that she was sure that Joan would willing grant it "yf you dyd butt knowe att how highe a rate I woulde estymate *you*r fauor, and how much I woulde Indeuor to deserue the contynuance therof."[190] While Anne Bacon had earlier been able to reconcile with her mother-in-law following similar affirmations of good intention and a willingness to obey, Joan judged Maria's offence in marrying her son to be too great for such forgiveness. The fact that Maria refused to consider the marriage invalid or admit to a fault did not help matters.

Maria's efforts to be reconciled with Joan Thynne came to naught and Maria's patience was eventually exhausted. By 1602 she was becoming increasingly frustrated with her mother-in-law and wrote to Joan in the middle of that year, "so much am I discouraged to finde that no intreatyes of myne Can prevayle to the obtayninge of ytt [Joan's good will] that I am determined henceforth, to Cease troublinge you."[191] She hoped that Joan would "in tyme inclyne *you*r harte to pyttye and pardon *you*r Sonne, and me for hys sake" but noted that, "vntyll such tym," she would trouble her no further.[192] In a subsequent letter Maria noted that she would continue "to craue your fauore and good oppinion, not onlye for my selfe, butt also for M*aste*r thine, who ys now the better parte of my selfe."[193] Angry exchanges (particularly from Joan) continued to characterize Maria and Joan's relationship and, eventually, Maria's charitable disposition gave out entirely. While Maria strove for years to win Joan over with deferential conduct, when she realized that these actions were ultimately futile, she reacted with a defiant assertion of the justness of her position. But it took Thomas coming into his inheritance in 1604 following the death of his father for Maria to arrive at such a point. When Maria became mistress of Longleat, it altered the relationship, and the balance of power, between her and Joan. Maria now had the unconstrained space in which to express her true feelings of frustration and no longer had to present herself as an obedient child seeking forgiveness. The behaviour expected of her as a youth with respect to her reputation transitioned as she and her husband moved through the life cycle and, as an independent householder in her own right, she was able to be more aggressive in the manner in which she defended her reputation.

Accordingly, in 1605 she wrote to her mother-in-law to complain of her malice and curtly informed her "good La*dy*: out of my Care to yo*u*r health lett me intreat you to temper yo*u*r Choller."[194] Maria indicted Joan's conduct and claimed that she was writing "disgracefullye or contempeyouslye" to her "in bussines w*hi*ch concernes you not."[195] Maria indicated that she would no longer stand for such treatment. After lobbing an insult at Joan by referring to her as "so corpulent a La*dy*," Maria angrily asserted,

> you talke to much of malice & revenge, yo*u*r wyll to shew malice maye be as greate as please you, butt yo*u*r power to revenge ys a bugg beare that one who knows hys owne strength no better then m*aste*r Thyn*ne* doth, wyll never be affrayde of.[196]

Far from feeling that she owed her mother-in-law a measure of obsequiousness now that she was mistress of Longleat, Maria asserted that she and Thomas were undeserving of such handling as,

> how farr yo*u*r bountyous lyberalitye hath extended towards hym in former tymes I know not, butt I haue called my memory to a stricte accompte

> & can*n*ot finde anye obligacion of debte recorded ther that hath binne substanciallye canceled.[197]

In writing these words, Maria struck at Joan as a mother and alleged that, as a result of her unnaturalness, neither Thomas nor she were much indebted to her. She closed her missive by taking her attack one step farther and calling Joan's status into question, writing that she did not feel the need to respond to further criticisms from one not "equall to my selfe by bearth."[198] Denigrating Joan's birth served here to both cast aspersions on her honour and strip her criticisms of legitimacy.

Interestingly, Maria and Thomas's clandestine marriage was not the first marital issue that threatened to divide the Thynne family. Years earlier, Sir John Thynne was briefly alienated from his father, also Sir John, over his attempts to wed none other than the mother of his son's clandestine bride, Lucy Marvin (later Lucy Touchet, Lady Audley). Originally, Sir John Thynne the elder had commenced negotiations with Sir James Marvin for the marriage of their children, but things turned sour when Thynne suspected that Marvin was trying to cheat him by offering, as Lucy's dowry, lands which were either already entailed to the Marvins or limited to their ownership.[199] Thynne had then started negotiating with Sir Rowland Hayward for a match between his daughter, Joan, and Thynne's son. But John the younger was unwilling to abandon the match with Lucy Marvin, much as his son was later unwilling to part from Lucy's daughter Maria.

It was this disobedience that led to the falling out between father and son. The seriousness of the rift prompted friends to intervene. Sir Henry Seymour wrote to the elder Thynne that, although he "will be loth to be a medler in any thing betweene the father and the sonne but for agood purpose," he felt that this conflict was one worthy of his intrusion, as it threatened to dishonour both father and son.[200] As the elder Sir John informed others, his son's actions were "contrary to my com*m*andment" and his involvement with "the young woman" was against "my will."[201] In the end, the match was broken off when John was threatened with disinheritance and he wed Joan Hayward, while Lucy married George Touchet, Lord Audley. As we have seen, when youths refused to conform to social expectations that they obey their parents, more hardline methods could be invoked. After being persuaded with financial repercussions that he should respect his father's wishes, John the younger wrote to Lucy Marvin's mother to end things. Even as he extricated himself from the match, he took pains to make Lucy aware that he only did so under duress – he did not wish for her to view his actions as entirely dishonourable. He thus promised her that, even though he must forsake the match with Lucy, she could rest assured that she has "hade sufficiente triall of the vnfayned good will w*hi*ch I haue alwayes borne bothe to your ladishippe and your daughter."[202] Thynne continued by emphasizing that he had only ended the talk of marriage because "I sawe my fathers dislike to be suche." It was his belief that he had no other choice but to respect his father's wishes in the matter.[203] As he noted, if he refused to back down his father had threatened to "out me to shifte for me selfe," and that confronted with "too extremities I chose ye lesse hurtefull."[204] Undoubtedly Sir John the younger wished his son would later show the same level of deference, even if arrived at under duress, that he had shown in his youthful years.

In addition, ironically anticipating her later conflicts with Maria, Joan herself quarreled with her mother-in-law years earlier. Following the death of his first wife and Sir John the younger's mother, Christian Gresham, John the elder remarried around 1566. His second wife, Dorothy Wroughton, and daughter-in-law Joan got along very poorly. Apparently Joan was not above spreading evil rumours about Dorothy and the situation became so acrimonious that outsiders intervened, something that can only have been detrimental to the family's honour. Margaret, Countess of Derby, thus wrote to Dorothy to alert her of the evil remarks being made about her by Joan, saying "I fynde it more then needefull to warne you of muche evell pretended againste you."[205] As Margaret informed her, "she [Joan] is altogether bente to disgrace you and belye you, and as I beleue doth greatly Inioure you and your house."[206] However, Margaret also believed that at least a portion of the fault lay with Dorothy because, as she told her, "you nickname her [Joan] vnto her face, and scorne and mocke her behynde her back."[207] She concluded that there was naughte in you but pride, mallise, and myschefe."[208] Nonetheless, realizing how detrimental such a rift was, and that the associated gossip it might engender could be to her friend's personal honour, the Countess counseled:

> if you loue your owne quiete and crediete take heade of such venymous vermente and nowe you be warned be armede. suffer not suche mothes quietly to harber in your goune tyll they freate a hole in your nearer garmente. I shalbe sory to fynde you carelesse in your owne causes.[209]

For her part, Joan blamed things on her mother-in-law and, in a letter to her husband (who was in London while Joan lived with her father- and mother-in-law), curtly remarked to him that "almost dayly my lady kepes her accustomede curtesy towards me."[210] She also hoped that soon she would no longer have to remain in a household where she was as vilely "abused as nowe."[211] Years later, as history repeated itself and Joan fought with her daughter-in-law Maria, she may perhaps not have remembered what a bitter experience her own earlier conflict with Dorothy had been. Or perhaps she remembered perfectly well and assumed that, just as she had maligned Dorothy behind her back, Maria must be engaging in similar behaviour, which would have intensified Joan's displeasure with her.

While both John and Joan (to varying degrees) were initially hopeful that their son would repent of the match, such hope was ill founded. Thomas refused to submit and the breach between the Thynnes and their son endured. Aside from a brief later attempt at reconciliation, Joan Thynne appears to never have entirely forgiven her son for his disobedience or his disregard of those he was "borne to honor perpetually."[212] This was likely not helped by the fact that there were some indications that, immediately after his father's death, Thomas Thynne was not conducting himself in a manner befitting that of a responsible householder or loyal child. Speaking to this, in the Longleat House archives a letter survives from a relation of Thomas's, Francis Thynne, cautioning him to see that his father was properly buried and remembered with all due solemnity. Francis enjoined Thomas that "the worlde (which caryed a gret note of yo*u*r father bothe for his lyvinge and place) dothe expecte that the solymnyties of his funerall shalbe p*er*formed w*i*th as grete showe as his state dothe require" and also warned him that, in order to "manyfeste the dutye of a lovinge sonne to a not vnkynde father," he needed to "haue althings p*er*formed to the vttermoste nothwithstandinge the charge that shall rise thereof."[213] Francis also felt it was necessary to remind Thomas that performing his proper duty as a son would be to "yo*u*r best credit."[214]

After John Thynne died intestate, Joan and Thomas fought openly over his intentions with respect to his wealth and property (and their respective inheritances). In 1605, Joan initiated a Chancery lawsuit against Thomas on behalf of her three other children, whom she felt Thomas was failing to provide for adequately. Joan claimed that John Thynne had intended to disinherit his son prior to his death, but that she had worked out a compromise with Thomas whereby he agreed to provide £1,000 to each of his sisters when they married or turned 21 in exchange for being recognized as Thynne's heir. When Thomas defaulted on these obligations, Joan filed suit against him. In a petition to the court she charged that her son "dealth vnkindelie w*it*h me" over the matter and maintained that she felt it necessary to proceed with the litigation because she was unable to cast aside "the naturall care of my younger children, who are hereby like to be vtterlie destitute" if Thomas had his way.[215] As was the case with Elizabeth Slifield, Elizabeth Knyvett, and Margaret Wotton, by advancing a self-presentation of herself as a dutiful ("natural") mother, Joan's petition attempted to prevent a loss of honour by proceeding against her own son in the courts by showing her actions as justified – she thus indicted his unnatural behaviour in contrast to her own. She sought to show that the family was fractured because of Thomas's failure to show her proper obedience, rather than because she was stubbornly unwilling to forgive his transgression. Joan's tactics were successful, as Thomas soon received a letter from the Lord Chancellor in which he was strongly urged to reconsider his behaviour towards "your owne naturall mother," which the Lord Chancellor labelled as "vnkynd & vnnaturall."[216] In response, Thomas denied that he had not made adequate provisions for his siblings. He countered by alleging that he was being asked, indeed, to make excessive provisions to them. Thomas sent the petition to James I and noted that he feared being thought of by the King as "willfull or obstinate," and affirmed again that he had fulfilled his responsibilities to his family.[217] Thomas, just as much as his mother, did not wish to be seen as unnatural in his treatment of family members.

While relations within the family were never mended, Joan and Thomas did come close to a *rapprochement* at one juncture. While her motivations are not known, two years after their conflict over John's lack of a will Joan did try to heal the rift with her son. In 1607 she attempted to broker a marriage for her daughter Dorothy to "a gentleman of a verie ancient & wors*hipfu*ll house" and tried to enlist her son's assistance on the grounds that the proposed bridegroom was a friend to Maria's family, and so the union would help in restoring unity to the family.[218] As Joan told Thomas, Dorothy's suitor was "an aliesman to yo*u*r Lad*y* w*hi*ch to be solemnized & donne might renew a mutuall loue on euerie side to the comforte of many."[219] Unfortunately, the relationships within the family were too damaged for feelings to be calmed and Joan soon returned to a hostile view of Thomas. Several years later she had further issues with the manner in which he conducted himself when it came to caring for his sisters. In 1611, following his failure to financially aid his sister Dorothy and assist her in finding a suitable husband, Joan was compelled to write to her son chiding him for his negligence, which, as she phrased it, "gave both her [Dorothy] and my selfe much discontentment."[220] She also urged him to "have a brotherly care for her good" and fulfil his duties because a failure to do so would affect his reputation.[221] For her part, Dorothy also attempted to heal the rift between her mother and brother. She wrote to Thomas during the height of his legal conflict with Joan that "I assure you she [Joan] hath often said in my hearing that you should be very hartelie welcome to her," in an attempt to persuade her brother to seek a face-to-face meeting with Joan in the hope that they could be reconciled.[222] They do not seem to ever have been.

Happy Families and Little Commonwealths?

A unified family, attuned to the proper social expectations with respect to deference and authority, was of great importance for early modern elites as a marker of honour. It was perceived to be a social duty for members of the nobility and the gentry in the period to maintain "their ancient houses and reputation, free from scandall of dishonour."[223] Male householders, as heads of these little commonwealths, had a good deal of their social identities vested in their roles as family leaders. Women, as wives and the co-heads of households, similarly derived a measure of their social status from the successful performance of their household duties, which often included preserving agreeable relationships within the family. The efforts of some elite men and women to mend fractured relationships between various members of their marital and natal families demonstrate that they had a prominent part to play in negotiating family conflicts in order to present their families as unified and harmonious units and thereby accrue honour for themselves.

However, the ongoing nature of many intra-familial conflicts, and the sheer number of them which are to be found in family paper collections, also illustrate the manner in which elite men and women employed the shared discourse of honour in order to maintain their own reputation in a conflict with a family member while simultaneously refusing to end such conflicts. At the heart of such quarrels was often a disagreement over which aspect of honour was more important to preserve and defend – the image of a unified family or that of a family in which all members adhered to proper notions of obedience and correct behaviour with respect to their individual family roles. This ensured that sometimes, when it came to matters of family reputation, things could get nasty in fairly short order. While skirmishes between husbands and wives were common, and sometimes became noteworthy in their level of nastiness, youths also often had a primary part to play in family conflicts. As Gouge and other authors recognized, "children for the most part being heady and rash for want of experience" were prone to question parental authority.[224] In many instances it was their actions that led to a fracturing of the family as parents were then put into the position of having to decide whether to forgive their children and preserve the family, or to battle them as their behaviour had touched their honour as householders and family heads. In the cases considered above in which repentance and affirmations of filial obedience were not forthcoming, we can see that very few of the men and women involved opted to let matters rest and forgive their wayward offspring. Instead, they clung doggedly to their wounded reputations as family heads whose authority had been contravened and sought out ways to coerce their children into obedience, with threats of disinheritance being the most common method.

When they were convinced of the justness of their position, elite men and women used the rhetoric of honour as associated with proper behaviour within the structure of the family as a weapon when engaging with their opponents, even when they were family. Whether battling with their children, each other, or those external to the core family relationships, several of the episodes considered here further point to the aggressive attitude found among many early modern elite men and women with regard to family reputation. While honour was to be found in preserving the peace (both within the family and within the community), it could also serve to spark and sustain quarrels. The idea of a unified family in which members respected the behavioural expectations associated with them has perhaps waned in importance as an element of honour (owing possibly in part to the eventual reconfiguration of the nature of bonds of authority and deference between spouses and between parents and children – although a lack of obedience among children remains a source of embarrassment to some). But it was very much a fixture of understandings of honour among the early modern English elite considered here. Yet the relative value individual elite men and women attached to this understanding of honour was negotiable based upon their needs and preferences in a given interaction. Accordingly, gentlewomen and gentlemen often brought other understandings of honour to the fore in their actions and self-presentations, especially in instances where they felt their personal reputations had been adversely affected by the behaviour of a family member.

Conclusion: The Importance of Honour

The Meanings of Honour

When Antony remarked in *Antony and Cleopatra*, "if I lose mine honour / I lose myself," he would have easily won the empathy of his early modern audiences. To lose honour as a member of the elite in early modern England was often to lose a measure of both one's standing among one's peers and the deference of one's subordinates. And because honour was "a certaine testimony of vertue shining of it selfe, giuen of som men by the Judgement of good men," and thus dependent on assessments made by others, it could be easily compromised.[1] This necessitated that it be managed carefully. Yet honour was not a static concept and, in investigating the ways in which members of the social elite tended to personal and familial honour within routine social interactions, the various and occasionally contradictory and contested meanings of honour become visible. Likewise, this work reveals that the various elements associated collectively with honour might carry different weight for different people in different settings and at different times. As Pollock has aptly noted, honour was "a multiplicity of overlapping discourses, an amalgam of attributes that could be mixed and employed as needed."[2] Accordingly, this study has offered not a tidy reconceptualization of honour meant to replace earlier analyses but, rather, something that reveals the flexibility and ambiguity inherent in the many understandings of honour that persisted across the period. Because it could result in so many performative and rhetorical manifestations, honour was a social construct in motion, constantly being defined and redefined through practice.

Honour was a diffuse value, intimately bound up with one's sense of self, and so foundational an element of identity that individuals often discussed matters relating to their honour or reputation without necessarily employing those terms. Throughout the examples discussed here it is apparent that while early modern elite men and women may have often used the term "honour" in restricted contexts, they nonetheless perceived it as constituted by a broad range of elements. These examples also illustrate that gentlemen and gentlewomen were daily engaged in an equally broad range of interactions and behaviours that they saw as related to their reputations. Honour can thus be a somewhat elusive concept. Yet, for the elite, it was clearly linked to influence, social worth, esteem, and deference. Gentlewomen and gentlemen recognized honour when they saw it at stake, and felt its loss when they were deprived of it. For them it had real and immediate, albeit negotiable, meanings. It was both an element in the construction of personal identity and family and reputation, and one with practical and very real benefits. Honour was a concept routinely invoked and enacted in daily social life – its multiple meanings are revealed through performance and presentations of self.

In a letter to his mother after a falling out over a financial matter, Francis Bradborne informed her, "I never gave my consent to troble but haue byn alwayes a peace maker."[3] His statement reveals one of the ways in which elites in the early modern period understood and talked about the multifaceted concept of honour. Throughout his letter, Francis wanted to safeguard his reputation as a gentleman of financial responsibility and as a good son who, even at the height of a conflict with his mother (which became fairly heated), appeared to want the restoration of loving bonds. Despite this insistence on his desire to be seen as someone who wanted settlement in the aftermath of a family quarrel, Francis's letter then moved to privilege another understanding of honour, that associated with the defence of good name, as he attempted to claim the moral high ground in the conflict by rounding on his mother and decrying her un-maternal and harsh treatment of him and her other children. In spite of his earlier insistence that he was a "peace maker," Francis here became very aggressive with his mother and showed himself as willing to violate the expectation that a son owed filial deference to his mother, which itself was understood to be an element of an honourable reputation. In harsh terms Francis condemned Elizabeth's "uniuste dealinge" and alleged that "ther is noe credet to yor worde."[4] While claiming honour as connected to his desire to end conflicts, Francis simultaneously mounted an attack on his mother and, while asserting his own proper behaviour as a dutiful son, he likewise denigrated his mother's actions as unnatural, a serious criticism of her character and one which violated understandings of honour as vested in a unified family. His missive speaks to the flexibility of honour and the manner in which some of the various meanings associated with it could be privileged with fluidity.

Understanding the importance of honour as associated with the collective of the family (even as his words fractured it in the defence of his own honour), Francis was unwilling to be labelled as one who subverted the proper ties of authority and deference within the family unit, and so denied his role in the weakening of family bonds in favour of shifting the blame to his mother. Displaying a similar awareness but a different reaction, when Sir Thomas Gresham quarreled with his brother-in-law, the elder Sir John Thynne, he was anxious to ensure that the rift did not cause his sister, Christian, to think too poorly of him. Aside from declaring that he had always endeavoured to treat his sister and her family with the utmost affection and respect, Gresham hoped that he had "stayed yo*u*r rashe Iugment towardes me whom nature movythe me to love becausse you are my sister."[5] Desiring to rehabilitate himself in his sister's eyes (while simultaneously calling her judgment into question by labelling it "rash"), he wrote that his "malicious" activities had been exaggerated and claimed that "whatsoever thosse slaunderers have mis-reported of me I praye god forgeve them and amend them."[6] Like Francis Bradborne, Gresham was aware of the damage that could be done to his reputation if he was seen to be involved in an open conflict with close family members. But the two men also had a keen sense of their own personal reputation as men of honesty, good conduct, and honour, although they employed different tactics in the defence of their reputations. Bradborne resorted to an attack on his mother, while Gresham sought to pacify his sister, although he couldn't resist taking a small swipe at her, and refused to countenance what he regarded as malicious gossip.

As these examples suggest, claims to honour could lead elites in early modern England to aggressive actions and forceful statements. In her conflict with Master Savage, Margaret, Countess of Bath, was no shrinking violet, nor, indeed, a mild-mannered and polite gentlewoman. After levelling a string of angry insults at Savage related to his conduct in the argument, coupled with a denigration of his status, Margaret simply and in exasperation exclaimed, "ye [are] no honest man."[7] Walter Bagot could be similarly pushed into forceful declarations of his own honour in opposition to that of others. As he avowed in a letter to his troublesome brother-in-law, Francis Kynnersley, "my fidelitie shall neuer bee impeached by any man."[8] For these elites, in these contexts, honour was to be found in the defence of good name, delivered in the form of an attack on an opponent. Yet, in other contexts, both Margaret and Walter spoke of and displayed honour as a value associated with demonstrations of civility and the avoidance of conflict, much as Francis Bradborne had done before he attacked.

Matters of honour and reputation held great importance for early modern men and women. Yet, as the examples briefly recounted above suggest, "honour" carried a range of meanings and was capable of generating an array of surface manifestations, as these various meanings and associated modes of behavioural expression could take on varying levels of importance depending on circumstances and the personalities and interests of those involved. Its level of pliability meant that the elite men and women considered here were able to utilize honour to legitimize their own activities and outlooks. This flexibility as a representational strategy ensured that it was an often-invoked concept. Yet, while honour was malleable, it would be a mistake to equate this with a lack of substance or to discount its weight in the lives of inhabitants of the period. Though diffuse in meaning, honour was bounded by broadly recognizable primary characteristics and consisted of certain core attributes (including a concern with status and lineage, an awareness of the importance attached to the exercise of authority, the appearance of self-mastery, the display of various behaviours associated with gentility, hospitality, political influence, education, estate management, the forging and maintenance of local and family relationships rooted in respect and sometimes deference, myriad activities associated with the household, and a willingness to defend – in moderation – one's good name) and carried great weight in both social interaction and self-presentation.

Examining the manner in which some of the various attributes associated with honour could be privileged over others, within different spaces, different historical contexts, and, more narrowly, with reference to the situational and individual dynamics of a given interaction within these broader settings, can be revealing of the social norms and cultural constructs at play with respect to both personal and collective behaviour. The ways in which honour and reputation were articulated can thus also serve as a lens through which to view and analyse an array of matters. They can also provide a means through which to better understand the techniques used in forms of self-fashioning and self-presentation as they evolved in accordance with dictates surrounding personal and public behaviour, and the relative importance of various spheres of interaction and the relative weight accorded to an array of social relationships.

Change without Transformation

This analysis reveals little direct evidence to support the idea that there was a marked transition among the elite from a chivalric/militaristic ethos – notwithstanding that the direct involvement of the peerage in military service was declining – to a court-centred/humanist-influenced model of honour, or that the understanding that honour as vested in name and status was falling out of fashion during the years between 1540 and 1640.[9] This is, perhaps, somewhat surprising. The sixteenth and seventeenth centuries were ones of great change in many ways in early modern England (owing, for example, to rising levels of urbanization, shifts in conceptions of piety and religious identity occasioned by the religious upheavals of the period, the expansion of the state, the rising wealth and associated prominence of some segments of society, England's increasing integration into European politics and economic structures, and its expansion into the Atlantic). While one might expect to see a commensurate level of transformative change in social attitudes with respect to values such as honour, the reality is that truly meaningful shifts in the ways in which reputation and honour were constituted and enacted did not occur. Across the medieval and early modern periods and, to an extent, into the modern period, elites saw their personal honour and that of their lines as vested in proper displays of civility, management of their families and estates, competent self-government, and the external maintenance of the social order. Such understandings of honour could transcend other values, religious sensibilities and political outlooks included, and bound elites together; indeed, this shared sense of honour could serve to smooth over differences and mitigate quarrels in some instances, even as it could promote conflict in others.

Yet, while the large-scale meanings associated with honour noted above remained relatively static, the manner in which they were manifested in social behaviour did ultimately change. Elites in the years before 1540, through to 1640, and arguably in the years immediately following, made a connection between a loss of honour and a commensurate diminution of personal reputation and improperly offered or received hospitality, a lack of deference between parents and children and between spouses, removal from local office, improperly managed households, a failure to properly discipline servants, and uncivil forms of behaviour, alongside clinging to an understanding of their honour as inseparable from their bloodline and/or position in the social hierarchy. Yet such things now seem somewhat outmoded and antiquated.

This speaks to the reality that the varying levels of importance attached to the constitutive elements of honour did shift in subtle ways between 1540 and 1640, and beyond. In this sense, it is useful to think of honour in the period considered here in a manner similar to Judith Bennett's suggestion that the status of women in history be addressed as one of "change without transformation."[10] Like other cluster concepts, which, "because of their semantic sweep and referential breadth, are laced to the past, tethered to the present, and yet stretch tendrils towards the future," the various constituent elements of honour and reputation reviewed here waxed and waned alongside each other in accordance with the changing circumstances in which elites could find themselves.[11] Sometimes one meaning associated with honour rose in importance above another, and this affected the manner in which reputation was constructed and in which claims to honour were articulated, but this occurred without the overall range of meanings associated with honour and the diverse areas seen as connected to reputation necessarily being transformed.

Notwithstanding, as the social roles in which elites participated (and the relative importance attached to those roles) changed, they could privilege some meanings of honour over others with increased frequency. For example, the noted expansion of institutions of local governance in the period coupled with the growth of the courts, not to mention the rise in litigiousness, led many gentlemen to increasingly see the holding of local office and the role of mediator in local disputes, rather than an adherence to a martial ethos (although this remained a facet of personal reputation), as things which gained them honour among their peers and deference from their subordinates. Bureaucratic involvement in local politics and governance thus increasingly became a means by which gentlemen could gain honour and also be known and recognized as honourable within their communities by virtue of their promotion to magisterial office.

Along these lines there is much to be said for Andy Wood's argument concerning a perceived crisis of legitimation occasioned by the ideological challenges of the Henrician and Edwardian reformations, the ensuing breakdown of consensus between the nobility and the "commons" (specifically following the rebellions of 1549), and the eventual breaking apart of that "commons" as wealthier members became incorporated into the ranks of the gentry and into the service of the state.[12] Increasingly, men once on the periphery of government were becoming part of it, and this elevated status brought not only increased wealth but often also enhanced respect from both peers and subordinates, and a commensurate desire to consolidate status and stake a reputation as a true elite. It likewise conferred responsibilities associated with the maintenance and upholding of the social order which most gentlemen, both long established and newly minted, took very seriously. This expansion of local governance, and the growing sense of importance attached to the holding of such offices, certainly affected the level of import attached to the understanding of honour as rooted in displays of paternalism and service, but it did not entail the emergence of an entirely new understanding that supplanted an earlier one. Service to the monarch or a local magnate (often in a military capacity but also in a bureaucratic sense – and this bureaucratic dimension of service certainly did assume elevated importance in the early modern period) had also been a means to advance one's reputation in earlier periods.

There were perhaps subtle changes in other areas as well. Keith Thomas, for example, has theorized that, by the eighteenth and nineteenth centuries, people were slightly less preoccupied with issues of hierarchy and precedence than they once had been and increasingly saw it as uncivil and unseemly to quarrel publicly over such matters.[13] Fletcher has further speculated that the terminology of "honour" and some of its associated attributes and behaviours may have fallen out of fashion in these centuries as a rising middle class and the growth of urban centres increasingly saw them as outmoded, old fashioned, and socially discriminatory.[14] The roots of this shift may lie in the sixteenth and seventeenth centuries as displays of civility began to take on more importance than articulations of status as a marker of elite honour, especially so as the boundaries of what constituted status were largely permeable and "proper" behaviour could confirm social position in the period. Likewise, institutional changes with their beginnings in the later part of the period considered here, such as the spread of banks that overtook more personal-based credit interactions and the processes by which jury selection became more impersonal with respect to knowledge of the accused, may have made personal reputation and articulations of the possession of honour and status in financial and legal transactions less important.[15] Yet, for all this, social elites in these later periods were never truly averse to claiming the advantages that their status and position within the hierarchy afforded them, and to insisting upon those privileges when they felt it warranted. So, while these slow transformative processes may have affected in part the level of importance attached to some displays of status and honour, it did not negate them, and, for the elite, the importance of displaying wealth and emphasizing status persisted during the roughly one hundred years considered here, and retained importance well beyond.[16]

Shifting patterns of economic interaction, which also resulted in reconfigurations of the social hierarchy and the associated interactions between social groups within that hierarchy, also led to delicate shifts in social identity; this also surely, but subtly, affected the manner in which honour was conceived of and enacted, even if it did not result in a clear transformation in the early modern period. For example, an increased emphasis on manifesting the outward behaviour associated with gentility as a means to denote and consolidate status (as suggested above) assumed a great deal of importance among some gentlemen and gentlewomen. Thus, when they levelled attacks on others they were often based on allegations that the conventions of appropriately civil behaviour had been breached. This understanding of honour persisted across the period and remained in place into the eighteenth and nineteenth centuries – to an extent it still remains important to many in terms of personal reputation and serves (among some) to demarcate the "better sort" from others.

In addition, the desire to consolidate their relatively new positions among the elite led many members of the lesser gentry and other men on the rise to establish estates and marry into established families as a means to demarcate themselves as gentlemen. This caused members of the more long-established aristocracy and the upper ranks of the gentry a measure of anxiety and perhaps resulted in a reactionary tendency among some elites to cleave to their sense that honour was vested in bloodline, name, and status, even as more newly established elites worked to consolidate and promote their own bloodlines and estates, and so augment their honour. The importance of status and lineage thus largely persisted as a foundational element in elite understandings of honour, both among long established and newly minted families. A prominent place in the social hierarchy, and all the attendant associations with good reputation and honour that that entailed, was consistently and frequently invoked by all of the individuals considered here, even those who had only recently seen their families elevated. These new gentlemen extolled their bloodlines as much as those members of the ancient aristocracy did, and both groups often coveted positions of service of the state as a way to ensure they were properly recognized as leaders and governors.

The various active involvements which elite women perceived as connected to their honour and personal reputation, such as motherhood, the effective exercise of authority in housewifery and domestic management, economic honesty, and involvement in networks of sociability, likewise did not undergo a profound change either in the period considered here or in the years following (and, arguably, these still remain foundational elements in many women's conceptions of honourable conduct). Sexual probity, while far from being the most important element of a woman's honour in the early modern period, also still remains an element by which women's reputations are assessed, and by which they assess themselves – although the importance attached to this element of honour was and is highly negotiable with respect to actual behaviour.

Conversely, what may eventually have shifted was the level of importance attached to sexual probity as a source of honour among men, although not in the period analysed here. Dabhoiwala argues that there was a complex transformation in the eighteenth century following the emergence of libertine culture that contributed to the view that men were more sexually libidinous than women and that this led to their sexual rapacity being increasingly socially accepted. Accompanying this was a complex and gradual shift in the manner in which female sexuality was understood so that, by the nineteenth century, women were seen as sexually restrained in contrast to the unbridled sexual impulses of men – a change from sixteenth- and seventeenth-century attitudes that characterized women as the more licentious sex.[17] A reputation for sexual dissoluteness was certainly seen as potentially damaging by many sixteenth- and seventeenth-century gentlemen; yet, like gentlewomen, when it came to actual lived experience, many ignored this in favour of the pursuit of their own desires. While the value attached to sexual continence among men eventually did ebb in terms of its importance as a source of honour, this was not due to the emergence of a new meaning associated with honour but, rather, came as the result of a reevaluation of the level of importance accorded to this one element of reputation as a result of shifting understandings of social behaviour and medical knowledge. In addition, among men, the interconnectedness between the value accorded to sexual circumspection and one's place in the life cycle has endured – sexual indiscretions among mature men, established in society with the trappings of family stability and attendant responsibilities, remain a source of condemnation.

Attitudes towards the most outward and oft-pointed-to manifestation of honour, the duel, certainly did change by the eighteenth and nineteenth centuries, and the roots of this change can be seen in the period considered here. While never wholeheartedly socially accepted as a mechanism for earning and defending honour, duels certainly did occur in the period and this form of ritualized violence enjoyed a certain level of popularity among some segments of the early modern population. Yet the practice became obsolete by the 1850s, following a brief period of popularity from 1570 to 1620 (as it was taken up with enthusiasm for several years by a small contingent of gentlemanly society and portions of provincial society) and what Cockburn describes as an "inexplicable surge" in frequency between 1680 and 1700, at least in Kent.[18] We can see this transition in the prevalence of duelling occurring as the result of a strengthening of the idea (already well-established in the sixteenth and seventeenth centuries and existing alongside occasional and limited toleration of the duel) that such incidents were threatening to the social order, impolite, and not conducive to maintaining a good reputation. Such involvements displayed a lack of sober self-control that was not only unbecoming in a gentleman but also called into question one's ability to effectively exercise authority over social subordinates and hence play a role in governance, whether within the household and family or within state apparatuses of government. Given the growing number of such magisterial positions available and the increasing value attached to holding such offices as a way to affirm status and extend one's level of influence, gentlemen increasingly endeavoured to display themselves as upholders rather than disrupters of good order. Attitudes towards duelling and other such contests of honour, while always characterized by a measure of ambiguity, thus hardened and such activities were increasingly perceived in a negative light by many. This is not to say that violence ceased to be a very real part of the social landscape, or that there was a marked change in attitudes towards violence between the medieval and early modern periods, however. It is to suggest, rather, that the privileging of the idea that honour among gentlemen was vested in self-control and temperate behaviour over the notion that it was rooted in a willingness to defend reputation and standing at all costs perhaps came to be enacted with ever increasing frequency and regularity.

Like all cultural ideals that inform both outward behaviour and personal attitudes, the varying constituent parts of honour, and the level of privilege variously attached to them, did change and shift slowly over time, often is ways that are imperceptible. The wide array of meanings that honour could have were never entirely abandoned in favour of some new understanding, both in the period considered here and beyond, though the level of importance attached to these meanings was subject to change. Honour as a concept was functionally broad and encompassed a range of differing and often inconsistent behaviours and values. This elasticity ensured not only a level of durability when it came to honour's popularity and level of importance as a social value in the years between 1540 and 1640, but also made it unnecessary for one understanding of honour to overturn another and push it into obscurity. In this sense, continuity, mingled with fluidity, characterized honour. This is revealed through a focus on the minutiae of social interaction and self-fashioning in the period and the ways in which the varying levels of importance attached to the constituent parts of honour shifted without necessarily being transformed. Honour for the individuals considered here was not a static concept or blanket code of behaviour that mandated a fixed set of performative imperatives; rather, it was something far more elastic and complex. The paradox associated with honour is that while it was consistently and emphatically claimed by elites as of the utmost importance, it was simultaneously something that no one could define or structure with any degree of precision. Yet in its malleability lay its strength.

Just as reputation and honour mattered a great deal to early modern gentlemen and gentlewomen, they matter to us still and have retained a measure of their importance as social values. Granted, the manner in which honour is discussed has changed. For example, in current parlance we speak now more of good name or credibility than honour, while "reputation" remains a term of great social currency. But the core concept retains its primacy of place.[19] Then as now, honour and other such values remain vaguely defined and inherently protean, highly dependent on individual personalities and contexts for their meaning. For the early modern English elite (and among other social orders, for that matter), honour was "a 'discourse' tool that could be used to justify behaviour."[20] It remains one.

Notes

Introduction

1 Gouge, *Of Domesticall Duties*, 247.
2 Within the broader span of the loosely defined early modern period (c. 1500–1800), the years focused upon in this work are c. 1540–1640; see 22–3.
3 Thomas, *The Ends of Life*, 148.
4 As Jerrilyn Greene Marston notes, honour was a "force which governed the lives" of gentlemen in the period, a statement equally applicable to gentlewomen ("Gentry Honor and Royalism in Early Stuart England," 22).
5 Vincent's sermon was published in 1685. See Vincent, *The Right Notion of Honour*, 1.
6 On honour as a primary component of political discourse, see Richard C. McCoy, "Old English Honour in an Evil Time: Aristocratic Principle in the 1620s," in Smuts, ed., *The Stuart Court and Europe*, 133–55. See also Smuts, *Culture and Power in England, 1585–1685*, 15–17, and Kane, *The Politics and Culture of Honour in Britain and Ireland, 1541–1641.*
7 Pollock, "Honor, Gender and Reconciliation in Elite Culture, 1570–1700," 8.
8 Work by Linda Pollock, Faramerz Dabhoiwala, Cynthia Herrup, Garthine Walker, Laura Gowing, Alexandra Shepard, Eleanor Hubbard, and others has drawn attention to some of the varied contexts in which the language of honour and reputation was invoked and the ways in which its meanings were negotiated and understood.
9 As Cynthia Herrup has aptly described, "honour was less a single value than a selection from a medley of values. It was both quality and commodity, inborn and achieved, self-generated and bestowed, activist

and stoical (Herrup, "'To Pluck Bright Honour From the Pale-Faced Moon'," 138–9). See also Fletcher, *Gender, Sex and Subordination in England, 1500–1800*, 126.

10 Pollock, "Honor, Gender and Reconciliation."

11 Some of the themes and incidents investigated throughout this work are also touched upon (though in different contexts and to different ends) in Thomas, "'The Honour & Credite of the Whole House'," 329–45.

12 Pollock, "The Practice of Kindness in Early Modern Elite Society," 124.

13 Social constructs such as honour are equally well suited to an analysis rooted in the methodologies of *Histoire Croisée*, as they are concepts that can be studied across temporal and geographical borders within the framework of being entangled ideas. See Werner and Zimmermann, "Beyond Comparison," 30–50, and Kocka, "Comparison and Beyond," 39–44.

14 Thomas, *The Ends of Life*, 177.

15 Pollock, "The Practice of Kindness," 123.

16 BOD, Ashmole 1184, Robert Ashley, *Of Honour*, c. 1596, f. 141r.

17 Bryson, *From Courtesy to Civility*, 107.

18 The most important proponent of this idea is Mervyn James (*Society, Politics and Culture* and *English Politics and the Concept of Honour*), but similar themes were earlier raised by Lawrence Stone in his *The Crisis of the Aristocracy, 1558–1641*. For other works that portray honour as transitioning throughout the medieval and early modern period, see Stewart, *Honor*, and Muir, *Mad Blood Stirring*; Muir's work, of course, examines honour in a very different context that the one considered here.

19 See Elias, *The Civilizing Process*. Despite its high level of influence and its usefulness as an explanatory model regarding the emergence of polite society, Elias's analysis (and its use by James) is open to criticism. See, for example, Bryson, *From Courtesy to Civility*, 11, and Rosenwein, "Theories of Change in the History of Emotions," in Liliequist, ed., *A History of Emotions, 1200–1800*, 7–20. Other scholars dispute James's idea of a transition in attitudes concerning honour, especially with respect to changing levels of elite violence; see Peltonen, *The Duel in Early Modern England*, Beaver, *Hunting and the Politics of Violence Before the English Civil War*, Beaver, "'Bragging and Daring Words': Honour, Property and Symbolism of the Hunt in Stowe, 1590–1642," in Braddick and Walter, eds., *Negotiating Power in Early Modern Society*, 149–65, and Caroline Hibbard, "The Theatre of Dynasty," in Smuts, ed., *The Stuart Court and Europe*, 156–76.

20 On the expansion of the state's monopoly on violence, see Carroll, *Blood and Violence in Early Modern France*, and Carroll, "The Peace in the Feud

in Sixteenth- and Seventeenth-Century France," 98–9. On the history of emotions, see Forth, Cribb, and Strange, eds., *Honour, Violence and Emotions in History*, Liliequist, ed., *A History of Emotions*, Champion and Lynch, eds., *Understanding Emotions in Early Europe*, Rosenwein, *Emotional Communities in the Early Middle Ages*, Rosenwein, "Worrying About Emotions in History," 821–45, Rosenwein, ed., *Anger's Past*, Frevert, *Emotions in History*, and Plamper, *The History of Emotions*.

21 On the idea of a transition in political life and modes of conduct as a result of an expanded understanding of civility and the role of education, see Bryson, *From Courtesy to Civility*, 24–35, 49–53, and 61–71.

22 For James, groupings at the centre of early modern politics, such as the Sidney circle, articulated this new conception of honour most cogently, while the best example of its antithesis could be found in Robert Devereux, Earl of Essex (1565–1601). Building on James's analysis, Felicity Heal notes that members of the Cecil circle were also key proponents and exemplars of this understanding of honour as rooted in service and civility. See Heal, "Reputation and Honour in Court and Country," 162. On the Earl of Essex, see Hammer, *The Polarization of Elizabethan Politics*, Dickinson, *Court Politics and the Earl of Essex, 1589–1601*, and Gajda, *The Earl of Essex and Late Elizabethan Political Culture*.

23 Francis Hastings to Robert Devereux, 9 September 1588, in Cross, ed., *The Letters of Sir Francis Hastings, 1574–1609*, 39, taken from MS HA 5090 at the Huntington Library.

24 Herrup, *A House in Gross Disorder*, 77.

25 Janet Dickinson, "Nobility and Gentry," in Doran and Jones, eds., *The Elizabethan World*, 285.

26 This has been suggested by Richard Cust in his "Honour, Rhetoric and Political Culture: The Earl of Huntingdon and His Enemies," in Amussen and Kishlansky, eds., *Political Culture and Cultural Politics in Early Modern England*, 90–2. See also Asch, *Nobilities in Transition, 1550–1700*, 80–1, 88, and 99–100, and Cust, "Honour and Politics in Early Stuart England," 57–94. Peltonen likewise contends that these two concepts of honour existed in tandem in early modern England (Peltonen, "Francis Bacon," 1–28).

27 Quentin Skinner, "Language and Political Change," in Ball, Farr, and Hanson, eds., *Political Innovation and Conceptual Change*, 6–23.

28 Dabhoiwala, "The Construction of Honour, Reputation and Status," 201.

29 Martin Ingram, "Sexual Manners: The Other Face of Civility in Early Modern England," in Burke, Harrison, and Slack, eds., *Civil Histories*, 98. On the need to pay close attention to language as a historical construct that

shifts over time and between places, see Burke and Porter, eds., *The Social History of Language*.

30 From the "challenge of deedes of Armes of Phillip Boyle knight" and the "challenge of Peires de Masse," in Anon., Undated Commonplace Book [Mid-Seventeenth Century], Osborn Fb 162 (BRBM), ff. 23v–24v, 63v–64v, 113r–114r, 114v, and 143v. See also Markham, *The Booke of Honour*, Sir Edward Dering, bart., *History of the Dering Family from the time of the Conquest*, c. 1635, Z.e.27 (FSL), and Anon., *Book on Heraldry*, c. 1590, V.a.466 (FSL), ff. 22r–54v. There are also countless ranked lists of peers and other elites to be found in commonplace books and other manuscripts from the period. See, for example, the lengthy lists of members of the English nobility found in the historical notebook and memorandum book owned by Edward and Henry Stafford that was compiled c. 1562 and is currently held by the Huntington Library, HM 202. Countless other commonplace books collected moral maxims on honourable conduct. See, for example, William Hill, Undated Commonplace Book [Mid-Seventeenth Century], Osborn b 234 (BRBM) and Thomas Dowbiggen, Undated Commonplace Book [Late Seventeenth Century], Osborn b 53 (BRBM).

31 For more on forms of address and their importance in framing social interactions within the hierarchical classification of society, see Postles, *Social Proprieties*. On honour in the context of intellectual credibility and scientific knowledge, see Shapin, *A Social History of the Truth*, and Chamberland, "Between the Hall and the Market," 69–90.

32 Richardson, *Pamela*, 193.

33 Martin Ingram, "Law, Litigants and the Construction of 'Honour': Slander Suits in Early Modern England," in Coss, ed., *The Moral World of the Law*, 139.

34 Interestingly, the meaning of honour as some sort of a code, a set of rules, does not appear until 1785, according to the *OED* (*OED*, s.v.).

35 Elyot, *The Dictionary of Syr Thomas Eliot Knyght*. Available online at http://leme.library.utoronto.ca/lexicon/text.cfm.

36 See Baret, *An Aluearie Or Triple Dictionarie, in Englishe, Latin, and French*. Available online at http://leme.library.utoronto.ca/lexicon/text.cfm.

37 FSL, V.b.125, Anon., *The Excellencie of Man, His Nobilitie, Praise, Glory, Honour, and Dignitie*, c.1610, f. 4r.

38 Ibid., ff. 10v, 28r.

39 Cooper, *Thesaurus linguae Romanae & Britannicae*. Available online at http://leme.library.utoronto.ca/lexicon/text.cfm.

40 Florio, *A Worlde of Wordes*. Available online at http://leme.library.utoronto.ca/lexicon/text.cfm.

41 Cotgrave, *A Dictionarie of the French and English Tongues*. Available online at http://leme.library.utoronto.ca/lexicon/text.cfm.

42 Wilson, *A Christian Dictionarie*. Available online at http://leme.library.utoronto.ca/lexicon/text.cfm.

43 Cawdrey, *A Table Alphabeticall*. Available online at http://leme.library.utoronto.ca/lexicon/text.cfm.

44 See Thomas, *Dictionarium linguae Latinae et Anglicanae*. Available online at http://leme.library.utoronto.ca/lexicon/text.cfm.

45 Marston, "Gentry Honor and Royalism," 25. Thus, for example, Robert Ashley's 1596 text, *Of Honour*, was heavily rooted in Aristotelian thought and, in particular, the concept of proper moderation in all forms of conduct. Ashley's work (based upon HL, MS EL 1117, rather than that held by the Bodleian) has been published by Virgil B. Heltzel. The text is analysed in more detail by Casellas in "The Social Function of the Renaissance Concept of Honour," 83–7. See also Heltzel, "Robert Ashley," 349–63. In Heltzel's estimation, Ashley's work constituted the first attempt by an Englishman to "deal with the concept of honor comprehensively and systematically" (Heltzel, "Robert Ashley," 349).

46 See Aristotle, *Nicomachean Ethics*, ed. Broadie and Rowie.

47 Peacham, *The Compleat Gentleman*, 3.

48 Peter Burke, "A Civil Tongue: Language and Politeness in Early Modern Europe," in Burke, Harrison, and Slack, eds., *Civil Histories*, 36.

49 BOD, Ashmole 1184, Ashley, *Of Honour*, c. 1596, f. 143r.

50 Donagan, "The Web of Honour," 366.

51 Thomas, *The Ends of Life*, 155.

52 See Stewart, *Honor*. Stewart's analysis adopts a cross-cultural approach to analyse honour from the Renaissance to the present day comparatively alongside the Bedouin idea of honour (or *'ird*).

53 Pollock, "Honor, Gender and Reconciliation," 5.

54 Smith, *De Republica Anglorum*.

55 Smith's work circulated in manuscript form prior to its publication and Harrison elaborated upon it. See Shepard, *Accounting For Oneself*, 3.

56 Furnivall, ed., *Harrison's Description of England in Shakespeare's Youth*, part I, chapter 5. The work of Smith and then Harrison was later expanded upon by other early demographers such as Gregory King. See also Wrightson, *English Society, 1580–1680*, 26–46, Wrightson, "Estates, Degrees and Sorts: Changing Perceptions of Society in Tudor and Stuart England," in Corfield, ed., *Language, History, and Class*, 30–52, and Shepard, *Accounting For Oneself*, 3–9, where the flexibility (and problematic nature, especially with reference to classifications of

members of the lower social orders) of contemporary categorizations of social classes is addressed.

57 Smith, *De Republica Anglorum*, 39–40.

58 On the link between social identity and material possessions in the period, see Shepard, *Accounting For Oneself*. According to Shepard, "social identity in early modern England was rooted in the possession of moveable estate" (35). As Shepard's analysis suggests, this remained true until the years following the Restoration when, as the result of changes to financial structures and the expansion of consumerism, the means by which evaluations of others, of self, and of self-worth were made began to subtly shift. Her analysis, likewise, suggests that the link between social identity and moveable property was just as potent as that between the possession of land and social identity.

59 See Heal and Holmes, *The Gentry in England and Wales, 1500–1700*, 6–19.

60 Shepard, *Accounting For Oneself*, 233.

61 Anna Bryson, "The Rhetoric of Status: Gesture, Demeanour and the Image of the Gentleman in Sixteenth- and Seventeenth-Century England," in Gent and Llewellyn, eds., *Renaissance Bodies*, 136.

62 Fletcher, *A County Community in Peace and War*, 22. See also Smith, *Land and Politics in The England of Henry VIII*, 43–84 and 123–64, where the difficulties of defining the gentry and nobility as bounded social groups are discussed, and Bernard, *The Power of the Early Tudor Nobility*. For other county studies which attempt to sketch the contours of the local gentry class, see Barnes, *Somerset, 1625–1640*, Everitt, *The Community of Kent*, Powis, *Aristocracy*, MacCulloch, *Suffolk and the Tudors*, and Chalklin, *Seventeenth-Century Kent*.

63 Bush, *The English Aristocracy*, 1.

64 Dickinson, "Nobility and Gentry," 286.

65 See Wood, *The 1549 Rebellions*, Hindle, *The State and Social Change in Early Modern England*, Withington, *Society in Early Modern England*, Heal and Holmes, *The Gentry in England and Wales*, 24–33, and Jones, *Governing by Virtue*, 27–43.

66 Newton, *North-East England*, 22, and Mertes, *The English Noble Household*, 4.

67 French, *The Middle Sort of People*, 200.

68 Rosenwein developed the idea of the "emotional community" and defines it as a group "in which people adhere to the same norms of emotional expression and value – or devalue – the same or related emotions" (Rosenwein, *Emotional Communities*, 3).

69 Withington, *Society in Early Modern England*, 219.

70 Kane, "From Irish Eineach to British Honor?," 416.

71 For a discussion of the benefits of an analysis of practice, see French and Rothery, "'Upon Your Entry into the World'," 403–4, and French and Rothery, *Man's Estate*, 1–38.
72 Stretton, *Women Waging Law in Elizabethan England*, 240.
73 In doing so, it builds upon and extends work done by Pollock in her "Honor, Gender and Reconciliation."
74 For a bibliography of prescriptive texts and behavioural guides published in the period, see Kelso, *Doctrine of the English Gentleman in the Sixteenth Century*, and Kelso, *Doctrine for the Lady of the Renaissance*.
75 Bryson, *From Courtesy to Civility*, 6.
76 See Goldberg, *Writing* Matter, 254–5. See also Herbert, *Female Alliances*, and Tague, *Women of Quality*.
77 See, for example, Keenan, "'Embracing Submission'?," 69–85.
78 Pollock, "The Practice of Kindness," 155.
79 Anne Kugler's work on the diaries of Sarah Cowper, for example, reveals the ways in which Cowper utilized prescriptive literature as a mechanism to criticize her husband for not allowing her a greater share of authority within the household. Cowper outlined her criticisms, and her extensive use of prescriptive literature, in a diary she began in her 50s. See Kugler, "Constructing Wifely Identity," 291–323, and Kugler, *Errant Plagiary*.
80 On early modern epistolary networks and their importance, see O'Neill, *The Opened Letter*.
81 See Daybell, *Women Letter-Writers in Tudor England*, 265.
82 On letters as sources, the materiality of letters, and the epistolary culture and conventions of the period, see Walter J. Ong, "Writing is a Technology that Restructures Thought," in Baumann, ed., *The Written Word*, 23–50, Daybell, *The Material Letter in Early Modern England*, Mack, *Elizabethan Rhetoric*, Bannet, *Empire of Letters*, and Schneider, *The Culture of Epistolarity*. On women's epistolary self-fashioning and associated gender tropes, see Daybell, "Gender, Obedience, and Authority," Daybell, ed., *Early Modern Women's Letter Writing, 1450–1700*, Daybell, *Women Letter-Writers in Tudor England*, and Couchman and Crabb, eds., *Women's Letters Across Europe*.
83 Women, for example, were often careful to present themselves as being in accord with proper feminine attitudes and modes of interaction in their correspondence. For analysis of this in one set of elite women's letters, the Thynne women, see Alison Wall, "Deference and Defiance in Women's Letters of the Thynne Family: The Rhetoric of Relationships," in Daybell, ed., *Early Modern Women's Letter Writing*, 77–93 and Williams, *Women's Epistolary Utterance*, 1–18.

84 See Barclay, "Negotiating Patriarchy," 86, and Bossis and McPherson, "Methodological Journeys Through Correspondence," 63–75.
85 Likewise, desiring to assess how honour operated in day-to-day social interactions, I have not attempted here to meaningfully engage with the potent use of honour in political discourse in the tumultuous decades after 1640 – this would be a separate study unto itself.

1 Men and Honour

1 Recent work on honour, for example, points to its more varied meanings and to the numerous other aspects of social interaction in which gentlemen saw issues of reputation at play.
2 While Philippa Maddern has persuasively shown that violence was not as endemic or socially destabilizing in the medieval period as earlier scholarship suggested (see Maddern, *Violence and Social Order*), violence was a very real component of the early modern social landscape, as scholars such as Stone, Sharpe, and Cockburn have shown (see n. 4 below). Likewise, physical confrontations over matters of reputation remain relatively common, although the efficiency and efficacy with which they are punished has evolved.
3 For the complexities of early modern conflict resolution, see the essays in Cummins and Kounine, eds., *Cultures of Conflict Resolution in Early Modern Europe*.
4 While physical conflict was very much a part of life in the early modern period (as remains the case), there are a series of difficulties inherent both in quantifying and explaining levels of violence. On this topic, and the debate surrounding the degree to which early modern English communities were conflict-ridden and the extent to which levels of violence declined as "modernity" took hold, see Stone, "Interpersonal Violence in English Society 1300–1800," 22–33, Sharpe, "The History of Violence in England: Some Observations," 206–15, Stone, "The History of Violence in England," 216–24, and Cockburn, "Patterns of Violence in English Society," 70–106. See also Ruff, *Violence in Early Modern Europe, 1500–1800*. Ruff argues, in accord with Stone, that levels of violence among the English aristocracy declined in the seventeenth century, as they increasingly embraced an ethos of courtier culture (a viewpoint shared by Sharpe in his *Crime in Early Modern England, 1550–1750*, 96–9; notwithstanding this, however, Sharpe does perceive a short-lived spike in homicides between 1580 and 1620 in the Home Counties [83–4]). Likewise, Gurr theorized a downward trend in homicide rates over a

span of centuries ("Historical Trends in Violent Crime," 295–353). See also K.J. Kesselring, "'Murder's Crimson Badge': Homicide in the Age of Shakespeare," in Smuts, ed., *The Oxford Handbook of the Age of Shakespeare*, 543–58.

5 Muldrew, "The Culture of Reconciliation," 919–20. Earlier examinations of anger and violence in early modern society often ran parallel in many senses to those of honour. They advanced a teleological argument: namely, that as "civility" took hold, anger and its associated behaviours, such as physical confrontation or honour-based violence, were increasingly repressed within social interactions (see Pollock, "Anger and the Negotiation of Relationships," 568).

6 While women were much more likely to mount verbal, rather than physical, attacks on those who aroused their ire, they too resorted to violence at times, and we should be wary of "the simple correlation of men's disputes with violence, women's with words" (Crawford and Gowing, eds., *Women's Worlds in Seventeenth-Century England*, 223). On violence and gender, see also Kesselring, "Bodies of Evidence," 245–62, and Walker, *Crime, Gender, and Social Order in Early Modern England*. On women's anger, see Kennedy, *Just Anger*.

7 Ibid., 576; see also Hibbard, "The Theatre of Dynasty," 157–63.

8 Anger could also be cast as the prerogative of authoritative men, the expression of which signalled their power when it was directed toward just ends. See Downame, *Foure Treatises*, 205.

9 Stafford, *The Guide of Honour*, 84.

10 While some have argued that neighbourliness was a value in decline among increasingly polarized communities after 1550, others maintain that it was "neither a waning relic … nor necessarily a declining ethos." The sources examined throughout this work suggest that neighbourliness (a value that, like honour, possessed a measure of flexibility with respect to its enactment) remained a dynamic and important value. On neighbourliness, see Steve Hindle, "A Sense of Place?: Becoming and Belonging in the Rural Parish, 1550–1650," in Shepard and Withington, eds., *Communities in Early Modern England*, 96–113, Naomi Tadmor, "Friends and Neighbours in Early Modern England: Biblical Translations and Social Norms," in Gowing et al., eds., *Love, Friendship, and Faith in Europe, 1300–1800*, 150–76, and Keith Wrightson, "The 'Decline of Neighbourliness' Revisited," in Jones and Woolf, eds., *Local Identities in Late Medieval and Early Modern England*, 19–49.

11 On violence and its social and political meanings, see Kesselring, *Mercy and Authority in the Tudor State*, Maddern, *Violence and Social Order*, Beaver,

Hunting and the Politics of Violence, Wood, "Collective Violence, Social Drama and Rituals on Rebellion in Late Medieval and Early Modern England," in Carroll, ed., *Cultures of Violence*, 99–116, and Amussen, "Punishment, Discipline and Power," 1–34.

12 Pollock, "Honor, Gender and Reconciliation," 8.

13 SHC, LM/COR/3/150, Dr John Griffith to William More, 18 April 1567.

14 James, *Society, Politics and Culture*, and Stone, *The Crisis of the Aristocracy*. For a general history of duelling, see Frevert, *Men of Honour*, and Kiernan, *The Duel in European History*.

15 See Asch, *Nobilities in Transition, 1550–1700*, 73, for the level of duelling at the French court. See also Billaçois, *The Duel*, 29–30, and Cockburn, "Patterns of Violence," 84.

16 See Peltonen, *The Duel in Early Modern England*, 93, and Peltonen, "'Civilized with Death': Civility, Duelling and Honour in Elizabethan England," in Richards, ed., *Early Modern Civil Discourses*, 51–67. On the duel's importation from Italy, see Quint, "Duelling and Civility in Sixteenth Century Italy," 231–4, and Selden, *The Duello or Single Combat*. Selden also produced a work on honour that articulated the view that all honour owed to gentlemen came via virtue and that all civil honours were granted solely by the sovereign, thus arguing against the honour of hereditary bloodlines (Selden, *Titles of Honor*).

17 The figures are taken, respectively, from Andrew, *Aristocratic Vice*, 47, and Pollock, "Honor, Gender and Reconciliation," 7. Marston similarly points to the low levels of actual duels that occurred in early modern England ("Gentry Honor and Royalism," 24–5). On statistics from Kent, where killings with bladed weapons accounted for 37 per cent of homicides between 1570 and 1620, followed by a quick decline and then a short-lived increase, see Cockburn, "Patterns of Violence," 84. As Cockburn notes, "the impact of duelling on the pattern of provincial homicide, though dramatic, was relatively short-lived" (84).

18 Peltonen, *The Duel in Early Modern England*, 82, 202–3, and 205.

19 Cockburn, "Patterns of Violence," 84.

20 The reasons for this are obscure; they may perhaps relate to the higher number of foreigners present in London, increasing the average person's exposure to duelling culture, or perhaps to the more claustrophobic and charged atmosphere with ample opportunities for competition that the city offered.

21 Stone, *The Crisis of the Aristocracy*, 112–13.

22 The Court had been founded for several centuries before it was revitalized by Northampton. During the 1630s it presided over an

unprecedented level of cases before being abolished by Parliament in the wake of the Civil War and then established again following the Restoration.

23 See Cust and Hooper, eds., *Cases in the High Court of Chivalry, 1634–1640*, and Squibb, *The High Court of Chivalry*. The records of the Court, which survive for 738 of some 1,000 cases heard between 1634 and 1640, are also accessible online at http://www.birmingham.ac.uk/schools/historycultures/departments/history/research/projects/court-of-chivalry/index.aspx/.

24 On the construction of gentility from the Middle Ages onward with reference to land-holding, see Keen, *Origins of the English Gentleman*.

25 On the printed criticisms of duelling in the eighteenth century, see Andrew, "The Code of Honour and Its Critics," 409–34, and Andrew, *Aristocratic Vice*, 43–81. Andrew suggests that duelling became more public, and thus more open to criticism, as a result of the expansion of the press in the eighteenth century. She argues that this was accompanied by a wide-ranging attack on the perceived vices of the aristocracy by the middling sort, who believed that elites flouted social conventions and the law with impunity and cloaked their transgressions in the meaningless language of honour – the example of Baron Mohun's activities offering, for many, an apt example of this (see n. 28, below).

26 On the role and prevalence of the duel among non-aristocratic circles, see Shoemaker, "The Taming of the Duel," 525–45, and Shoemaker, "Male Honour and the Decline of Public Violence in Eighteenth-Century London," 190–208.

27 Stephen Banks concludes that duelling in England, while never occurring at high levels, had died out completely by 1845 (Banks, "Killing with Courtesy," 528–58) and Donna Andrew concurs (Andrew, *Aristocratic Vice*, 243). See also Banks, *A Polite Exchange of Bullets*.

28 See Stater, *Duke Hamilton Is Dead*, and Stater, *High Life, Low Morals*.

29 Peltonen has demonstrated this in an examination of printed arguments on duelling published between 1500 and 1700 (Peltonen, *The Duel in Early Modern England*, 35–44). For an analysis of attitudes toward duelling after 1700, see Andrew, "The Code of Honour and Its Critics."

30 Beaver, *Hunting and the Politics of Violence*, 15–31.

31 In this line of thinking, far from being an indicator of unconstrained violence and social misbehaviour, the duel could be interpreted as a set of principles that served to restrain expressions of anger related to honour and, in doing so, preserve gentility as linked to self-mastery and stable conduct (Peltonen, *The Duel in Early Modern England*, 52; see

also Robert A. Nye, "How the Duel of Honour Promoted Civility and Attenuated Violence in Western Europe," in Forth, Cribb, and Strange, eds., *Honour, Violence and Emotions in History*, 183–202). Other scholars have reinterpreted the role of bloodfeuds in a similar manner, suggesting that they could function to maintain order and minimize outbreaks of violence. See Brown, *Bloodfeud in Scotland 1573–1625*, and Fletcher, *Bloodfeud*.

32 The most popular duelling manual of the period, written by an Italian who, like Rocco Bonita, established a fencing school in London in the 1590s, was Saviolo's *Vincentio Sauiolo His Practise In Two Bookes*.

33 The importance of the perception of self-mastery as a foundational component of masculine identity has featured prominently in several recent works on the history of masculinity. See Reinke-Williams, "Manhood and Masculinity in Early Modern England," 685–93.

34 On humoural compositions, see commentators such as Lemnius, *The Secret Miracles of Nature*, Book IV.

35 Helkiah Crooke, *Mikrokosmographia, A Description of the Body of Man* (1616), as cited in Kesselring, "Bodies of Evidence," 254. Crooke was physician to King James VI and I.

36 As Pollock has noted, anger was, and remains, a highly gendered emotion. See Pollock, "Anger and the Negotiation of Relationships," 578, Frevert, *Emotions in History*, 87–147, and Susan Broomhall, "Destroying Order, Structuring Disorder: Gender and Emotions," in Broomhall, ed., *Gender and Emotions in Medieval and Early Modern Europe*, 1–13. On the destructive potential of affective states, see the introduction by Broomhall and Finn to their *Violence and Emotions in Early Modern Europe*, 1–18, and Christine Battersby, "The Man of Passion: Emotion, Philosophy and Sexual Difference," in Gouk and Hills, eds., *Representing Emotions*, 139–54.

37 Ambrose Randolph to Lady Jane Cornwallis, 21 November 1634, in Bacon, *The Private Correspondence of Jane, Lady Cornwallis, 1613–44*, 197.

38 Ibid.

39 Fletcher, *A County Community*, 54–5.

40 In many ways, the early modern legal system was extraordinarily tolerant of violence and convictions were rare.

41 Herrup, *A House in Gross Disorder*, 27. Herrup uses this language in reference to the crimes of rape and sodomy.

42 On the discretionary nature of the law, see Herrup, "Law and Morality in Seventeenth Century England," 102–23, and Herrup, *The Common Peace*. Ingram, in *Church Courts, Sex and Marriage in England, 1570–1640*, and Beattie, in *Crime and the Courts in England, 1660–1800*, have also

addressed the theme of discretion within both criminal prosecutions and presentments to the church courts.

43 While lawmakers often viewed such acts of violence as inexcusable and legislated against them accordingly, jurors and those involved with the actual administration of the law could be more inclined to offer moderate sentences when injury or death was perceived to have arisen in the context of a fairly conducted conflict – while such things could not be entirely excused legally, they were also not necessarily worthy of punishment that accorded with the full rigours of the law.

44 Edward Coke, "An Acte to Take Away the Benefit of Clergy From Some Kinde of Manslaughter" (or the "Statute of Stabbing") in *Institutes of the Laws of England*, 56. Chancemedley remained an offense distinct from voluntary manslaughter (rooted in provocation) until the mid-nineteenth century (see Horder, "The Duel and the English Law of Homicide," 28–9; see also Horder, *Provocation and Responsibility*).

45 Coke, *Statute of Stabbing*.

46 Horder, "The Duel and the English Law of Homicide," 422.

47 Hindle, *The State and Social Change*, 131.

48 See Herrup, "Law and Morality," 111.

49 Ibid., 202.

50 Anon. [attributed to Henry Howard], *A Publication of His Ma[jes]ties Edict*.

51 Andrew, *Aristocratic Vice*, 22.

52 Bacon, *The Charge of Sir Francis Bacon*, 12.

53 Ibid., 42 and 55.

54 Anon., *A Publication of His Ma[jes]ties Edict*, 103.

55 In asserting a monopoly on violence and control, states must necessarily officially condemn both crime and private justice. Likewise, while the heightened frequency of governmental condemnations of duelling may also be taken to indicate its widespread nature, they can also just as easily be read as a sign of the regime's near obsession with the preservation of order.

56 BRBM, Osborn b 230, Anon. [attributed to William Sandys], Undated Commonplace Book [Mid-Seventeenth Century].

57 Ibid., f. 48r.

58 Ibid.

59 Ibid.

60 Ibid., f. 215r.

61 Martyn, *Youths Instruction*, 18.

62 BRBM, Osborn b 230, Anon. [attributed to William Sandys], Undated Commonplace Book [Mid-Seventeenth Century], f. 47r.

63 Withington, "Public Discourse, Corporate Citizenship, and State Formation in Early Modern England," 1018. See also Withington, *The Politics of Commonwealth*.

64 Withington, *Society in Early Modern England*, 217. Members of the aristocracy also historically claimed a right to involvement in governance.

65 Wood, *The 1549 Rebellions*, 188.

66 The refusal to hold a particular office often involved the payment of a fee and, while not all gentlemen were universally eager to accept various appointments, many recognized the potential for influence and possible financial benefits (or penalties, if refused) inherent in such posts.

67 See Braddick, *State Formation*, 29–35, Eastwood, *Government and Community*, 119, Hindle, *The State and Social Change*, 19–21, Patrick Collinson, "The Monarchical Republic of Queen Elizabeth I," in Collinson, ed., *Elizabethan Essays*, 31–57, Hindle, "Hierarchy and Community in the Elizabethan Parish," 835–51, and Clark and Slack, "Introduction," in Clark and Slack, eds., *Crisis and Order in English Towns, 1500–1700*, 22. See also n. 65 in the introductory chapter.

68 Hindle, *The State and Social Change*, 175. See also Hindle, "Hierarchy and Community in the Elizabethan Parish," 848.

69 Fletcher, *Gender, Sex and Subordination*, 145. On the idea that government in this period was essentially local, see Jones, *The English Reformation*, 135. While the expansion of opportunities for local office was a feature of the early modern period, it is worthwhile to emphasize that ample opportunities for service within communities and to local magnates also existed in the medieval period and were seen by gentlemen then as important means by which to augment their local reputations.

70 Thomas, *The Ends of Life*, 151. See also Anthony Fletcher, "Honour, Reputation and Local Office Holding in Elizabethan and Stuart England," in Fletcher and Stevenson, eds., *Order and Disorder in Early Modern England*, 92–115.

71 See Fletcher, *Gender, Sex and Subordination*, 147, and Wall, "'The Greatest Disgrace'," 312–32.

72 Sharp, *Memorials of the Rebellion of 1569*, 318.

73 James, *Society, Politics and Culture*, 296–7.

74 There were, of course, exceptions to this, often revolving around how elevated one's status was and the complexities of deep-rooted patronage relationships.

75 Hicks, "Talbot, Gilbert," accessed 26 September 2014, http://www.oxforddnb.com/view/article/26930.

76 Ibid.

77 Ibid. Gilbert, while possessing an ancient bloodline and claims to a vast estate, had many enemies by his death in 1616 as the result of his litigious manner, spendthrift habits, and argumentative nature.
78 On violence and masculinity in early modern drama and literature, see Low, *Manhood and the Duel*, Saul, *Chivalry in Medieval England*, 305–24, and Davis, *Chivalry and Romance in the English Renaissance*.
79 See, for example, Lloyd, *A Brief Discourse*.
80 Foyster, "Male Honour, Social Control and Wife Beating in Late Stuart England," 215.
81 See Shepard, *Meanings of Manhood* and Foyster, *Manhood in Early Modern England*.
82 Lemnius, *The Secret Miracles*, Book IV, 274.
83 Shepard, *Meanings of Manhood*, 48–69.
84 Ibid., 128.
85 A certain degree of permissiveness with respect to violence was present in relation to the young in much the same way that excessive drinking was more acceptable among them. But among men who were perceived to have reached their maturity, drunkenness, like violence, was seen as subversive of the social order, as it indicated an insufficient mastery of self. See Alexandra Shepard, "'Swil-bols and Tos-pots': Drink Culture and Male Bonding in England 1560–1640," in Gowing et al., eds., *Love, Friendship, and Faith*, 110–30.
86 SHC, LM/COR/3/99, Francis Walsingham to William More, 7 July 1569.
87 Ibid.
88 SHC, LM 6729/2/25, Thomas Egerton, Lord Keeper, to Robert Devereux, Earl of Essex, 1601.
89 Ibid.
90 FSL, L.a.45, Anthony Bagot to Richard Bagot, 1 March 1592/3.
91 On the subjects of youth, authority, disobedience, and the maturation process, see Paul Griffiths, "Tudor Troubles: Problems of Youth in Elizabethan England," in Doran and Jones, eds., *The Elizabethan World*, 316–34, Griffiths, *Youth and Authority*, and Ben-Amos, *Adolescence and Youth in Early Modern England*.
92 Shepard, "'Swil-bols and Tos-pots'," 115. As Herrup notes, "self-mastery was the characteristic that distinguished a responsible adult male" (*A House in Gross Disorder*, 71).
93 See Marston, "Gentry Honour and Royalism," 32. See also Andrew, "The Code of Honour and its Critics," 414, and, on duelling within the military in the eighteenth and nineteenth centuries, see Andrew, *Aristocratic Vice*, 58–70.

94 Thomas, *The Ends of Life*, 44–77. See also Rapple, *Martial Power and Elizabethan Political Culture*, chapter 1 and 38–46 specifically. While the direct involvement of the elite in military engagements was declining across the period (notwithstanding the spike which occurred during the Civil Wars), at times during the seventeenth century a nevertheless high proportion of living peers had seen military service (see Manning, *Swordsmen*).

95 Beaver, *Hunting and the Politics of Violence*, 15–31 and Peter Sherlock, "Militant Masculinity and the Monuments of Westminster Abbey," in Broomhall and Van Gent, eds., *Governing Masculinities*, 131–52.

96 On the early modern English soldiery fighting in defence of Protestantism, see Trim, "Calvinist Internationalism," 1024–48 (and for a counter view, see Rapple, *Martial Power*).

97 Donagan, "The Web of Honour," 371.

98 FSL, X.d.428 (9), Henry Cavendish to Elizabeth Talbot, Countess of Shrewsbury, c. 1570.

99 Ibid.

100 Ibid.

101 Ibid.

102 Ibid.

103 Ibid.

104 Durant, *Bess of Hardwick*, 20.

105 Gilbert was both Henry's brother-in-law (Henry was married to Gilbert's sister, Grace, and Gilbert was married to Henry's sister, Mary), and his step-brother, as Gilbert's father, George, the sixth Earl of Shrewsbury, was married to Henry's mother, Elizabeth Talbot.

106 Pollock, "Honor, Gender and Reconciliation," 7.

107 The episode is chronicled in the commonplace book of John Brown. See BRBM, Osborn Fb 155, John Brown, Undated Commonplace Book, 225. Another account of the conflict appears in the Ellesmere Papers, this one dated to 1602, very soon after the events it describes occurred. See HL, MS EL 404, Account of a Quarrel Between the Earl of Northumberland and Sir Francis Vere, before 21 April 1602.

108 BRBM, Osborn Fb 155, John Brown, Undated Commonplace Book, 225.

109 Ibid.

110 Ibid., 227.

111 Ibid., 228.

112 Ibid., 229.

113 Ibid., 230.

114 Quint, "Duelling and Civility," 257.

115 See n. 107, above.

116 This was one of the more notorious episodes of duelling in the Jacobean period and, as Peltonen discusses, resulted in the regime taking "more decisive action to abolish duelling," including spurring the revitalization of the Court of Chivalry (Peltonen, *The Duel in Early Modern England*, 83–4).

117 FSL, X.d.165, Edward Sackville to Edward Bruce, Lord Bruce of Kinloss, 1613. A similar account of the conflict can be found in HL, MS EL 244, Account of the Duel Between Edward Sackville, Earl of Dorset, and Lord Bruce of Kinloss, 1613.

118 Venetia may have been Sackville's lover prior to her marriage to Digby and this, a well-circulated rumour, provides additional context for the duel between Bruce and Sackville. By the time of her union to Digby, Sackville's affection for Venetia may have fizzled, as he maintained a friendly relationship with Digby after the marriage. Digby's memoirs interestingly mention an incident in which he challenged Sackville to a duel over Sackville's alleged possession of a picture of Venetia, and Sackville refused to fight; the two men remained friends after this contest of honour fizzled out rather ingloriously. See Longueville, *The Life of Sir Kenelm Digby*, 110–12.

119 BL, Stowe MS 150, Thomas Ferrers to Humphrey Ferrers, 19 July 1598, f. 114r.

120 BL, Stowe MS 150, Humphrey Ferrers to Unknown Recipient, 3 December 1596, f. 95r.

121 Ibid.

122 BL, Stowe MS 150, John Harpur to Humphrey Ferrers, 5 April 1597, f. 100r.

123 Ibid.

124 Hicks, "Talbot, Gilbert," accessed 26 September 2014, http://www.oxforddnb.com/view/article/26930.

125 BL, Add MS 32464, John Holles to Edmund Sheffield, 20 July 1599, ff. 17r–17v.

126 BL, Add MS 70505, A Discourse of S*ir* Iohn Holles Concerning His Meeting W*ith* M*aste*r Markham, 1598, ff. 81r-83v.

127 John Holles to Edmund Anderson, 6 November 1598, in Seddon, ed., *Letters of John Holles, 1587–1637*, vol. I, 12.

128 BL, Add MS 32464, Discourse on the Duel with Gervase Markham, n.d., f. 169r. See also BL, Add MS 70505, A Discourse of S*ir* Iohn Holles Concerning His Meeting W*ith* M*aste*r Markham, 1598, ff. 6r–7v.

129 John Holles to Edmund Anderson, 6 November 1598, in Seddon, ed., *Letters of John Holles*, vol. I, 12.

130 Ibid.

131 BL, Add MS 32464, Discourse on the Duel with Gervase Markham, n.d., f. 169v.

132 Ibid., f. 171r.

133 John Holles to Edward Stanhope, 22 November 1598, in Seddon, ed., *Letters of John Holles*, vol. I, 14. Another account of the fight appears in a brief letter that Holles wrote to Callisthenes Brook. See BL, Add MS 32464, John Holles to Callisthenes Brook, 29 December 1598, ff. 5r–8r.

134 John Holles to John Holles the younger, 4 March 1616, in Seddon, ed., *Letters of John Holles*, vol. I, 118.

135 For more on Elizabeth Hatton, see Norsworthy, *Lady of Bleeding Heart Yard*.

136 John Holles to John Holles the younger, 2 June 1616, in Seddon, ed., *Letters of John Holles*, vol. I, 130.

137 John Holles to Henry Yelverton, December 1616, in Seddon, ed., *Letters of John Holles*, vol. I, 148.

138 On Holles's career disappointments, see Morrill, "Holles, Denzil," accessed 17 November 2014, http://www.oxforddnb.com/view/article/13550.

139 See BL, Add MS 32464, John Holles to Thomas Lake, 25 July 1617, ff. 149r–149v, in which Holles laments his failure to secure royal favour during his career. In addition to the numerous trenchant political letters which he authored, Holles was likely also involved in the production of several libels against those who he perceived to be his enemies. See Cogswell, "'The Symptones and Vapors of a Diseased Time'," 310–35. He also tangled with men close to the centre of power, such as William Cecil, Lord Burghley. See BL, Add MS 32464, John Holles to William Cecil, Lord Burghley, 23 June 1598, f. 2v.

140 For documentation relating to the case, see HL, MS HA, Legal Papers, Notes on a Case Between Henry Hastings, Earl of Huntingdon and William Fawnt, Boxes 5–8. See also Cogswell, *Home Divisions*.

141 Cogswell, *Home Divisions*, 43–6.

142 Ibid., 164.

143 HL, MS HA, Legal Papers, Box 7, Folder 5, Notes on a Case Between Henry Hastings, Earl of Huntingdon, and William Fawnt, 1635.

144 HL, MS HA, Legal Papers, Box 5, Folder 14, Notes on a Case Between Henry Hastings, Earl of Huntingdon, and William Fawnt, 1632–1635.

145 Cogswell, *Home Divisions*, 223.

146 HL, MS HA, Legal Papers, Box 8, Folder 3, Notes on a Case Between Henry Hastings, Earl of Huntingdon, and William Fawnt, 1638.

147 Ibid.

148 This incident was subsequently described by John Egerton's falconer in testimony against Morgan, see NA, SP 46/174/86, Evidence of Henry ap Edward, April–June 1610. See also NA, SP 46/174/114, Paper Giving the History of the Morgan-Egerton Quarrel, c. 1611.

149 NA, SP 46/174/22, Edward Egerton to Edward Morgan, 16 August 1608.

150 HL, MS EL 200, Edward Morgan to Edward Egerton, 1608.

151 Ibid.

152 NA, SP 46/174/23, Edward Morgan to Edward Egerton, 16 August 1608.

153 HL, MS EL 199, Edward Morgan to Edward Egerton, 8 August 1608. Egerton wrote this as a note added to a letter sent to him by Morgan in which he extended a second invitation to duel.

154 HL, MS EL 200, Edward Morgan to Edward Egerton, 1608.

155 HL, MS EL 215, John Egerton to Thomas Egerton, Lord Chancellor and Baron Ellesmere, 28 July 1611.

156 Ibid.

157 HL, MS EL 216, Thomas Egerton, Lord Chancellor and Baron Ellesmere, to John Egerton, after 28 July 1611.

158 Ibid.

159 See NA, SP 46/174/24, John Egerton to Edward Morgan, 20 April 1610 for Egerton's challenge and NA, SP 46/174/25, Edward Morgan to John Egerton, 20 April 1610, for Morgan's response (a second copy of the response also exists as NA, SP 46/174/27, Edward Morgan to John Egerton, 20 April 1610).

160 HL, MS EL 220, Account of Edward Morgan's Attempts to Avoid Trial for the Murder of John Egerton, 1611. See also NA, SP 46/75/263, Petition of Roland Egerton, 1611. Another version of the petition survives as NA, SP 46/75/270, Petition of Roland Egerton, 1611.

161 NA, SP 46/75/231, Breviate of Information Against Thomas Petre, c. 1611.

162 HL, MS EL 219, Ellesmere Papers, Certificate of the Viewing of the Body of John Egerton, 1611.

163 Ibid.

164 NA, SP 46/75/228, History of the Case Against Edward Morgan, c. 1611. See also NA, SP 46/75/92, Paper Giving the History of the Morgan-Egerton Quarrel, c. 1611 and NA, SP 46/75/157, Breviate of Proofs Against Edward Morgan, c. 1611.

165 NA, SP 46/174/120, List of Precedents for Condemnations for Murder After Duels, c. 1611.

166 HL, MS EL 222, Pardon of Edward Morgan, 1611.
167 SHC, LM 6729/7/77, Nicholas St John to William More, 24 April 1584. See also SHC, LM/COR/3/370, Nicholas St John to George More, 24 June 1584.
168 SHC, LM 6729/8/96, Anthony Browne, Viscount Montague, to William More, 28 June 1584.
169 Fletcher, *Gender, Sex and Subordination*, 95.
170 Bossy, *Peace in the Post-Reformation*. Bossy suggested that the level of success of post-Reformation churches was partially vested in their provision of effective mediation to adherents. See also Bossy, ed., *Disputes and Settlements*. Additionally, on arbitration, see Roebuck, *The Golden Age of Arbitration*.
171 HL, MS EL 64, William Foorth to Thomas Egerton, Lord Keeper, 18 January 1598/9.
172 See Wrightson, "Mutualities and Obligations," 157–94. See also n. 12 above.
173 This is an element of honour to which Pollock has earlier drawn attention (see Pollock, "Honor, Gender and Reconciliation," 24).
174 Dod and Cleaver, *A Treatise or Exposition Upon the Ten Commandements*, 139.
175 Cust, ed., *The Papers of Sir Richard Grosvenor*, 35.
176 Edward Willoughby to Thomas Darby, n.d., in Welch, ed., *Willoughby Letters*, 82, taken from the Middleton MS, Mi L 18a.
177 Ibid.
178 Ibid., 83.
179 Thomas Darby to Edward Willoughby, n.d., in ibid., 84.
180 Ibid., 86–7.
181 Ibid., 94.
182 J.A. Sharpe, "'Such Disagreement Betwyx Neighbours': Litigation and Human Relations in Early Modern England," in Bossy, ed., *Disputes and Settlements*, 175. See also Muldrew, "The Culture of Reconciliation," 918–22.
183 Capp, *When Gossips Meet: Women, Family, and Neighbourhood in Early Modern England*, 214.
184 See Muldrew, "The Culture of Reconciliation," 921.
185 SHC, LM 6729/1/35/2, Thomas Copley to William More, 14 July 1569. See also SHC, LM 6729/1/36, William Cordell to William More and Thomas Browne, 9 May 1577.
186 On the rise of civil litigation in the period, see Hindle, *The State and Social Change*, 66–93, C.W. Brooks, "Interpersonal Conflict and Social Tension: Civil Litigation in England, 1640–1830," in Beier et al., eds., *The First Modern Society*, Brooks, *Lawyers, Litigation and English Society Since 1450*, 10–1, and Brooks, *Pettyfoggers and Vipers*, 48–111. On litigation and the

straining of neighbourly bonds, see Tim Stretton, "Written Obligations, Litigation, and Neighbourliness, 1580–1680," in Hindle, Shepard, and Walter, eds., *Remaking English Society*, 189–209.

187 FSL, L.b.693, George More to Unknown Recipient, 10 April 1631.

188 HL, MS HA 2509, Alice Stanley, Viscountess Brackley, to Henry Hastings, Earl of Huntingdon, 26 January 1601/2.

189 SHC, LM 6729/1/45/1, John Fortescue to William More, George More, William Morgan of Chilworth, Laurence Stoughton, John Derick, and Thomas Smith, Mayor of Guildford, 30 August 1596. In addition to various requests to have More serve as a mediator in local conflicts, he was frequently commended by powerful men at court (such as Robert Dudley, Earl of Leicester, Charles Howard, Earl of Nottingham, and Sir Nicholas Bacon, Lord Keeper) for the care he took in his duties as a JP. See, for example, SHC, LM 6729/9/114, Nicholas Bacon, Lord Keeper, to William More, 25 October 1568, SHC, LM 6729/3/88, Robert Dudley, Earl of Leicester, to Henry Neville and William More, 26 March 1575, and SHC, LM 6729/9/82, Charles Howard, Earl of Nottingham, to William More, 30 July 1596–1600.

190 SHC, LM 6729/13/35, Robert Dudley, Earl of Leicester, to William More, 3 September 1582.

191 Ibid.

192 FSL, L.a.103, Walter Bagot to Unknown Recipient, 2 May 1597.

193 Ibid.

194 Ibid.

195 FSL, L.a.133, Walter Bagot to Unknown Recipient, c. 1610 [?].

196 Ibid. Walter's father Richard was also asked to serve as a mediator in several conflicts. See, for example, FSL, L.a.190, William Basset to Richard Bagot, 15 January 1594/5.

197 SHC, LM 6729/1/45/1, John Fortescue to William More, George More, William Morgan of Chilworth, Laurence Stoughton, John Derick, and Thomas Smith, Mayor of Guildford, 30 August 1596.

198 Withington, *Society in Early Modern England*, 217.

199 Peacham, *The Compleat Gentleman*, 9.

200 Ibid.

2 Women and Honour

1 HH, CP 90/151 (letter 2), Elizabeth Russell to Robert Cecil, 1601.

2 See, as an example of the gendered dimension of honour present in some works, Smuts, *Culture and Power in England*, 8. For an overview of the

manner in which female honour has often been characterized in historical analyses, see Capern, *The Historical Study of Women*, 63–9. See also Fletcher, *Gender, Sex and Subordination*, 101–25.

3 See Walker, "Expanding the Boundaries of Female Honour in Early Modern England," 235–45, Stretton, *Women Waging Law*, Dabhoiwala, "The Construction of Honour, Reputation and Status," Heal, "Reputation and Honour in Court and Country," Harris, *English Aristocratic Women, 1450–1550*, Gowing, *Domestic Dangers* and "Women, Status and the Popular Culture of Dishonour," 225–34, Reinke-Williams, *Women, Work, and Sociability in Early Modern London*, Hubbard, *City Women*, Pollock, "Honor, Gender and Reconciliation," and Alexandra Shepard, "Honesty, Worth and Gender in Early Modern England, 1560–1640," in French and Barry, eds., 87–105. Likewise, work that reevaluates the role of sexual reputation in female constructions of honour is not limited to early modern England; see, for example, Taylor, *Honor and Violence in Golden Age Spain*.

4 Dabhoiwala, "The Construction of Honour," 208, and Fletcher, *Gender, Sex and Subordination*, 89.

5 Julian Pitt-Rivers, "Honour and Social Status," in Peristiany, ed., *Honour and* Shame, 42.

6 See Gowing, *Domestic Dangers*, 113, Ingram, "Law, Litigants and the Construction of 'Honour'," 135–6, and Sharpe, *Defamation and Sexual Slander*, 18.

7 Gilmore, "Introduction," in Gilmore, ed., *Honor and Shame*, 5. See also Gilmore, *Manhood in the Making*.

8 See Stone, *Sex, Honor, and Power*.

9 See Herzfeld, *Anthropology Through the Looking-Glass*, 63–4.

10 Ibid. See also Pina-Cabral, "The Mediterranean as a Category of Regional Comparison," 399–406, who has labelled such characterizations as "singularly ethnocentric" (402).

11 Herzfeld, *Anthropology Through the Looking-Glass*, 65.

12 See Fletcher, *Gender, Sex and Subordination*, 154–72.

13 Sharpe, *Defamation and Sexual Slander*, 15.

14 Thomas, *The Ends of Life*, 170.

15 Gowing, *Domestic Dangers*, 2.

16 See, for example, Capp, *When Gossips Meet*, 185–225. Likewise, Gowing reflects that "honour and dishonour are *not* the two ends of one axis – what was considered dishonouring didn't reflect what did constitute honour" (Gowing, "Women, Status and the Popular Culture of Dishonour," 225; italics Gowing's). See also Gowing, "Language, Power

and the Law: Women's Slander Litigation in Early Modern London," in Kermode and Walker, eds., *Women, Crime and the Courts*, 26–47.

17 See Fletcher, *Gender, Sex and Subordination*, 124.

18 See Gowing, *Domestic Dangers*, 59.

19 Gowing, "Language, Power and the Law," 27–8.

20 Shepard, *Meanings of Manhood*, 157. Sharpe makes a similar suggestion in his *Defamation and Sexual Slander*, 22. See also Shepard, *Accounting For Oneself*, 25–6.

21 Gowing, "Women, Status and the Popular Culture of Dishonour," 226. As Dabhoiwala has similarly noted with respect to whether there was a unified code of male sexual morality, sexual mores associated with men were also far from unitary in the period ("The Construction of Honour, Reputation and Status," 204 and 212).

22 Shepard, *The Meanings of Manhood*, 165. Women also occasionally utilized the courts to sue over allegations of witchcraft, which they saw as damaging to their reputations and which had the potential to land them in very serious legal trouble. See Rushton, "Women, Witchcraft, and Slander," 116–32.

23 Shepard, *Accounting For Oneself*, 137.

24 For discussion of elements of male sexual reputation, see, for example, Foyster, *Manhood in Early Modern England*, Shepard, *Meanings of Manhood*, Fletcher, *Gender, Sex and Subordination* (in particular 104–5), and Capp, "The Double Standard Revisited," 70–100. See also Thomas, "The Double Standard," 195–216. Illicit sex and other forms of behaviour that denoted inadequate self-control were seen as potentially disruptive of the social order. Thus, "though domestic advice dwelt extensively on men's mastery of others, it also emphasized that this was predicated on their mastery of themselves," including sexual self-mastery (Shepard, *Meanings of Manhood*, 77–8).

25 As Shepard relates in her analysis of the records of the University courts of Cambridge, 20 per cent of the cases brought by townsmen and 30 per cent of those brought to the courts by university men were about matters of sexual slander (Shepard, *Meanings of Manhood*, 152–85; 166 in particular). Shepard, in her most recent work, likewise sees a prominent level of overlap in the ways in which the sexes were discredited, demonstrating that the credit of male witnesses of limited means in court cases was impeached based on sexual dishonesty as often as it was on factors such as drunkenness; likewise, accusations of sexual impropriety were not as frequently used to impeach the credibility of female witnesses of limited means as one might expect, although they did possess a certain primacy of place (Shepard, *Accounting for Oneself*, 136).

26 See Capp, "The Double Standard Revisited," 70–100, Capp, *When Gossips Meet*, 253–5, and Ingram, "Ridings, Rough Music and the 'Reform of Popular Culture'," 79–113. Intemperate sexual behaviour could also result in accusations of bastard children, and the potential associated financial consequences, and mar a reputation for proper, Christian conduct.
27 Dabhoiwala, "The Construction of Honour, Reputation and Status," 205 and 212–13. See also Dabhoiwala, *The Origins of Sex*, especially chapters three and four, 141–233.
28 Heller, *The Mother's Legacy in Early Modern England*, 63–86, and Capp, "The Double Standard Revisited," 72.
29 The woman is identified as Stanley by Anna Whitelock in her *The Queen's Bed*, 288.
30 BL, Lansdowne MS 885, Robert Devereux, Earl of Essex, to Anne Bacon, December 1596, f. 88r.
31 Ibid.
32 Rickman, *Love, Lust, and License in Early Modern England*, 68.
33 See Dabhoiwala, "The Construction of Honour, Reputation and Status," 202–3 and 208–9. Indeed, for some women, such as royal mistresses, sexual involvements, far from marring honour, could bestow it in the form of increased wealth and enhanced social standing (ibid., 210–11).
34 Harris, *English Aristocratic Women*, 84–6.
35 This episode is covered by Rickman, *Love, Lust, and License*, 29–34. See also Paul Hammer, "Sex and the Virgin Queen, 77–97.
36 LH, TH/VOL/V, Morice Brown to John Thynne, 23 March 1580, f. 173r.
37 Lee's wife, Anne Paget, died in 1590.
38 A bill in Parliament in 1552 annulled the marriage of Parr and Bourchier. This was overturned by a Marian Parliament in 1553. It was alleged that Elizabeth Brooke was intimately involved in the plot to place Lady Jane Grey on Mary I's throne after the death of Edward VI, and so it is no surprise that she found no favour with Mary. See also Capp, "Bigamous Marriage in Early Modern England," 540.
39 CUL, Hengrave 88/2/91, George Carew to Mary Darcy, n.d.
40 CUL, Hengrave 88/2/92, Mary Darcy to George Carew, n.d.
41 Ibid.
42 Ibid.
43 Ibid.
44 CUL, Hengrave 88/2/77, Mary Darcy to Elizabeth Kitson, 3 January 1594/5.
45 Ibid.
46 Ibid.

47 Ibid.
48 Additional information on the relationship between Blount and Penelope can be found in Freedman, *Poor Penelope*, Varlow, *The Lady Penelope*, and Capp, "Bigamous Marriage," 541.
49 BL, Lansdowne MS 885, Discourse Written by the Earl of Devonshire in Defense of his Marriage with the Lady Rich, n.d. (but between their 1605 marriage and Blount's 1606 death), f. 86v.
50 Ibid.
51 Ibid.
52 Ibid., f. 86r.
53 Dudley Carleton to John Chamberlain, 20 August 1606, in Lee, Jr., ed., *Dudley Carleton to John Chamberlain*, 90.
54 HL, MSS EL 251, Margaret Howard, Countess of Nottingham, to Andrew Sinclair, 1606.
55 Ibid.
56 Ibid.
57 Ibid.
58 Ibid.
59 An example of the strong link between the Bagots and the Devereuxes can be found in an anxious letter written by Walter Bagot to the Earl of Essex. Bagot was ill and wrote to Essex to implore him to care for his children should he die, saying "I daylie rather expecte a deliverance owt of this troublesome life," and hoped that Essex would show favour to "this poore familie of Blithfield" (HH, CP 176/81, Walter Bagot to Robert Devereux, Earl of Essex, 28 January 1598/9).
60 Recall, for example, Lady Mary Darcy's anxious reaction when she believed her mother was angry with her.
61 See Pollock, "'Teach Her to Live Under Obedience'," 231–58.
62 FSL, L.a.68, Richard Bagot to Richard Broughton, 3 June 1587.
63 Ibid.
64 Ibid.
65 Ibid.
66 Ibid.
67 This has been showcased forcefully in the work of others. See, for example, Harris, *English Aristocratic Women*.
68 This Mary Tyrrell may be the same Mary Tyrrell who, in 1571, married the second son of the Earl of Lincoln – although if she was not, there may have been a family connection.
69 SHC, LM 6729/9/117, Elizabeth Clinton, Countess of Lincoln, to Margaret More, 15 November 1568.
70 Ibid.

71 SHC, LM 6729/9/182, Elizabeth Clinton, Countess of Lincoln, to William More, November, 1568 [?].

72 Ibid.

73 Ibid.

74 SHC, LM 6729/9/120, Edward Clinton, Earl of Lincoln, to William More, 28 September 1570.

75 SHC, LM 6729/9/119, Elizabeth Clinton, Countess of Lincoln, to Margaret More, 2 February 1570/1.

76 Sarah Eve Kelly, "The Other Elizabethan Settlement," 75–104. See also Hammer, "Sex and the Virgin Queen," 82.

77 Conversely, the testimony of servants (commonly believed to be gossips who delighted in the foibles of their masters and mistresses) against their employers could be a nail in their coffin should they be accused of inappropriate behaviour.

78 FSL, L.e.503, Bridget Eyre to Humphrey Ferrers, c. 1600.

79 Ibid.

80 Ibid.

81 This point is made persuasively by Walker in "Expanding the Boundaries of Female Honour," 235. Walker also demonstrates that in situations such as serving as witnesses in court cases (when they were called upon to demonstrate their suitability to serve as a witness by demonstrating their good morality) women usually cast their claims to social capital on the basis "of their honorable, hardworking and honest undertakings in their households" (240). This is further borne out by Shepard in her *Accounting for Oneself.*

82 SHC, LM 6729/6/22, Robert Horne, Bishop of Winchester, to William More, 20 July 1578. While lack of "honesty" was often used as a synonym for a woman's loose morals, in the context of this letter Horne used it to refer to her reputation for upright dealing and truth telling, or lack thereof.

83 Rich, *The Excellency of Good Women*, 5.

84 Ibid., 2.

85 BL, Add MS 48064 (Yelverton MS 70), John Penry to his Daughers, 10 April 1593, ff. 23v-24r.

86 Ibid., f. 24r.

87 BL, Add MS 48064 (Yelverton MS 70), John Penry to Eleanor Penry, 6 April 1593, ff. 19r–21v.

88 Ibid., f. 19r.

89 See Carlson, "English Funeral Sermons as Sources, 567–97. Patrick Collinson was critical of the genre's ability to provide insights into past

beliefs and patterns of piety due to the strict constraints of genre that he believed surrounded them, although Carlson has persuasively challenged these assertions. See Collinson, *Godly People*, 523–4.

90 Cressy, *Birth, Marriage and Death*, 572, n. 39.

91 For a list of funeral sermons relating to elite women, see the appendix to Carlson's article as well as Lake, "Feminine Piety and Personal Potency," 143–65, Retha M. Warnicke, "Eulogies For Women: Public Testimony of Their Godly Example and Leadership," in Travitsky and Seeff, eds., *Attending to Women in Early Modern England*, 168–86, and Willen, "Godly Women in Early Modern England," 561–80.

92 Geree, *The Ornament of Women*.

93 Rich, *The Excellency of Good Women*, 2.

94 FSL, L.b.547, Advice to a Newly Married Gentleman, c. 1540, f. 1r. The perception that women, owing to their more frivolous dispositions, were inclined to excessive and unnecessary spending served as a primary motivator for statements such as this. Likewise, women were aware that this was a perception that they needed to grapple with when it came to their self-representations (for example, see Tague, *Women of Quality*, 133–61).

95 Ibid.

96 BL, Add MS 70505 (Portland Papers), John Holles, The Counsell of a Father to His Son, n.d., f. 8r.

97 Ibid.

98 Ibid.

99 See, for example, FSL, L.d.17, Anne Bacon to Thomas Gresham, c. 1572 and FSL, L.d.62, Anne Bacon to Thomas Gresham, n.d. Anne also enjoyed a good rapport with Gresham's wife, Lady Gresham, and wrote to her frequently (see, for example, FSL, L.d.18, Anne Bacon to Anne Gresham, February [?] 1572/3 and FSL L.d.19, Anne Bacon to Anne Gresham, March [?] 1572/3). In addition, Anne maintained a close relationship with her natural mother and often wrote to her to update her on her health, household affairs, and her progression with her "training" (see FSL, L.d.20, Anne Bacon to Winifred Dutton, mid-June 1573). She also wrote to both women simultaneously on occasion (see FSL, L.d.21, Anne Bacon to Anne Gresham and Winifred Dutton, early June [?] 1573).

100 Harris, *English Aristocratic Women*, 64.

101 FSL, L.d.48, Nathaniel Bacon to Anne Bacon, late 1571–early 1572.

102 Ibid.

103 Harris, *English Aristocratic Women*, 32–35 and 64–5. As Harris notes, wifehood in the period constituted a career that incorporated both

reproductive and managerial functions essential to the success and survival of elite houses (61).

104 Kugler, "Constructing Wifely Identity," 296. See also Tague, *Women of Quality*, 97–132.

105 Gouge, *Of Domesticall Duties*, 253.

106 Ibid., 152.

107 Dod and Cleaver, *A Godly Forme of Houshold Government*, 168.

108 Gouge, *Of Domesticall Duties*, 21.

109 CUL, Hengrave 88/2/6, Thomas Kitson to Susan Bourchier, 1 March 1567/8.

110 FSL, L.d.16, Anne Bacon to Winifred Dutton and Anne Gresham, c. 1572.

111 Ibid.

112 Ibid.

113 Ibid.

114 FSL, L.d.23, Anne Bacon to Thomas Gresham, September [?] 1573.

115 FSL, X.d.502 (5), Henry Neville to Nathaniel Bacon, 3 March 1589/90.

116 Barclay, "Negotiating Patriarchy," 99. See also Barclay, *Love, Intimacy and Power*.

117 Dolan, *Marriage and Violence*, 114. As Dolan notes, the idea of the early modern companionate marriage was "riddled with contradictions" (ibid., 15).

118 Pollock, "Anger and the Negotiation of Relationships," 576–7 and Tague, *Women of Quality*, 97–132. Kugler has also addressed this issue in her work on Sarah Cowper (Kugler, "Constructing Wifely Identity" and *Errant Plagiary*).

119 Nicholas Breton, *The Good and the Badde* (1615), as cited in Keeble, ed., *The Cultural Identity of Seventeenth Century Woman*, 80.

120 See Maclean, *The Renaissance Notion of Woman*, 42, Lemnius, *The Secret Miracles*, Book IV, and Lambarde, *Eirenarcha*, 244.

121 Lemnius, *The Secret Miracles*, Book IV, 274.

122 Richard Baxter, *A Christian Directory* (1673), as cited in Keeble, ed., *The Cultural Identity of Seventeenth Century Woman*, 74. Baxter was a seventeenth-century theologian and poet.

123 LH, TH/VOL/VIII, Maria Thynne to Thomas Thynne, c. 1604–6, f. 1r and FSL L.a.598, Lettice Kynnersley to Walter Bagot, 14 September 1608 [?].

124 As Dolan notes, women had to commit themselves to the "fiction" of their own inferiority in marriage (Dolan, *Marriage and Violence*, 102).

125 TH/VOL/VIII, Maria Thynne to Thomas Thynne, c. 1604–6, f. 1r.

126 Ibid.

127 Ibid.

128 See Gouge, *Of Domesticall Duties*, 152, and Dod and Cleaver, *A Godly Forme of Houshold Government*, 168. These authors were building on earlier Protestant literature that likewise conferred authority over maidservants on women. See, for example, Heinrich Bullinger's 1543 *The Golden Boke of Christen Matrimonye* (as noted in Dolan, *Marriage and Violence*, 106).

129 TH/VOL/VIII, Maria Thynne to Thomas Thynne, c. 1604–6, f. 1r.

130 *Ibid*. See also Fletcher, *Gender, Sex and Subordination*, 156.

131 TH/VOL/VIII, Maria Thynne to Thomas Thynne, after Aug. 1604, f. 2r.

132 Ibid.

133 TH/VOL/VIII, Maria Thynne to Thomas Thynne, c. 1604–6, f. 1r.

134 Ibid.

135 As an example of Thomas's keen interest in household administration, one repository of household records associated with the couple contains approximately 925 account statements and other items, some 454 of which were personally signed and annotated by Thomas. See LH, TH/VOL/LXI, Accounts and Receipts, c. 1603–22.

136 HL, MS HA 4821, Elizabeth Hastings, Countess of Huntingdon, to Henry Hastings, Earl of Huntingdon, c. 1607.

137 Ibid.

138 FSL, L.a.598, Lettice Kynnersley to Walter Bagot, 14 September 1608 [?].

139 Ibid.

140 See Friedman, "Portrait of a Marriage," 545–6.

141 Elizabeth Willoughby to Francis Willoughby, early 1586, Lansdowne 46/33, f. 66r in Friedman, "Portrait of a Marriage," 554.

142 Ibid., Elizabeth Willoughby to John Littleton, 1585, Lansdowne 46/30, f. 60v, 549.

143 Ibid.

144 Ibid., 549–50.

145 On elite men's roles in the making of marriages as a way to project and bolster the collective honour of their families, see Marston, "Gentry Honor and Royalism," 30–1.

146 SHC, LM/COR/4/22, Thomas Sackville, Earl of Dorset, to George More, 28 April 1607. See also SHC, LM 6729/2/22, Thomas Sackville, Earl of Dorset, to George More, 16 June 1607.

147 Ibid.

148 FSL, L.a.167, Walter Bagot to Unknown Recipient, 1622 [?] and FSL, L.a.168, Walter Bagot to Unknown Recipient, 1622 [?].

149 FSL, L.a.169, Walter Bagot to Master Chamberlaine, 12 April 1622 [?] and FSL, L.a.170, Walter Bagot to Unknown Recipient, 1623 [?].

150 FSL, L.a.171, Walter Bagot to Unknown Recipient, 1623 [?].

151 FSL, L.d.22, Anne Bacon to Mistress Billingford, n.d.

152 Ibid. For another example of women's involvement in matrimonial negotiations, see FSL, X.d.428 (5), Charles Cavendish to Elizabeth Talbot, Countess of Shrewsbury, 18 June, c. 1600, where the Countess is involved with the match of the daughter of a Master and Mistress Dales and her advice on the matter is requested. It was a sign of deference owed to a social superior that the Countess's opinion was sought.

153 HL, HA 2507, Alice Stanley to Henry Hastings, Earl of Huntingdon, 4 February 1600/1.

154 HL, HA 2508, Alice Stanley to Henry Hastings, Earl of Huntingdon, after 1601.

155 Pollock, "Honor, Gender and Reconciliation," 23.

156 Simon Adams, "Scudamore, Mary," accessed 15 November 2014, http://www.oxforddnb.com/view/article/69882.

157 Atherton, *Ambition and Failure in Stuart England*, 28.

158 Ibid.

159 LH, TH/VOL/V, Joan Thynne to John Thynne, 18 June 1601, f. 108r.

160 SHC, LM 6729/7/115, Elizabeth Wolley to William More, n.d. (after 1577).

161 Ibid.

162 On Queen Elizabeth's relationships with her women, see Whitelock, *The Queen's Bed*, and Kelly, *The Other Elizabethan Settlement*.

163 SHC, LM 6729/7/115, Elizabeth Wolley to William More, n.d. (after 1577).

164 LH, SE/BOX/IV, List of Goods Belonging to Frances, Duchess of Somerset, 31 December 1674, f. 231r.

165 Stephen Wright, "Pakington, Sir John," accessed 10 December 2014, http://www.oxforddnb.com/view/article/21145.

166 Harris, *English Aristocratic Women*, 99.

167 Hearn, *Marcus Gheeraerts II*, 41.

168 Ibid., 41–3.

169 Reynolds, *In Fine Style*, 54.

170 On early modern women's attitudes and apprehensions with respect to pregnancy, see Linda A. Pollock, "Embarking on a Rough Passage: The Experience of Pregnancy in Early Modern England," in Fildes, ed., *Women as Mothers in Pre-Industrial England*, 39–67.

171 See Hearn and Croft, "'Only Matrimony Maketh Children to be Certain'," 19–24. See also Hearn, ed., *Dynasties*, and Hearn, "A Fatal Fertility?," 39–43.

172 Llewellyn, "Honour in Life, Death and in the Memory," 184. See also Llewellyn, *The Art of Death*, and Sherlock, *Monuments and Memory*.

173 See, for example, the table of lineage that survives in the papers of Margaret Bourchier, Countess of Bath, during the reign of Elizabeth I. CUL, Hengrave 90, Papers, Inventories, and Legal Proceedings Relating to Margaret, Countess of Bath, 1510–1562.

174 For women's attitudes to property and their sense of ownership of items and land, even though not always officially recognized by the law, see Churches, "Women and Property in Early Modern England," 165–80, Erickson, *Women and Property in Early Modern England*, Shepard, *Accounting For Oneself*, 56–62, and Bailey, "Favoured or Oppressed?," 351–71. See also Harris, *English Aristocratic Women*, 80–2. Clifford's experiences are detailed in her diaries (which survive as four separate and incomplete manuscripts, including a late eighteenth-century transcript in the Sackville collection at the Kent Record Office, the third volume of the *Books of Record* in the Hothfield MSS in the Cumbria Record Office, the so-called Kendal Diary, and a manuscript entitled "Last Months" in the possession of the Hasell McCosh family of Cumbria). For a synthesis of these various pieces, see Clifford, ed., *The Diaries of Lady Anne Clifford*. See also Fletcher, *Gender, Sex and Subordination*, 166–8.

175 See Mary Chan and Nancy E. Wright, "Marriage, Identity, and the Pursuit of Property in Seventeenth-Century England: The Cases of Anne Clifford and Elizabeth Wiseman," in Wright, Ferguson, and Buck, eds., *Women, Property, and the Letters of the Law in Early Modern England*, 162–82. See, in particular, 165 and 168.

176 Jessica L. Malay, "Anne Clifford: Appropriating the Rhetoric of Queens to Become the Lady of the North," in Oakley-Brown and Wilkinson, eds., *The Rituals and Rhetoric of Queenship*, 157–70.

177 On Elizabeth's work at Hardwick, see Sara French, "A Widow Building in Elizabethan England: Bess of Hardwick at Hardwick Hall," in Levy, ed., *Widowhood and Visual Culture in Early Modern Europe*, 161–76.

178 For more on architecture and its connections to social display in the period, see Cooper, "Ranks, Manners and Display," 291–310, and Airs and Tyack, eds., *The Renaissance Villa in Britain, 1500–1700.*

179 Cooper, "Ranks, Manners and Display," 291.

180 Elizabeth Goldring, "Talbot, Elizabeth [Bess of Hardwick]," accessed 13 April 2013, http://www.oxforddnb.com/view/article/26925. See also Durant, *Bess of Hardwick*.

181 HH, CP 88/120, Elizabeth Russell to Robert Cecil, 12 October 1601. Elizabeth, one of the Cooke sisters famed for their erudition, was the widow of Sir Thomas Hoby prior to her marriage to Lord Russell. Lord Russell predeceased his father, the Earl of Bedford, thus denying

Elizabeth the opportunity to be a Countess. In her later years she proved to be a rather fractious individual and was involved in a host of lawsuits, many connected to claims to land ownership and property rights.

182 HH, CP 90/151 (letter 2), Elizabeth Russell to Robert Cecil, 1601.

183 Ibid.

184 HL, MS EL 46, Elizabeth Russell to Thomas Egerton, Lord Keeper, between 1595 and 1604.

185 Ibid.

186 Ibid.

187 Holmes, "The Strange Case of a Misplaced Tomb," 18–36.

188 On this aspect of women's active involvement in honour culture, see Pollock, "Honor, Gender and Reconciliation," 26.

189 Daybell, *Women Letter-Writers in Tudor England*, 188.

190 CUL, Hengrave 88/1/75, Margaret, Countess of Bath, to Master Savage, n.d.

191 Ibid.

192 Ibid.

193 Ibid.

194 Ibid.

195 Ibid.

196 Ibid.

197 Ibid.

198 Ibid.

199 HH, CP 56/89, Dorothy Wharton to Robert Cecil, 2 November 1597.

200 Ibid.

201 Ibid.

202 HH, CP 76/37, Mary Rogers to Robert Cecil, 4 February 1600/1.

203 Ibid.

204 Ibid.

205 FSL, L.a.657, Dorothy Okeover to Walter Bagot, 23 February 1617/18.

206 Ibid.

207 SHC, LM 6729/1/64, Robert Lyvesey to William More, 7 March 1579. With respect to relationships between maids and mistresses that were characterized by exploitation and cruelty, Capp has produced a listing of allegations of maidservants beaten and murdered by their mistresses (see Capp, *When Gossips Meet*, 143 and 149–84), and his research has also shown that allegations of physical abuse were more frequently levelled at female employers. Additionally, in her recent sampling of 3,601 people identified as victims of homicide between 1500–1680, and the 4,374 people implicated in their deaths, Kesselring found that

women were said to have killed 28 of the victims identified as servants, in contrast to the 22 killed by men (see Kesselring, "Bodies of Evidence," 249). It is possible that women, perhaps aware of their authority in this arena in a heightened way given that they were denied authority in most other realms, may have been more likely to harshly correct servants with violence than men. In a sense, while they could not wear the breeches within the household, they could wield the rod – although such exercises of violence were, of course, not uncomplicated (see Dolan, *Marriage and Violence*, 104–16). Conversely, other works have suggested that relationships between mistresses and their maidservants were more positive than previous historiography has outlined (such as Reinke-Williams, *Women, Work, and Sociability*). Despite their possibly friendly nature, at their core relationships between maids and mistresses were ones of authority and deference. As Gouge noted of servants, "no inferiors are more bound to obedience than servants: it is their main and most peculiar function to obey their masters" (Gouge, *Of Domesticall Duties*, 438).

208 SHC, LM 6729/1/64, Robert Lyvesey to William More, 7 March 1579.
209 Ibid.
210 Ibid.
211 Ibid.
212 FSL, L.a.856, Thomas Skrymsher to Walter Bagot, c. 1605.
213 Ibid.
214 Ibid.
215 SHC, LM/COR/3/607, Morgan Benyon to William More, 30 July [?] 1597.
216 Ibid.

3 Honour in the Community and at Home

1 On the local nature of government, see Jones, *The English Reformation*, 135.
2 Withington, *Society in Early Modern England*, 219.
3 SHC, LM 6729/3/48, Charles Howard, Earl of Nottingham, to the JPs of Surrey, 13 August 1601.
4 Ibid.
5 Ibid.
6 Ibid.
7 FSL, L.a.130, Walter Bagot to Thomas Smethwick, c. 1610 [?].
8 Ibid.
9 FSL, L.a.430, Richard Draycote to Walter Bagot, c. 1610.
10 Ibid.

11 LH, TH/VOL/VI, Edward Stafford, Baron Stafford, to Justice Henry Townshend, 27 July 1587, f. 48r.
12 Ibid.
13 LH, TH/VOL/VI, Privy Council to John Thynne, 16 March 1594/5, f. 302r.
14 Ibid.
15 FSL, L.a.23, Edward Aston to Richard Bagot, 4 December 1591 [?].
16 FSL, L.a.489, Thomas Fitzherbert to Richard Bagot, 3 October 1592.
17 Ibid.
18 Ibid.
19 FSL, L.b.309, Robert Cole to William More, 4 April 1580.
20 Ibid.
21 Ibid.
22 Ibid.
23 Ibid.
24 SHC, LM 6729/1/87, Nicholas Saunder to William More, 16 September 1580.
25 Ibid.
26 SHC, LM/COR/4/7, Thomas Sackville, Lord Buckhurst, to George More, Master Aungier, and Master Stoughton, Justices of the Peace of Surrey, 14 August 1601.
27 Ibid.
28 Ibid.
29 Ibid.
30 SHC, LM 6729/2/19, Thomas Sackville, Lord Buckhurst, to George More, 14 August 1601.
31 Ibid.
32 FSL, L.a.867, Edward Stafford, Baron Stafford, to Richard Bagot, February 1589/90.
33 FSL, L.a.78, Richard Bagot to Edward Stafford, Baron Stafford, 1 March 1589/90.
34 Ibid.
35 LH, TH/VOL/VIII, Joan Thynne to Thomas Thynne, 24 September 1611, f. 36r.
36 Fletcher, *Gender, Sex and Subordination*, 137.
37 LH, TH/VOL/V, Joan Thynne to John Thynne, 28 April 1602, f. 116r.
38 Ibid.
39 Wall, ed., *Two Elizabethan Women*, xxiv.
40 Wall, "Elizabethan Precept and Feminine Practice," 31–3.
41 Indeed, careful financial management often took on an additional layer of importance for gentlewomen, as failures in this area were often

interpreted with reference to the gendered perception that women were more prone to engage in fiscal irresponsibility and overindulgence in petty vanities that compromised the good standing of a family (see Fletcher, *Gender, Sex and Subordination*, 18–23).

42 For a full analysis of women's work, economic roles, and credit relationships in the period, see McIntosh, *Working Women in English Society, 1300–1620*.

43 Finn, "Women, Consumption and Coverture in England, c. 1760–1860," 703–22. Additionally, freemen's wives were permitted to operate as *femes soles*.

44 The issue of credit, both with reference to the household economy and the broader community, has been insightfully examined in recent analyses that have emphasized that credit and the cultural expectations and anxieties surrounding it were a primary facet of honour. See, for example, Craig Muldrew's nuanced examinations of the culture of credit, *The Economy of Obligation* and "Credit and the Courts, 23–38. Muldrew shows the importance of reputation as a means to secure credit and create economic bonds and argues that social relationships and economic ones came to be increasingly conflated and interwoven in the period before undergoing an eventual transition as economic interactions became more impersonal (*The Economy of Obligation*, and 156 in particular; for a differing interpretation, see Shepard, *Accounting For Oneself*, 277–302). See also McIntosh, *Working Women in English Society*, 85–114.

45 Muldrew, "'A Mutual Assent of Her Mind'?," 48.

46 Pollock has looked at this episode in the context of early modern understandings and displays of anger in her "Anger and the Negotiation of Relationships," 579–81, and also briefly with respect to honour in her "Honor, Gender and Reconciliation," 22 and 25.

47 FSL, L.e.769, Elizabeth Bradborne to Francis Bradborne, c. 1600.

48 FSL, L.e.763, Francis Bradborne to Elizabeth Bradborne, c. 1600.

49 Ibid.

50 Ibid.

51 LH, TH/VOL/VIII, Lucy Touchet to Maria Thynne, early 1610, f. 59r.

52 Ibid.

53 Ibid.

54 Kitson was apprenticed to a mercer and merchant adventurer of London in his youth and remained active as a merchant until his death. He enjoyed a great deal of success within his profession as, in 1534–5, he exported 625 cloths; only ten other merchants exported larger quantities. He also enjoyed a prosperous civic career and served as sheriff of London in 1533–4 and was knighted in 1533.

55 See, for example, CUL, Hengrave 88/1/10, Alexander Colles to Margaret Long, 27 December 1547 and CUL, Hengrave 88/1/11, Alexander Colles to Margaret Long, n.d. Both letters consist of Colles, Margaret's man of business and household agent, updating her on an array of local affairs and inquiring into matters of estate management. For an example of Margaret arranging for supplies and other household provisions, see CUL, Hengrave 88/1/53, Thomas Washington to Margaret Bourchier, Countess of Bath, 14 July 1555.

56 See, for example, CUL, Hengrave 88/1/18, Henry Brown to Margaret Bourchier, Countess of Bath, 7 October 1550.

57 See, for example, CUL, Hengrave 88/1/19, Margaret Bourchier, Countess of Bath, to John Bourchier, Earl of Bath, 17 October 1550, CUL, Hengrave 88/1/23, Margaret Bourchier, Countess of Bath, to John Bourchier, Earl of Bath, n.d., CUL, Hengrave 88/1/48, Margaret Bourchier, Countess of Bath, to John Bourchier, Earl of Bath, 16 March 1553/4, and CUL, Hengrave 88/1/65, Margaret Bourchier, Countess of Bath, to John Bourchier, Earl of Bath, 17 March 1556/7.

58 CUL, Hengrave 88/1/23, Margaret Bourchier, Countess of Bath, to John Bourchier, Earl of Bath, 15 February n.y.

59 Ibid.

60 Ibid. Margaret also offered her husband counsel with respect to his legal affairs. See CUL, Hengrave 88/1/23, Margaret Bourchier, Countess of Bath, to John Bourchier, Earl of Bath, 21 November 1552.

61 CUL, Hengrave 88/1/54, Margaret Bourchier, Countess of Bath, to John Bourchier, Earl of Bath, 21 February n.y.

62 Ibid. See also CUL, Hengrave 88/1/63, John Bourchier, Earl of Bath, to Margaret Bourchier, Countess of Bath, 22 April 1557.

63 CUL, Hengrave 88/1/49, John Bourchier, Earl of Bath, to Margaret Bourchier, Countess of Bath, 31 May 1554. See also Harris, *English Aristocratic Women*, 70–2.

64 CUL, Hengrave 88/1/26, Thomas Kitson to Margaret Bourchier, Countess of Bath, n.d.

65 Ibid.

66 CUL, Hengrave 88/1/132, Jane Hawsley to Margaret Bourchier, Countess of Bath, 5 September 1558.

67 There was a certain measure of tension between the period's prevailing rhetoric of paternalism and good lordship and the fact that many landholders were, in one sense or another, exploiting their tenants. Landowners were often treading a precarious line between losing honour

as a result of seeming like a grasping landlord and pursuing their own economic self-interest when it came to making improvements on their estates. See Bernard, *The Power of the Early Tudor Nobility*, 187–9, and Heal and Holmes, *The Gentry in England and Wales*, 102–4.

68 Stow, *A Summarie of the Chronicles of England*, 348. Derby was also praised by Stow for his open hospitality and kindness within the local community.

69 CUL, Hengrave 88/1/87, John Bourchier, Earl of Bath, to Margaret Bourchier, Countess of Bath, 23 March 1556/7.

70 Elizabeth's first short marriage, while she was still a child, was to the heir of a neighbouring estate named Robert Barley or Barlow. The marriage endured for at least a year before Robert's death and may have been arranged to prevent land owned by the Barlow or Barley family from falling into the hands of the crown. Robert's death led to many years of litigation (including three Chancery cases) in order to secure some measure of the estate for Elizabeth. The particulars of this legal wrangling are covered in Durant, *Bess of Hardwick*, 8–11.

71 See LH, TH/VOL/III, Elizabeth Talbot, then Elizabeth Cavendish, to John Thynne, February, 1557/8 and LH, TH/VOL/III, Elizabeth Talbot, then Elizabeth Cavendish, to John Thynne, 25 February 1557/8. Cavendish was suspected by the Marian regime of certain financial irregularities associated with one of his court offices (an allegation that may have had some merit but which also may have been motivated by hostility toward him for his notable Protestant sympathies; see Durant, *Bess of Hardwick*, 28–30). Fortunately for Elizabeth, Mary I did not long outlive Cavendish and her successor, Elizabeth I, never insisted upon full repayment of the amount owed to the crown, although Elizabeth's next husband, William St Loe, did repay a portion of it.

72 FSL, X.d.428 (48), Elizabeth Leche to Elizabeth Talbot, then Elizabeth St Loe, c. 1565.

73 FSL, X.d.428 (83), Elizabeth Talbot, then Elizabeth St Loe, to James Crompe, 8 March 1560 [?].

74 FSL, L.a.843, Elizabeth Talbot, Countess of Shrewsbury, to Richard Bagot, 19 September 1594.

75 Ibid.

76 BRBM, Osborn MS 92, Box 1, Folder 1, Christopher Standish to James Standish, 22 July 1480–1485.

77 FSL, LM 6729/1/77, Elizabeth Onslow to George More, 21 August 1607 [?].

78 Ibid.

79 FSL, L.a.147, Walter Bagot to Unknown Recipient, 9 May 1611.
80 HL, MS STT 2006, Miles Temple to Hester Temple, 4 December 1639.
81 HL, MS STT 2001, Miles Temple to Hester Temple, 11 February 1635/6.
82 See, for example, HL, MS HA 5369, Henry Hastings, Earl of Huntingdon, to Francis Hastings, 14 May 1584 and HL, MS HA 5377, Henry Hastings, Earl of Huntingdon, to Francis Hastings, 8 February 1584/5 as well as HL, MS HA 5364, MS HA 5365, MS HA 5366, MS HA 5367, MS HA 5368, MS HA 5369, MS HA 5370, MS HA 5371, MS HA 5371, MS HA 5372, MS HA 5373, MS HA 5374, MS HA 5375, MS HA 5376, MS HA 5382, MS HA 5384, MS HA 5385, MS HA 5388, MS HA 5390, MS HA 5392, MS HA 5394, MS HA 5395, MS HA 5397, MS HA 5398, MS HA 5399, and MS HA 5403 in which Huntingdon refers to financial matters and displays evidence that he was clearly closely monitoring his credit situation through references to payments made, payments due, etc.
83 HL, MS HA 5094, Francis Hastings to Henry Hastings, Earl of Huntingdon, 17 September 1592.
84 HL, MS HA 5413, Henry Hastings, Earl of Huntingdon, to Francis Hastings, 24 September 1592.
85 See Patterson, *Urban Patronage in Early Modern England*, 202.
86 Henry Hastings, Earl of Huntingdon, Certaine Directions For My Sonne to Observe in the Course of His Life, in the Historical Manuscripts Commission, *Hastings MSS*, vol. IV, 333–4.
87 Ibid., 332.
88 LH, TH/VOL/V, Joan Thynne to John Thynne, 5 March 1603, f. 122v.
89 HL, MS HA 7903, Mary Jollife to Theophilus Hastings, Earl of Huntingdon, 5 November 1672.
90 Dod and Cleaver, *A Godly Forme of Houshold Government*, 386–7.
91 Braithwaite, *The English Gentleman*, 160.
92 And, given that these types of prescriptive ideals were lofty ones, many servants undoubtedly fell short of the mark.
93 Tadmor, "The Concept of the Household-Family in Eighteenth-Century England," 120.
94 Herbert, *Female Alliances*, 81 and 78–116. On the range of attachments, emotional interactions, and anxieties that could be present in social relationships between maids and their mistresses, see, for example, Marko Lamberg, "Suspicion, Rivalry and Care: Mistresses and Maids in Stockholm Between 1450 and 1650," in Broomhall, ed., *Emotions in the Household*, 170–84, and Laura Gowing, "The Haunting of Susan Lay," 183–201.

95 See Dolan, *Dangerous Familiars*, 59–88, and Gowing, "The Haunting of Susan Lay." Elizabeth Pepys's occasionally fraught interactions with the family's servants offer an apt illustration of this.

96 V.B Hetzel, ed., "Richard, Earl of Carbery's Advice to His Son," *Huntington Library Bulletin*, 11 (1937), 102 as quoted by Richardson, *Household Servants in Early Modern England*, 63.

97 Francis Dillingham, "Christian Oeconomy Or Household Government," in his *A Golden Keye*, f. 49v. As Paul Griffiths notes, "households leaked gossip and secrets like running water" (Griffiths, "Tudor Troubles," 326).

98 Gouge, *Of Domesticall Duties*, 152.

99 See, for example, ibid., 651.

100 Dod and Cleaver, *A Godly Forme of Houshold Government*, 384.

101 See Reinke-Williams, *Women, Work, and Sociability in Early Modern London*, 82.

102 As Marjorie McIntosh writes, "service furnished emotional contacts as well." See McIntosh, "Servants and the Household," 19, and Meldrum, *Domestic Service and Gender*.

103 Gouge, *Of Domesticall Duties*, 651.

104 Jones, *A Briefe Exhortation to All Men*, 25.

105 As Herrup has described it, on a prescriptive level "physiological frailty made women constitutionally unsuited for authority," yet on a practical basis (and, paradoxically, with the encouragement of other prescriptive works) women did, of course, routinely exercise authority within the household (Herrup, *A House in Gross Disorder*, 71); women's power over servants, and associated power to discipline, was indeed sometimes harshly asserted (see Kesselring, "Bodies of Evidence").

106 TH/VOL/VIII, Maria Thynne to Thomas Thynne, c. 1604–6, f. 1r.

107 LH, TH/VOL/V, Joan Thynne to John Thynne, 30 September 1600, f. 97v.

108 Ibid., ff. 97v–98r.

109 Ibid., f. 98r.

110 SHC, LM 6729/8/12, Anthony Browne, Viscount Montague, to William More, 23 June 1564.

111 SHC, LM 6729/8/55, Anthony Browne, Viscount Montague, to William More, 3 August 1575.

112 Most notably Heal in her *Hospitality in Early Modern England*.

113 Ben-Amos, "Gifts and Favors," 315.

114 BL, Add MS 70505 (Portland Papers), John Holles, The Counsell of a Father to His Son, n.d., f. 8r.

115 BL, Add MS 19191, Household Expenses of Elizabeth Kitson, 1592, ff. 66r–76r and LH, TH/VOL/XLIX, List of Weekly Expenses at Longleat at

Various Times, 1561, ff. 9r–11r and f. 14r both provide extensive listings of the provisions felt necessary to have on hand for guests. See also LH, TH/VOL/LXXIX, Inventory of Household Furniture by Joan Thynne, n.y., which lists the various pieces of furniture and household decorations at Longleat, many of which were publically displayed and used to both entertain and impress guests.

116 On women's sociability in a slightly later period, see Tague, *Women of Quality*, 162–93.

117 Herbert, *Female Alliances*. See also Frye and Robertson, eds., *Maids and Mistresses, Cousins and Queens*.

118 HL, MS HA 2507, Alice Stanley, Viscountess Brackley, to Henry Hastings, Earl of Huntingdon, 4 February 1600/1.

119 Ibid.

120 Ibid.

121 FSL, L.b.547, Advice to a Newly Married Gentleman, c. 1540, f. 7.

122 BL, Add MS 36901 (Aston Papers, vol. I), Margaret Cave Knollys to Master Lee, 10 June 1587, f. 12r.

123 Expressions of social status and distinction can be found in virtually all aspects of early modern hospitality, from the reception of guests, to seating arrangements at table, to the type and quantity of dishes served. See, for example, Adam Fox, "Food, Drink and Social Distinction in Early Modern England," in Hindle, Shepard, and Walter, eds., *Remaking English Society*, 165–87.

124 See Heal, *The Power of Gifts*.

125 See Beaver, *Hunting and the Politics of Violence*. In Beaver's estimation, the giving of venison had an almost sacred quality that conferred honour (15–17).

126 Mauss, *The Gift*, 31. See also Davis, *The Gift in Sixteenth-Century France*.

127 Ben-Amos, "Gifts and Favors," 295–338.

128 This point is discussed by Heal in her "Food Gifts," 41–70.

129 Ibid., 55.

130 SHC, LM 6729/7/22, William Cole to William More, 25 June 1570.

131 Ibid.

132 On patronage, see Peck, *Court Patronage and Corruption*, and Peck, "'For a King not to be Bountiful were a Fault'," 31–61.

133 See Cross, "The Third Earl of Huntingdon and Elizabeth Leicestershire," 6–21.

134 Patterson, *Urban Patronage in Early Modern England*, 197–208.

135 HL, MS HA 4815, Elizabeth Hastings, Countess of Huntingdon, to Henry Hastings, Earl of Huntingdon, 1607. See Patterson, *Urban Patronage in Early Modern England*, 205–6.

136 HL, MS HA 4815, Elizabeth Hastings, Countess of Huntingdon, to Henry Hastings, Earl of Huntingdon, 1607.

137 Patterson, *Urban Patronage in Early Modern England*, 207.

138 Davis, *The Gift in Sixteenth-Century France*, 124.

139 See Heal, "Reputation and Honour in Court and Country," 169–78. The episode is also discussed, with reference to the structures of hospitality, in Heal, *Hospitality in Early Modern England*, and in Cambers, "'The Partial Customs of Those Frozen Parts'," 169–79. See also Moody, ed., *The Private Life of an Elizabethan Lady*, and BL, MS Egerton 2614, Margaret Hoby, The Diary of Lady Margaret Hoby.

140 Heal, *Hospitality in Early Modern England*, 12–14.

141 BL, MS Egerton 2614, Margaret Hoby, The Diary of Lady Margaret Hoby, undated entry, f. 89v.

142 Ibid.

143 Moody, ed., *The Private Life of an Elizabethan Lady*, 239. The letter can be found in *The Cecil Papers: Calendar of the MS of the Most Honourable the Marquis of Salisbury*, vol. X, 302–4.

144 BL, MS Egerton 2614, Hoby, The Diary of Lady Margaret Hoby, 30 May 1600, f. 39r.

145 SHC, LM 6729/8/13, Anthony Browne, Viscount Montague, to William More, 4 August 1564.

146 Ibid.

147 Ibid.

148 While Kitson, as her elder half-sibling and a man, was, in theory, entitled to a certain measure of deference from her, Susan was of a higher social status than he, being the daughter of his mother's third marriage to the Earl of Bath; this likely mitigated the degree of deference she felt it necessary to accord him (see also Daybell, *Women Letter-Writers in Tudor England*, 184; Daybell identifies Susan as Kitson's sister-in-law).

149 CUL, Hengrave 88/2/10, Susan Bourchier to Thomas Kitson, 30 December 1567.

150 Ibid.

151 Ibid.

152 Ibid.

153 CUL, Hengrave 88/2/6, Thomas Kitson to Susan Bourchier, 1 March 1567/8.

154 Ibid.

155 Ibid.

156 See the following chapter for further discussion of this quarrel.

157 CUL, Hengrave 88/1/24, Anne Jermyn to Anne Spring, 7 August 1558.

158 Ibid.
159 Ibid.
160 Ibid.
161 Ibid.
162 CUL, Hengrave 88/1/117, Margaret Bourchier, Countess of Bath, to Anne Jermyn, August 1558.
163 Ibid.
164 Ibid.
165 Ibid.
166 FSL, L.a.1, Humphrey Adderley to Walter Bagot, 24 May 1620.
167 FSL, L.a.134, Walter Bagot to a Sister, probably Dorothy Okeover, c. 1610 [?].
168 Ibid.
169 Ibid.

4 Honour and the Family

1 SHC, LM/1617, Autobiographical Notes by William More, 1586.
2 The importance of the family as a site of honour for elites in early modern England is further considered in Thomas, "'The Honour & Credite of the Whole House'," 329–45, and Pollock, "Honor, Gender and Reconciliation," 16–21.
3 CUL, Hengrave 88/2/85, Thomas Cornwallis to Elizabeth Kitson, 23 October 1594.
4 Fletcher, *Gender, Sex and Subordination*, 127.
5 HL, STT 1909, Alexander Temple to Thomas Temple, 25 May 1619.
6 Pollock, "Honor, Gender and Reconciliation," 16–21.
7 Heal and Holmes, *The Gentry in England and Wales*, 51–2.
8 Susan Amussen, "Gender, Family and the Social Order, 1560–1725," in Fletcher and Stevenson, eds., *Order and Disorder in Early Modern England*, 203. This link between state and family, as Amussen discusses, was not unproblematic and it was an analogy, not an equation. For example, while it was often employed as a means to stress the subordination of women, servants, and children, and critique household heads who failed to preserve order through the proper governing of subordinates, it was used much less frequently to critique the behaviour of family heads who themselves threatened the prosperity and ordering of the house through, for example, squandering of funds or mistreatment of other family members. Despite these complicating factors in the family/state analogy, "the family was, at least until the late seventeenth century, an

institution whose internal relationships were important to society" (ibid.). For examples of prescriptive texts linking the early modern family to the state and society, see Gouge, *Of Domesticall Duties*, Griffith, *Bethel*, and the writings of Robert Filmer. Most political and social theorists in the period before Locke made this connection and the analogy was ubiquitous in the period.

9 Pollock, "Honor, Gender and Reconciliation," 23.

10 HL, MS HA 5094, Francis Hastings to Henry Hastings, Earl of Huntingdon, 17 September 1592.

11 Ibid.

12 Ibid.

13 Ibid.

14 HL, MS HA, Personal Papers, Box 14, Folder 18, Household Regulations of Henry Hastings, Earl of Huntingdon.

15 SHC, LM/COR/4/80, Frances More to Poynings More, February 1626/7.

16 Ibid.

17 SHC, LM 6729/1/113, Francis Carew to William More, 25 February 1627/8.

18 Ibid.

19 CUL, Hengrave 88/2/11, Susan Bourchier to Thomas Kitson, 31 January 1568/9.

20 CUL, Hengrave 88/2/12, Susan Bourchier to Thomas Kitson, 13 February 1568/9.

21 Ibid.

22 CUL, Hengrave 88/2/32, Thomas Kitson to Susan Bourchier, 28 July 1571.

23 Ibid.

24 CUL, Hengrave 88/2/39, Thomas Kitson to Susan Bourchier, n.d.

25 On women's role in the maintenance of family honour, see, for example, Marston, "Gentry Honor and Royalism," 27, and Pollock, "Honor, Gender and Reconciliation," 25.

26 See Pollock, "Honor, Gender and Reconciliation," 26.

27 FSL, L.a.21, Edward Aston to Richard Bagot, 2 July c. 1590.

28 Henry Hastings, Earl of Huntingdon, Certaine Directions For My Sonne to Observe in the Course of His Life, 332.

29 Ibid.

30 HL, MS EL 213, Instructions from Lord Chancellor Ellesmere to His Son, 1610–1611.

31 Dod and Cleaver, *A Godly Forme of Houshold Government*, 167.

32 HL, MS EL 213, Instructions from Lord Chancellor Ellesmere to His Son, 1610–1611.

33 Ibid.

34 This conflict is also analysed, through the lens of early modern arbitration, by Boorman in his "Arbitration and Elite Honour in Elizabethan England," 1–21.
35 French, "A Widow Building in Elizabethan England," 165, and Durant, *Bess of Hardwick*, 57–8.
36 See Durant, *Bess of Hardwick*, 72–88, and Boorman, "Arbitration and Elite Honour," 4.
37 FSL, X.d.428 (99), George Talbot, Earl of Shrewsbury, to Elizabeth Talbot, Countess of Shrewsbury, c. 1575 [?].
38 See Durant, *Bess of Hardwick*, 113 and 120, and Boorman, "Arbitration and Elite Honour," 4.
39 HH, CP 164/92_4, George Talbot, Earl of Shrewsbury, to Elizabeth, Countess of Shrewsbury, 5 August 1586, f. 1r.
40 Elizabeth Goldring, "Talbot, Elizabeth [Bess of Hardwick]," accessed 13 April 2013, http://www.oxforddnb.com/view/article/26925.
41 *Calendar of State Papers, Domestic, 1581–1590*, 451–5.
42 HH, CP 164/92_4, George Talbot, Earl of Shrewsbury, to Elizabeth, Countess of Shrewsbury, 5 August 1586, f. 1r.
43 Ibid.
44 Ibid.
45 Gouge, *Of Domesticall Duties*, 247.
46 Ibid., 252. While (as Francis Boorman has noted) it is certainly true that it was the Earl who seemed to rail more publically and vociferously against his wife, at least based on the evidence of the surviving correspondence, it seems probable that the Countess was as critical of her husband as he was of her. While Elizabeth professed that she was the aggrieved party and was mystified as to the causes of her husband's harshness to her, Shrewsbury suspected that his wife's words contained a disguised malice, however outwardly submissive her tone might seem; and, of course, the employment of rhetorical strategies characterized by obedience and deference by women was not at all uncommon in the period (see Boorman, "Arbitration and Elite Honour," 10).
47 FSL, X.d.428 (3), Nicholas Booth to Thomas Kniveton, 4 April c. 1580.
48 HH, CP 164/92_8, Orders Betwixt the Earl of Shrewsbury and the Countess His Wife, 7 August 1586, f. 1r.
49 Ibid.
50 Ibid.
51 Ibid.
52 FSL, X.d.428 (111), Gilbert Talbot to Elizabeth Talbot, Countess of Shrewsbury, July 1577.

53 Ibid.
54 Ibid. See also FSL, X.d.428 (112), Gilbert Talbot to Elizabeth Talbot, Countess of Shrewsbury, 1 August 1577, in which Gilbert reports further conversations he has had with his father to his stepmother.
55 Linking poor behaviour to low status, a recurring theme in many of the incidents investigated here, was a common means of attacking the conduct of another. It speaks in a sense to the manner in which honour was seen as vested both in name and status as well as conduct.
56 See Pollock, "Honor, Gender and Reconciliation," 25.
57 Daybell, *Women Letter-Writers in Tudor England*, 182–3.
58 See, for example, FSL, L.a.596, Lettice Kynnersley to Walter Bagot, 23 March 1605/6, FSL, L.a.597, Lettice Kynnersley to Walter Bagot, 20 May 1608 [?], and FSL L.a.598, Lettice Kynnersley to Walter Bagot, 14 September 1608 [?].
59 FSL, L.a.598, Lettice Kynnersley to Walter Bagot, 14 September 1608 [?].
60 Ibid.
61 Ibid.
62 Gouge, *Of Domesticall Duties*, 152.
63 FSL, L.a.598, Lettice Kynnersley to Walter Bagot, 14 September 1608 [?].
64 FSL, L.a.593, Isabel Kynnersley to Walter Bagot, 27 July 1609.
65 Ibid.
66 FSL, L.a.604, Lettice Kynnersley to Walter Bagot, 8 April 1618 [?].
67 Ibid.
68 FSL, L.a.600, Lettice Kynnersley to Elizabeth Bagot, 20 May 1610 [?].
69 FSL, L.a.603, Lettice Kynnersley to Walter Bagot, 19 October c. 1610.
70 FSL, L.a.602, Lettice Kynnersley to Walter Bagot, 14 September c. 1610
71 Ibid.
72 FSL, L.d.15, Anne Bacon to Anne Bacon, late 1571 to early 1572.
73 Ibid.
74 Ibid.
75 FSL, X.d.428 (51), Elizabeth Stuart, Countess of Lennox, to Elizabeth Talbot, Countess of Shrewsbury, 22 July 1577.
76 Ibid.
77 CUL, Hengrave 88/2/59, Margaret Kitson to Elizabeth Kitson, 1 April n.y.
78 Ibid.
79 Ibid.
80 Ibid.
81 CUL, Hengrave 88/2/60, Margaret Kitson to Elizabeth Kitson, n.d., where Margaret again writes in an attempt to secure her mother's

forgiveness and also suggests that her sister Mary was implicated in her ill behaviour. Margaret implores her mother to forgive both her and her sister. In a separate letter to her mother and father, Mary Kitson pegged the blame more squarely on her sister and remarked upon "my sisters evyll behavoure"; to restore her reputation in the eyes of her parents she was not above impugning the reputation of her sister. See CUL, Hengrave 88/2/61, Mary Kitson to Elizabeth Kitson and Thomas Kitson, 1 April n.y.

82 Peacham, *The Compleat Gentleman*, 16.

83 Owen Feltham, *Resolves: A Duple Century* (1628), as cited in Herrup, *A House in Gross Disorder*, 81.

84 FSL, L.a.2, Ralph Adderley to Nicholas Bagnal, 10 April 1567.

85 Ibid.

86 Ibid.

87 Newdigate, *The Case of an Old Gentleman*, 1.

88 Ibid., 2.

89 SHC, LM/1321, Petition of Elizabeth Slifield to John Puckering, Lord Keeper, 1591–1598 [?].

90 Ibid.

91 Ibid.

92 FSL, L.d.385, Elizabeth Knyvett to Anne Townshend, 14 September 1626.

93 BL, SPI/129, 1538, f. 19r. The episode is discussed in Harris, *English Aristocratic Women*, 115–16.

94 Patricia Crawford, "The Construction and Experience of Maternity in Seventeenth-Century England," in Fildes, ed., *Women as Mothers in Pre-Industrial England*, 11–13. The worst sort of unnaturalness was manifested in infanticide, a crime with a complex history (see Wrightson, "Infanticide in European History," 1–20, Gowing, "Secret Births and Infanticide," 87–115, Kilday, *A History of Infanticide in Britain*, Dolan, *Dangerous Familiars*, 121–70, Hoffer and Hull, *Murdering Mothers*, and Jackson, ed., *Infanticide*).

95 SHC, LM/COR/3/569, Memorandum by William More, 4 July [?] 1580.

96 George Talbot, Earl of Shrewsbury, to Gilbert Talbot, 17 June 1587, in Lodge, ed., *Illustrations of British History*, 302–3.

97 Sir Henry Lee to Gilbert Talbot, 13 August 1587, in Lodge, ed., *Illustrations of British History*, 304.

98 Pollock, "Honor, Gender and Reconciliation," 23. Jennifer Heller also echoes this theme and has found that a concern with impetuous behaviour was recurring in the advice that mothers wrote to their children (Heller, *The Mother's Legacy*, 63–86).

99 Durant, *Bess of Hardwick*, 20.

100 Elizabeth Goldring, "Talbot, Elizabeth [Bess of Hardwick], accessed 13 April 2013, http://www.oxforddnb.com/view/article/26925, and Durant, *Bess of Hardwick*, 82–7.
101 HH, CP 99/114, Elizabeth Talbot, Countess of Shrewsbury, to Robert Cecil, 13 April 1603.
102 FSL, X.d.428 (10), Henry Cavendish to Elizabeth Talbot, Countess of Shrewsbury, 6 November c. 1585. Henry wrote that "my com*m*ynge vp was … to seeke vyrtu and honor in Armes," a reference to his largely unrealized hopes of gaining military advancement.
103 FSL, X.d.428 (81), Edward Talbot to Elizabeth Talbot, Countess of Shrewsbury, 12 May 1604.
104 Elizabeth also had problems with her other son, Charles Cavendish. Charles's behaviour, never notably good, had so declined by 1575 that Elizabeth's husband the Earl of Shrewsbury felt compelled to write to her and request that she do something about her son's escapades. See FSL, X.d.428 (96), George Talbot, Earl of Shrewsbury, to Elizabeth Talbot, Countess of Shrewsbury, 7 June 1575.
105 Portions of this incident are briefly analysed by Pollock in her "Honor, Gender and Reconciliation," 17.
106 FSL, L.a.67, Lewis Bagot to Walter Bagot, 1611 [?].
107 Ibid.
108 See FSL, L.a.355, John Chadwick to Walter Bagot, 30 January 1611/12.
109 Ibid.
110 Ibid.
111 Ibid.
112 FSL, L.a.67, Lewis Bagot to Walter Bagot, 1611 [?].
113 FSL, L.a.135, Walter Bagot to Master Skipwith, 1611.
114 Ibid.
115 Ibid.
116 Ibid.
117 Ibid.
118 Ibid.
119 Ibid.
120 FSL, L.a.67, Lewis Bagot to Walter Bagot, 1611 [?].
121 FSL, L.a.850, Jane Skipwith to Walter Bagot, 20 September 1610.
122 Ibid.
123 Ibid.
124 FSL, L.a.854, Jane Skipwith to Walter Bagot, 19 September 1610 [?].
125 Ibid.
126 Ibid.

127 FSL, L.a.568, Anthony Kynnersley to Walter Bagot, 23 March 1605/6. See also Pollock, "Honor, Gender and Reconciliation," 19.
128 FSL, L.a.162, Walter Bagot to Unknown Recipient, c. 1620. See also Pollock, "Honor, Gender and Reconciliation," 18.
129 FSL, L.a.162, Walter Bagot to Unknown Recipient, c. 1620.
130 FSL, L.a.119, Walter Bagot to Anthony Kynnersley, 19 March 1605/6.
131 Stafford, *The Guide of Honour*, 84.
132 FSL, L.a.120, Walter Bagot to Anthony Kynnersley, 23 March 1605/6.
133 FSL, L.a.122, Walter Bagot to Francis Kynnersley, 21 May 1607.
134 FSL, L.a.121, Walter Bagot to Francis Kynnersley, c. 1605/6 [?].
135 Ibid.
136 Ibid.
137 Ibid.
138 Ibid.
139 Ibid.
140 Ibid.
141 FSL, L.a.597, Lettice Kynnersley to Walter Bagot, 20 May 1608 [?].
142 FSL, L.a.608, Lettice Kynnersley to Walter Bagot, 1622 [?].
143 FSL, L.a.599, Lettice Kynnersley to Walter Bagot, 9 May 1610 [?].
144 FSL, L.a.151, Walter Bagot to Anthony Kynnersley, 1 September 1619.
145 Recall the example of Mary Bagot's illicit match to William Trew recounted in an earlier chapter.
146 FSL, L.a.240, Richard Broughton to Richard Bagot, 13 May 1577.
147 SHC, LM 6729/8/70, Anthony Browne, Viscount Montague, to William More, 30 March 1578.
148 See Harris, *English Aristocratic Women*, 70–2, for additional information on Margaret and her matrimonial career.
149 Ingram, *Church Courts, Sex and Marriage*, 136.
150 Joy Rowe, "Kitson Family (*per*. c.1520–c.1660)," accessed 23 November 2014, http://www.oxforddnb.com/view/article/73910, and Gage, *The History and Antiquities of Hengrave in Suffolk* for information on this match and the Kitson family generally.
151 The transcribed text of the tract can be found in Nicolas, ed., *The Poetical Rhapsody*, 388–407. The original is located in Harleian MS 249.
152 On this clandestine marriage and the ongoing feud between the Thynne and Marvin/Touchet families over Wiltshire politics that made the match between Thomas and Maria so unpalatable to the Thynnes, see Wall, "For Love, Money, or Politics?," 511–33.
153 Financial considerations also played a role and later, in a suit filed in Chancery, Joan Thynne made reference to her and John's expectation that

Thomas's bride would bring a dowry worth between £4,000 and £5,000, from which they intended to partially provide dowries for Thomas's two sisters and which was not forthcoming from the Touchet family. The Touchets did, however, eventually take steps to provide Maria with a more modest dowry (Wall suggests that these efforts may have stemmed from the their perception that Maria's lack of a dowry was dishonouring; see Wall, "For Love, Money, or Politics?," 516–17).

154 Extended family members and local allies were also involved in the simmering feud. For example, shortly after the secretive marriage ceremony, an ally of the Marvin/Touchet family, the Danvers, shot and murdered John Thynne's brother-in-law at an inn (ibid., 519).

155 LH, TH/VOL/VIII, Maria Thynne to Joan Thynne, 15 September 1601, f. 12r.

156 LH, TH/VOL/V, Joan Thynne to Thomas Higgins, 15 April 1595, f. 80r.

157 Heal and Holmes, *The Gentry in England and Wales*, 60.

158 LH, TH/VOL/V, Joan Thynne to John Thynne, 8 May 1595, f. 84r.

159 LH, TH/VOL/V, Joan Thynne to Thomas Higgins, 15 April 1595, f. 80r.

160 LH, TH/VOL/V, Joan Thynne to John Thynne, 20 April 1595, f. 82r.

161 LH, TH/VOL/VI, Thomas Higgins to Richard Halliwell, 6 May 1595, f. 308r.

162 Ibid.

163 LH, TH/VOL/V, Joan Thynne to John Thynne, 8 May 1595, f. 84r.

164 Ibid., f. 84v.

165 Ibid.

166 Ibid.

167 Ibid.

168 LH, TH/VOL/V, Joan Thynne to John Thynne, 30 May 1595, f. 73r.

169 Ibid.

170 LH, TH/VOL/V, John Thynne to Joan Thynne, 26 July 1601, f. 110r.

171 Ibid.

172 LH, TH/VOL/V, Joan Thynne to Thomas Higgins, 15 April 1595, f. 80r.

173 LH, TH/VOL/V, Thomas Thynne to John Thynne, 21 January 1594, f. 77r.

174 Ibid.

175 See Wall, "For Love, Money, or Politics?," 511–33.

176 LH, TH/VOL/VII, Elizabeth Hayward to John Thynne, 1601, f. 200r.

177 LH, TH/VOL/VII, Joan Thynne to Lucy Touchet, 8 August 1602, f. 237r.

178 LH, TH/VOL/VIII, Maria Thynne to Joan Thynne, 14 May 1603, f. 22r.

179 Ibid.

180 LH, TH/VOL/VII, Lucy Touchet to Joan Thynne, 13 June 1602, f. 232r.

181 Ibid.

182 Ibid.

183 Ibid.
184 LH, TH/VOL/VII, Joan Thynne to Lucy Touchet, 8 August 1602, f. 237r.
185 Ibid.
186 LH, TH/VOL/VIII, Maria Thynne to Joan Thynne, 15 September 1601, f. 12r.
187 Ibid.
188 For more on these strategies, see Williams, *Women's Epistolary Utterance*, 155–88.
189 LH, TH/VOL/VIII, Maria Thynne to Joan Thynne, 15 September 1601, f. 12r.
190 LH, TH/VOL/VIII, Maria Thynne to Joan Thynne, 24 February 1601/2, f. 14r. See also LH, TH/VOL/VIII, Maria Thynne to Joan Thynne, 13 June 1602, f. 16r.
191 LH, TH/VOL/VIII, Maria Thynne to Joan Thynne, 27 July 1602, f. 18r.
192 Ibid.
193 LH, TH/VOL/VIII, Maria Thynne to Joan Thynne, 11 December 1602, f. 20r.
194 LH, TH/VOL/VIII, Maria Thynne to Joan Thynne, 1605 [?], f. 10r.
195 Ibid.
196 Ibid.
197 Ibid.
198 Ibid.
199 See LH, TH/VOL/XLIX, Proposals for Marriage Between John Thynne and Lucy Marvin, 1574, f. 280r and f. 282r.
200 LH, TH/VOL/I, Henry Seymour to John Thynne, 25 January 1574/5, f. 85r.
201 LH, TH/VOL/I, John Thynne to Unknown Recipient, 1574, f. 154r.
202 LH, TH/VOL/I, John Thynne to Lucy Marvin, March 1575, f. 158r.
203 Ibid.
204 Ibid.
205 LH, TH/VOL/IV, Margaret Stanley, Countess of Derby, to Dorothy Thynne, 3 March 1576/7, f. 147r. In 1579 Margaret was banished from court for allegedly using sorcery to predict Queen Elizabeth's death.
206 Ibid.
207 Ibid.
208 Ibid.
209 Ibid.
210 LH, TH/VOL/V, Joan Thynne to John Thynne, 7 December 1576, f. 12r.
211 Ibid.
212 LH, TH/VOL/VII, Joan Thynne to Lucy Touchet, 8 August 1602, f. 237r.
213 LH, TH/VOL/XL, Francis Thynne to Thomas Thynne, 22 November 1604, f. 103r.
214 Ibid.

215 LH, TH/VOL/LVIII, Petition of Joan Thynne, n.d. (after 1605), f. 9r.

216 LH, TH/VOL/VIII, Thomas Egerton, Lord Chancellor, to Thomas Thynne, 15 June 1605, f. 74r.

217 LH, TH/VOL/LVIII, The Aunswere of Sir Thomas Thynn Knighte to the Peticion of the Ladie Iohan Thynn His Mother, n.d. (after 1605), f. 11r.

218 LH, TH/VOL/VIII, Joan Thynne to Thomas Thynne, 11 April 1607, f. 26r.

219 Ibid. See also LH, TH/VOL/VIII, Joan Thynne to Thomas Thynne, 25 October 1608, f. 30r.

220 LH, TH/VOL/VIII, Thynne Papers, Joan Thynne to Thomas Thynne, October–November 1611, f. 37r.

221 Ibid.

222 LH, TH/VOL/VIII, Dorothy Thynne to Thomas Thynne, 12 October 1606, f. 24r.

223 Peacham, *The Compleat Gentleman*, 16.

224 Gouge, *Of Domesticall Duties*, 449.

Conclusion

1 BOD, Ashmole 1184, Ashley, *Of Honour*, c. 1596, f. 137r.

2 Pollock, "Honor, Gender and Reconciliation," 5.

3 FSL, L.e.763, Francis Bradborne to Elizabeth Bradborne, c. 1600.

4 Ibid.

5 LH, TH/VOL/I, Thomas Gresham to Christian Thynne, n.d., f. 250r.

6 Ibid.

7 CUL, Hengrave 88/1/75, Margaret Bourchier, Countess of Bath to Master Savage, n.d.

8 FSL, L.a.122, Walter Bagot to Francis Kynnersley, 21 May 1607.

9 It is worth noting here that any clear distinction made between a militaristic ethos and courtly conduct influenced by humanism may be a somewhat forced one. For example, as has been suggested to the author, appropriate conduct at court was often associated with the type of subservience that humanism proper resisted, while humanism itself did much to legitimate the ritualized violence of quasi-militaristic activities such as duelling.

10 Bennett, "Confronting Continuity," 88.

11 Pollock, "The Practice of Kindness," 148–9.

12 See Wood, *The 1549 Rebellions*.

13 Thomas, *The Ends of Life*, 179–82.

14 Fletcher, *Gender, Sex and Subordination*, 322–46. Ute Frevert has similarly argued that honour fell out of favour as a social value beginning in the

eighteenth century because it was tied to antiquated notions of social stratification and so it lost its legitimacy in the face of modernity (Frevert, *Emotions in History*, 80–1).

15 Thomas, *The Ends of Life*, 182. Along these lines, Craig Muldrew has argued that there was a long-term shift from a world of "negotiated community," where relationships were intensely personal and face-to-face and, as a consequence, had to be constantly managed and maintained, to one of "architectural community" in which people came to depend more on the existence of impersonal institutions rather than neighbours (Muldrew, "From a 'Light Cloak' to an 'Iron Cage': Historical Changes in the Relation Between Community and Individualism," in Shepard and Withington, eds., *Communities in Early Modern England*, 156–79).

16 For example, Shepard, in contrast to Muldrew, argues that market and credit relationships did not, in fact, become less personal or reputation-oriented into the eighteenth century; personal behaviour and reputation still mattered a great deal with respect to judgments about creditworthiness (*Accounting For Oneself*, 277–302).

17 Dabhoiwala, "The Construction of Honour, Reputation and Status," 205 and 212–13. See also Bryson, *From Courtesy to Civility*, 243–75, and Dabhoiwala, *The Origins of Sex*, 141–233.

18 Cockburn, "Patterns of Violence," 84. See also Sharpe, *Crime in Early Modern England*, 83–4. Undoubtedly, while formal duels declined in frequency, the habit of engaging in unscripted brawls and physical confrontations over matters of reputation remained very much intact.

19 Thomas, *The Ends of Life*, 186.

20 Norman Jones, "Governing Elizabethan England," in Doran and Jones, eds., *The Elizabethan World*, 28.

Bibliography

Primary Sources

I. Manuscripts

BEINECKE RARE BOOK AND MANUSCRIPT LIBRARY

Anonymous. Undated Commonplace Book [Mid-Seventeenth Century].	Osborn Fb 162
– [Attributed to William Sandys].	Osborn b 230 Undated Commonplace Book
[Mid-Seventeenth Century].	
Brown, John. Undated Commonplace Book.	Osborn Fb 155
Dowbiggen, Thomas. Undated Commonplace	Osborn b 53 Book
[Late Seventeenth Century].	
Hill, William. Undated Commonplace Book [Mid-Seventeenth Century].	Osborn b 234
Standish Family of Duxbury Hall Papers	Osborn MS 92

BODLEIAN LIBRARY

Ashmolean Manuscripts	MS 1184

BRITISH LIBRARY

Collections of Historical and Other Letters	Stowe MS 150
Diary of Lady Margaret Hoby	Egerton MS 2614
Household Expenses of Elizabeth Kitson	Add MS 19191
Letter Book of John Holles	Add MS 32464
Aston Papers	Add MS 36901

Papers of Robert Beale — Add MS 48064 (Yelverton MS 70)
Letter Book and Commonplace Book of Sir John Holles — Add MS 70505

CAMBRIDGE UNIVERSITY LIBRARY

Hengrave Manuscripts — Hengrave 88, 90

FOLGER SHAKESPEARE LIBRARY

Anonymous. Book on Heraldry, ca. 1590. — V.a.466
– The Excellencie of Man, His Nobilitie, Praise, Glory, Honour, and Dignitie, ca. 1610. — V.b.125
Bacon-Townshend Papers — L.d.
Bagot Papers — L.a.
Bruce of Kinloss, Edward Bruce. Letters to and from Edward Sackville to Arrange a Duel. — X.d.165
Cavendish-Talbot Papers — X.d.428
Dering, Sir Edward, bart. History of the Dering Family from the Time of the Conquest, ca. 1635. — Z.e.27
Loseley Papers — L.b.
Ferrars Papers — L.e.
Bradborne Papers — L.e.

HATFIELD HOUSE

Cecil Papers — CP

HUNTINGTON LIBRARY

Ellesmere Manuscripts — MS EL
Hastings Manuscripts — MS HA
Stafford, Edward and Henry Stafford. Memorandum Book and Historical Notebook, ca. 1562. — HM 202
Stowe Temple Manuscripts — MS STT

ACCESSED ON MICROFILM AND HELD AT LONGLEAT HOUSE

Seymour Papers — SE
Thynne Papers — TH

NATIONAL ARCHIVES

Carnsew Papers — SP 46/71
Egerton-Morgan Papers — SP 46/174, SP 46/75
Star Chamber Records — STAC 5/H50/4

SURREY HISTORY CENTRE

Loseley Papers LM 6729, LM/COR

II. Early Printed Books

Anonymous [Attributed to Henry Howard]. *A Publication of His Ma[jes]ties Edict, and Severe Censure Against Private Combats and Combatants.* London: Printed by Robert Barker, 1613 [STC 8498].

Bacon, Francis. *The Charge of Sir Francis Bacon, Knight, His Majesties Attourney Generall, Touching Duells.* London: Printed for Robert Wilson, 1614 [STC 1125].

Baret, John. *An Aluearie Or Triple Dictionarie, in Englishe, Latin, and French: Very profitable for all such as be desirous of any of those three Languages. Also by the two Tables in the ende of this booke, they may contrariwise, finde the most necessary Latin or French wordes, placed after the order of an Alphabet, whatsoeuer are to be founde in any other Dictionarie: and so to turne them backwardes againe into Englishe when they reade any Latin or French Aucthors, & doubt of any harde worde therein.* London: Printed for Henry Denham, 1574 [STC 1410].

Braithwaite, Richard. *The English Gentleman, Containing Sundry Excellent Rules or Exquisite Observations, Tending to Direction of Every Gentleman.* London: Printed by John Haviland, 1630 [STC 3563].

Cawdrey, Robert. *A Table Alphabeticall, conteyning and teaching the true writing, and vnderstanding of hard vsuall English wordes, borrowed from the Hebrew, Greeke, Latine, or French, &c. With the interpretation thereof by plaine English words, gathered for the benefit & helpe of Ladies, Gentlewomen, or any other vnskilfull persons. Whereby they may the more easilie and better vnderstand many hard English wordes, which they shall heare or read in Scriptures, Sermons, or elswhere, and also be made able to vse the same aptly themselues.* London: Printed by J. Roberts for Edmund Weaver, 1604 [STC 4884].

Cooper, Thomas. *Thesaurus linguae Romanae & Britannicae tam accurate congestus, vt nihil penè in eo desyderari possit, quod vel Latinè complectatur amplissimus Stephani Thesaurus, vel Anglicè, toties aucta Eliotae Bibliotheca: opera & industria Thomae Cooperi Magdalenensis ... Accessit dictionarium historicum & poëticum propria vocabula virorum, mulierum, sectarum, populorum, vrbium, montium, & caeterorum locorum complectens, & in his iucundissimas & omnium cognitione dignissimas historias.* London: Printed by Henry Denham for Henrici Bynnemani, 1584 [STC 5689].

Cotgrave, Randle. *A Dictionarie of the French and English Tongues.* London: Printed by Adam Islip, 1611 [STC 5830].

Dillingham, Francis. *A Golden Keye, Opening the Locke to Eternall Happiness.* London: Printed by J. Windet for John Tapp, 1609 [STC 6886].

Dod, John and Cleaver, Robert. *A Godly Forme of Houshold Government for the Ordering of Priuate Families, According to the Direction of Gods Word*. London: Printed by R. Field for Thomas Man, 1621 [STC 5387.5].

– *A Treatise or Exposition Upon the Ten Commandements, Grounded Upon the Scriptures Canonicall*. London: Printed by T. East and J. Harrison for Thomas Man, 1603 [STC 6967].

Downame, John. *Foure Treatises*. London: Printed by Felix Kyngston for William Welby, 1609 [STC 7141].

Elyot, Thomas. *The Dictionary of Syr Thomas Eliot Knyght*. London: Printed for Thomæ Bertheleti, 1538 [STC 7659].

Florio, John. *A Worlde of Wordes, Or Most Copious, and Exact Dictionarie in Italian and English*. London: Printed by Arnold Hatfield for Edward Blount, 1598 [STC 11098].

Geree, Stephen. *The Ornament of Women. Or, a Description of the True Excellency of Women Delivered in a Sermon at the Funerall of M. Elizabeth Machell, on Easter Munday Being the 15 of April 1639*. London: Printed by T. Badger for L. Fawne and S. Gellibrand, 1639 [STC 11763].

Gouge, William. *Of Domesticall Duties*. London: Printed by John Haviland for William Bladen, 1622 [STC 12119].

Griffith, Matthew. *Bethel: Or, A Forme For Families*. London: Printed by Richard Badger for Richard Allot and Jacob Bloome, 1633 [STC 12369.5].

Jones, William. *A Briefe Exhortation to All Men to Set Their Houses in Order*. London: Printed by William Jones, 1631 [STC 14741].

Lambarde, William. *Eirenarcha*. London: Printed by Thomas Wight, 1599 [STC 15152].

Lemnius, Levinus. *The Secret Miracles of Nature: In Four Books*. 1559. London: Printed by J. Streater, 1658 [STC Wing L1044].

Lloyd, Richard. *A Brief Discourse of the Most Renowned Actes and Right Valiant Conquests of Those Puisant Princes, Called the Nine Worthies*. London: Printed by R. Warde, 1584 [STC 16634].

Markham, Francis. *The Booke of Honour*. London: Printed by Augustine Matthewes and John Norton, 1625 [STC 17331].

Martyn, William. *Youths Instruction*. London: Printed by John Beale for Richard Redmer, 1613 [STC 17531].

Newdigate, Richard. *The Case of an Old Gentleman Persecuted by His Own Son*. London: Publisher unknown, 1707 [STC T98012].

Peacham, Henry. *The Compleat Gentleman*. London: Printed by John Legat for Francis Constable, 1622 [STC 19502].

Rich, Barnabe. *The Excellency of Good Women, The Honour and Estimation That Belongeth Vnto Them*. London: Printed by Thomas Dawson, 1613 [STC 20982].

Saviolo, Vincentio. *Vincentio Sauiolo His Practise In Two Bookes. The First Intreating of the Vse of the Rapier and Dagger. The Second, of Honour and Honourable Quarrels.* London: Printed by Thomas Scarlet for John Wolfe, 1595 [STC 21788].

Selden, John. *The Duello or Single Combat: From Antiquitie Derived Into This Kingdome of England.* London: Printed by G.E. for J. Helmet, 1610 [STC 22171].

– *Titles of Honor.* London: Printed by William Stansby for John Helme, 1614 [STC 22171].

Stafford, Anthony. *The Guide of Honour, or, The Ballance Wherein She May Weigh Her Actions.* London: Printed by Thomas Cotes for S. Cartwright, 1634 [STC 23124.5].

Thomas, Thomas. *Dictionarium linguae Latinae et Anglicanae. In hoc opere quid sit præstitum, & ad superiores λεξικογραφονς adiectum, docebit epistola ad Lectorem.* Canterbury: Printed by Thomae Thomasii for Richardum Boyle, 1587 [STC 24008].

Vincent, Nathaniel. *The Right Notion of Honour.* London: Printed for Richard Chiswell, 1685 [STC Wing V424B].

Wilson, Thomas. *A Christian Dictionarie, Opening the signification of the chiefe wordes dispersed generally through Holie Scriptures of the Old and New Testament, tending to increase Christian knowledge. Whereunto is annexed: A perticular Dictionary For the Reuelation of S. John. For the Canticles, or Song of Salomon. For the Epistle to the Hebrues.* London: Printed for William Jaggard, 1612 [STC 25786].

III. Modern Editions and Collections

Anonymous. *Memorials of the Bagot Family Compiled in 1823.* Blithfield: W.M. Hodgetts, 1824.

Aristotle. *Nicomachean Ethics.* Edited by Sarah Broadie and Christopher Rowie. Oxford: Oxford University Press, 2001.

Ashley, Robert. *Of Honour.* Edited by Virgil B. Heltzel. c. 1596. San Marino: Huntington Library, 1947.

Bacon, Lady Jane. *The Private Correspondence of Jane, Lady Cornwallis, 1613–44.* Edited by Lord Braybrooke. London: S. and J. Bentley, Wilson and Fley, 1842.

Calendar of State Papers, Domestic Series, 1581–1590. Edited by Robert Lemon and Mary Anne Everett Green. London: Longman, 1865.

Carleton, Dudley. *Dudley Carleton to John Chamberlain: 1603–1624, Jacobean Letters.* Edited by Maurice Lee, Jr. New Brunswick: Rutgers University Press, 1972.

Clifford, Lady Anne. *The Diaries of Lady Anne Clifford*. Edited by D.J.H. Clifford. London: Alan Sutton, 1990.

Coke, Sir Edward. *Institutes of the Laws of England: Concerning High Treason, and Other Pleas of the Crown and Criminal Causes, 3rd Part*. London: W. Clarke, 1817.

Crawford, Patricia, and Laura Gowing, eds. *Women's Worlds in Seventeenth-Century England: A Sourcebook*. London: Routledge, 2000.

Cust, Richard, ed. *The Papers of Sir Richard Grosvenor, 1st Bart. (1585–1645)*. Chester: Record Society of Lancashire and Cheshire, 1996.

Cust, Richard, and Andrew J. Hooper, eds. *Cases in the High Court of Chivalry, 1634–1640*. London: Harleian Society, 2006.

Frederick J. Furnivall, ed. *Harrison's Description of England in Shakespeare's Youth*. London: New Shakespeare Society, 1877–81.

Gage, John. *The History and Antiquities of Hengrave in Suffolk*. London: J.F. Dove, 1822.

Hastings, Sir Francis. *The Letters of Sir Francis Hastings, 1574–1609*. Edited by Claire Cross. Frome: Butler and Tanner, 1969.

Historical Manuscripts Commission, *Hastings MSS*, Volume IV.

Hoby, Lady Margaret. *The Private Life of an Elizabethan Lady: the Diary of Lady Margaret Hoby, 1599–1605*. Edited by Joanna Moody. Stroud: Sutton, 1998.

Holles, John, Second Earl of Clare. *Letters of John Holles, 1587–1637*. Edited by P.R. Seddon. Nottingham: Thornton Society, 1975, 3 volumes.

Keeble, Neil, ed. *The Cultural Identity of Seventeenth Century Woman: A Reader*. Abingdon: Routledge, 1994.

Lodge, Edmund, ed. *Illustrations of British History, Biography, and Manners, in the Reigns of Henry VIII, Edward VI, Mary, Elizabeth, and James I*. London: John Chidley, 1838, volume II.

Nicolas, Nicholas Harris, ed. *The Poetical Rhapsody: To Which Are Added Several Other Pieces by Francis Davison With Memoirs and Notes*. London: William Pickering, 1826.

Richardson, Samuel. *Pamela or Virtue Rewarded*. 1740. Manchester: Russell and Allen, 1811.

Smith, Sir Thomas. *De Republica Anglorum: A Discourse on the Commonwealth of England*. 1583. Edited by L. Alston. Cambridge: Cambridge University Press, 1906 [STC 22857].

Stow, John. *A Summarie of the Chronicles of England, Diligently Collected, Abridged, and Continued Unto This Present Yeare of Christ, 1604*. 1604. Edited by Barrett L. Beer. Lampeter: Edward Mellen, 2007 [STC 23329].

Wall, Alison, ed. *Two Elizabethan Women: The Correspondence of Joan and Maria Thynne, 1575–1611*. Devizes: Wiltshire Record Society, 1983.

Welch, Mary A., ed. *Willoughby Letters of the First Half of the Sixteenth Century*. Nottingham: Derby and Sons for the Thornton Society Record Series, 1967.

Cited Secondary Sources

Adams, Simon. "Scudamore, Mary, Lady Scudamore (c.1550–1603)." *Oxford Dictionary of National Biography*. Oxford University Press, 2006; online edition, 2008. Accessed 15 November 2014. http://www.oxforddnb.com/view/article/69882.

Airs, Malcolm, and Geoffrey Tyack, eds. *The Renaissance Villa in Britain, 1500–1700*. Reading: Spire Books, 2007.

Amussen, Susan D. *An Ordered Society: Gender and Class in Early Modern England*. Oxford: Blackwell, 1988.

– "Punishment, Discipline and Power: The Social Meanings of Violence in Early Modern England." *Journal of British Studies* 34 (1995): 1–34.

Amussen, Susan D., and Mark A. Kishlansky, eds. *Political Culture and Cultural Politics in Early Modern England: Essays Presented to David Underdown*. Manchester: Manchester University Press, 1995.

Andrew, Donna T. *Aristocratic Vice: The Attack on Duelling, Suicide, Adultery, and Gambling in Eighteenth Century England*. New Haven: Yale University Press, 2014.

– "The Code of Honour and Its Critics." *Social History* 5 (1980): 409–34.

Anglo, Sydney, ed. *Chivalry in the Renaissance*. Woodbridge: Boydell, 1990.

Asch, Ronald G. *Nobilities in Transition, 1550–1700: Courtiers and Rebels in Britain and Europe*. London: Arnold, 2003.

Atherton, Ian. *Ambition and Failure in Stuart England: The Career of John, First Viscount Scudamore*. Manchester: Manchester University Press, 1999.

Bailey, Joanne. "Favoured or Oppressed? Married Women, Property and 'Coverture' in England, 1660–1800." *Continuity and Change* 17 (2002): 351–71.

Ball, Terence, James Farr, and Russell L. Hanson (eds.), *Political Innovation and Conceptual Change*. Cambridge: Cambridge University Press, 1989.

Banks, Stephen. "Killing with Courtesy: The English Duelist, 1785–1845." *Journal of British Studies* 47 (2008): 528–58.

– *A Polite Exchange of Bullets: The Duel and the English Gentleman, 1750–1850*. Woodbridge: Boydell, 2010.

Bannet, Eve Tavor. *Empire of Letters: Letter Manuals and Transatlantic Correspondence, 1680–1820*. Cambridge: Cambridge University Press, 2005.

Barclay, Katie. *Love, Intimacy and Power: Marriage and Patriarchy in Scotland, 1650–1850*. Manchester: Manchester University Press, 2011.

– "Negotiating Patriarchy: The Marriage of Anna Potts and Sir Archibald Grant of Monymusk, 1731–1744." *Journal of Scottish Historical Studies* 28 (2008): 83–101.

Barnes, Thomas Garden. *Somerset, 1625–1640: A County's Government During the "Personal Rule."* Cambridge: Harvard University Press, 1961.

Baumann, Gerd, ed. *The Written Word: Literacy in Transition, the Wolfson College Lectures 1985*. Oxford: Clarendon Press, 1986.

Beattie, J.M. *Crime and the Courts in England, 1660–1800*. Oxford: Oxford University Press, 1986.

Beaver, Daniel. *Hunting and the Politics of Violence Before the English Civil War*. Cambridge: Cambridge University Press, 2008.

Beier, A.L., David Cannadine, and J.M. Rosenheim, eds. *The First Modern Society: Essays in English History in Honour of Lawrence Stone*. Cambridge: Cambridge University Press, 1989.

Ben-Amos, Ilana Krausman. "Gifts and Favors: Informal Support in Early Modern England." *Journal of Modern History* 72 (2000): 295–338.

Bennett, Judith. "Confronting Continuity." *Journal of Women's History* 9 (1997): 73–94.

Bernard, G.W. *The Power of the Early Tudor Nobility: A Study of the Fourth and Fifth Earls of Shrewsbury*. Brighton: The Harvester Press, 1985.

Billaçois, François. *The Duel: Its Rise and Fall in Early Modern France*. 1986. Translated by Trista Selous. New Haven: Yale University Press, 1990.

Boorman, Francis. "Arbitration and Elite Honour in Elizabethan England: A Case Study of Bess of Hardwick." *Journal of Dispute Resolution* 1 (2016): 1–21.

Bossis, Mireille, and Karen McPherson. "Methodological Journeys Through Correspondence." *Yale French Studies* 71 (1986): 63–75.

Bossy, John, ed. *Disputes and Settlements: Law and Human Relations in the West*. Cambridge: Cambridge University Press, 1983.

– *Peace in the Post-Reformation: The Birkbeck Lectures, 1995*. Cambridge: Cambridge University Press, 1998.

Braddick, Michael J. *State Formation in Early Modern England, c. 1550–1700*. Cambridge: Cambridge University Press, 2000.

Braddick, Michael J., and John Walter, eds. *Negotiating Power in Early Modern England: Order, Hierarchy and Subordination in Britain and Ireland*. Cambridge: Cambridge University Press, 2001.

Brigden, Susan. *New Worlds, Lost Worlds: The Rule of the Tudors, 1485–1603*. New York: Penguin, 2000.

Brooks, C.W. *Lawyers, Litigation and English Society Since 1450*. London: Hambledon Press, 1998.

– *Pettyfoggers and Vipers of the Commonwealth: The "Lower Branch" of the Legal Profession in Early Modern England*. Cambridge: Cambridge University Press, 2004.

Broomhall, Susan, ed. *Gender and Emotions in Medieval and Early Modern Europe: Destroying Order, Structuring Disorder*. Farnham: Ashgate, 2015.

– ed. *Emotions in the Household, 1200–1900*. Basingstoke: Palgrave Macmillan, 2008.

Broomhall, Susan, and Sarah Finn, eds. *Violence and Emotions in Early Modern Europe*. Abingdon: Routledge, 2015.

Broomhall, Susan, and Jacqueline van Gent, eds. *Governing Masculinities in the Early Modern Period: Regulating Selves and Others*. Farnham: Ashgate, 2011.

Brown, Keith M. *Bloodfeud in Scotland 1573–1625: Violence, Justice and Politics in an Early Modern Society*. Edinburgh: John Donald Publishers, 1986.

Bryson, Anna. *From Courtesy to Civility: Changing Codes of Conduct in Early Modern England*. Oxford: Clarendon Press, 1998.

Burke, Peter, Brian Harrison, and Paul Slack, eds. *Civil Histories: Essays Presented to Sir Keith Thomas*. Oxford: Oxford University Press, 2000.

Burke, Peter, and Roy Porter, eds. *The Social History of Language*. Cambridge: Cambridge University Press, 1987.

Bush, M.L. *The English Aristocracy: A Comparative Synthesis*. Manchester: Manchester University Press, 1984.

Cambers, Andrew. "'The Partial Customs of Those Frozen Parts': Religious Riot and Reconciliation in the North of England." *Studies in Church History* 40 (2004): 169–79.

Capern, Amanda. *The Historical Study of Women: England, 1500–1790*. Basingstoke: Palgrave Macmillan, 2008.

Capp, Bernard. "Bigamous Marriage in Early Modern England." *The Historical Journal* 52 (2009): 537–56.

– "The Double Standard Revisited: Plebian Women and Male Sexual Reputation in Early Modern England." *Past and Present* 162 (1999): 70–100.

– *When Gossips Meet: Women, Family, and Neighbourhood in Early Modern England*. Oxford: Oxford University Press, 2004.

Carlson, Eric Josef. "English Funeral Sermons as Sources: The Example of Female Piety in Pre-1640 Sermons." *Albion* 32 (2000): 567–97.

Carroll, Stuart. *Blood and Violence in Early Modern France*. Oxford: Oxford University Press, 2006.

– ed. *Cultures of Violence: Interpersonal Violence in Historical Perspective*. Basingstoke: Palgrave Macmillan, 2007.

– "The Peace in the Feud in Sixteenth- and Seventeenth-Century France." *Past and Present* 178 (2003): 74–115.

Casellas, Jesús López-Peláez. "The Social Function of the Renaissance Concept of Honour: An Introduction." *Journal of the Spanish Society for English Renaissance Studies* 8 (1997): 83–7.

Chalklin, Christopher W. *Seventeenth-Century Kent: A Social and Economic History.* London: Longman, 1965.

Chamberland, Celeste. "Between the Hall and the Market: William Clowes and Surgical Self-Fashioning in Elizabethan London." *Sixteenth Century Journal* 41 (2010): 69–90.

Champion, Michael, and Andrew Lynch, eds. *Understanding Emotions in Early Europe*. Turnhout: Brepols, 2015.

Cockburn, J.S. "Patterns of Violence in English Society: Homicide in Kent, 1560–1985." *Past and Present* 130 (1991): 70–106.

Churches, Christine. "Women and Property in Early Modern England: A Case Study." *Social History* 23 (1998): 165–80.

Clark, Peter, and Paul Slack, eds. *Crisis and Order in English Towns, 1500–1700.* London: Routledge, 1973.

Cogswell, Thomas. *Home Divisions: Aristocracy, the State and Provincial Conflict.* Stanford: Stanford University Press. 1998.

– "'The Symptones and Vapors of a Diseased Time': The Earl of Clare and Early Stuart Manuscript Culture." *Review of English Studies* 57 (2006): 310–35.

Collinson, Patrick, ed. *Elizabethan Essays*. London: Hambledon Press, 1994.

– *Godly People: Essays on English Protestantism and Puritanism*. London: Hambledon Press, 1983.

Cooper, Nicholas. "Rank, Manners and Display: The Gentlemanly House, 1500–1750." *Transactions of the Royal Historical Society* 12 (2002): 291–310.

Corfield, Penelope, ed. *Language, History, and Class*. Oxford: Blackwell, 1991.

Coss, Peter R., ed. *The Moral World of the Law*. Cambridge: Cambridge University Press, 2000.

Couchman, Jane, and Ann Crabb, eds. *Women's Letters Across Europe, 1400–1700: Form and Persuasion*. London: Aldershot, 2005.

Cressy, David. *Birth, Marriage and Death: Ritual, Religion and the Life-Cycle in Tudor and Stuart England*. New York: Oxford University Press, 1997.

Cross, Claire. "The Third Earl of Huntingdon and Elizabeth Leicestershire." *Transactions of the Leicestershire Archaeological Society* 36 (1960): 6–21.

Cummins, Stephen and Laura Kounine, eds. *Cultures of Conflict Resolution in Early Modern Europe*. Farnham: Ashgate, 2016.

Cust, Richard. "Honour and Politics in Early Stuart England: The Case of Beaumont v. Hastings." *Past and Present* 149 (1995): 57–94.

Dabhoiwala, Faramerz. "The Construction of Honour, Reputation and Status in Late Seventeenth- and Early Eighteenth-Century England." *Transactions of the Royal Historical Society* 6 (1996): 201–13.

– *The Origins of Sex: A History of the First Sexual Revolution*. New York: Oxford University Press. 2012.

Davis, Alex. *Chivalry and Romance in the English Renaissance*. Rochester: D.S. Brewer, 2003.

Davis, Natalie Zemon. *The Gift in Sixteenth-Century France*. Wisconsin: University of Wisconsin Press, 2000.

Daybell, James, ed. *Early Modern Women's Letter Writing, 1450–1700*. Basingstoke: Palgrave Macmillan, 2001.

– "Gender, Obedience, and Authority in Sixteenth-Century Women's Letters." *Sixteenth Century Journal* 41 (2010): 49–67.

– *The Material Letter in Early Modern England: Manuscript Letters and the Culture and Practices of Letter-Writing, 1512–1635*. Basingstoke: Palgrave Macmillan, 2012.

– *Women Letter-Writers in Tudor England*. Oxford: Oxford University Press, 2006.

Dickinson, Janet. *Court Politics and the Earl of Essex, 1589–1601*. London: Pickering and Chatto, 2012.

Dolan, Frances. *Dangerous Familiars: Representations of Domestic Crime in England, 1550–1700*. Ithaca: Cornell University Press, 1994.

– *Marriage and Violence: The Early Modern Legacy*. Philadelphia: University of Pennsylvania Press, 2008.

Donagan, Barbara. "The Web of Honour: Soldiers, Christians, and Gentlemen in the English Civil War." *The Historical Journal* 44 (2002): 365–89.

Doran, Susan, and Norman Jones, eds. *The Elizabethan World*. London: Routledge, 2011.

Durant, David. *Bess of Hardwick: Portrait of an Elizabethan Dynast*. London: Weidenfeld and Nicolson, 1977.

Eastwood, David. *Government and Community in the English Provinces, 1700–1870*. Basingstoke: Macmillan, 1997.

Elias, Norbert. *The Civilizing Process*. 1939. Translated by Edmund Jephcott. New York: Pantheon Books, 1982.

Erickson, Amy Louise. *Women and Property in Early Modern England*. London: Routledge, 1993.

Everitt, Alan Milner. *The Community of Kent and the Great Rebellion, 1640–60*. Leicester: Leicester University Press, 1966.

Fildes, Valerie, ed. *Women as Mothers in Pre-Industrial England*. Abingdon: Routledge, 1990.

Finn, Margot. "Women, Consumption and Coverture in England, c.1760–1860." *Historical Journal* 39 (1996): 703–22.

Fletcher, Anthony. *A County Community in Peace and War: Sussex 1600–1660.* London: Longman, 1975.

– *Gender, Sex and Subordination in England, 1500–1800.* New Haven: Yale University Press, 1995.

Fletcher, Anthony, and John Stevenson, eds. *Order and Disorder in Early Modern England.* Cambridge: Cambridge University Press, 1985.

Fletcher, Richard. *Bloodfeud: Murder and Revenge in Anglo-Saxon England.* Oxford: Oxford University Press, 2003.

Forth, Christopher E., R.B. Cribb, and Carolyn Strange, eds. *Honour, Violence and Emotions in History.* London: Bloomsbury, 2014.

Foyster, Elizabeth A. "Male Honour, Social Control and Wife Beating in Late Stuart England." *Transactions of the Royal Historical Society* 6 (1996): 215–24.

– *Manhood in Early Modern England: Honour, Sex, and Marriage.* London: Longman, 1999.

Freedman, Sylvia. *Poor Penelope: Lady Penelope Rich, An Elizabethan Woman.* Abbotsbrook: Kensal Press, 1983.

French, Henry. *The Middle Sort of People in Provincial England, 1600–1750.* Oxford: Oxford University Press, 2007.

French, Henry, and Jonathan Barry, eds. *Identity and Agency in England, 1500–1800.* New York: Palgrave Macmillan, 2004.

French, Henry, and Mark Rothery. *Man's Estate: Landed Gentry Masculinities, 1660–1900.* Oxford: Oxford University Press, 2012.

– "'Upon Your Entry into the World': Masculine Values and the Threshold of Adulthood Among Landed Elites in England 1680–1800." *Social History* 33 (2008) 402–22.

Frevert, Ute. *Emotions in History: Lost and Found.* Budapest: Central European University Press, 2011.

– *Men of Honour: A Social and Cultural History of the Duel.* London: Polity Press, 1995.

Friedman, Alice. "Portrait of a Marriage: The Willoughby Letters of 1585–86." *Signs* 11 (1986): 542–55.

Frye, Susan, and Karen Robertson, eds. *Maids and Mistresses, Cousins and Queens: Women's Alliances in Early Modern England.* Oxford: Oxford University Press, 1999.

Gajda, Alexandra. *The Earl of Essex and Late Elizabethan Political Culture.* Oxford: Oxford University Press, 2012.

Gent, Lucy, and Nigel Llewellyn, eds. *Renaissance Bodies: The Human Figure in English Culture, c. 1540–1660.* London: Reaktion Books, 1990.

Gent, Jacqueline Van, and Susan Broomhall, eds. *Governing Masculinities in the Early Modern Period: Regulating Selves and Others*. Farnham: Ashgate, 2011.

Gilmore, David D., ed. *Honor and Shame and the Unity of the Mediterranean*. Washington: American Anthropological Association, 1987.

– *Manhood in the Making: Cultural Concepts of Masculinity*. New Haven: Yale University Press, 1991.

Goldberg, Jonathan. *Writing Matter: From the Hands of the English Renaissance*. Stanford: Stanford University Press, 1990.

Goldring, Elizabeth. "Talbot, Elizabeth [Bess of Hardwick], Countess of Shrewsbury (1527?–1608)." *Oxford Dictionary of National Biography*. Oxford University Press, 2004. Accessed 13 April 2013. http://www.oxforddnb.com/view/article/26925.

Gouk, Penelope, and Helen Hills, eds. *Representing Emotions: New Connections in the Histories of Art, Music and Medicine*. Farnham: Ashgate, 2005.

Gowing, Laura. *Domestic Dangers: Women, Words, and Sex in Early Modern London*. Oxford: Clarendon Press, 1996.

– "The Haunting of Susan Lay: Servants and Mistresses in Seventeenth-Century England." *Gender and History* 14 (2002): 183–201.

– "Secret Births and Infanticide in Seventeenth-Century England." *Past and Present* 156 (1997): 87–115.

– "Women, Status and the Popular Culture of Dishonor." *Transactions of the Royal Historical Society* 6 (1996): 225–34.

Gowing, Laura, Michael Cyril William Hunter, and Miri Rubin, eds. *Love, Friendship, and Faith in Europe, 1300–1800*. Basingstoke: Palgrave Macmillan, 2005.

Griffiths, Paul. *Youth and Authority: Formative Experiences in England, 1560–1640*. Oxford: Oxford University Press, 1996.

Gunn, Steven. *Early Tudor Government, 1485–1558*. London: Macmillan, 1995.

Gurr, T.R. "Historical Trends in Violent Crime: A Critical Review of the Evidence." *Crime and Justice* 3 (1981): 295–353.

Hammer, Paul. *The Polarization of Elizabethan Politics: The Political Career of Robert Devereux, Second Earl of Essex, 1585–1597*. Cambridge: Cambridge University Press, 1999.

– "Sex and the Virgin Queen: Aristocratic Concupiscence and the Court of Elizabeth I." *Sixteenth Century Journal* 31 (2000): 77–97.

Harris, Barbara J. *English Aristocratic Women, 1450–1550: Marriage and Family, Property and Careers*. Oxford: Oxford University Press, 2002.

Heal, Felicity. "Food Gifts, the Household and the Politics of Exchange in Early Modern England." *Past and Present* 199 (2008): 41–70.

– *Hospitality in Early Modern England*. Oxford: Clarendon Press, 1990.

– "Reputation and Honour in Court and Country: Lady Elizabeth Russell and Sir Thomas Hoby." *Transactions of the Royal Historical Society* 6 (1996): 161–78.

– *The Power of Gifts: Gift Exchange in Early Modern England*. Oxford: Oxford University Press, 2014.

Heal, Felicity, and Clive Holmes. *The Gentry in England and Wales, 1500–1700.* Stanford: Stanford University Press, 1994.

Hearn, Karen, ed. *Dynasties: Painting in Tudor and Jacobean England, 1530–1630.* New York: Rizzoli, 1996.

– "A Fatal Fertility? Elizabethan and Jacobean Pregnancy Portraits." *Costume* 34 (2000): 39–43.

– *Marcus Gheeraerts II: Elizabethan Artist in Focus*. London: Tate Publishing, 2002.

Hearn, Karen, and Pauline Croft. "'Only Matrimony Maketh Children to be Certain': Two Elizabethan Pregnancy Portraits." *The British Art Journal* 3 (2002): 19–24.

Heller, Jennifer Louise. *The Mother's Legacy in Early Modern England*. Farnham: Ashgate, 2011.

Heltzel, Virgil B. "Robert Ashley: Elizabethan Man of Letters." *Huntington Library Quarterly* 10 (1947): 349–63.

Herbert, Amanda. *Female Alliances: Gender, Identity, and Friendship in Early Modern Britain*. New Haven: Yale University Press, 2014.

Herrup, Cynthia. *The Common Peace: Participation and the Criminal Law in Seventeenth-Century England*. Cambridge: Cambridge University Press, 1989.

– *A House in Gross Disorder: Sex, Law, and the 2nd Earl of Castlehaven*. New York: Oxford University Press, 1999.

– "Law and Morality in Seventeenth Century England." *Past and Present* 106 (1985): 102–23.

– "'To Pluck Bright Honour From the Pale-Faced Moon': Gender and Honour in the Castlehaven Story." *Transactions of the Royal Historical Society* 6 (1996): 137–59.

Herzfeld, Michael. *Anthropology Through the Looking-Glass: Critical Ethnography in the Margins of Europe*. Cambridge: Cambridge University Press, 1987.

Hicks, Michael. "Talbot, Gilbert, Seventh Earl of Shrewsbury (1552–1616)." *Oxford Dictionary of National Biography*. Oxford University Press, 2004; online edition, 2008. Accessed 26 September 2015. http://www.oxforddnb.com/view/article/26930.

Hindle, Steve. "Hierarchy and Community in the Elizabethan Parish: The Swallowfield Articles of 1596." *The Historical Journal* 42 (1999): 835–51.

– *The State and Social Change in Early Modern England, c.1550–1640*. New York: Macmillan, 2000.

Hindle, Steve, Alexandra Shepard, and John Walter, eds. *Remaking English Society: Social Relations and Social Change in Early Modern England*. Woodbridge: Boydell, 2013.

Hoffer, Peter C., and N.E.H. Hull. *Murdering Mothers: Infanticide in England and New England, 1558–1803*. New York: New York University Press, 1981.

Holmes, Clive. "The Strange Case of a Misplaced Tomb: Family Honour and Law in Late Seventeenth-Century England." *Midland History*, 31 (2006), 18–36.

Horder, Jeremy. "The Duel and the English Law of Homicide." *Oxford J Legal Studies* 3 (1992): 419–30.

– *Provocation and Responsibility*. Oxford: Clarendon Press, 1992.

Hubbard, Eleanor. *City Women: Money, Sex and the Social Order in Early Modern London*. Oxford: Oxford University Press, 2014.

Ingram, Martin. *Church Courts, Sex and Marriage in England, 1570–1640*. Cambridge: Cambridge University Press, 1987.

– "Ridings, Rough Music and the 'Reform of Popular Culture' in Early Modern England." *Past and Present* 105 (1984): 79–113.

Jackson, Mark, ed. *Infanticide: Historical Perspectives on Child Murder and Concealment, 1550–2000*. Aldershot: Ashgate, 2002.

James, Mervyn. *English Politics and the Concept of Honour*. *Past and Present*, Supplement, 3 (1978).

– *Society, Politics and Culture: Studies in Early Modern England*. Cambridge: Cambridge University Press, 1986.

Jones, Norman. *The English Reformation: Religion and Cultural Adaptation*. Oxford: Oxford University Press, 2002.

– *Governing by Virtue: Lord Burghley and the Management of Elizabethan England*. Oxford: Oxford University Press, 2015.

Jones, Norman, and Daniel Woolf, eds. *Local Identities in Late Medieval and Early Modern England*. Basingstoke: Palgrave Macmillan, 2007.

Kane, Brendan. "From Irish Eineach to British Honor? Noble Honor and High Politics in Early Modern Ireland, 1500–1650." *History Compass* 7 (2009): 414–30.

– *The Politics and Culture of Honour in Britain and Ireland, 1541–1641*. Cambridge: Cambridge University Press, 2010.

Keen, Maurice. *Origins of the English Gentleman: Heraldry, Chivalry and Gentility in Medieval England, c. 1300–c. 1500*. London: Tempus Publishing, 2002.

Keenan, Siobhan. "'Embracing Submission'? Motherhood, Marriage and Mourning in Katherine Thomas's Seventeenth-Century 'Commonplace Book'." *Women's Writing* 15 (2008): 69–85.

Kelly, Sarah Eve. "The Other Elizabethan Settlement: The Virgin Queen as *Materfamilias*, 1548–1603." MA Thesis, University of Alberta, 2007.

Kelso, Ruth. *Doctrine for the Lady of the Renaissance*. 1956. Urbana: University of Illinois Press, 1978.

– *Doctrine of the English Gentleman in the Sixteenth Century, With a Bibliographical List of Treatises on the Gentleman and Related Subjects Published in Europe to 1625*. Urbana: University of Illinois Press, 1929.

Kennedy, Gwynne. *Just Anger: Representing Women's Anger in Early Modern England*. Carbondale: Southern Illinois University Press, 2000.

Kermode, Jenny, and Garthine Walker, eds. *Women, Crime and the Courts in Early Modern England*. Chapel Hill: University of North Carolina Press, 1994.

Kesselring, Krista J. "Bodies of Evidence: Sex and Murder (or Gender and Homicide) in Early Modern England, c. 1500–1680." *Gender and History* 27 (2015): 245–62.

– *Mercy and Authority in the Tudor State*. Cambridge: Cambridge University Press, 2003.

Kiernan, Victor Gordon. *The Duel in European History: Honour and the Reign of Aristocracy*. Oxford: Oxford University Press, 1988.

Kilday, Anne-Marie. *A History of Infanticide in Britain, c.1600 to the Present*. Basingstoke: Palgrave Macmillan, 2013.

Kocka, Jürgen. "Comparison and Beyond." *History and Theory* 42 (2003): 39–44.

Kugler, Anne. "Constructing Wifely Identity: Prescription and Practice in the Life of Lady Sarah Cowper." *Journal of British Studies* 40 (2001): 291–323.

– *Errant Plagiary: The Life and Writing of Lady Sarah Cowper, 1644–1720*. Stanford: Stanford University Press, 2002.

Lake, Peter. "Feminine Piety and Personal Potency: The 'Emancipation' of Mrs Jane Ratcliffe." *The Seventeenth Century* 2 (1987): 143–65.

Langford, Paul. "The Uses of Eighteenth-Century Politeness." *Transactions of the Royal Historical Society* 12 (2002): 311–31.

Levy, Allison, ed. *Widowhood and Visual Culture in Early Modern Europe*. Aldershot: Ashgate, 2003.

Liliequist, Jonas, ed. *A History of Emotions, 1200–1800*. London: Pickering and Chatto, 2012.

Llewellyn, Nigel. *The Art of Death: Visual Culture in the English Death Ritual c. 1500–c. 1800*. London: Reaktion Books, 1991.

– "Honour in Life, Death and in the Memory: Funeral Monuments in Early Modern England." *Transactions of the Royal Historical Society* 6 (1996): 179–200.

Longfellow, Erica. "Public, Private, and the Household in Early Seventeenth-Century England." *Journal of British Studies* 45 (2006): 313–34.

Longueville, Thomas. *The Life of Sir Kenelm Digby*. London: Longmans, Green, and Co., 1896.

Low, Jennifer. *Manhood and the Duel: Masculinity in Early Modern Drama and Culture*. Basingstoke: Palgrave Macmillan, 2003.
MacCulloch, Diarmaid. *Suffolk and the Tudors: Politics and Religion in an English County, 1500–1600*. Oxford: Clarendon Press, 1986.
Mack, Peter. *Elizabethan Rhetoric: Theory and Practice*. Cambridge: Cambridge University Press, 2002.
Maclean, Ian. *The Renaissance Notion of Woman*. New York: Cambridge University Press, 1980.
Maddern, Philippa. *Violence and Social Order: East Anglia, 1422–1442*. Oxford: Clarendon Press, 1992.
Manning, Roger B. *Swordsmen: The Martial Ethos in the Three Kingdoms*. New York: Oxford University Press, 2003.
Marston, Jerrilyn Greene. "Gentry Honor and Royalism in Early Stuart England." *Journal of British Studies* 13 (1973): 21–43.
Mauss, Marcel. *The Gift: Forms and Functions of Exchange in Archaic Societies*. 1922. London: Routledge, 1990.
McIntosh, Marjorie. "Servants and the Household Unit in an Elizabethan English Community." *Journal of Family History* 9 (1984): 2–23.
– *Working Women in English Society, 1300–1620*. Cambridge: Cambridge University Press, 2005.
Meldrum, Timothy. *Domestic Service and Gender, 1660–1750: Life and Work in the London Household*. Harlow: Pearson Education Limited, 2000.
Mertes, Kate. *The English Noble Household, 1250–1600: Good Governance and Politic Rule*. Oxford: Blackwell, 1988.
Morrill, John. "Holles, Denzil, First Baron Holles (1598–1680)." *Oxford Dictionary of National Biography*. Oxford University Press, 2004; online edition, 2008. Accessed 17 November 2014. http://www.oxforddnb.com/view/article/13550.
Muir, Edward. *Mad Blood Stirring: Vendetta and Factions in Friuli During the Renaissance*. Baltimore: Johns Hopkins University Press, 1993.
Muldrew, Craig. "Credit and the Courts: Debt Litigation in a Seventeenth-Century Urban Community." *Economic History Review* 46 (1993): 23–38.
– "The Culture of Reconciliation: Community and the Settlement of Economic Disputes in Early Modern England." *The Historical Journal* 39 (1996): 915–42.
– *The Economy of Obligation: The Culture of Credit and Social Relations in Early Modern England*. New York: St Martin's Press, 1998.
– "'A Mutual Assent of Her Mind'? Women, Debt, Litigation and Contract in Early Modern England." *History Workshop Journal* 55 (2003): 47–71.
Munden, Roger. "George More, 1553–1632: County Governor, Man-of-Business and Central Government Office Holder." *Surrey Archaeological Collections* 83 (1996): 97–124.

Newton, Diana. *North-East England, 1569–1625: Governance, Culture and Identity.* Woodbridge: Boydell, 2006.

Norsworthy, Laura. *Lady of Bleeding Heart Yard: Lady Elizabeth Hatton, 1578–1646.* London: J. Murray, 1935.

Oakley-Brown, Liz, and Louise J. Wilkinson, eds. *The Rituals and Rhetoric of Queenship: Medieval to Early Modern*. Dublin: Four Courts Press, 2009.

O'Neill, Lindsay. *The Opened Letter: Networking in the Early Modern British World.* Philadelphia: University of Pennsylvania Press, 2014.

Patterson, Catherine. *Urban Patronage in Early Modern England: Corporate Boroughs, the Landed Elite, and the Crown, 1580–1640*. Stanford: Stanford University Press, 1999.

Peck, Linda Levy. *Court Patronage and Corruption in Early Stuart England*. London: Routledge, 1990.

– "'For a King not to be Bountiful were a Fault': Perspectives on Court Patronage in Early Stuart England." *Journal of British Studies* 25 (1986): 31–61.

Peltonen, Markku. *The Duel in Early Modern England: Civility, Politeness, and Honour*. Cambridge: Cambridge University Press, 2003.

– "Francis Bacon, the Earl of Northampton, and the Jacobean Anti-Duelling Campaign." *The Historical Journal* 44 (2001): 1–28.

Peristiany, J.G., ed. *Honour and Shame: The Values of Mediterranean Society*. London: Weidenfeld and Nicolson, 1965.

Pina-Cabral, João de. "The Mediterranean as a Category of Regional Comparison: A Critical View." *Current Anthropology* 30 (1989): 399–406.

Plamper, Jan. *The History of Emotions: An Introduction*. Oxford: Oxford University Press, 2015.

Pollock, Linda A. "Anger and the Negotiation of Relationships in Early Modern England." *The Historical Journal* 47 (2004): 567–90.

– "Honor, Gender and Reconciliation in Elite Culture, 1570–1700." *Journal of British Studies* 46 (2007): 3–29.

– "The Practice of Kindness in Early Modern Elite Society." *Past and Present* 211 (2011): 121–58.

– "'Teach Her to Live Under Obedience': The Making of Women in the Upper Ranks of Early Modern England." *Continuity and Change* 4 (1989): 231–58.

Postles, David. *Social Proprieties: Social Relations in Early Modern England (1500–1680)*. Washington: New Academia, 2006.

Powis, Jonathan. *Aristocracy*. Oxford: Blackwell, 1984.

Quint, David. "Duelling and Civility in Sixteenth Century Italy." *I Tatti Studies: Essays in the Renaissance* 7 (1997): 231–78.

Rapple, Rory. *Martial Power and Elizabethan Political Culture: Military Men in England and Ireland, 1558–1594*. Cambridge: Cambridge University Press, 2009.

Reinke-Williams, Tim. "Manhood and Masculinity in Early Modern England." *History Compass* 12 (2014): 685–93.

– *Women, Work, and Sociability in Early Modern London*. Basingstoke: Palgrave Macmillan, 2014.

Reynolds, Anna. *In Fine Style: The Art of Tudor and Stuart Fashion*. London: Royal Collection Trust, 2013.

Richards, Jennifer, ed. *Early Modern Civil Discourses*. Basingstoke: Palgrave Macmillan, 2003.

Richardson, R.C. *Household Servants in Early Modern England*. Manchester: Manchester University Press, 2010.

Rickman, Johanna. *Love, Lust, and License in Early Modern England: Illicit Sex and the Nobility*. Burlington: Ashgate, 2008.

Roebuck, Derek. *The Golden Age of Arbitration: Dispute Resolution Under Elizabeth I*. London: HOLO Books, 2015.

Rosenwein, Barbara H., ed. *Anger's Past: The Social Uses of an Emotion in the Middle Ages*. Ithaca: Cornell University Press, 1998.

– *Emotional Communities in the Early Middle Ages*. Ithaca: Cornell University Press, 2006.

– "Worrying About Emotions in History." *The American Historical Review* 107 (2002): 821–45.

Rowe, Joy. "Kitson Family (per. c.1520–c.1660)." *Oxford Dictionary of National Biography*. Oxford University Press, 2004; online edition, 2014. Accessed 23 November 2014. http://www.oxforddnb.com/view/article/73910.

Ruff, Julius R. *Violence in Early Modern Europe, 1500–1800*. Cambridge: Cambridge University Press, 2001.

Rushton, Peter. "Women, Witchcraft, and Slander in Early Modern England: Cases from the Church Courts of Durham, 1560–1675." *Northern History* 18 (1982): 116–32.

Saul, Nigel, *Chivalry in Medieval England*. Cambridge: Harvard University Press, 2011.

Schneider, Gary M. *The Culture of Epistolarity: Vernacular Letters and Letter Writing in Early Modern England, 1500–1700*. Newark: University of Delaware Press, 2005.

Shapin, Steven. *A Social History of the Truth: Civility and Science in Seventeenth-Century England*. Chicago: University of Chicago Press, 1994.

Sharp, Cuthbert. *Memorials of the Rebellion of 1569*. London: J.B. Nichols, 1840.

Sharpe, J.A. *Crime in Early Modern England, 1550–1750*. London: Longman, 1984.

– *Defamation and Sexual Slander in Early Modern England: The Church Courts at York*. York: University of York Press, Borthwick Papers, No. 58, 1980.

– "The History of Violence in England: Some Observations." *Past and Present* 108 (1985): 206–15.

Shepard, Alexandra. *Accounting For Oneself: Worth, Status, and the Social Order in Early Modern England.* Oxford: Oxford University Press, 2015.

– *Meanings of Manhood in Early Modern England*. Oxford: Oxford University Press, 2003.

Shepard, Alexandra, and Phil Withington, eds. *Communities in Early Modern England: Networks, Place, Rhetoric*. Manchester: Manchester University Press, 2000.

Sherlock, Peter. *Monuments and Memory in Early Modern England*. Burlington: Ashgate, 2008.

Shoemaker, Robert B. "Male Honour and the Decline of Public Violence in Eighteenth-Century London." *Social History* 26 (2001): 190–208.

– "The Taming of the Duel: Masculinity, Honour and Ritual Violence in London, 1660–1800." *The Historical Journal* 45 (2002): 525–45.

Smith, R.B. *Land and Politics in the England of Henry VIII: The West Riding of Yorkshire, 1530–1546*. Oxford: Clarendon Press, 1970.

Smuts, R. Malcolm. *Culture and Power in England, 1585–1685*. Basingstoke: Macmillan, 1999.

– ed. *The Oxford Handbook of the Age of Shakespeare*. Oxford: Oxford University Press, 2016.

– ed. *The Stuart Court and Europe: Essays in Politics and Political Culture.* Cambridge: Cambridge University Press, 1996.

Squibb, G.D. *The High Court of Chivalry: A Study in the Civil Law of England*. Oxford: Clarendon Press, 1959.

Stater, Victor. *Duke Hamilton Is Dead!: A Story of Aristocratic Life and Death in Stuart Britain*. London: Hill and Wang, 1999.

– *High Life, Low Morals: The Duel that Shook Stuart Society*. London: Pimlico, 2000.

Stewart, Frank Henderson. *Honor*. Chicago: University of Chicago Press, 1994.

Stone, Ken. *Sex, Honor, and Power in the Deuteronomistic History*. Sheffield: Sheffield Academic Press, 1996.

Stone, Lawrence. *The Crisis of the Aristocracy, 1558–1641*. Oxford: Clarendon Press, 1965.

– "The History of Violence in England: Some Observations – A Rejoinder." *Past and Present* 108 (1985): 216–24.

– "Interpersonal Violence in English Society 1300–1800." *Past and Present* 101 (1983): 22–32.

Stretton, Timothy. *Women Waging Law in Elizabethan England*. Cambridge: Cambridge University Press, 1998.

Tadmor, Naomi. "The Concept of the Household-Family in Eighteenth-Century England." *Past and Present* 151 (1996): 111–40.

Tague, Ingrid. *Women of Quality: Accepting and Contesting Ideals of Femininity in England, 1690–1760*. Woodbridge: Boydell, 2002.

Taylor, Scott K. *Honor and Violence in Golden Age Spain*. New Haven: Yale University Press, 2008.

Thomas, Courtney Erin. "'The Honour & Credite of the Whole House:' Family Unity and Honour in Early Modern England." *Cultural and Social History* 10 (2013): 329–45.

Thomas, Keith. "The Double Standard." *Journal of the History of Ideas* 1959 (20): 195–216.

– *The Ends of Life: Roads to Fulfillment in Early Modern England*. New York: Oxford University Press, 2009.

Travitsky, Betty S., and Adele F. Seeff, eds. *Attending to Women in Early Modern England*. Cranbury: Associated University Press, 1994.

Trim, David. "Calvinist Internationalism and English Officer Corps, 1562–1642." *History Compass* 4 (2006): 1024–48.

Varlow, Sally. *The Lady Penelope: The Lost Tale of Love and Politics in the Court of Elizabeth I*. London: André Deutsch, 2007.

Walker, Garthine. *Crime, Gender, and Social Order in Early Modern England*. Cambridge: Cambridge University Press, 2008.

– "Expanding the Boundaries of Female Honour in Early Modern England." *Transactions of the Royal Historical Society* 6 (1996): 235–45.

Wall, Alison. "Elizabethan Precept and Feminine Practice: The Thynne Family of Longleat." *History* 75 (1990): 23–38.

– "'The Greatest Disgrace': The Making and Unmaking of JPs in Elizabethan and Jacobean England." *English Historical Review* 481 (2004): 312–32.

– "For Love, Money, or Politics? A Clandestine Marriage and the Elizabethan Court of Arches." *The Historical Journal* 38 (1995): 511–33.

Werner, Michael, and Bénédicte Zimmermann. "Beyond Comparison: *Histoire Croisée* and the Challenge of Reflexivity." *History and Theory* 45 (2006): 30–50.

Whitelock, Anna. *The Queen's Bed: An Intimate History of Elizabeth's Court*. New York: Sarah Crichton Books, 2013.

Willen, Diane. "Godly Women in Early Modern England: Puritanism and Gender." *The Journal of Ecclesiastical History* 43 (1992): 561–80.

Williams, Graham T. *Women's Epistolary Utterance: A Study of the Letters of Joan and Maria Thynne, 1575–1611*. Amsterdam: John Benjamins Publishing Company, 2013.

Withington, Phil. *The Politics of Commonwealth: Citizens and Freemen in Early Modern England*. Cambridge: Cambridge University Press, 2005.

– "Public Discourse, Corporate Citizenship, and State Formation in Early Modern England." *The American Historical Review* 112 (2007): 1016–38.

– *Society in Early Modern England: The Vernacular Origins of Some Powerful Ideas.* Cambridge: Polity Press, 2010.

Wood, Andy. *The 1549 Rebellions and the Making of Early Modern England.* New York: Cambridge University Press, 2007.

Wright, Nancy E., Margaret W. Ferguson, and A.R. Buck, eds. *Women, Property and the Letters of the Law in Early Modern England.* Toronto: University of Toronto Press, 2004.

Wright, Stephen. "Pakington, Sir John (1549–1625)." *Oxford Dictionary of National Biography.* Oxford University Press, 2004; online edition, 2007. Accessed 10 December 2014. http://www.oxforddnb.com/view/article/21145.

Wrightson, Keith. *English Society, 1580–1680.* 1982. London: Routledge, 2004.

– "Infanticide in European History," *Criminal Justice History* 3 (1982): 1–20.

– "Mutualities and Obligations: Changing Social Relationships in Early Modern England." *Proceedings of the British Academy* 139 (2005): 157–94.

Index

Note: page numbers in italics indicate an illustration.